-BOTANY IN A DAY-
THOMAS J. ELPEL'S
HERBAL FIELD GUIDE TO
PLANT FAMILIES

4th Edition

*Dedicated to Dad; you showed me
my first edible wild plants.*

HOPS Press
Hollowtop Outdoor Primitive School
12 Quartz Street
Pony, Montana 59747
http://www.hollowtop.com

Illustrations in this book are digitally adapted from these public domain sources:
-Text-Book of Western Botany. Ivison, Blakeman & Co.: New York & Chicago. 1885.
-An Illustrated Flora of the Northern United States, Canada, and the British Possessions. Volumes I, II, III. Nathaniel Lord Britton, Ph.D. & Hon. Addison Brown. 1896, 1897, 1898.
-Standard Cyclopedia of Horticulture. Volumes I-VI. L. H. Bailey. Macmillan: New York. 1900, 1914.
-A Text-Book of Botany. John M. Coulter A.M. Ph.D. 1910.
-A Manual of Poisonous Plants. Volume II. L. H. Pammel, Ph.D. 1911.
-Indian Medicinal Plants. K. R. Kirtikar & B. D. Basu. 1918.
-Flora of Montana Part II. W. E. Booth & J. C. Wright. Montana State University, Bozeman, Montana. 1959.
-Key to Important Woody Plants of Eastern Oregon and Washington. Doris W. Hayes & George A. Garrison. USDA Handbook No. 148. 1960.
-Important Western Browse Plants. William A. Dayton. USDA Handbook No. 101. July 1931.
-Plant Relations. John M. Coulter, A.M., Ph.D. D. Appleton & Co. New York. 1899.
- A Textbook of Botany, Volume II: Ecology. John M. Coulter Ph.D., Charles R. Barnes Ph.D., Henry C. Cowles Ph.D. American Book Company. New York, Cincinnati, Chicago. 1911.-
-How to Know the Wild Flowers. Mrs. William Starr Dana. Charles Scribner's Sons. New York. 1909.
-A Practical Course in Botany. E. F. Andrews. American Book Company. New York, Cincinatti, Chicago. 1911.
-Familiar Trees and Their Leaves. F. Schuyler Mathews. D. Appleton & Co. New York. 1898.

<u>Botany in a Day</u>
Thomas J. Elpel's Herbal Field Guide to Plant Families

Copyright: 1st Edition. Comb Bound. May 1996. 25 copies printed.
Revised & Expanded 2nd Edition. Comb Bound. April 1997. 500 copies printed.
Revised & Expanded 3rd Edition. First in Paperback. March 1998. 2,000 copies printed.
Revised & Expanded 4th Edition, January 2000. ISBN: 1-892784-07-6. 5,000 copies printed.
Minor Corrections. 4th Edition, 2nd Printing. October 2001. 7,500 copies printed.

Legal Note: There is a big difference between knowing the properties of plants and knowing how to apply them to the body. This guide is intended for the identification of plants and their properties only; it is <u>not</u> a field guide to the human body. The author is not responsible for your accidents. Also keep in mind that every plant book has errors, and every person who uses a plant book makes errors. It is very important that you cross-check both the identification and the uses of these plants with other sources.

Publisher's Cataloging-in-Publication Data
Elpel, Thomas J. 1967-
    Botany in a Day: Thomas J. Elpel's Herbal Field Guide to Plant Families / Thomas J. Elpel. —4th ed.

    Includes bibiliographical references and index.
    ISBN: 1-892784-07-6 $22.50 Pbk. (alk. paper)
    1. Plants—Identification. 2. Botany—North America. 3. Medicinal Plants. 4. Edible Plants.
    I. Elpel, Thomas J. II. Title.
    QK110.E46 2000   581.023   99-068343

All of the interior pages of <u>Botany in a Day</u> are printed with soy-based inks on 100% recyled paper, bleached without chlorine. Remember to recycle your papers!

HOPS Press
Hollowtop Outdoor Primitive School, LLC
12 Quartz Street
Pony, MT 59747
www.hollowtop.com

Contents

$1.00 from every copy of this book sold is being donated to 3riverspark.org

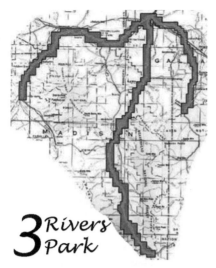

3Rivers Park

Canoeing, Rafting, Fishing, Hiking, Bicycling, Horseback Riding, Hunting, Camping, Bird Watching, Wildlife Viewing
-A Place for People-

The scenic Three Rivers Watershed in southwest Montana consists of all land that drains into the Jefferson, Madison, and Gallatin rivers, forming the headwaters of the Missouri River. It is an exciting and beautiful place to live and work, naturally drawing in a steady stream of new-comers to the area. In fact, everyone seems to want a piece of this special place, as evidenced by the houses that pop up on every little hilltop with a view or in green meadows along the rivers. Unfortunately, there are also "No Trespassing" signs sprouting up across the landscape, blocking out hunters, hikers, and fishermen on tens of thousands of acres of private lands that used to be informally open to public use.

What we have seen so far is just the "tip of the iceberg" compared to what is coming. We can expect to witness a population explosion within the watershed from about 100,000 people today to more than a million later this century. Everyone wants a piece of the action, but pieces may soon be all that are left!

There is plenty of room for all to enjoy and to share this special place, but we will all enjoy it a lot more if we plan ahead. This organization, **3riverspark.org**, was formed by Thomas J. Elpel and Chris Powell to envision and create a better tomorrow for this special part of the world. 3Rivers Park is our answer to preserving critical riparian habitat within the watershed for wildlife and for people, so that the future will be a fun place to live for our children and for our children's children.

The park boundaries (exaggerated on this map) were designated by following the approximate range of the cottonwood groves along the three rivers, with additional acreage for other adjacent lands with unique recreational or biological qualities. The park encompasses the entire length of the Jefferson, Madison, and Gallatin Rivers outside of federal lands. Almost all of the park remains in private hands, except for several fishing access points and the public right-of-way along the rivers between the high water marks.

The challenge we face is to halt the deterioration of the river corridors, moving development back from the waters edge, while purchasing the acreage or recreational easements on the acreage that lies within park boundaries. For more information on this undertaking, or to contribute towards the vision, please contact:

3riverspark.org
PO Box 972
Bozeman, MT 59771-0972
http://www.3riverspark.org

Forward

As a teenager in junior high and high-school I had the luxury of time. Like most kids, I had few responsibilities and lots of freedom. I spent much of my time studying plants. I collected specimens while on walks with my grandma. I brought the plants home and studied them for hours, using a number of books to identify them and learn about their uses. If I could not identify a plant then I brought it in to the herbarium at the university for assistance. Over the years I learned to identify most of the plants in southwest Montana and a substantial portion of them across the northern latitudes of America. I learned to recognize many plants from the time they were tiny seedlings in the spring until they were dead, leafless stalks in the fall.

As a self-taught botanist/herbalist, I approached plants one-at-a-time. There are hundreds of thousands of species of plants in the world, and I approached them one-by-one, as if each one had nothing to do with any others. It seemed that all plants were completely different, with no rhyme or reason as to what they were or what they could be used for. It seemed like there should be some rationale to the plant world, but I did not find it in my library of plant books.

Then we hosted a medicinal herb class through our outdoors school. The instructor was a local herbalist by the name of Robyn Klein. She identified individual plants for the group and explained the uses of each. On this walk she showed us several members of the Rose family and talked about them. She told us that most members of the Rose family were astringent, and that an astringent tightens up tissues and closes off secretions. An astringent herb she told us, would help close a wound, tighten up inflammations, dry up digestive secretions (an aid for diarrhea)—and about twenty other things that you will see in the coming pages. In a few short words she explained what an astringent does and gave us the uses of virtually every member of this one family. On this walk she went on to summarize several other families of plants in a similar way. She cracked open a door to a whole new way of looking at plants.

I was totally dismayed that I had been studying for all those years and no book ever mentioned that there were patterns or any kind of logic to the plant world. In short, Robyn's class totally changed everything I ever knew about plants. From there I had to *relearn* every plant I already knew in a whole new way. I set out to study the patterns in plants, learning to identify the plants and their uses together as groups and families. I wrote this book not merely because I wanted to share what I knew, but because I wanted to read it myself. The only way I could really learn plant patterns was to gather all the information I could find into one place and see what patterns were revealed.

I present this book to you on the belief that knowledge is a good thing. If we are going to take good care of the world we live in then we need to be informed about this world. Knowing plants is one way of being informed. Yet until now it was impractical for most people to seriously study plants. The immensity of the field of study required an almost full-time commitment just to grasp the fundamentals.

One principle I have learned while writing and teaching is that the ease or difficulty of learning a subject is not so much a factor of the complexity or volume of the information, but rather of its packaging. Even the most complex mathematical concepts can be simple to understand if they are packaged and presented well. Similarly, learning a thousand different plants and many of their uses can be a snap when presented with the right packaging.

This book is designed to short-cut the study of botany and herbology. The beginning naturalist will quickly have a foundation for the future. The more experienced may find their knowledge suddenly snapped into focus with a new and solid foundation under that which is already known.

Thomas J. Elpel
May 10, 1996

Region Covered

This field guide is designed to give the reader the "big picture" of botany and medicinal plant properties. It deals more with *patterns* among related plants than with the details of specific plants. Because the style of the book is broad, the coverage is also broad. Montana plants provided the core of the book, but the scope is so wide that I once tried to obtain the rights to use drawings of British plants for the illustrations!

Many species in Montana and across North America are identical to those in the British Isles and other countries of similar latitude. Other species are different, but they are closely related and have similar characteristics and uses. This field guide started as a simple list of virtually every plant in the state of Montana. I compiled the list originally for my own reference and built on it from there. The same or similar plants are found all across the northern latitudes, and in the higher elevations as you move farther south. Unique plants exist in every locality, yet the *majority* of plants where you live are likely to be the same *or similar* to those covered in this text.

Basically, any place that has real winters with hard freezes will have a great number of plants in common with ours. The vegetation does not radically change until you travel far enough south and low enough in elevation to get below the "frost-belt" of the country.

Below the frost-belt you will continue to find many of the same and similar plants, but you will also find whole new families of plants not found in the north. With each revision of the book I have worked to expand the coverage from coast-to-coast and farther south. Eventually I hope to cover all the plant families in North America north of Mexico.

The biggest problem with every plant book is in trying to identify a plant that is *not covered in the text*. There is a tendency to *make a plant fit* the description in the text, and that can be a very dangerous mistake in learning and using plants. From that standpoint, this book is the most useful in the northern Rocky Mountains and slightly less useful the farther you are away from this area. I have even heard of people using it successfully in places as far away as Central America, Africa, and Austrailia!

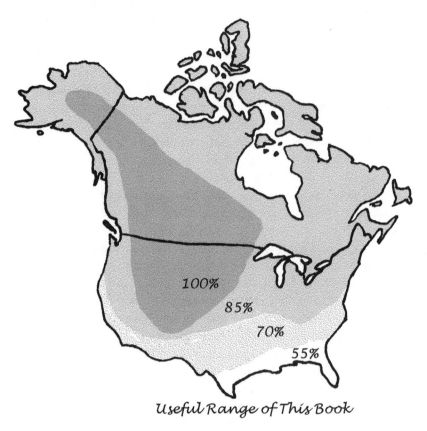

100%

85%

70%

55%

Useful Range of This Book

Start Here!

1. Find a comfortable, quiet place to read for about an hour. You will need to read the following pages on *Plant Names and Classification* and the *Evolution of Plants* before you begin identifying specimens. These chapters outline the basic vocabulary and the broadest divisions of the Plant Kingdom in simple, easy-to-read language. This background is essential for understanding how and why plants are placed in groups the way they are. Did you know, for instance, that common grass is considered a "flowering" plant? After you read these chapters you will be able to look at the plants around you begin the identification process.

I also recommend reading through the *Edible and Medicinal Plant Properties* chapter before you begin. A basic understanding of plant properties will often aid you in identifying a plant. Please wait on utilizing any plants until you build up confidence in your identification skills.

2. Once you have finished this reading assignment you are ready to start looking for patterns in plants. Begin with a few of the major families which are high-lighted in **bold** in the *Index of Plant Families by Common Names* in the back of this book. The **Mint**, **Mustard**, **Parsley**, **Lily**, **Rose**, and **Aster** families are especially good to start with. Read about these families and learn their characteristics, then go for a walk and look for plants—wild or domestic—that fit the patterns. A glossary of flower terms is available on the inside cover of this book if you need help remembering a word.

Do not concern yourself with individual plant names at first; just concentrate on learning the patterns of the families. You will be farther ahead in the long run. See how many plants you can find in each of the families you are studying. *Now* you are doing botany!

3. Continue building on your knowledge of plant families. As you become comfortable with the first few families you can begin studying others. Stick with the families high-lighted in bold in the index until you are comfortable with most or all of them, before you start learning the rest.

There are many places to look for patterns in plants. Look at wild flowers and weeds and study the flowers in your yard. Look at pictures in other plant guides and notice those plants that fit the patterns of the families you are studying. Floral shops, greenhouses, nurseries and botanic gardens are other good places to study plant patterns. Some gardens have living displays of plants from all around the world. There you will recognize plants from other continents that belong to the families you are studying!

If you are on a nature trail or in a nursery—any place where plants are labeled with their Latin names—you can look up their names in the *Index of Plants by Genus*. Read about the family characteristics and look for those patterns in the specimen before you.

You may use the key included in this book at any time, although it is no substitute for learning the patterns of the families. Start with showy, distinctive flowers first—and simply match them against the patterns in the key.

4. As you become confident with patterns in a family you may start identifying individual plants in that family. You can do this easily by searching through the drawings and photos of plants *within the proper family*. Instead of randomly searching through hundreds or thousands of pictures, you can look through the one or two dozen plants within the family you have identified. Some illustrations are provided for that purpose in this text, but you should also use this book in conjunction with other picture books that have the plants organized by family.

Many plant guides are organized alphabetically or by the color of the flower; these books can ultimately hinder your progress in learning plants. Look for books that are organized according to families. At the very least, make sure the book includes the family name with each plant. A few of my favorite field guides are available through our website at **www.hollowtop.com**.

Plant Names and Classification

Latin names of plants may seem intimidating at first, but do not fear them; they are true allies in learning about plants. Consider that a plant normally has only *one Latin name*, but it may have *dozens of common names*. Further, a common name may be used for several different and totally unrelated plants. For instance, several plants are called "loosestrife", yet without the Latin name you can never know exactly which plant you are talking about.

There is no need to memorize every Latin name, you need to refer to them only when you want to communicate about the plant to another person, or if you want to research that plant in other books. I have included many common names in this book, and I encourage you to write in any other common names that you like better. In fact, you can make up *your own* common names, if it helps you to remember them. I do!

As long as you can remember the common name then you can return to it in the book and look up the Latin name to cross-reference with other sources. The Latin names are standardized all over the world, so you will see exactly the same terms used by people in China, Kenya, Vietnam, and Sweden. Latin was chosen for this purpose because it is a "dead" language. No group of people still speaks the language, so it is not evolving and changing—thus the names should always stay the same. And since it is a dead language, nobody really cares how you pronounce the words, so just stumble through them however you can. You may be surprised by how many of the names you will memorize as a result of looking them up in the indexes of other books.

Every plant has a unique name in Latin, and the name is always in two parts. For example, "sweet cicely" a local plant with a potent anise-like flavor, is called *Osmorhiza occidentalis*. The first name is the *genus* name (plural: *genera*), and it is always capitalized. The second part is the *species* name, and it is always lower-case. Both are always italicized.

As Robyn Klein likes to point out, these two-part Latin names are much like the system of first and last names we use to describe each other. For example, I belong to the genus *Elpel*, and my species name is *Thomas*. Other "species" of the *Elpel* genus include: *Cherie, Nick, Alan, Marc,* and *Jeanne*. The species names are meaningless on their own, because many people have the same names around the world. But the names *Cherie Elpel* or *Nick Elpel* are quite unique.

In a similar way, there are five different species of sweet cicely just in Montana. These are very closely related plants, so they all have the same genus name, *Osmorhiza*; only their species names are different. Fortunately you do not have to write out *Osmorhiza* for each species. You can abbreviate the genus name after the first time you have used it. For instance, the other species of *Osmorhiza* in Montana are *O. longistylis, O. chilensis, O. purpurea,* and *O. depauperata*. If you want to talk about the whole group at once then you just write out "*Osmorhiza spp.*". This abbreviation means **sp**ecies **p**lural.

This book is designed to illustrate the patterns among related plants, so I have almost exclusively relied on the genus names. I have only used the species names in a few cases where there are significant differences between the species, or only one species in a genus. Instead of listing every single species, I have merely indicated the number of species there are (see sidebar).

What do the numbers and dots mean?

After each plant listed in this book you will see some numbers in parenthesis. The numbers indicate how many species from that genus are present in the world, in North America, and in Montana. For example, "*Viola*—Violet, Pansy (450/60/13) " indicates that there are 450 different species of violet in the world, 60 species in North America, and 13 species just in Montana. Your state may have more or less than this number. In most cases every plant in a genus will have similar properties and uses. For example, all 450 species of violet in the world are probably edible. At least it is highly improbable that any of them are seriously poisonous.

Some plants in the text are marked with a "D"; this means they are grown domestically, but do not normally occur in the wild. A dash "-" is inserted for any species that I could not find more information for

The dot "•" after many of the names indicates that those are plants I recognize. You are encouraged to mark the plants that you learn as well. You might use a high-lighter marker on the names, and you may want to make a note of the location to help jog your memory the next time you come across the name in the book. You can also high-light the names in the index.

PLANT NAMES AND CLASSIFICATION

Another level of classification, above the *species* and *genus*, is the **family**. For example, we belong to the Primate family, along with apes, chimpanzees, and orangutans. There are some major differences between us, yet there is also a distinct pattern of similarity, and genetically we have a lot in common. Likewise, wheat and corn are distinctly different, yet also similar, and both belong to the Grass family—and have similar uses. This book is designed especially to familiarize you with these plant families. You will learn to recognize patterns to identify the families, and you will often be able to make educated guesses about the properties of unknown new plants, based on the uses of others within the family.

If a family is especially large, or if its members sufficiently distinct from one another, then there may also be **subfamilies** and **tribes** within the family. For example, alfalfa belongs to the *Clover Tribe* of the *Pea Subfamily* within the *Pea Family*. This indicates that alfalfa is slightly more related to clover than it is to soybeans, which are of the *Bean Tribe*, also within the *Pea Subfamily* and the *Pea Family*. Fortunately most families are not grouped this way!

A higher level of classification, above the *species, genus,* and *family*, is the **order**. For example, the plants of the Pea Family and the Rose Family are very different from each other, yet there is a remote pattern of similarity, at least to botanists. Therefore, both of these families, plus the *Stonecrop, Gooseberry* and *Saxifrage* families, all belong to the *Rose Order*. However, for the purposes of field identification, the orders are sufficiently different from one another that there are few useful patterns to work with.

The next level of classification is the **subclass**. The subclass is a grouping of orders with increasingly remote similarities. This information is included in the upper margin of each page to give you an idea of the larger framework of the botanical hierarchy. (Pay no attention to it at first. It will mean more to you after you have confidently learned most of the families.)

Above the subclass is the **class**. There are only two classes of flowering plants, the monocotyledons (with one seed-leaf) and the dicotyledons (with two seed-leaves), as discussed in the next section about the evolution of plants.

A still higher level of classification is called the **division**. These groupings are highly arbitrary and are different in just about every botany book you look at. For instance, I have chosen to separate the Enclosed Seed Plants Division from the Naked-Seed Division, but sometimes they are both placed together into the Seed Plants Division. None of this makes a hoot of difference when you are out looking at plants. I simply picked the structure that would make it easiest to illustrate the major similarities and differences between the many types of plants.

Finally, all plants belong to the Plant Kingdom where they are distinguished from the Animal Kingdom and the Fungus Kingdom.

In review, the hierarchy of the Plant Kingdom, from top to bottom is:

Division (-*phyta*)
    Class (-*eae, opsida*)
        Subclass (-ae)
            Order (-*ales*)
                Family (-*aceae*)
                    Subfamily (-*ae*)
                        Tribe (-*eae*)
                    Genus
                        Species

The suffixes in parenthesis are used to distinguish each level of classification. For example, the entire name of the tomato is: *Angiospermophyta Dicotyledoneae Asteridae Polemoniales Solanaceae Lycopersicon esculentum*

In English that means:
Flowering Plants Division - Two-Seed Leaves Class - Aster Subclass -Phlox Order -
Nightshade Family - Tomato Genus - Edible Species
(The family is not grouped into subfamilies or tribes.)

Of course, all you need is *Lycopersicon esculentum* to look up the tomato in the index of another book!

5

The Evolution of Plants

I. A Puzzle Without all the Pieces

Piecing together the story of evolution is challenging, especially since 99.9% of everything that ever lived is now extinct. To try to understand evolution through the species of plants and animals that are alive today is like trying to interpret a long novel from the last paragraph. You can see the outcome, but do not know how the story unfolded.

The plot lies hidden in fossil records where plants and animals have been buried and turned to stone over vast eons of time. Although this story is conveniently laid down in the linear sequence of geologic time, it is unfortunately a very fragmented tale. At best, the fossil record is the equivalent of finding a few scattered words and phrases to the story. Most living organisms rot away without leaving a trace. Fossilized specimens are the exception rather than the rule.

Another challenge to reading the story of life is that the links in the evolutionary record are rarely found. Scientists originally assumed that entire gene pool of each species was continuously undergoing gradual change. However there were problems with that idea. Specifically, it is extremely difficult for any individual mutation to merge into the whole population. There is a tendency for mutant genes to be diluted away across a population. Also, naturalists noticed the absence of gradual change in the fossil record. There always seemed to be a sudden, dramatic change from one fossil layer to the next. The reason for this is because new species evolve "on the margin".

Imagine a wide valley several hundred miles across, surrounded by mountains on all sides. Now suppose that only one type of grass seed were deposited into this valley. Coincidentally, the whole expanse of the valley is the ideal habitat for this particular type of grass. The valley fills up and evolution stalls. There are still mutations, but the grass is already optimized for the environment so the mutations fail to survive. How-

> "evolution proceeds both gradually and suddenly. It is revealed in the fossil record as long periods of stability with periodic jumps to completely new species. "

ever, on the margins of the valley there is a great diversity of habitats. Possibly it is wetter in the mountains on one side than on the other, or one area may be warmer or colder. There could be different chemistry in the soil. The valley grass may survive in each of these areas, but it wouldn't prosper. Over time there would be gradual mutations and a few of these abnormalities would be more optimized to the environments on the margins, eventually creating new species.

Then a sudden change comes to the valley. Let's say the climate changes, causing this particular valley to become slightly warmer and wetter. The valley becomes more favorable to a grass species from the margin, resulting in an apparent "jump" in evolution from one species to another. The previously dominate species is limited back to the margin or completely eliminated while the new species suddenly invades the habitat. Thus evolution proceeds both gradually and suddenly. It is revealed in the fossil record as long periods of stability with periodic jumps to completely new species. (Scientists researching trilobites found a jump in the fossil record from those with 17 pairs of eyes to those with 18 pairs of eyes. It took years of searching to find the margin where both types were present.)

II. Life Begins

Life started in the oceans an estimated 3.6 billion years ago as single-celled organisms without a nucleus. These included bacteria and blue-green algae which are still with us today. These organisms reproduce asexually, each of them splitting in half to form two exact replicas of the original. Blue-green algae used the sun's energy to convert resources into living tissue; they grew, copied themselves asexually and populated the surface of the oceans. Each algae divided into exact duplicates of itself, so mutations were few and far between. That was pretty much the sum of life on earth until about 1.5 billion years ago, when cells developed specialized parts.

It was possibly the result of several bacteria joining together that eventually led to specialization within a single cell. Cells developed separate organs or "organelles" for storing DNA, digesting nutrients, burning sugar to produce energy, and for copying the DNA into new proteins. These proteins are shipped wherever they are needed inside the cells for repairs. This new cell with specialized parts became the basis for all new life forms, including you

THE EVOLUTION OF PLANTS

ERA	PERIOD	MIL. YEARS	EVOLUTIONARY EVENT
Cenozoic	Quarternary	0-1.65	Modern humans
	Tert./Neogene	1.65-23	Human ancestors, asters, pinks
	Tert./Paleogene	23-65	Primates, grasses, lilies, roses, peas, grapes
Mesozoic	Cretaceous	65-143	Flowering plants, broad-leaf trees, palms
	Jurassic	143-213	First birds
	Triassic	213-248	Dinosaurs and mammals
Paleozoic	Permian	248-290	First modern insects
	Pennsylvanian	290-323	Coal age —cycads, ginkos, primitive conifers
	Mississippian	323-362	Coal age —cockroaches, reptiles
	Devonian	362-408	Ferns, horsetails, club mosses, amphibians
	Silurian	408-440	Vascular plants, abundance of fish
	Ordovician	440-510	Plant/fungus symbiosis begins on land.
	Cambrian	510-600	Marine life: invertebrates, shells, predators
PreCambrian	Proterozoic	600-900	Bisexual reproduction/multi-celled life
		900-1,500	Cells with nucleus
	Archean	1,500-3,600	Fungi, bacteria, blue-green algae
	Pre-Archean	3,600-4,500	Earth's Crust and Oceans Form. No Life.

and I. The only major difference between plant and animal cells is that plants have an extra set of organelles called "chloroplasts". The chloroplasts harness energy from sunlight and use it to combine water and carbon dioxide into sugar molecules. This stored energy is passed on to the other organelles for the rest of the process. Our cells get by without chloroplasts because we eat the plants (or other animals that have eaten the plants) that do that step for us.

This innovation of specialized cell parts allowed genetic information to be copied more readily and sped up the process of evolution, but just barely. Another 600 million years passed before the advent of another new idea: bisexual reproduction.

Bisexual reproduction allowed slightly different versions of genetic knowledge to be combined into new, living products. This accelerated the evolutionary process and led to the development of multi-cellular organisms within another 300 million years, the beginning of the Cambrian Explosion. These first creatures were essentially fluid-filled blobs with no bones, eyes, mouths, or brains. They may have had chloroplasts to produce their own energy.

The fluid-filled ocean blobs only lasted 70 million years before being wiped out by another new idea: the predator, also part of the Cambrian Explosion. (In this context a "predator" is any animal eating either plants or other animals.) Exactly how the first predators came about is still a mystery, but they quickly wiped out the defenseless blobs. Evolution suddenly favored nature's mistakes and mutants. Whole oceans of habitat awaited any organisms that mutated a defensive ability against predators. This, in turn, encouraged the evolution of more advanced predators, into a sort of feed-back cycle that quickly filled the oceans with all kinds of life, such as jelly fish, sponges, worms, shelled animals, and arthropods. (Arthropods were the ancestors of insects, spiders, and crustaceans.)

Surprisingly, the predator effect may have been the force that started the rapid colonization of land a mere 60 million years later, starting in the Ordovician Period. Previously, life in the ocean was sustained by the *external flow of nutrients*. Simple plants in the ocean survived by absorbing nutrients from the water. These nutrients reached the plants through disturbances at sea. Upwellings brought minerals up from the bottom while ocean currents brought minerals out from shore. Plants survived in these paths of disturbance, and animals survived by eating the plants. Otherwise, the ocean was (and still is) largely a desert because the minerals are not equally distributed.

To make the transition to land, plants had to evolve from floating in the nutrient stream to carrying the nutrient stream inside. It is theorized that this evolutionary jump was accomplished by the plants forming a symbiotic relationship with fungus, according to paleontological researchers Mark and Dianna McMenamin.

Fungus is neither plant nor animal. It is a third type of life that produces enzymes capable of breaking down dead organic matter, living tissue, and even rock. In theory, the presence of plant-eating animals made the open ocean a more hostile environment, thus favoring any plant life that could survive along the turbulent shore-line. I

extracting carbohydrates back from the plant.

Today, ninety percent of all plants associate with fungus in the soil, and eighty percent could not survive without their fungal partners. In many cases the fungus lives in the core of the plant. Some simple plants like the club mosses lack a complete vascular system for circulating water and nutrients, but their fungal partners live inside the stems and provide that function.

The McMenamins researched the fossil record for signs of symbiosis between plants and fungus, and found evidence of a link among the earliest fossils. They examined slices of cells from high quality fossils and found fungal hyphae inside the plant cells. The plant-fungus association internalized the nutrient stream and gave the proto-plant independence from the ocean currents to grow and evolve along the shore and ultimately on land. The force of evaporation served as a pump to move the nutrient stream up from the soil through the plants.

> *"ninety percent of all plants associate with fungus in the soil, and eighty percent could not survive without their fungal partners. "*

The symbiotic relationship between plants and fungi set the stage for yet another explosion of new life forms. Within a 100 million years life on land had become more diverse than in the oceans. In the remaining 350 million years since then, life on land has evolved at an ever increasing speed. Today there are twice as many species on land as in the ocean. Although the surface of the planet is one-third land and two-thirds water, the land area produces a whopping fifty times as much biomass (organic matter) as the oceans.

III. The Land Plants

Very few links have been found in the evolutionary development of the modern plants, but the available living and fossilized plants do suggest a logical progression from simple to complex vegetation. The following list provides a generalized out-line of the evolutionary process:

- **Spore plants without a vascular system**
- **Spore plants with a vascular system**
- **Plants with seeds**
- **Flowering Plants with seeds enclosed in an ovary**
- **Deciduous trees and deciduous (annual) plants**
- **Monocots and Dicots**
- **Complex Flowers**
- **Composite flowers**

Please note that **Lichens** evolved independently from other plants as an association between fungus and algae. The algae is a layer of single-celled plants near the surface, just below a gelatinized layer of fungal hyphae. The algae captures nutrients that land on its surface and provides energy through photosynthesis, while the fungus absorbs moisture and provides a protective structure for the algae. These are otherwise independent organisms capable of surviving without each other, and they only form lichens when both are present. Lichens were historically included in the Plant Kingdom, but modern botanists have moved them to the Fungus Kingdom. I believe they do not properly belong in either, and should be separated into their own group, as illustrated in the Key to Kingdoms and Divisions (see page 14).

The varied and often bright colors of the lichens comes from acid crystals stored in their tissues. The acid is used to etch holes in wood, rock, buildings, and other surfaces to give the lichens something to grab on to. Thread-like appendages are then inserted to anchor the lichens. Most of the so-called "mosses", especially those found in trees, are actually lichens. True mosses are distinctively green like other plants. See pages 28 and 29 for more information about lichens.

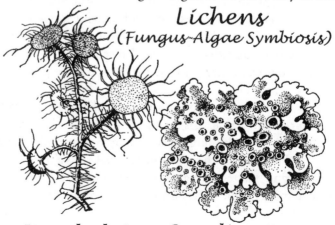

Lichens
(Fungus-Algae Symbiosis)

Usnea barbata   *Parmelia conspersa*

THE EVOLUTION OF PLANTS

-Spore Plants without a Vascular System

The simplest land plants are those that reproduce with spores and have no vascular (circulatory) system. These plants are limited in size because they lack the internal structure to transport water and nutrients. These plants are separated into their own Division called the *Bryophyta*, meaning the "Moss Division". Simple mosses like peat moss (*Sphagnum*) and "liverworts" are included in this division, and are not within the scope of this book. A good identification guide for the Moss Division is *Mosses Lichens & Ferns of Northwest North America* by Dale Vitt, Janet Marsh, and Robin Bovey. The key is technical, but there are also hundreds of color pictures.

It is unclear whether the *Bryophyta* were part of the evolutionary link to the higher plants. Members of the *Bryophyta* are soft-bodied plants that leave little trace in the fossil record, so the first samples found are relatively recent in the geologic record. It is possible that the *Bryophyta* evolved independently, well after other plants were established on land.

Specific information about the properties of mosses

Mosses & Liverworts
(Non-Vascular Spore Plants)

and liverworts is hard to come by, but *Sphagnum* and other mosses are typically highly acidic and antibiotic. The bodies of people that have drowned in peat bogs in the past have been almost perfectly preserved by the acidic quality. *Sphagnum* moss has often been used to dress wounds—with better results than ordinary sterilized pads.

-Spore Plants with a Vascular System

The first plants with a vascular system may have evolved from now extinct members of the Moss Division, but more likely they developed independently through an association between plants and fungi, where the fungi provided mineral nutrients and the plants provided energy through photosynthesis. This association helped to internalize the nutrient stream so that water and nutrients could be transported through the plant. The force of evaporation became the pump to pull fluids out of the fungus and through the plants. We call this "transpiration" as the water is lost to the atmosphere through the leaves.

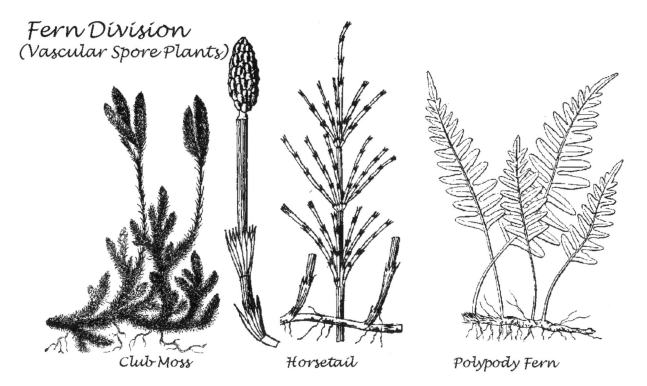

Fern Division
(Vascular Spore Plants)

Club Moss   Horsetail   Polypody Fern

THE EVOLUTION OF PLANTS

The intimate relationship between plants and fungus has undoubtedly led to genetic exchanges over time. (Among the lichens I understand that the algae and fungi share as much as thirty percent of their genetic material in common. The reason they have not advanced more than they have must be because the algae consist of simple single-celled organisms which do not readily mutate into anything more complex.) There is a tremendous evolutionary advantage in being able to share genetic information between wholly unrelated species. Imagine if *you* exchanged DNA with a bird, an apple, or a mushroom, for instance. Most exchanges would certainly lead to fatal defects, but any successful exchange would tend to accelerate the evolutionary process much more than simply exchanging genes with another member of your own species.

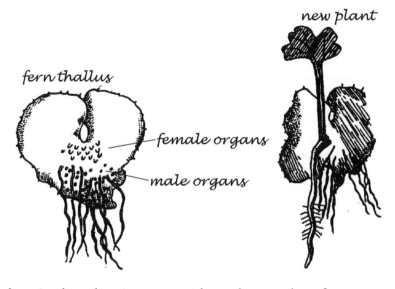

fern thallus

female organs

male organs

new plant

The development of the vascular system allowed plants to stand upright and to reach for the sky, a distinct evolutionary advantage over the lowly members of the Moss Division. Our first forests were comprised of these spore-producers with vascular systems; they are called the *Pteridophyta*, meaning the "Fern Division". This division includes ferns, club-moss, horsetails and many extinct plants.

In this first forest the club-mosses and horsetails grew into giant trees, often over a 100 feet tall! These plants thrived at a time when the earth's climate was moderated by ocean currents circulating warm equatorial waters up around the poles. The spore plants flourished in the tropical climate for millions of years and laid down the organic matter that eventually became our coal deposits.

The plants of the Fern Division split off from one another so long ago in the fossil record that most modern botanists separate them into different divisions. Nevertheless, the historical grouping is suitable for our purposes. See pages 30-35 for more information on the plants of the Fern Division.

-Plants with Seeds

Primitive plants like club mosses, horsetails, and ferns reproduce with spores. The spores drop to the ground and grow into a minute vegetative part called the "thallus". This term is used to describe a vegetative structure that is not differentiated into either leaves or a stem. The thallus produces sexual organs, including female egg cells and male swimming sperms to fertilize them. After fertilization the thallus grows into a new plant, as illustrated above.

Evolution eventually led to this process occurring on the plant, originally in a seed fern, now extinct, and later in conifers and the flowering plants. Conifers for example, produce two sizes of cones from modified clusters of leaves wth spore sacks at the base of each "leaf". Large cones produce big spores which develop into a thallus-like structure and produce egg cells, called ovules, within the cones. The smaller cones produce tiny spores which also develop into a thallus-like structure, but they produce the male sperm cells called **pollen**. Instead of tails to swim, the sperm or pollen is encased in a tough coat to resist drying. The cones open and release the pollen to the wind to find and fertilize the egg cells.

The pollen reaches the egg cells and fertilizes them within the protective structure of the plants. The fertilized cells begin to develop into a minute plant, but then the growth is stopped, and the new plant is shed as a "seed". In favorable conditions the seed absorbs

Naked Seed Division
Pine Family
Fir Tree

moisture, swells, and resumes growth. This gives the seedling plants a considerable advantage over those that are borne from spores.

In a crude analogy, you might say that spore plants are like the reptiles that lay their eggs and leave, whereas seed plants are more like mammals that gestate the eggs internally and give birth to a partially developed being. It is a tactical advantage for the seed plants as they are way ahead of the spore plants when they reach the soil. In addition, the seed provides a means of storing starch. The seedling relies on this energy reserve for rapid growth while it establishes itself among the competition.

The *Gymnospermophyta* were the first plants to evolve beyond spores to produce true seeds. The name means "Naked-Seed Division". It is called that because the egg cells of these plants are slightly exposed to the air and are fertilized by the pollen landing directly on their surface. Among conifers, for example, the female cones become elongated for a very short time when the male cones are releasing pollen. This exposes the ovules to the pollen in the wind. The shape of the cones causes air currents to swirl around them to help catch this pollen. The shape of the pollen and the shape of the cones are aerodynamically matched to each other, so each species captures its own pollen. After pollination the scales grow rapidly and again cover the ovules, allowing them to mature into seeds.

The Naked-Seed Plants first included the **cycad** and **ginkgo**, and later the **sequoia**, **cypress**, and **pines**. For more information on plants of the Naked-Seed Division turn to pages 36-39. The more recently evolved flowering plants, by contrast, have the egg cells tightly protected inside the ovary, and the pollen must grow through a long tube, called the "pistil" to reach them.

-Flowering Plants with Seeds Enclosed in an Ovary

It is difficult to imagine a world without flowers where the only color is green. Yet our first flowers appeared only about a 100 million years ago. Flowers co-evolved with the insects. Early insects may have tracked pollen across one plant—or between separate plants—from the male sporangia to the female egg cells. Eventually the plants developed nectaries and showy petals to attract and feed the insects, and the insects developed wings to move from flower to flower. This brought about the bees, moths, butterflies, mosquitoes and flies. It was once speculated that an ancestor of *Ephedra* (see page 39) was the link between the conifers and the flowering plants. The *Ephedras* are naked seed plants with colored bracts, much like petals. However, these plants appeared late in the fossil record, after

The Flowering Plants

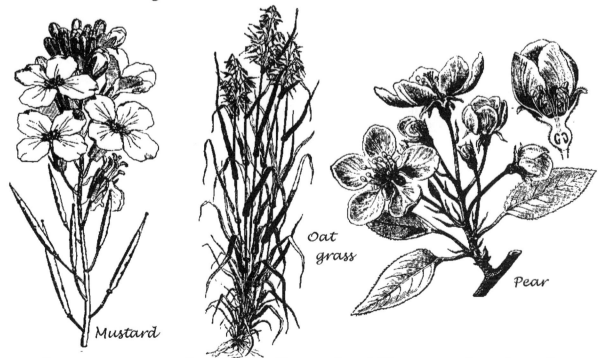

Mustard

Oat grass

Pear

Flowers, grasses, and trees are all considered "flowering plants". Each produces stamens and pistils and matures their seeds in an enclosed ovary.

THE EVOLUTION OF PLANTS

the arrival of the flowering plants.

What is known for certain is that flowers evolved through a modification of the branch buds and leaves of ancestral plants. Botanists determined that the flowers developed from the branch buds based on their positions on the plants. Moreover, on many plants the buds can become *either* branches *or* flowers, depending on environmental conditions.

Another step in the evolutionary process was to enclose the developing seed deeper inside the parent plant. The female flower parts formed a fully enclosed ovary, fertilized through a tube called a "pistil". The pistil has a soft core. Pollen lands on the tip of the pistil and grows a sort of "root" down through the pistil to reach the ovule. The pollen has two nuclei; the first nucleus controls growth through the pistil, while the second carries the genetic information and passes it along to the ovule.

The chemicals used by the pollen to burrow through the pistil are identical to some that are produced by fungi, thus it is suspected that plants acquired the genes to do this through their intimate relationship with fungi.

The development of the enclosed ovary led to a whole new division of plants called the *Angiospermophyta*, meaning the "Enclosed-Seed Plants Division" (Usually called the "Flowering Plants".) The ovary in plants is approximately the equivalent of the womb in the human female. The development of the ovary gave the fledgling seed more protection from outside dangers.

The ovary also became a flexible means of creating many new dispersal systems. For instance, berries and other fruits are swollen ovaries, usually designed to be eaten as a means to transport and plant the seeds. The ovaries around maple seeds develop into wings to disperse the seeds on the wind. The ovaries of some plants develop into spring-like systems to propel the seeds away. The evolution of the mammals is closely linked to the development of the plant ovary and its fleshy fruits, nuts, and grains.

Liriodendron tulipifera

Magnolia grandiflora

You might be surprised that grass and many other non-showy plants are considered "flowers", but they do produce true stamens and pistils, and they develop their seeds in an enclosed ovary. They have merely adapted to wind pollination and lack the need for the showy petals to attract insects. Please see the **Glossary of Flower Terms** on the inside cover of this book for additional information on floral parts.

Despite being recently evolved, the Angiosperms are by far the largest Division of plants, with the most species and greatest volume of plants around the world. The exact evolutionary link to the conifers is not known, but remnants of the evolutionary progression can still be found in modern flowering plants. Members of the Magnolia family in particular, bear their seeds in a large cone-like structure at the center of the flowers. One member of the family, the Tulip Tree, has green, chorophyll-bearing petals. To a lesser degree the plants of the Buttercup family produce similar flowers. Many deciduous trees also continue to bear their seeds in cone-like structures.

Beginning botanists usually expect that the trees would be completely separate families from the herbs. They are surprised, for instance, that the strawberry and the apple would be in the same family. The reason for this is because plants are grouped according to similarities in their floral parts, rather than in the vegetation.

To understand this, imagine a dandelion growing in the shade and another one growing in full sunlight. The one in the shade is going to appear lush, with leaves up to a foot long, while the dandelion in the sun will be a much smaller, more compact plant. The amateur naturalist might not even recognize them as the same plant. Yet the flowers on both plants are

Water Lily

sepals to petals to stamens transition

going to be identical. The leaves and stems are very flexible to change and easily adapt to new and different conditions. Over time there is more evolutionary pressure on the vegetation than on the flowers. Thus, any given family can have vastly different vegetation, but similar blossoms.

Interestingly, botanists have determined that floral parts have evolved as modifications of the leaves. The sepals on most plants are green and leaf-like, while in others they have taken on the color of the petals. In the water lily there is a visible transition from sepals on the outside to petals and then stamens on the inside. Thus the petals are modifications of the sepals, and the stamens are modifications of the petals. Plant breeders often manipulate these features of the flowers. Virtually every plant in the Rose family for instance, has 5 petals, including the wild roses. Yet plant breeders have developed roses with multiple layers of petals. Those extra petals were bred from the stamens!

-Deciduous Vegetation

Another development that came with the Angiosperms was deciduous vegetation. This adaptation may have come about due to climate change. The world climate was moderated during the Carboniferous Period (The Coal Age) by warm ocean currents flowing from the equator up over the North Pole. The climate today is much harsher. Flowering trees have adapted to the new climate by dropping their leaves and becoming dormant in the winter time. They shed old, worn-out leaves to enrich their own soil while also safe-guarding against potential damage from heavy snows. In the spring they burst forth with vigorous new leaves.

Simple and Compound Pistils
How many chambers does an ovary have?

A simple pistil has a single-celled ovary called a "carpel". Most primitive plants like this magnolia have numerous simple pistils (called "apocarpous") in a cone-like form.

Evolution leads to fusion of the parts so that most plants now have one "compound pistil" consisting of several united carpels, also called "syncarpous".

Further fusion of the carpels may eliminate the partition walls, leading to a compound pistil that has only one "chamber". In this example the ovules are attached in three points, indicating that it is composed of three carpels.

For the purposes of this book you will rarely need to look at the ovary, except to determine if there are numerous simple pistils or one compound pistil. However, to help you work with other books I have included information on the number of carpels and chambers with each family.

Alder

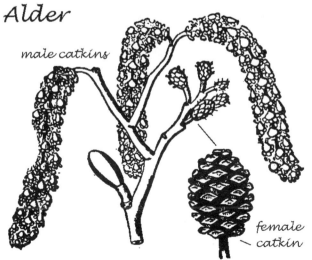

male catkins

female catkin

-Alder seeds are fully enclosed in the cone-like "catkins".
-The leaves are deciduous.

In a similar way, many flowering plants became wholly "deciduous", completing their entire life-cycle in the span of one or two years. A club moss, by contrast, may take 20 years to complete its reproductive cycle, from a spore to a new plant! A short life-cycle is a huge evolutionary advantage because it allows plants to change and adapt quickly.

We tend to think of survival as *preservation*, but true survival is *adaptation*. Any species that fails to change to fit new circumstances is ultimately as doomed as the dinosaurs. But make note: not all dinosaurs became "extinct". The DNA of a few species survives today in all our thousands of birds. A few dinosaurs survived by continuing to evolve. Similarly, our flowering plants today are highly flexible and adaptable. They are the most recently evolved type of plants, yet already they cover the earth's surface with hundreds of thousands of different species—they survive and thrive on change.

THE EVOLUTION OF PLANTS

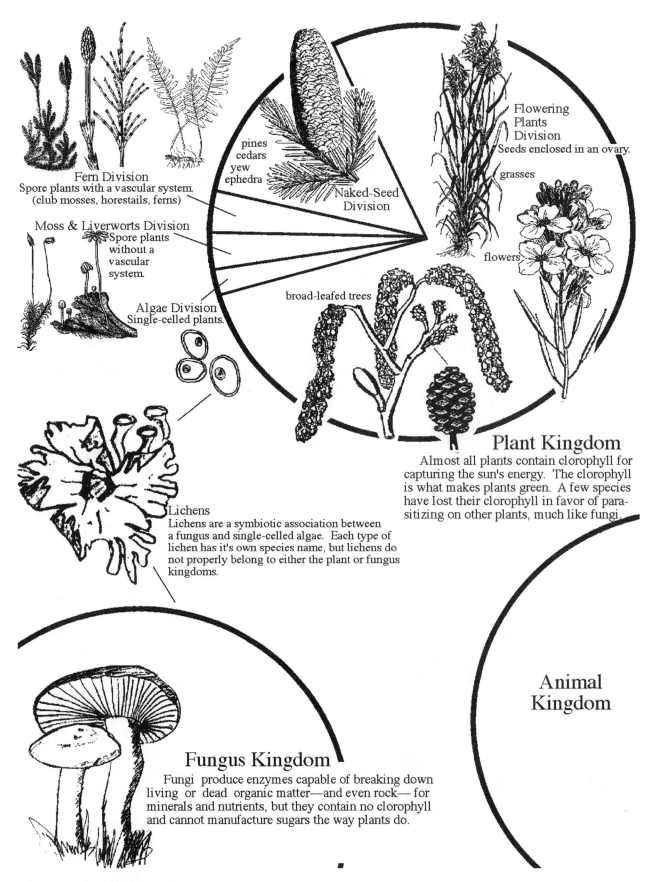

Fern Division
Spore plants with a vascular system.
(club mosses, horestails, ferns)

Moss & Liverworts Division
Spore plants without a vascular system.

Algae Division
Single-celled plants.

pines
cedars
yew
ephedra

Naked-Seed Division

Flowering Plants Division
Seeds enclosed in an ovary.

grasses

flowers

broad-leafed trees

Plant Kingdom
Almost all plants contain clorophyll for capturing the sun's energy. The clorophyll is what makes plants green. A few species have lost their clorophyll in favor of parasitizing on other plants, much like fungi.

Lichens
Lichens are a symbiotic association between a fungus and single-celled algae. Each type of lichen has it's own species name, but lichens do not properly belong to either the plant or fungus kingdoms.

Fungus Kingdom
Fungi produce enzymes capable of breaking down living or dead organic matter—and even rock— for minerals and nutrients, but they contain no clorophyll and cannot manufacture sugars the way plants do.

Animal Kingdom

Use this page as a reference "key" to remember which Division of the Plant Kingdom your specimen belongs to.

THE EVOLUTION OF PLANTS

-Monocotyledons and Dicotyledons

The newly evolved Angiosperms quickly split into two classes of plants, those with one seed leaf, the *Monocotyledoneae* and those with two seed leaves, the *Dicotyledoneae*. These are easy to remember because "mono-" means "one" and "di-" means "two". (The rest

> *Most monocot plants have leaves with parallel veins, like grass, while most dicot plants have net-veined leaves.*

of the word "cotyle-don-eae" means "seed-leaf-class".) As an example, corn is a "monocot" because only one leaf sprouts from the seed. Beans on the other hand, are "dicots" because the bean seed splits open to form two leaves. *All the flowering plants are based on one or the other of these two genetic algorithms.* Paleontologists have determined that the first flowering plants were dicots, and the monocots branched off from there soon after. For that reason, the monocots are listed behind the dicots in this book.

There are some striking differences between these two classes, and it is usually easy to determine which class a plant belongs to. Most monocot plants have leaves with *parallel veins*, like grass, while virtually all dicot plants have *net-veined* leaves. Even those dicots that initially appear to have parallel venation like plantain (*Plantago*) actually have a smaller net-like pattern in between the larger veins. There are always exceptions, so if you are uncertain then look at other features of the plant to be sure.

The majority of dicot plants have floral parts in fours and fives, but again there are some exceptions. Most monocot plants on the other hand, have floral parts in threes, except for a few exceptions. If a plant has both parallel veins in the leaves *and* floral parts in multiples of threes it is definitely a monocot. If you are still uncertain about a plant then you might look at the roots. The monocots tend to have spreading roots like grass, that grow horizontally just under the soil surface, while the dicots tend to have branching taproots that go straight down into the soil. Also, monocot plants rarely branch out above ground the way dicots do.

It really is easy to pick out the differences between monocots and dicots. Just go out and look at plants for fifteen to twenty minutes and you will get the idea.

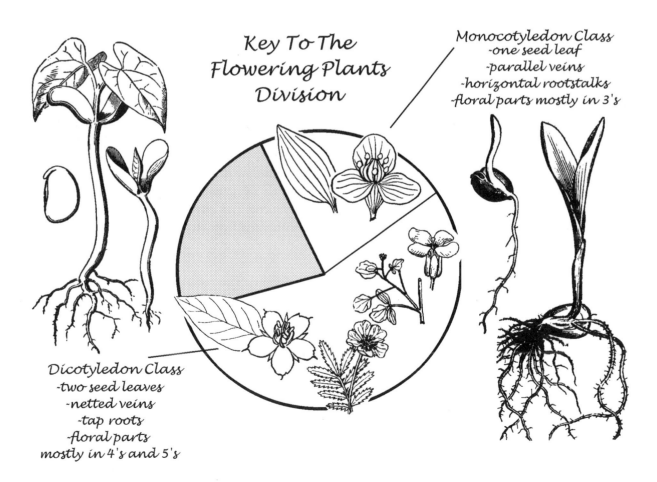

Key To The Flowering Plants Division

Monocotyledon Class
-one seed leaf
-parallel veins
-horizontal rootstalks
-floral parts mostly in 3's

Dicotyledon Class
-two seed leaves
-netted veins
-tap roots
-floral parts mostly in 4's and 5's

Simple and Advanced Flowers
(This is not an actual evolutionary progression.)

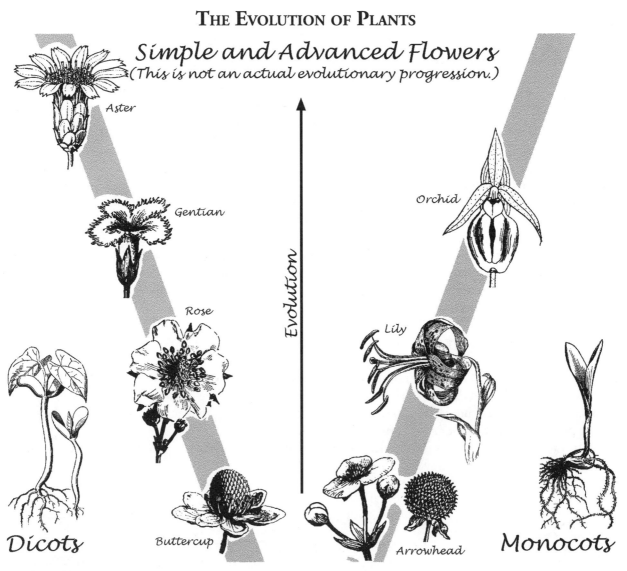

-**Complex Flowers**

Continued evolution of the flowering plants led from simple flowers with numerous separate parts to specialized flowers with fewer, often fused parts: Simple or "primitive" flowers usually have numerous sepals, petals, stamens and pistils, while more advanced flowers typically have reduced numbers of each, and the parts are often fused together. Modern plants evolved from now-extinct species, but some plants have retained many of the ancestral characteristics. The diagram above uses living plants to illustrate a generalized evolutionary progression from primitive to advanced flowers. Notice also that the primitive monocots and dicots are very much alike. Despite being botanically separated into completely different classes, they are actually somewhat related.

-**Composite Flowers: The Aster Family**

At the top of the dicot line, as shown above, is the Aster family. The Asters may initially seem like simple flowers with numerous parts, but in fact they are some of the most evolved plants on earth.

Most families of plants have floral parts in a similar order: a ring of sepals on the outside, then a ring of petals, a ring of stamens, and the pistil or pistils in the middle. Some parts may be missing, but the basic order is always the same. The Aster family is very different, however. The "sepals" are really bracts (modified leaves), and these often appear in multiple layers. The "petals" make it appear that there is just one big flower, but look inside and you will discover a head of many very small flowers—dozens or even hundreds of them! In the sunflower for example, *every seed* is produced by *one small flower within the larger head*. These itsy-bitsy flowers each have microscopic sepals and petals—although these have been modified enough that they have a whole botanical nomenclature of their own. In fact, each of the main "petals" is a flower too, often with stamens and a pistil! To learn more about the Asters, turn to the Aster family, pages 143-154.

How to Use the Keys

1. What Division of the Plant Kingdom does your specimen belong to?

The previous section on the evolution of plants provides an overview of the major groupings within the Plant Kingdom. When you have finished your reading assignment you should be able to pick up virtually any plant and make an educated guess as to which major group it belongs to. If you need a reminder, just return to the "Key to Divisions of the Plant Kingdom" on page 14.

Most divisions of the Plant Kingdom are relatively small so you can turn directly to the appropriate section of the book and read through the family descriptions to decide where your plant belongs. But if you have a specimen from the Flowering Plants Division then you will need to continue through the keys to narrow down the choices.

2. Is your plant a Monocot or a Dicot?

If your plant belongs to the Flowering Plants Division then you need to determine whether it belongs to the Monocotyledon or Dicotyledon Class. Remember, monocot plants usually have parallel-veined leaves and flower parts mostly in 3's. Dicot plants mostly have net-veined leaves and parts in 4's and 5's. For a refresher on the differences between monocots and dicots, or if you have an unusual specimen about which you are uncertain, then turn back to page 15 for a review.

If your plant is a Monocot, then turn to the *Key to Monocot Flowers* on page 26. Monocot plants with showy flowers are covered in the top section. Monocots with grassy flowers are in the bottom section. If you are uncertain which section yours belongs to, then try both. Next go to the **Index of Plant Families by Common Names** in the back of this book to find the right page for the family. If your plant is a Dicot then continue reading here.

3. Is your Dicot plant a member of the Aster family?

The Aster family is the largest family of flowering plants in the northern latitudes. World-wide there are 920 genera and 19,000 species, including 346 genera and 2,687 species in the United States and Canada. Just as a matter of probability, it makes sense to determine whether or not your plant is a member of the Aster family before checking any others. But more than that, the Asters can be misleading with their "composite" flowers. Aster flowers superfi-

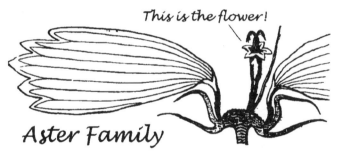

This is the flower!

Aster Family

cially appear to have numerous sepals or numerous petals, but they are really composed of many smaller flowers with parts in 5's. You must weed out all members of the Aster family before proceeding through the Dicot Keys. Please turn to page 143 for a thorough refresher on the Aster family. If your plant is definitely not a member of the Aster family, then continue reading here.

4. How to use the Dicot Keys.

If your dicot flower is not a member of the Aster family then turn to the appropriate key on these pages and search the text and pictures for the closest match you can find. Please note that not every family is illustrated in the key. In some families, however, a number of flowers are illustrated to show the range of possibilities. Your flower may not exactly match the samples shown, but just pick the family that seems the most like your specimen. Look up the page number for that family in the **Index of Plant Families by Common Names** in the back of this book. Turn to the page indicated and read carefully the family description to make sure your flower fits in that family.

Keep in mind that there are limitations to this kind of a key and some flowers are not well-represented here. Always double-check your conclusions. You may need to go back to the key and pick another family with similar characteristics. It is easy to make a plant "fit" into a family when you are trying to find an identity. I usually wait a few days before utilizing a new plant, because time and perspective can change the way the plant is perceived. It is important to know for certain what plants you are dealing with before using them for food and medicine.

(continued on the next page...)

How to Use the Dicot Keys (...continued)

The key included in this text is designed to be as non-technical and user-friendly as possible, without sacrificing too much accuracy. Identifying your plants will be easiest if you first make a few notes about the flower you are identifying. Simply write down the number of **sepals, petals, and stamens**, and notice whether the flowers are **regular or irregular** in shape. Look carefully to see if the sepals or petals are **united or separate**. (Look closely, because they may only be united at the base!) Also notice how the leaves are positioned on the plant (**alternate, opposite, basal,** or **whorled**). Turn to the *Glossary of Flower Terms* inside the front cover or the *Glossary of Leaf Terms* inside the back cover to help you remember the parts. Additional information is required to identify some families.

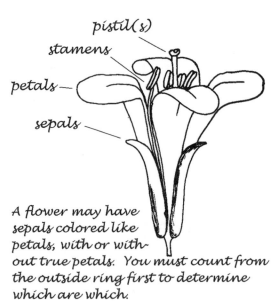

A flower may have sepals colored like petals, with or without true petals. You must count from the outside ring first to determine which are which.

Always remember to look at the individual flower. A clover blossom for example, is a tight cluster of dozens of small flowers. Pick one of those flowers out and you will quickly discover that it is irregular in shape. Compare it to the samples in the Key to Irregular Dicot Flowers and you will see that the flower looks like a pea blossom and belongs to the Pea family.

Keep in mind that <u>**flower parts occur in rings, always in the same order**</u>, from the outside in towards the middle. The outside ring is always the sepals (be careful not to confuse them with bracts that are present in some species). The next row is the petals, then the stamens, and finally the pistil is in the middle. Some of the parts may be missing, but all of the parts that are present will be in that order. If, for example, you find a flower without green sepals, then look close and you may find *two* overlapping rings of "petals". The outer ring is actually the sepals colored to look like petals!

On the other hand, *you may not find a second ring*, in which case you have a flower with sepals, but no petals, *even if the sepals are colored like petals*. No matter what they look like, a single ring always indicates sepals, not petals. These are important distinctions for properly using the keys. A flower with five colored sepals and no actual petals would be found in the *Key to Regular Dicot Flowers with 3 or 0 Petals* and <u>not</u> in the other keys.

Key to Regular Dicot Flowers with Numerous Petals
(Numerous means 11 or more)

Cactus

Purslane (bitterroot)

Buttercup

Waterlily

Numerous sepals, petals, and stamens. Succulent plants with spines. Desert habitats. .... Cactus
30 sepals, 30 petals, 30 or 60 stamens. Succulent plants, usually in grainy soil. .... Stonecrop
2-9 sepals, 5-18 petals, 4-50 stamens. Succulent plants, usually in intense sunlight. .... Purslane
3-15 sepals, 0-15 petals, numerous stamens. 3+ pistils in a cone-like head and/or with hooked tips. ...... Buttercup
3-numerous sepals, petals, and stamens. Always in the water, usually with broad, floating leaves. .... Waterlily

KEY TO IRREGULAR DICOT FLOWERS
(INCLUDING REGULAR FLOWERS WITH SPURS.)

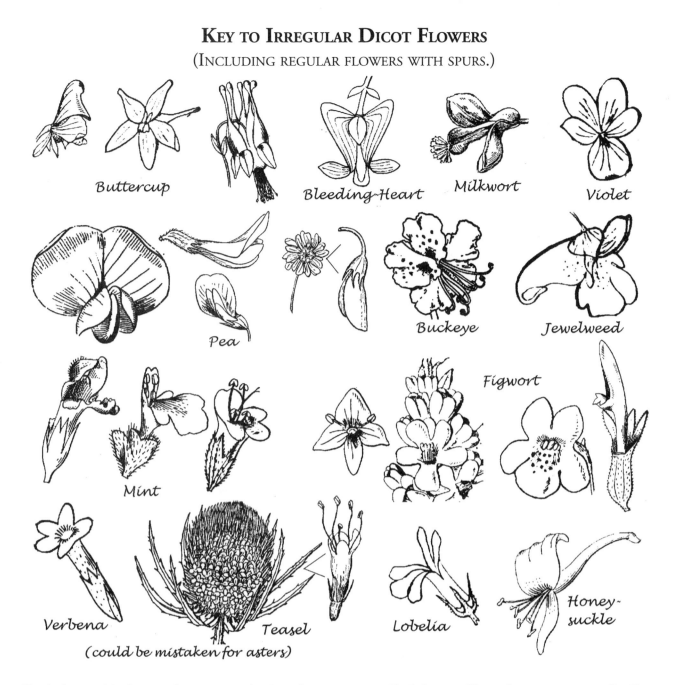

Buttercup   Bleeding-Heart   Milkwort   Violet

Pea   Buckeye   Jewelweed

Figwort

Mint

Verbena   Teasel   Lobelia   Honey-suckle

(could be mistaken for asters)

Shrubs/trees with alternate leaves. 5 sepals, 5 petals, 10 stamens. Fruit is a pea-like pod .... Pea/Senna

Sepals 0+, petals separate, some with spurs. Numerous stamens. 3 or more pistils with hooked tips. ..... Buttercup

2 very small sepals, 4 petals (2 outside and 2 inside). 4 or 6 stamens. Leaves alternate. .... Bleeding-Heart

3 outer sepals and 2 inner petal-like sepals, 3 petals. 8 stamens (or less) fused together as a sheet .... Milkwort

3 united sepals, 0 petals. Sepals fused together to make a curved tube. 6-celled ovary. .... (*Aristolochia*) Birthwort

3 or 5 unequal sepals, one forming a spur. 5 petals (2 united, 3 separate). .... Jewelweed

4-5 united sepals and petals. Irregular, usually with two petal lobes up and three down. .... Figwort

5 united sepals. 4 or 5 separate petals. Trees with large palmate leaves and big seeds with "eyes". .... Buckeye

5 united sepals and petals, usually with two petal lobes up and three down. Square stems. Opposite leaves. .. Mint

5 united sepals. 5 petals (bottom two may be united) forming a "banner, wings, and keel" (see family). .... Pea

5 separate sepals and petals. Petals in two pairs plus bigger bottom petal, sometimes with a spur. .... Violet

5 separate sepals and 5 united petals, with two petal lobes up and three down. Alternate leaves. .... Lobelia

Tubular flowers, usually in pairs. Mostly bushes or vines with opposite leaves. .... Honeysuckle

Small, slightly irregular flowers. Leaves opposite or whorled. Squarish stems. .... Verbena

Small, slightly irregular flowers in dense heads resembling the Aster family. Opposite leaves. .... Teasel

Key to Regular Dicot Flowers with 3 or 0 Petals

(Caution: Some have colored bracts or sepals!)

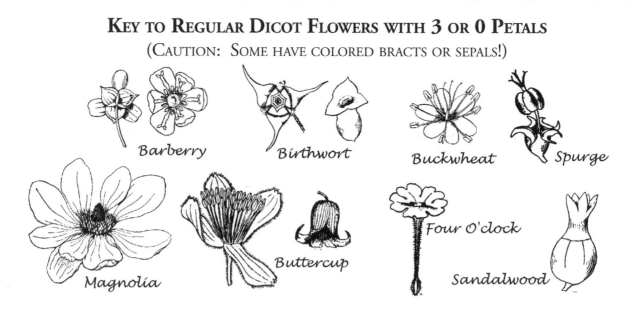

Barberry   Birthwort   Buckwheat   Spurge

Magnolia   Buttercup   Four O'clock   Sandalwood

Start here:

3 green bracts, 6 yellow sepals and petals, appearing as 4 sets of 3. Evergreen leaves. .... Barberry

Sepals (or bracts) colored like petals:

3 sepals. 3 or more petals. Numerous stamens. Trees with large flowers and pine-cone like fruits .... Magnolia

3 united sepals, tubular. 0-3 small petals. 12 stamens. 6-celled ovary. Moist forest habitat. .... Birthwort

3-6 sepals. 0 petals. 6 or 9 stamens. Seeds usually 3-sided.   Leaves alternate and/or basal. .... Buckwheat

0-5 sepals. 0-5 petals. Colored bracts. Plants with milky juice, mostly in warm habitats. .... Spurge

4 sepals, separate or united. 0 petals. Numerous stamens. 3 or more simple pistils with hooked tips. ... Buttercup

4 separate sepals. 0 petals. 2-12 stamens. 1-3 simple pistils. Small, white flowers. *Sanguisorba spp.* .... Rose

4-5 united sepals. 0 petals. tubular. Desert habitats. .... Four-O'Clock

4-5 united sepals. 0 petals.   Small plants, parasitic on the roots of others. .... Sandalwood

Plants or vines with green flowers:

Submerged aquatic plants with whorled leaves. .... Mare's Tail

Green plants with berries. Parasitic on tree branches. .... Mistletoe

Palmate leaves. Vines with "papery cones" in *Humulus spp.* .... Hemp

Squarish stalks and opposite leaves, usually with stinging hairs. .... Stinging Nettle

Disturbed or alkaline soils. Flowers globular or prickly. .... Goosefoot

Disturbed or alkaline soils. Flowers prickly.. .... Amaranth

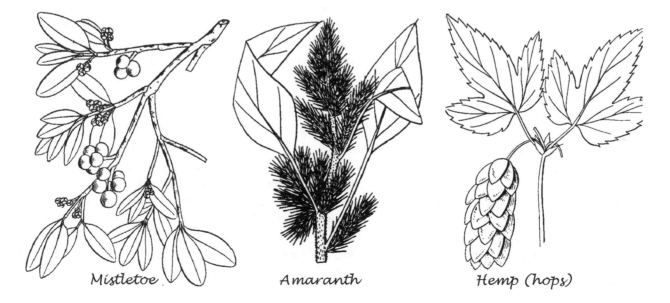

Mistletoe   Amaranth   Hemp (hops)

Key to Regular Dicot Flowers with Four Petals

(Includes some flowers with 6, 8, or 12 Petals)

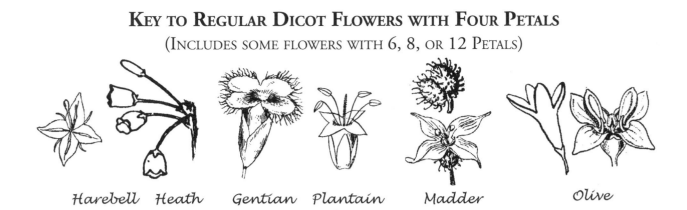

Harebell Heath Gentian Plantain Madder Olive

Flowers with 4 united petals:

Sepals united. Shrubs or trees with opposite leaves. 2 stamens. .... Olive
Sepals united. Flowers tubular with dish-shaped faces. Leaves opposite or alternate. .... Phlox
Sepals united. Basal leaves only, looks like parallel venation. Small greenish flowers on slender spike. .... Plantain
Sepals united or separate. Mostly bell-shaped flowers. Fruit a capsule or berry. Usually evergreen. .... Heath
Sepals united or separate. Flowers slightly irregular, in dense heads resembling the Aster family. .... Teasel
Sepals separate. Leaves opposite or whorled. Bell-shaped flowers, sometimes with dish-shaped faces. .... Gentian
Sepals separate. Alternate leaves. May have milky juice. *Triodanis spp.* (not common). .... Harebell
Sepals separate. Whorled leaves. Small green or white flowers. Mature fruit looks like green testicles. . ..... Madder

Flowers with 4 separate petals.

2-3 sepals. 4-12 petals. Numerous stamens. Stems usually with milky sap. Desert habitats. .... Poppy
2 sepals. 4-6 petals and 1 or 2x as many stamens. Succulent plants, usually in areas of intense sunlight. ... Purslane
4 sepals, petals, and stamens. 3 or more simple pistils. Succulent plants, usually in grainy soil. .... Stonecrop
4 sepals, petals, and stamens. Slightly irregular. Pea-like plants with mustard-like pods. Desert habitats. .... Caper
4 sepals and petals, 6 stamens. Mostly weedy, annual plants with a slight mustard odor. .... Mustard
4 sepals and petals, 4 or 8 stamens. Usually a 4-parted stigma. .... Evening Primrose
4 or 6 sepals and petals and 2x as many stamens in two sets, short and tall. Leaves opposite or whorled. Loosestrife
4 or 5 sepals and petals and twice as many stamens. Evergreen, with basal leaves. Bell-shaped flowers .... Pyrola
Vining plants with tendrils, alternate leaves, and clusters of berries. .... Grape
Shrubs with showy flowers. Sepals united. Fruit a capsule. Usually opposite leaves. .... Hydrangea
Shrubs, trees, or small woody plants. Small sepals. Large showy bracts. Fruit a berry or a drupe. .... Dogwood
8-10 sepals. 8-10 petals. Numerous stamens and pistils. *Dryas spp.* .... Rose

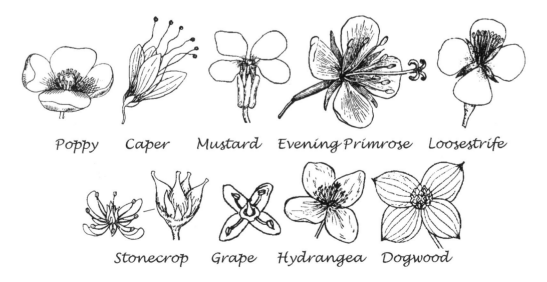

Poppy Caper Mustard Evening Primrose Loosestrife

Stonecrop Grape Hydrangea Dogwood

Key to Regular Dicot Flowers with Five United Petals
(Includes some flowers with 10 Petals)

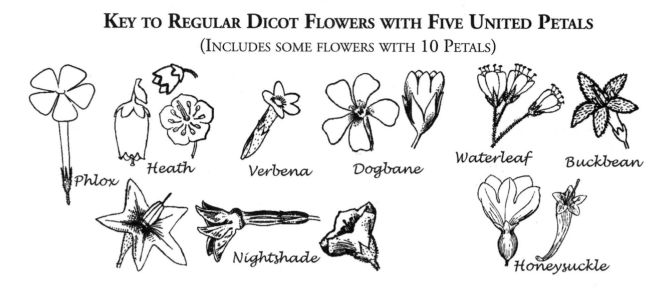

0 sepals: Small flowers, often with single spurs. Leaves opposite and/or basal. Roots with pungent odor. Valerian

Sepals united or separate:
Tubular flowers with a flat face (see above). Usually narrow leaves. Mostly in western states. .... Phlox
Fruit a tomato-like berry or 2-celled capsule with numerous seeds. Alternate leaves. .... Nightshade

Sepals united:
Mostly bell-shaped flowers. Fruit a capsule or berry. Usually alternate leaves. Mostly evergreen. .... Heath
Small flowers with 4 stamens. Leaves opposite or whorled. Slightly irregular. .... Verbena
Milky sap. Opposite leaves. .... Dogbane
Hairy plants, often curled like a scorpion tail. Stamens dangle beyond flowers. .... Waterleaf
3-parted, clover-like leaves. Sepals united at base only. Boggy habitats. Uncommon. .... Buckbean
Opposite leaves. Usually bushes. Flowers or berries in pairs or clusters. Pithy stems. .... Honeysuckle

Sepals separate:
Alternate leaves. Vining plants with tendrils and big 3 or 4 celled fruits in desert habitats. . ... Gourd
Alternate leaves. Mostly vines, often with milky juice. Star pattern in flowers (see picture below). . Morning-Glory
Alternate leaves. Bell-shaped flowers with five stamens. Usually milky juice. .... Harebell
Alternate leaves. Usually hairy plants. Ovary matures into 4 separate nutlets (less by abortion). .... Borage
Alternate, basal, or whorled leaves. Stamens aligned between petals. Fruit is a capsule. Moist habitats. ... Primrose
Whorled leaves. Small green or white flowers. Mature fruit looks like small, fuzzy green testicles. . ... Madder
Opposite or whorled leaves. 5 stamens. Bell or dish-shaped flowers. .... Gentian
Opposite leaves. Flowers slightly irregular, in dense heads resembling the Aster family. .... Teasel

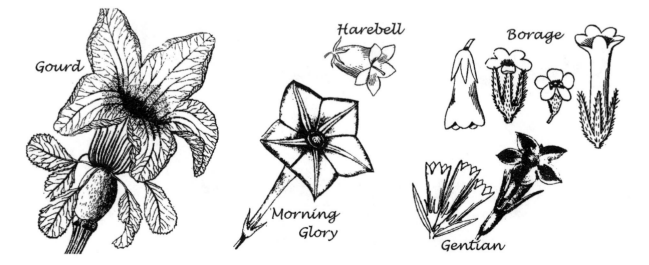

Key to Regular Dicot Flowers with Five Separate Petals

(Includes some flowers with 10 Petals)

Start Here:

Shrubs with showy flowers. 4-10 sepals, 4-5 (10) petals. 4+ stamens. Fruit a capsule. Opposite leaves..Hydrangea

Shrubs, trees, or woody plants. Small sepals. Often large showy bracts. Fleshy fruit. Opposite leaves. . Dogwood

Shrubs with alternate, palmate leaves. 4-5 sepals, 4-5 petals, 5 stamens. Fruit a berry. .... Gooseberry

Shrubs/trees with alternate leaves. 5 sepals, 5 petals, 5, 10, 15+ stamens. Leaves/leaflets oval and serrated. ..... Rose

Shrubs/trees with alternate leaves. Flowers small, white or green, in showy clusters. 3-celled fruit. .... Buckthorn

Shrubs/trees with alternate leaves. Usually small flowers in dense clusters. Fruit is a pea-like pod .... Pea/Mimosa

Vining plants with alternate leaves, tendrils, and clusters of berries. .... Grape

Succulent plants. 5 sepals, 5 petals, 5 or 10 stamens. 3 or more simple pistils. Usually in grainy soil. ..... Stonecrop

Succulent plants. 2 sepals. 4-6 petals and 1 or 2x as many stamens. Usually in intense sunlight. .... Purslane

Sticky leaves. 5 sepals, 5 petals, 5 stamens. Basal leaves. Insectivorous plants in moist forests. Rare. .... Sundew

Hairy plants, sometimes sticky. 5 sepals, 5 or 10 petals, numerous stamens. Fruit a capsule. .... Loasa

3-parted shamrock leaves. 5 sepals, 5 petals, 10 stamens. 5-celled ovary. Favorswarm, moist soil. ...... Wood Sorrel

Evergreen leaves. 4-5 sepals, 4-5 petals, and twice as many stamens. Mostly bell-shaped flowers. .... Pyrola

If none of the above fit your sample continue here:

Leaves alternate. 3-15 sepals, 0-15 petals, numerous stamens. 3+ simple pistils with hooked tips. .... Buttercup

Leaves alternate. 3-5 sepals (+ bracts), 5 petals, numerous stamens fused in a column. Mucilaginous. .... Mallow

Leaves alternate. 5 sepals (may look like 10), 5 petals. 5,10, or numerous stamens. Often serrated leaves. ...... Rose

Leaves alternate. 5 sepals, 5 petals, 5 or 10 stamens. Fruits fuzzy orange, or smooth and white.. .... Sumac

Leaves alternate. 5 sepals, 5 petals, 5 stamens. Hollow stalks and compound umbels. .... Parsley

Leaves alternate. 5 sepals, 5 petals, 5 stamens. Woody plants with umbels. Moist forests. .... Ginseng

Leaves alternate, basal or whorled. 4-9 sepals, 4-9 petals and 4-9 stamens, aligned between petals. .... Primrose

Leaves alternate or basal. 5 sepals, 5 petals, 5 or 10 stamens. Oblong ovary w/ 2 styles. Small flowers. ..... Saxifrage

Leaves alternate or opposite. 5 sepals, 5 petals, 5 or 10 stamens. Seed capsules split and curl upward. ... Geranium

Leaves alternate or opposite. 5 sepals, 5 petals, 5 stamens. Capsule looks like the sections of an orange. .... Flax

Leaves opposite. 5 sepals, 5 petals, 5 or 10 stamens. Sepals united or separate. Petal ends are usually split.. ... Pink

Leaves opposite. 5 sepals, 5 petals, 10+ stamens. Yellow petals often with red or orange spots. .... St. Johnswort

Leaves opposite and pinnate . 5 sepals, 5 petals, 5, 10, 15 stamens. 5-celled ovary. Desert habitats. .... Caltrop

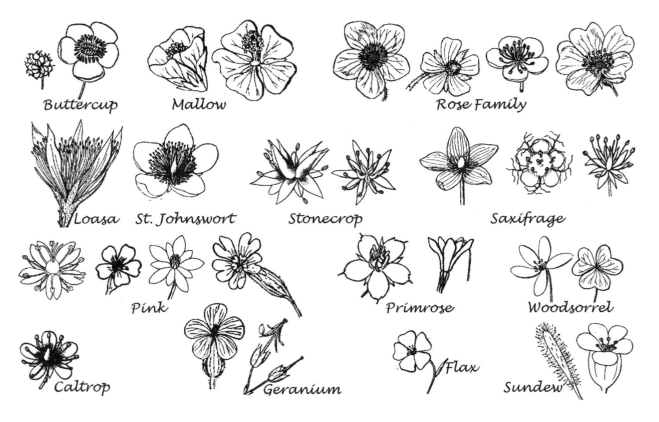

Buttercup   Mallow   Rose Family

Loasa   St. Johnswort   Stonecrop   Saxifrage

Pink   Primrose   Woodsorrel

Caltrop   Geranium   Flax   Sundew

23

KEY TO DICOT TREES AND SHRUBS BY THEIR FRUITS
(FAMILIES WITH SHOWY FLOWERS ARE ALS INCLUDED IN THE FLOWER KEY)

Start here:

Fruit is a pea-like pod. Mostly small trees with alternate, pinnate leaves. ....Pea
Fruits clustered in usually large, cone-like structures. Big flowers. Alternate, simple leaves. ....Magnolia
Fruits clustered in cone-like catkins. Individual fruits are nuts or winged seeds. Alternate, serrated leaves. .... Birch
Fruits clustered in catkins. Individual fruits are small capsules. Alternate leaves ....Willow
Fruits spiny. Alternate leaves with milky sap. *Maclura spp.* ....Mulberry
Fruits dry seeds or single-celled capsules. 5 persistent sepals. Alternate, serrated, rose-like leaves ....Rose

If none of the above fit your sample, then continue below:

Fruit is a winged seed: (not including seeds from catkins)

Winged seeds develop in pairs. Opposite leaves, palmate or sometimes pinnate. ....Maple
Winged seeds in loose clusters. Seeds separated by stems. Opposite, pinnate leaves. *Fraxinus spp.*................ Olive
Seed positioned in middle of wing. Alternate, simple leaves, often asymmetrical. *Ulmus spp.*..........................Elm

Fruit is a nut or nut-like: (walnut, acorn, etc.)

Seeds large and nut-like with one "eye". Wrapped in leathery or spiny casing. Leaves opposite, palmate... Buckeye
Hard-shelled nuts in husks. Inside looks like walnuts or pecans. Alternate, pinnate leaves. . ...Walnut
Mostly acorn-like nuts, usually attached to a cap. Cap may have spines. Alternate leaves............................Beech
Nuts with attached bracts. Alternate, serrated leaves. (Hazelnut Subfamily) .... Birch

Fruit is a capsule:

3-6 celled capsule (or united at base) with numerous seeds. Showy flowers. Mostly opposite leaves. ..... Hydrangea
2 celled capsule with 1 or 2 bony seeds per cell. Woody or leathery capsules, sometimes in ball shape. Witch Hazel
2 celled capsule with 2 seeds per cell. Opposite, simple leaves. ....Olive
3 celled capsule (sometimes 2 or 4). Simple, usually alternate leaves. Small flowers. ....Buckthorn
4-5 (up to 10) cells with numerous seeds. Alternate, simple leaves. Usually evergreen. Mostly shrubs.........Heath

Shrubs and Trees with Fleshy Fruits (berries, etc.): (These have simple leaves unless otherwise noted.)

Aggregate fruit, like a raspberry. Bushes or brambles. Alternate, serrated leaves. *Rubus spp.*...........................Rose
Aggregate fruit. Trees or shrubs. Alternate leaves. Milky sap. *Morus spp.* ....Mulberry
Fig-like fruit. Trees or shrubs. Alternate leaves. Milky sap. Southern states. *Ficus spp.* ....Mulberry
Pulpy fruit with sepals still attached on the bottom, forming a "star". Alternate, usually serrated leaves..........Rose

If none of the above fit your sample, then continue below:

Fruit is a berry with several to numerous small seeds: (Cross-check with the section below.)

Alternate leaves. Berry translucent with lines running end to end. Sepals remaining. Shrubs. ....Gooseberry
Alternate leaves. Usually evergreen. Mostly small shrubs. Circular indentation or star at end of berry.........Heath
Alternate or opposite leaves. Berry visibly 3-celled (sometimes 2 or 4), with 1 or 2 seeds per cell . . ..Buckthorn

Fruit is a berry with one or a few stony seeds: (Cross-check with the section above.)

Alternate leaves—either three-lobed or pinnate. Shrubs. Red or white berries (poison ivy). ....Sumac
Alternate leaves—simple or pinnate, with spines on margin. Evergreen shrubs. Bright yellow inner bark. Barberry
Alternate leaves. Berry with a "seam" down one side like a cherry. *Prunus spp.* ....Rose
Alternate leaves. Loose cluster of dry fruits from a single stem attached to the middle of a bract. Trees... Basswood
Alternate leaves. The leaves are often asymmetrical. Trees or shrubs. *Celtis spp.*............................... Elm
Alternate or opposite leaves—usually silvery in color or with orange dots underneath. May have thorns. .. Oleaster
Opposite leaves. Flowers with 4 sepals, 4 petals, 2 stamens. 2-celled ovary usually with 2 seeds per cell....... Olive
Opposite leaves—sometimes alternate or whorled. Flowers often with showy, colored bracts. .... Dogwood
Opposite leaves—simple, pinnate, or palmate. Berries in pairs or clusters. Shrubs with pithy stems. . Honeysuckle

KEY TO DICOT TREES AND SHRUBS BY THEIR FRUITS
(FAMILIES WITH SHOWY FLOWERS ARE ALS INCLUDED IN THE FLOWER KEY)

Plants are grouped into families according to their flower structure. Flowers are usually very consistent across a family, while fruits tend to be much more variable. The Rose family, for instance, includes many plants with dry seeds or one-celled capsules, but also fleshy fruits as varied as strawberries, apples and cherries. I chose to include this *Key to Trees and Shrubs by their Fruits* only because the fruits are often much *more visible* than the flowers. Some trees and shrubs have flowers without petals, and I have opted to leave them out of the flower key, but included them here. Other trees and shrubs with showy flowers are included in this key and the flower key.

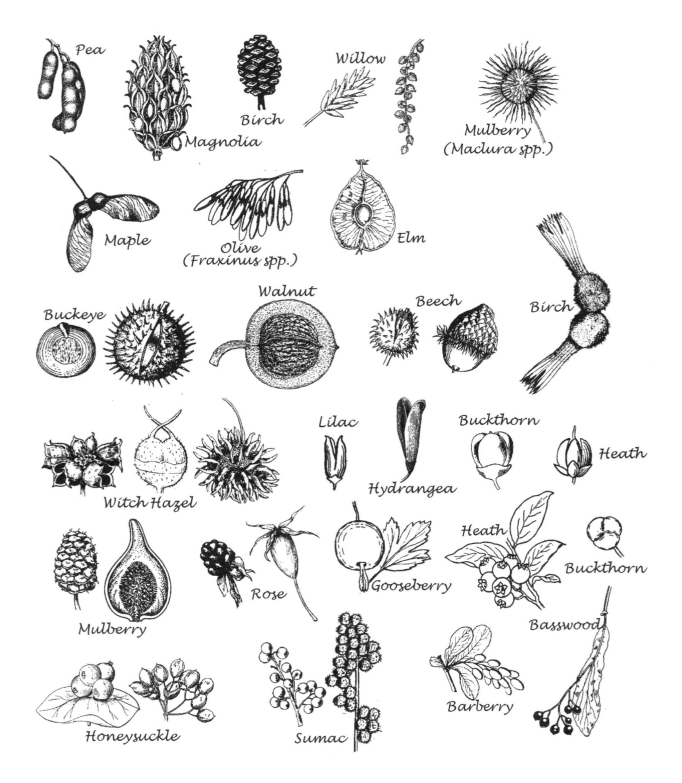

Pea

Magnolia

Birch

Willow

Mulberry
(Maclura spp.)

Maple

Olive
(Fraxinus spp.)

Elm

Buckeye

Walnut

Beech

Birch

Witch Hazel

Lilac

Hydrangea

Buckthorn

Heath

Mulberry

Rose

Gooseberry

Heath

Buckthorn

Basswood

Honeysuckle

Sumac

Barberry

Monocot Plants with Showy Flowers

Aquatic plants with flower parts in 3's and 6-numerous simple pistils, usually on a cone-like head. *Arrowhead Family.*

Aquatic plants of fresh or saltwater with flower parts in 4's and 1-4 simple pistils. *Pondweed Family.* (Also listed below.)

Plants with mucilaginous stems and slightly irregular flowers with parts in 3's. The sepals and petals are easily distinguished from each other. *Spiderwort Family.*

Flowers tightly clustered together in a spike, often wrapped in a large green or white modified leaf (a "spathe"). Fruit is a berry. *Arum Family.*

Flowers with 3 sepals and 3 petals usually identical in size and color, plus usually six stamens. Fruit is a is a 3-celled capsule or berry. (Most showy, regular monocot flowers belong to this group.) *Lily Family.*

Lily-like flowers, but only 3 stamens. Leaves arise from the base of the plant in a flat plane. *Iris Family.*

Distinctly irregular monocot flowers (sometimes not showy). Inferior ovary swells to become seed capsule. *Orchid Family.*

Monocot Plants with Non-Showy Flowers

Aquatic plants with minute flowers clustered on a spike or in a ball, with male flowers at the top and female flowers below. *Cattail Family.*

Aquatic plants (sometimes in damp meadows) with grassy leaves. Flower parts in 3's, with 3-6 simple pistils (sometimes basally united). *Arrowgrass Family.*

Submerged aquatic plants with narrow, serrated leavers. Submerged unisexual flowers with a single stamen enclosed by a bract, or a single pistil, sometimes enclosed by a bract. *Water Nymph Family.*

Aquatic plants of fresh or salt water with flower parts mostly in 4's and 1-4 simple pistils. (Also listed above.) *Pondweed Family.*

Grassy plants with knee-like joints ("nodes") present on the main flower stem. *Grass Family.*

Grass-like plants with triangular flower stems and no nodes. (Some have round, pithy stems.) *Sedge Family.*

Grass-like plants with small, green, lily-like flowers and parts in 3's. *Rush Family.*

Minute aquatic plants floating in the water, without noticeable stems or flowers. *Duckweed Family.*

-Notes Page-

The Lichens

Lichens are a symbiotic association between algae and fungus. The algae is a layer of usually single-celled plants near the surface, just below a gelatinized layer of fungal hyphae. The algae captures nutrients that land on its surface and provide energy through photosynthesis, while the fungus absorbs moisture and provides a protective structure for the algae. These are otherwise independent organisms, capable of surviving without each other. About 30 genera of algae have been found in lichens. The most common algae partners are single-celled plants from the genus *Trebouxia*. Blue-green algae from the genera *Nostoc* and *Stigonema* are also common in lichens.

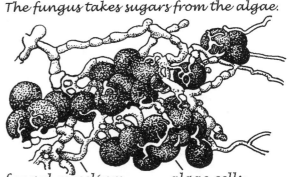

The fungus takes sugars from the algae.

fungal mycelium   algae cells

Lichens can insert threads a half inch into solid rock. These threads are not true roots, but anchors. The fungus produces a potent acid, which is combined with an alcohol from the algae to form acid crystals. The varied and often bright colors of the lichens come from these acid crystals. The acid is used to etch holes in the rock, and threads are inserted for anchors (Platt). Most of the so-called "mosses", especially those found in trees, are actually lichens. The true mosses are distinctively green like other plants.

Lichens gather nutrients through their surfaces directly from the air and rain. This habit gives the lichens an adaptability to live almost anywhere, even on rocks, trees, or buildings. On the other hand, lichens are highly susceptible to air-borne pollutants, which they absorb in toxic concentrations.

It is challenging to identify the many lichen families and genera. Much of the identification is done using high-powered microscopes or chemical tests, using *calcium hypochlorite* (like bleaching powder), *potassium hydroxite* (like "Liquid Plumber"), *aqueous potassium iodide* (iodine tincture), and *paraphenylenediamine* (highly toxic). For specific identification of the Lichens, I recommend *Mosses Lichens & Ferns of Northwest North America* by Dale Vitt, Janet Marsh and Robin Bovey. The book has a technical key, but it also has lots of vivid color photographs. For the purposes of this book I have chosen to lump the lichens together to see what, if any, patterns are revealed across the whole.

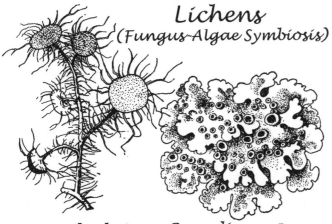

Lichens
(Fungus-Algae Symbiosis)

Usnea barbata   *Parmelia conspersa*

The Lichens include at least 8 orders, 45 families, and 15,000 to 20,000 species. Information on the edible and medicinal uses of the lichens is scattered. Many lichens are known to have potent *antibiotic* properties, and many are *edible*. In fact, all lichens found in the arctic are reportedly edible (Angier). However, some lichens do contain *toxic substances*, so you should not randomly graze on them.

Some lichens can be used to produce brilliant *dyes*. Litmus was originally derived from several species of *Roccella* found in Africa. Litmus is a purple substance that turns red in acid and blue in alkali. Many lichens were fermented in ammonia from urine to obtain the dyes. In most cases the dyes would set without the need for a mordant. Other lichens produced colors for dye when combined with chemicals like chrome, alum, or tannic acid.

The stringy lichens that hang from trees, such as *Alectoria* and *Usnea*, were used by northwest coast Indians for padding in diapers or to weave clothing when they lacked access to skins. Other plant fibers were woven in with the lichens for greater strength. The lichens also worked as a seive to strain the impurities out of hot pitch (Turner).

PARMELIALES ORDER

GYROPHORACEAE

Gyrophora —Rock Tripe: The lichen is edible, especially when boiled with meat (Sturtevant).

Umbiliceria—Rock Tripe: Rock tripe is edible cooked, especially after soaking in a couple changes of cold water to remove the bitterness. They are said to be mucilaginous, great for thickening stews (Angier). It also has antibiotic properties (Angier). *U. esculenta* is considered a delicacy in Japan (Rogers).

LECANORACEAE

Lecanora—Cup Moss, Manna: The plants are edible (Sturtevant). One species, growing in the middle-east is the "manna lichen". During drought years the plant may be broken apart by the wind and blown across the land. This lichen became immortalized in the Bible when it showered down on the starving Israelis as the "manna rain".

PARMELIACEAE

Cetraria—Reindeer Moss: *Cetraria islandica* has a history of use across the northern latitudes. The lichen contains a great deal of mucilage; it is also very bitter (Schauenberg), but edible after extensive soaking or cooking. The lichen can be soaked over-night and for most of a day, in two changes of cold water to remove the acids, then strained and eaten (Angier). The bitter principles are beneficial to the digestive system. In Switzerland the lichen is added to meats and pastries to retard spoilage. It is also used as a source of glycerol for soap making (Rogers), and it is a source of gelatin (Asch). Forty kilograms of the material produces 1 kilogram of an antibiotic. In Finland it is used to treat athlete's foot and ringworm (Rogers). The lichen is still packaged and sold in stores in Iceland as a thickener for soup. (Vitt).

Letharia—Wolf Lichen • This bright yellow tree lichen contains a highly toxic acid. It was once combined with animal fat and nails and used in Europe to kill wolves (Vitt). It is also used as a dye plant.

Parmelia—The lichen is boiled for use as a dye (Gilmore).

USNEACEAE

Alectoria—Black Tree Lichen • Black tree lichen is stringy and moss-like. Montana Indians washed and soaked the lichen, then cooked it for one to two days in a steam pit. The cooked lichen was eaten or dried and powdered and used as a mush or thickener later. Flathead Indian families reportedly ate 25 pounds of the lichen each year (Hart) I once gathered a quantity of *Alectoria* and prepared it. The most difficult part was removing the pine needles prior to cooking, and I concluded it would be imperitive to find a stand of clean lichens to start with. I boiled the lichens on the stove in numerous changes of water until it was reduced to a mass of black slime. While I think it has real potential as a food source, I ate very little from this first sampling, then dried the rest.

Bryoria—Several species of *Bryoria* were eaten by the natives of British Columbia. The lichens were soaked, then cooked in a steam pit for 48 hours until reduced to a jelly-like substance. After cooling it was sliced and eaten, or dried for storage (Vitt).

Evernia— The plant is edible (Sturtevant). A thick tea is used on running sores (Murphey).

Usnea— Old Man's Beard • *Usnea* can be boiled for use as a dye (Gilmore). The lichen contains antibiotic substances. Studies indicate that *Usnea* may be more effective than penicillin in inhibiting the growth of streptococcus, pneumococcus, and various strains of tuberculosis. The lichen can be used straight off the tree as an antimicrobial compress and dressing for open wounds. (Tilford). Laboratory studies with mice showed that the lichen had potent anti-tumor potential (Rogers).

PELTIGERALES ORDER

STICTACEAE

Sticta — The lichen is edible (Sturtevant).

CLADONIALES ORDER

CLADONIACEAE

Cladonia—Pixie Cup Lichen • The *Cladonias* contain didymic acid, used as an antibiotic against tuberculosis (Mabey). They are reported to be edible (Sturtevant). Eskimos used the lichens as wicks in their blubber oil lamps (Rogers).

Cladina—Reindeer Lichen Some species were boiled and the tea was taken for colds or as a laxative (Vitt)

Lycopodiaceae—Club Moss Family

The northern hemisphere was covered with vast, swampy forests from about 200 to 250 million years ago. These forests included now-extinct species of the Club Moss Family that grew to more than 100 feet in height! Note that peat moss (*Sphagnum centrale*) has no vascular system and belongs to the Mosses and Liverworts Division.

The Club Mosses have horizontal branching stems, either above or below ground. These send up erect shoots ranging in size from a 1/2 inch to over a foot tall in some species. The club mosses produce spores in a cone-like structure at the end of a stalk. The spores are shed, then germinate to become a minute "thallus". This word is used to describe a plant part that is not differentiated into leaves or a stem. The thallus produces male and female egg cells. The fertilized egg cells develop into new plants. The reproductive cycle is exceedingly slow in the club mosses. Twenty years or more can pass between the dropping of the spores and the final germination of the new plant. World-wide there are 2 genera and 450 species. Only *Lycopodium* is native to North America.

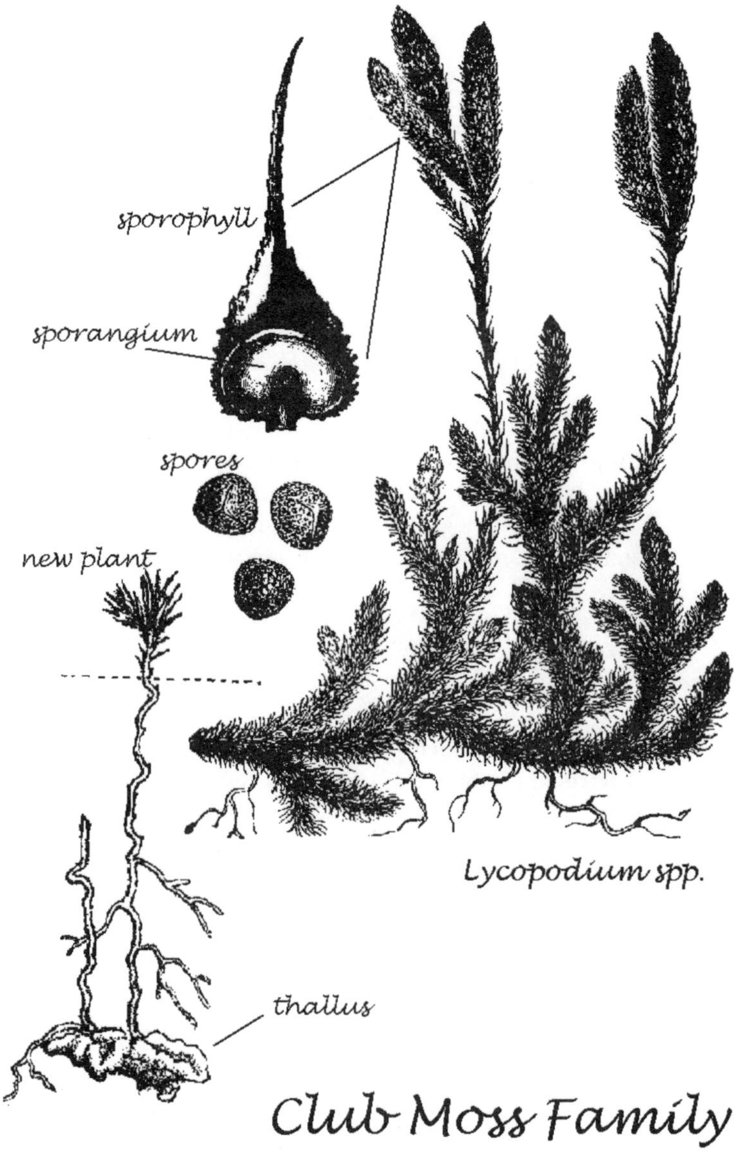

Lycopodium—Club Moss (450/-/8) • Club moss spores have been used as a homeostatic for nosebleed or other hemorrhaging and to absorb fluids from damaged tissues (Lust). The spores were once used as flash powder for stage performances (Smith). Picking and drying the moss will cause it to produce a large, final crop of spores.

L. clavatum reportedly contains toxic alkaloids (Schauenberg), but Native Americans used the tea as an analgesic to relieve pain after childbirth (Willard). The Chinese used the pollen as a dusting powder to coat suppositories and to keep pills from sticking together.. Today club moss spores are sold as "vegetable sulphur"; the powder is dusted onto diaper rashes, bed sores, and herpes eruptions. The spores contain a waxy substance that sooths and repells water. Reportedly you can dip a spore-coated hand in water and remain completely dry. The spores are also used as a dusting powder for condoms. The roots were used as a mordant to set dyes (Rogers).

sporophyll

sporangium

spores

new plant

Lycopodium spp.

thallus

Club Moss Family

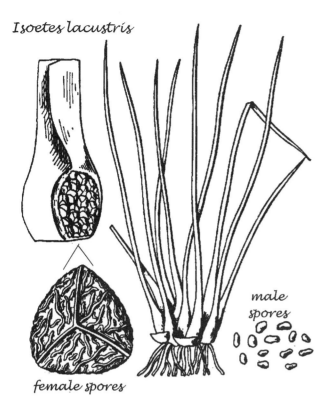

Isoetes lacustris

female spores

male spores

Isoetaceae—Quillwort Family

The Quillworts are small plants, typically found growing on the bottom of fresh-water ponds and lakes. They have hollow "quill-like" leaves, with a spore sack (sporangia) at the base of each leaf. The outer leaves produce male spore sacks and the inner leaves produce the female spore sacks. World-wide there are 2 genera and 77 species. Only *Isoetes* is found in North America.

Isoetes—Quillwort (75/-/5) Quillwort is often planted in aquariums.

Selaginellaceae—Spike Moss Family

Members of the Spike Moss family have small leaves arranged in four rows along the stems. Each leaf has a small, scale-like appendage at the base of the upper surface. This is believed to be a hold-over from an ancestral species, with no function in the living plants. The Spike Mosses produce male and female spores on the plant. These develop into the thallus and are fertilized before being shed. World-wide there is 1 genus and some 700 species.

Selaginella—Spike Moss (700/-/4) One species of Selaginella is called the "resurrection plant". During times of drought the plant rolls its leaves into a tight ball. Upon exposure to moisture it immediately uncurls and continues growing. It is often cultivated as a curiosity. Note that another resurrection plant, called *Anastatica* belongs to the Mustard family (Asch). There is also a resurrection fern.

Medicinally, the mashed plant can be simmered in milk and used internally or externally for snake or spider bites (Rogers).

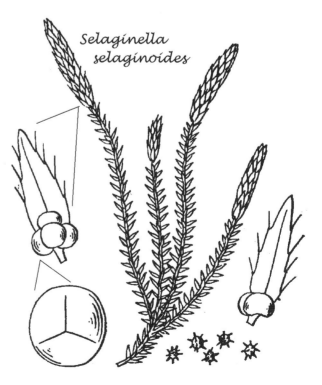

Selaginella selaginoides

31

Equisetaceae—Horsetail family

The horsetail produces two different stalks. One is the fertile "joint-grass", the other is the sterile "horse-tail". The fertile stalk produces a cone-like structure at the top, which is covered with spore-producing scales. The spores are wrapped with small bands. These bands unwrap in dry weather to function as parachute to carry the spores through the wind. Multiple spores frequently become entangled and travel together. The spores germinate into a thallus, cross-fertilize, then develop into a new plant. The world *thallus* is used to describe a plant part that is not differentiated into leaves or a stem.

The Horsetail family is small, comprised of 1 genus and 23 species world-wide. In earlier times this group was much larger and more diverse, with many species growing into giant trees. These ancient plants formed a significant portion of our coal deposits. Some deposits consist principally of compressed masses of spores. This rock is called "cannel". It can be cut and polished for ornaments.

Today there is only one tree-like species of horsetail. It is a native of the American tropics and grows to about 30 feet tall. The horsetails have an abrasive quality to them because they absorb silica from the soil to give strength to the plant structure.

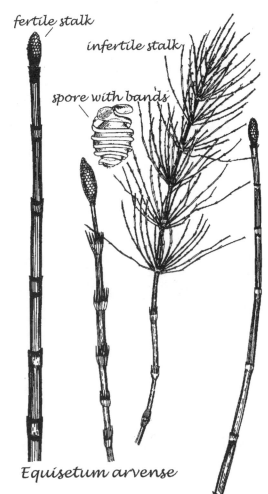

fertile stalk

infertile stalk

spore with bands

Equisetum arvense

Equisetum—Horsetail, Joint Grass, Scouring Rush (23/-/8) • The horsetail contains significant quantities (5-8%) of silica and silicic acids plus saponins (Tyler); it makes an excellent abrasive pad for cleaning camp cookware. This silica content is beneficial for the hair and fingernails (Bigfoot). The roots of some species are starchy and edible (Sturtevant).

Medicinally, a tea of the plant is mildly diuretic and astringent, useful for urinary tract infections, intestinal bleeding, excess menstruation, or external bleeding. Horsetails are also rich in calcium and other constituents believed beneficial for mending fractured bones and connective tissues

Note: the fresh plant contains thiaminase, an enzyme which destroys vitamin B-1 stored in the body. Cooking destroys the enzyme and renders the plant safe.. However, the high silica content can irritate the urinary tract and kidneys with excessive use. Also, the plants are known to accumulate heavy metals and chemicals from polluted soil. (Tilford).

Ophioglossaceae—Grape Fern Family

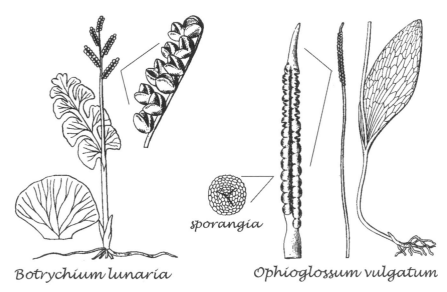

sporangia

Botrychium lunaria

Ophioglossum vulgatum

The Grape Fern Family is more primitive than the other ferns. They can be distinguished by the way the leaves (fronds) develop. Other ferns unroll their new leaves, but the grape ferns open them laterally. Also, the sporangia among the Grape Ferns are globe-shaped sacks on a stalk or at the base, as opposed to the true ferns with their "dots" on the underside of the leaves. World-wide there are 4 genera and 70 species. Our native genera are listed below. *Ophioglossaceae* is also known as the Adder's Tongue family.

Botrychium—Grape Fern (40/-/10)

One species is known to be boiled and eaten in the Himalayas and New Zealand (Sturtevant). A tea of the root has emetic, expectorant, and diaphoretic properties (Fern). The tea induces a gentle, warm sweat while soothing the nervous system. It is also mildly diuretic (Rogers).

Ophioglossum—Adder's Tongue, Grape Fern (30+/-/1) The leaves of at least one species are edible. Medicinally, the juice of the leaves is taken for internal bleeding and bruises (Fern).

Salviniaceae—Water Fern Family

Salvinia natans

The Water Ferns are small, floating ferns. The leaves may appear in pairs or rows. The Water Ferns may be confused with members of the unrelated Duckweed family (*Lemnaceae*). N ote the submerged sporangia on the illustration here. If the sporangia are present then it is definitely a Water Fern.

World-wide there are 2 genera and 16 species. *Salvinia* may be found in Florida and other southern states. *Azolla* is found across the continent. Some botanists split these genera into separate families.

Azolla—Mosquito Fern (6/6/0)
Salvinia—Water Fern (10/10/0)

33

Polypodiaceae—Fern Family

Ferns are distinctive and easily recognized. They reproduce with spores, which are formed on the underside of the leaves. These spores are produced asexually and spread by the wind. The spore germinates when it comes in contact with moist ground and develops into a minute structure called a "thallus". This term is used to describe a plant part that cannot be differentiated into leaves or a stem. The thallus produces female egg cells and male "spermatozoids". The male parts swim to and fertilize the egg cells, but only one egg cell matures to become a new fern. World-wide there are an estimated 170 genera and 7,000 to 8,000 species in the Fern family, including 36 genera and more than 200 species in North America. As treated here, the Fern family includes Adiantaceae, Aspleniaceae, and Dennstaedtiaceae. Please note that there are several other families of ferns not included in this text.

Caution is advised using ferns. Some species contain *carcinogens*. Many ferns also contain an enzyme that robs the body of B vitamins, but the enzyme is deactivated by cooking or drying (Fern).

Adiantum—Maidenhair (200/-/1) A tea of the leaves is expectorant and refrigerant, used for coughs and colds (Lust). A tea of the leaves or root is used as a menstrual stimulant (Moore), or as a hair rinse to add shine and body (Tilford).

Asplenium—Spleenwort (-/-/2) A tea of the plant is used to remove obstructions from the liver and spleen, and gravel from the bladder (Kadans).

Athyrium—Lady Fern (180/-/2) *Athyrium* contains a constituent similar to filicic acid (Densmore).

Dryopteris—Shield Fern (150/-/4) The plant contains potent acids. A tea of the root is used to expel worms, but must be followed by a purgative shortly afterwards to keep from poisoning the body. It should never be mixed with alcohol. The tea is also used as a foot bath for varicose veins (Lust). A poultice of the fresh, grated root is helpful for inflammation of the lymphatic glands. (Rogers).

Matteucia—Ostrich Fern (3/-/0) The young fiddleheads are edible, but fresh they contain thiaminase, which destroys Vitamin B in the body, so they must be cooked. Native Americans in Canada roasted the roots, then peeled away the outside and ate the cores.

Pellaea—Cliff Brake (80/-/3) A tea of the plant can be taken for tuberculosis and other lung infections (Bigfoot).

Polypodium—Polypody (75/-/1) The root contains a resinous bitter substance, volatile oils, and a sugary mucilage (Schauenberg). A tea of the root is used for worms, fever, respiratory problems, and as a purgative (Lust). A strong tea of the root of the licorice fern (*P. glycyrrhiza*) is useful as an anti-inflammatory, especially as a mild alternative to antihistamines (Moore). *P. vulgare* reportedly contains osladin, a substance 300 times sweeter than sugar (Rogers).

Polystichum—Holly Fern, Sword Fern (135/-/5) The roasted roots are edible (Sturtevant). The fronds were used in cooking to line steam pits (Turner).

Pteretis—Brake Fern (250/-/0) Ostrich fern is native to the northeast quarter of the country. The young fiddleheads are edible raw or cooked after the hairs are rubbed off and the plants soaked clean (Hall).

Pteridium—Bracken Fern (1/1/1) *P. aquilinum*, the young fronds can be eaten raw or cooked, but may contain a carcinogen (Bell). They are reported to have a mucilaginous quality, making a good stew thickener. . The root contains saponin (Fern), but can be roasted and pounded for its edible starch (Angier). The mature fern may be toxic (Olsen).

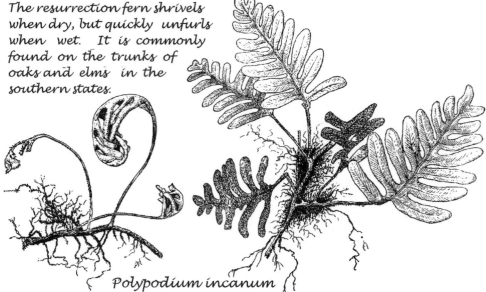

The resurrection fern shrivels when dry, but quickly unfurls when wet. It is commonly found on the trunks of oaks and elms in the southern states.

Other selected genera:
Aspidotis—Indian's Dream (2/-/1) … *Cheilanthes*—Lip Fern (180/-/2) … *Cryptogramma*—Rock Brake (4/-/2) … *Cystopteris*—Bladder Fern (18/-/2) … *Gymnocarpium*—Oak Fern (-/-/1) … *Thelypteris*—Beech Fern (4/-/1) … *Woodsia*—(40/-/2)

Polypodium incanum

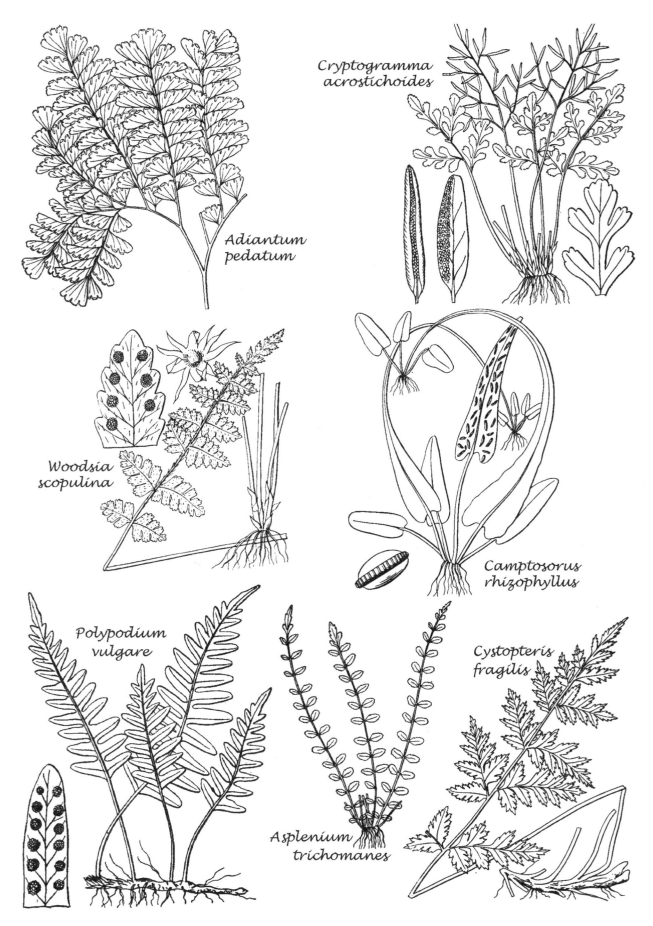

Cryptogramma
acrostichoides

Adiantum
pedatum

Woodsia
scopulina

Camptosorus
rhizophyllus

Polypodium
vulgare

Cystopteris
fragilis

Asplenium
trichomanes

Pinaceae—Pine Family

Members of the Pine family are "naked seed" plants even though the seeds are highly protected under the scales of developing cones. The female cones briefly become elongated, exposing the ovules to the pollen in the wind. The shape of the cones causes air currents to swirl around them to help catch this pollen. The pollen and the cones are aerodynamically matched to each other, so each species captures its own pollen. After pollination the scales grow rapidly and again cover the ovules, allowing them to mature into seeds. Primitive conifers first came into being about 300 million years ago, but most or all of them are extinct now. The Pine Family as we know it originated about 100 million years ago. World-wide there are 10 genera and 250 species. Our native genera are listed below. Amber is the fossilized pitch from this family.

The Pine family produces *edible* seeds that are rich in oils, although they are small and difficult to gather from most species. The needles may be used as in tea for a beverage, or medicinally for a diuretic. The Pine family is highly *resinous*, useful for its expectorant properties, but over-consumption may lead to kidney complications. Be sure to read more about resins in the Medicinal Properties section of this book.

Abies—Fir, Balsam Fir (50/-/2) • Fir contains turpentine, made of essential oils and resin. The oleoresin is stimulant, diuretic, and sometimes diaphoretic and externally rubefacient (Densmore). The needles can be used as an aromatic bath for rheumatism and nervous diseases (Klein). Steeped fir needles makes on of my favorite wilderness teas.

Larix—Larch, Tamarack (10/-/2) • The Larch sometimes exudes a sweet, edible sap (Sturtevant). The needles, bark, and resin all contain varying amounts of volatile oils, essentially turpentine. Drink a tea of the needles as a carminative to expel gas, or add the tea to your bath water for inflamed joints. The tea is also anthelmintic, diuretic, and laxative. Excess consumption can injure the kidneys (Lust). Larix contains a volatile oil made up of pinene, larixine, and the ester bornylacetate (Densmore).

Picea—Spruce (50/-/2) • A tea of the shoots is expectorant and diaphoretic, ideal for coughs and bronchitis (Lust).

Pinus—Pines (70+/-/5) • Pine nuts are perhaps the best kept secret of all the wild edibles there are. You may be familiar with the pine nut as a gourmet food from the pinion pine of the southwest, but the nuts from other pines are equally delicious and nutritious! All pine nuts are quite edible, but some like the lodgepole are impractical to harvest. The whitebark (*P. albicaulis*) and limber pines (*P. flexillis*) have a known history of use. Other pines around the country have certainly been used as well, you just have to get out and try the different trees to find which ones are most practical to harvest.

   The season for pine nuts is short. You need to watch the cones ripen on the trees and pick them as they start to open up, but before they drop the nuts. Lash a short stick to the end of a longer stick to make a hook, then use the hook to pull cones down from the trees. The cones may need to be dried more to open them up; this can be done by placing them in a warm, sunny spot, or by placing them in a pit which has been warmed with a fire. Be sure to scrape out all the hot coals before placing the cones in the pit. The nuts are pretty easy to shake or tap out once the cones open up. The hull is usually processed off the pinion nuts, but ours are quite edible with the hull intact. You can eat the pine nuts whole or ground, and raw or cooked. They are delicious in any way.

   The pine nuts do shrivel up as they dry, so the earlier in the season that you can get them the better. You can even harvest them early when the cones are very green, except that the nuts are much harder to get out at that time. Be sure to read *Participating in Nature* for additional notes on processing pine nuts.

   Medicinally, the pines are quite resinous and aromatic; the tea is useful as an expectorant, but can irritate the kidneys. It is reported that the needles of some pines cause abortions in cattle, so caution is advised here. Externally, the resin has a disinfectant quality, like Pinesol. The bark of some species contains powerful anti-oxidants.

Pseudotsuga—Douglas fir (7/-/1) • The seeds of the Douglas fir are edible, like pine nuts, just smaller. The season for them is very short. You have to watch the trees and collect the seeds just as the cones open up. You can shake the seeds out directly into a container, or you can pick the cones a little early and dry them out before you shake or tap out the seeds. We tried some various methods of harvesting fir seeds in bulk, shaking the branches and catching the seeds on tarps or in baskets, but found this to be impractical. The big problem was sorting out the seeds from the trash. The needles, bits of cone, flower parts, and seeds are all about the same weight, making the winnowing extremely difficult. My conclusion is that the seeds are worth tasting, but not worth harvesting and storing.

Tsuga—Hemlock Tree (15/-/2) Please note that there is no relationship between the hemlock tree and the poison hemlocks of the Parsley family. Tsuga is astringent, diuretic, and diaphoretic. A tea of the bark or twigs is used for sore mouth or throat, and kidney or bladder problems. Externally it is used as a wash for sores (Lust). The inner bark was reportedly used by the Indians for food in the springtime (Sturtevant).

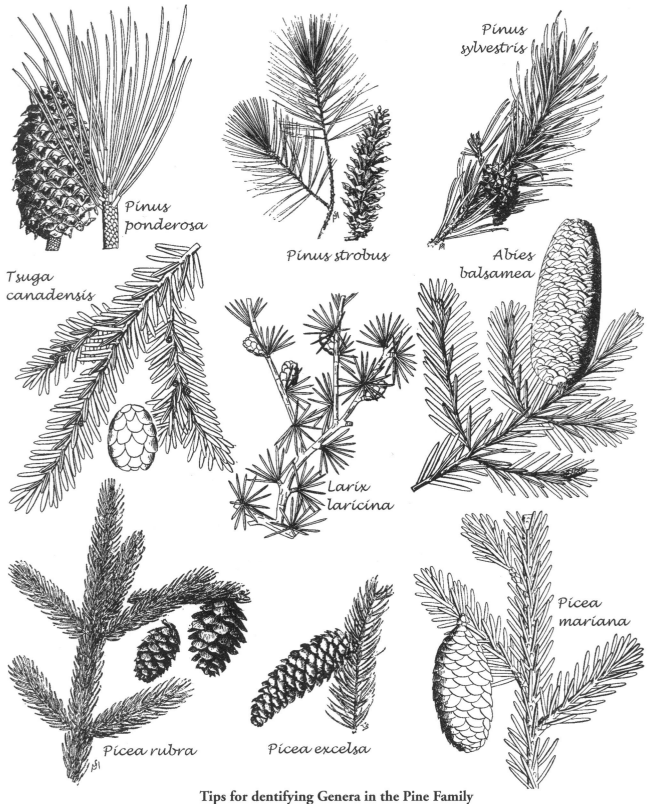

Pinus
sylvestris

Pinus
ponderosa

Pinus strobus

Abies
balsamea

Tsuga
canadensis

Larix
laricina

Picea
mariana

Picea rubra

Picea excelsa

Tips for dentifying Genera in the Pine Family
-Pines have 1-5 needles wrapped together at the base by a thin membrane.
-Larches have bright green, deciduous needles arranged in a spiral at the branch buds.
-The spruces usually have sharp, pointed needles.
-The firs have soft, "furry" needles.
-Douglas fir can be distinguished from other firs by the presence of "tridents" on the cones.
-Hemlock trees have short, flat, blunt needles attached by a small stem.

Cupressaceae—Cypress or Cedar Family

If you have ever smelled cedar or juniper wood, then you know the Cypress Family. The trees or shrubs of this family have small, scaley leaves and separate male and female cones, sometimes on separate trees. The seed-bearing cones are woody in most genera. The juniper "berry" is really a cone with fleshy scales.

All members of the family are richly aromatic, especially useful as an insence. World-wide there are 19 genera and 130 species, including 5 genera in North America.

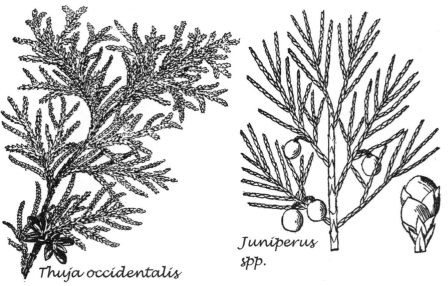

Thuja occidentalis

Juniperus spp.

Calocedrus (Libocedrus)—Insence Cedar (3/-/0) A tea of the aromatic twigs can be sipped for stomach troubles or inhaled to aid a head cold (Fern).

Chamaecyparis—White Cedar (7/-/0) White cedar is used in sweatlodges to aid rheumatism and arthritis, and other aches. It may also be used as a wash or bath. The tea is a powerful diuretic (Fern).

Cupressus—Cypress (15/-/0) A tea of the leaves is used internally or externally to stop bleeding, and for colds (Fern).

Juniperus—Juniper, Red Cedar (60/-/4) • Juniper berries can be eaten raw or used in tea. The bitter berries are the main ingredient in gin. Most people would consider them unpalatable, but I have acquired a taste for them over the last 15 years. Juniper berries contain volatile oils and resins; they are eaten as a carminative to expel gas, and the distilled oil is rubbed on painful joints. Additionally, juniper berries are diuretic, but may irritate the kidneys with prolonged use. They are not recommended for pregnant women (Lust, Tyler). A boiled tea of the fruits and leaves is a treatment for coughs (Gilmore). You may be able to decrease the risk of catching a virus by keeping juniper berries in the mouth while around others who are infected (Bigfoot). Also try chewing the berries when drinking unclean water.

Juniper needles can be added to the bath water for a stimulating effect on rheumatism. A southwestern species of juniper produces a thick, fibrous bark that is ideal tinder material for fire-starting.

Thuja—Cedar, Arbor-Vitae (5/-/1) • Cedar contains toxic volatile oils. It is used as a diaphoretic (promotes sweating), emmenagogue (promotes menstruation), and as an irritant poultice to stimulate healing to rheumatic pains. It should not be used without medical supervision (Lust). It is also expectorant.

Taxodiaceae—Bald Cypress Family

The Bald Cypress Family is small in numbers, but big in stature. The cypress swamps of Florida are well-known both for the distinctive ecology and the distinctive aerial roots that brace the trees upright in the water. On the other side of the country, the giant sequoia of California is the largest living thing on earth. The nearby redwoods are also huge in size. The trees shed a portion of their narrow leaves or twigs each year, so they are considered deciduous, even though they retain enough leaves to appear "evergreen". Look around the base of the trees for signs of the shedding twigs and leaves. Worldwide there are 10 genera and 16 species. The genera below are native to North America.

Taxodium distichum

Taxodium—Bald Cypress (3/-/0) Resin from the cones is used as an analgesic. The bark can be used to make cordage (Fern).

Sequoia—Redwood (1/1/0) *S. sempervirens*, the tea is aromatic and astringent. It is useful as an expectorant to help expel mucou, and as a mild disinfectant to the urrinary for bladder infections (Moore).

Sequoiadendron—Giant Sequoia (1/1/0) *S. giganteum*, the giant sequoia has aromatic vegetation and probably similar uses to its close cousins the redwoods.

Taxaceae—Yew Family

If you see a a shrub or tree with conifer-like branches and red or green berry-like fruits, then it is certainly a member of the Yew Family. The fruit is called an "aril"; produced by the swelling of the seed stalk around the seed. The *Taxus* genus is especially easy to recognize with its red, cup-shaped fruits.

World-wide there are 5 genera and 20 species. The genera below are native to North America.

Taxus spp.

Taxus—Yew (10/-/1) • Yew wood is prized for bow-making. The berries may be edible when ripe (Sturtevant), but all other parts of the yew tree contain poisonous alkaloids. It is listed as expectorant and purgative, but its use is not recommended without medical supervision (Lust). It also increases blood pressure (Phillips). In recent years a potent cancer medicine, called taxol, was derived from the bark of the tree. The preparation required most of the bark from a tree. Like most cancer medicines, this one was as toxic to the body as it was to the cancer. It is now produced in the laboratory.

Torreya— "California Nutmeg", Stinking Yew (6/-/1) The fruit of the California nutmeg resembles the true nutmeg in shape only and not in taste. The plants are not related. Indians roasted and ate the big seeds (Crittenden).

Ephedraceae—Mormon Tea Family

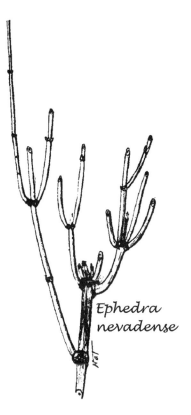

Ephedra nevadense

The Ephedras produce naked seeds like the pines, but they form on a colored, cup-like structure, called a perianth. Thus it superficially appears that these plants are an evolutionary link between the conifers and the true flowering plants. However, these are a recently evolved class of plants, and the fossil record indicates that the flowering plants developed before them.

The Ephedras are leafless desert shrubs with jointed, green stems forming in whorls at nodes along the stalk. Unlike other members of the Naked Seed Division, the Ephedras lack resin canals. The male cones have 2-8 anthers. The female cones have bracts covering the two maturing seeds. World-wide there is 1 genus and 40 species.

Ephedra—Mormon Tea, Brigham Tea, Ma Huang (40/-/0) • *Ephedra* is common in the desert southwest. It is mostly used as a beverage tea. The red berry is reported to be sweet and edible (Asch). Medicinally the plant is diuretic (Lust). The tea is recommended for diabetes, asthma, heart ailments and syphilis (Bigfoot).

A Chinese species, *E. sinica*, contains a potent stimulant alkaloid called ephedrine. Ephedrine stimulates the central nervous system and is thus used as a headache medicine, much like caffeine. Over-consumption can lead to nervousness, tension and insomnia. Other side effects of ephedrine include high blood pressure, reduced appetite, and reduced sexual desire (Emboden). Ephedrine has a dilating effect on the bronchials, but a constricting effect on the blood vessels.

Ephedra is often added to natural weight-loss and energy formulas. The stimulant effect is supposed to increases the burning of fats. At least fifteen people have died from over-dosing on ephedrine pills. Our southwestern species contain some ephedrine, but in much more minute amounts than the Chinese plants. Ephedrine is now produced synthetically for use as a decongestant in cold medications (Tyler).

Magnoliaceae—Magnolia Family

The trees and shrubs of the Magnolia family are distinctive with their showy flowers and the pine cone-like structure that the seeds develop in. Botanically there are 3 sepals and 3 or more petals, although the sepals and petals may be difficult to distinguish from one another in some species. The flowers are bisexual with numerous stamens arranged in a spiral, plus numerous simple pistils (apocarpous), also arranged in a spiral to make the "cone" in the center of the flower. The pistils are positioned superior to the other parts. Each pistil matures into a "follicle", a one-celled capsule with a seam down the side. In the *Magnolia* genus the seeds sometimes fall free from the follicle to hang suspended from fine threads.

World-wide there are 12 genera and 230 species in the family. The genera below are native to North America. The tulip tree and magnolia are native to the eastern states, but magnolias are often planted domestically in west-coast communities. *Michelia* is grown as an ornamental in some parts of the country.

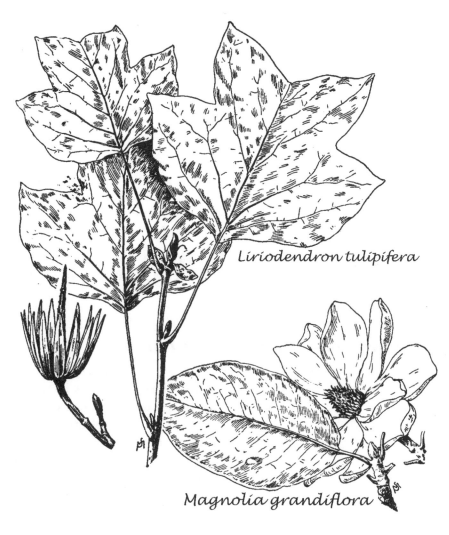

Liriodendron tulipifera

Magnolia grandiflora

Key Words
Broad-leaf trees with "flowering pine cones".

Liriodendron—Tulip Tree, Yellow "Poplar" (2/-/0) Some Native Americans ate the bark to expel worms and gave the seeds to children for the same purpose. The tulip tree has also been used to reduce fevers, as a diuretic, and for rheumatism (Weiner). The root has been used in Canada to take away the bitterness in brewing alcohol (Sturtevant).

Magnolia— (77/-/0) • The bark of the magnolia is known for its aromatic and astringent properties. A tea of the bark is used medicinally as a diaphoretic, and for indigestion or diarrhea. Reportedly, drinking the tea can help break the tobacco habit (Lust).

Aristolochiaceae—Birthwort Family

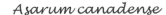

Asarum canadense

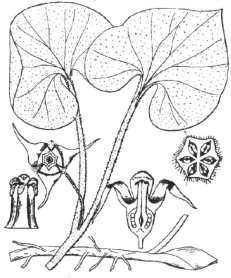

If you find a low-growing dicot plant in the moist forests of the northern latitudes with tubular flowers and parts in multiples of 3, it is almost certainly a member of the Birthwort family.

Our members of this family have either regular or irregular, bisexual flowers with 3 united sepals, 0 or 3 minute petals, and typically 12 stamens. The ovary is positioned inferior and consists of 6 united carpels (syncarpous) with the partition walls present, forming an equal number of chambers. It matures as a capsule with numerous seeds. Most members of this family are tropical plants. Worldwide there are 7 genera, representing about 400 species. The genera below are native to North America.

Medicinally, the pattern of this family is potent ***volatile oils***. The spicy nature of these plants warms the body and stimulates sweating (diaphoretic). Warming the body naturally increases blood flow, so these plants are also listed as having a vasodilator effect. Increased menstruation (emmenagogue) and uterine stimulation (oxytocic) are direct effects of increased blood flow. The contraceptive effect of Asarum may be due to the anthelmintic (worm-killing) effects of the potent volatile oils. Be sure to read more about volatile oils in the Medicinal Properties section of this book.

<u>Key Words</u>
Dicot plants with tubular flowers and parts in 3's.

Aristolochia—Birthwort (-/13/0) Birthwort contains a volatile oil, an alkaloid (Weiner), and a strong and toxic acid. The teas is used for infected wounds (Schauenberg). The birthworts are bitter, diaphoretic, and vasodilating, used to stimulate digestion, sweating, and white blood cell activity. A tea of the root is used as an "oxytocic" to stimulate uterine contractions during childbirth. Caution is advised in using this herb (Lust). The raw root was chewed and applied as a poultice for snake bite (Weiner)

Asarum—Wild Ginger (-/14/1) • The true ginger belongs to the Ginger family, *Zingiberaceae*, but *Asarum* is used similarly. Thin slices can be used in oriental cooking. The powdered root is used as a spice (Hall). Our Montana species has small, thread-like roots, but the leaves are flavorful and can be used in cooking in place of the roots (Tilford).

Medicinally, *Asarum* is a digestive stimulant, and like commercial ginger, it can be used to relieve stomach ache (Coon). *A. canadense* is listed as diaphoretic, carminative, expectorant, and irritant. A tea of the root was used by some American Indian women as a contraceptive. A European species, *A. europaeum,* is purgative and diuretic. It is considered too dangerous for use without supervision (Lust).

Aristolochia serpentaria

Nuphar advena

Nymphaea odorata

Nelumbo lutea

Nymphaeaceae—Water-lily Family

If you have ever seen a pond of lily pads then you have certainly seen members of this family. These are perennial, aquatic plants with thick horizontal rootstocks and large leaves that float on the surface of the water. They have solitary flowers on long stalks with 3-12 sepals and 3 to numerous petals. The ovary is positioned superior and consists of 3 or more separate or united carpels (apocarpous or syncarpous). It matures as a follicle (a dry fruit with a seam down one side), a nutlet, or a leathery, capsule-like "berry". World-wide there are about 7 genera and 68 species, including 4 genera in North America. Note that aquatic members of the Gentian family have similar leaves.

Each of these plants produces large, starchy roots and some are *edible*, but some species have powerful and undefined medicinal qualities making them unpalatable as food. Otherwise, the predominant medicinal patterns of this family are *mucilaginous* and *astringent*. Do not gather any plants for food or medicine from polluted waters. Most water plants cleanse pollutants out of the water and accumulate it in their tissues.

<u>Key Words</u>
Aquatic plants with large floating leaves.

Brasenia—Water Shield (1/1/1) *B. schreberi*, the starchy roots are boiled, peeled and eaten (Kirk).

Nelumbo—Lotus, Nelumbo (2/2/0) The acrid roots are edible after washing, and the seeds are edible (Sturtevant).

Nuphar—Yellow Pond Lily (13+/13/2) • Apparently a related European species has an edible root (Craighead), and *Nuphar avena*, growing in eastern America may be edible (Hall), but the common western species, *Nuphar variegatum* is strongly medicinal. Other authors have seemingly assumed that our species has an edible root, but apparently none have actually waded into the swamp to test that assumption. A friend and I made ourselves quite ill attempting to eat the root on a camping trip; other practicing primitives have reported similarly. Boiling in multiple changes of water does little to improve the root.

Pond lily seeds are also reported to be edible. The pods are collected, dried, and pounded to remove the seeds. The seeds are popped like popcorn, but with only mild heat, then winnowed to separate them from the hard shells, and ground into meal (Hart). In my experience the seeds have the same (although less intense) nauseating aroma of the roots. Clearly there needs to be more research done on this plant.

Medicinally, the Montana Indians boiled and mashed the starchy roots as poultices for sores, cuts, or rheumatism. The tea could be drunk to open up the urinary tract, or it could be added to bath water for rheumatism (Hart). *N. lutea* of Europe contains terpenoid alkaloids with hypotensive and antispasmodic effects (Schauenberg).

Nymphaeae—Water Lily (40/5/2) The roots and seeds of several species are reported to be edible (Sturtevant). The young leaves and flower buds are edible as a potherb. The larger leaves can be used to wrap food in for baking. A tea of the root or leaf is gargled for sore throat; also used as an eye wash, or as an astringent, mucilaginous lotion (Coon). Some species may contain cardiac glycosides and alkaloids (Schauenberg). Caution is advised.

Ranunculaceae—Buttercup Family

Key Words
Dicot flowers with 3 or more hooked pistils.

The Buttercup family is like a window back in time. If you travel back a hundred million years to see the first flowering plants you will find species similar to those of the Buttercup family today. That's what paleobotanists have found by studying the fossil record. Of all the families of flowering plants, today's Buttercups and their allies like the Magnolias have retained the most ancestral characteristics.

The Buttercups are considered very "simple" because the floral parts—the petals, sepals, stamens, and pistils—are all of an indefinite number and separate from one another. More advanced plant families have reduced, more specific numbers of floral parts, and the parts are often fused together.

The Buttercup family may be considered "simple" from an evolutionary standpoint, but it includes some flowers that are highly complex in appearance, such as the Delphinium and Columbine. Yet these flowers are still considered "simple" because all the parts are independently attached.

You will discover that the most common pattern of the family is the apparent *lack* of a pattern! Buttercups can have anywhere from 3 to 15 sepals, often colored like petals, and there can be anywhere from 0 to 23 actual petals. There are often, but not always, "numerous" stamens and numerous simple pistils (apocarpous), and the flo-

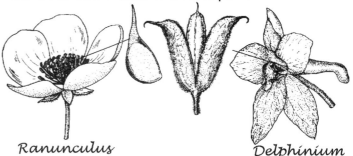

Pistils have a "spur" that remains as the ovary matures into a seed or seed capsule.

Ranunculus   *Delphinium*

ral parts are all independently attached below a superior ovary. Most have bisexual flowers, except some species of meadow rue (*Thalictrum*) and *Clematis*. Worldwide there are 35-70 genera in the Buttercup family and about 2000 species. Twenty-three genera are found in North America.

For the purposes of **identification**, the most obvious pattern across the family is the appearance of *3-numerous pistils with a small "spur" at the top*. Next time you see a peony (*Paeonia*), columbine (*Aquilegia*), or *Clematis,* stop and look at the pistils inside. You will see the spur when the flowers are first blooming, and the effect usually remains as the pistil matures into a seed or seed capsule. Most of the more evolved plant families have only one pistil at the center of each flower. Also note that the pistils often appear on a *cone-like receptical* in the middle of the flower. Note: A few species from the Rose family may be confused with the Buttercups.

The predominant property in the plants of the Buttercup family is an *acrid* protoanemonin glycoside oil. Most of the species are listed as poisonous, but *most* all are safe to *taste*. The buttercup taste is biting and acrid, stronger in some plants than others. Taste it and spit it out.

The acrid properties of the buttercups are unstable and are destroyed by drying or cooking, so the very mild buttercups are *edible* as salad greens or potherbs. But be careful not to over-do even these, as the residual acrid properties may cause a mild inflammation of the kidneys or liver. Mucilaginous plants can be ingested to counter-effect the acrid buttercups. Medicinally, the *acrid* nature of the plants makes them great for stimulating poultices, similar to a "mustard plaster". These poultices can be used on bruises, aches, or arthritis to stimulate healing activity inside, but be careful, because the poultices can cause blistering if left in place too long. The poultice can even stimulate activity in cases of mild paralysis. The acrid quality is also beneficial for getting rid of lice. Be sure to read more about acrid substances in the Medicinal Properties section of this book.

Goldenseal (*Hydrastis*) is a popular medicinal herb from this family. It is favored for the very bitter and highly antiseptic **berberine alkaloid**, also found in a few related genera and in the Barberry family.

WARNING: A number of plants in this family, especially *Aconitum* and *Delphinium* contain concentrations of toxic **terpenoid alkaloids**. These alkaloids *depress* the central nervous system; they are often used for nervous disorders, antispasmodics and sedatives. Some of these plants can be cautiously used internally (by professionals only!) as heart and respiratory sedatives.

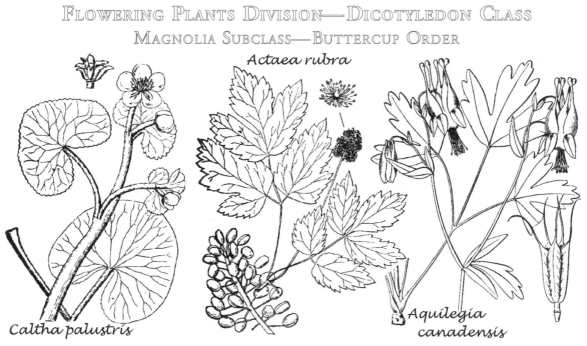

Actaea rubra

Caltha palustris

Aquilegia canadensis

Helleborus Subfamily

The subfamilies of the Buttercup family are distinguished from one another by their fruits. Members of the Helleborus subfamily produce berries or "follicles" (one-celled capsules that open along a single seam).

Aconitum—Monkshood (275/8/1) • Water hemlock from the Parsley family may be the most poisonous plant in North America, but a species of monkshood (*A. ferrox*) from Nepal is considered the most poisonous plant in the world. Even touching or smelling the plant can cause serious poisoning (Schauenberg). North American species of monkshood are much less toxic, but still deadly poisonous (Lust). The root is the most toxic part. A tincture or linament of the flowering plant may be used externally as an analagesic, if the skin is unbroken. It should not be used during pregnancy (Moore). Monkshood can be used internally, but only under expert supervision.

Actaea—Baneberry (-/-/1) • Children have been poisoned by eating the waxy, shiny red or white berries. Otherwise, baneberry is similar to black cohosh (see *Cimicifuga* below), but apparently lacks the estrogenic compounds. A poultice or linament of the root is useful as an anti-inflammatory and analgesic for sprains and swellings (Moore).

Aquilegia—Columbine (70/23/5) • The leaves or flowers are edible in a salad or steamed (Willard), but there is a risk of toxicity (Tilford). The root, seeds, and probably the leaves of some species are acrid and may be used raw for a stimulating poultice (Sweet)

Caltha—Marsh Marigold (20/3/1) • Marsh Marigold can be eaten as a salad or potherb (Harrington). It is acrid enough to stimulate mucus flow throughout the body (Moore). *C. palustris* contains berberine (Densmore).

Cimicifuga—Black Cohosh, Bugbane (-/5/0) The root and leaves of black cohosh (different from blue cohosh) are valued as peripheral vasodilators and for their anti-inflammatory, antispasmodic, sedative properties. Black cohosh is used especially for dull aches and muscle or menstrual cramping. The root also contains estrogenic compounds useful to lessen the surges of the luteinizing hormone and the related hot flashes during menopause (Moore).

Coptis—Gold Thread, Canker Root (-/4/1) • The roots of gold thread contain the bitter alkaloid berberine like its well-knownand over-harvested cousin goldenseal (see *Hydrastis* below). It may be used in the same ways, but take care to avoid over harvesting it. Gold thread has a long history of use in treating cold sores, hence its other common name.

Delphinium—Larkspur, Delphinium (300/67/13) • A vinegar or rubbing alcohol tincture of the plant is used for lice. But do not apply to highly irritated skin or the toxic alkaloids may be absorbed by the body (Moore).

Hydrastis—Goldenseal (-/-/0) Goldenseal is native to the eastern states. It contains the bitter alkaloid berberine, also found in *Coptis* (above) and in the related Barberry family. A tea of the powdered rootstock is astringent, antiseptic, diuretic, and laxative. In my experience, a tea of the powdered root is a very effective antiseptic and anti-inflmmatory at the onset of a sore throat. The fresh plant is acrid. Snuffing the powder up the nose will relieve congestion (Lust). It has a vasoconstrictor effect (Kadans). Excess consumption can over-stimulate the nervous system, producing nervous convulsions, miscarriage, and an excessive build-up of white corpuscles in the blood.

Trollius—Globe Flower (-/1/1) • Like other members of the family, the root and plant of the globe flower have a rubefacient property when fresh, but loses the property when dry.

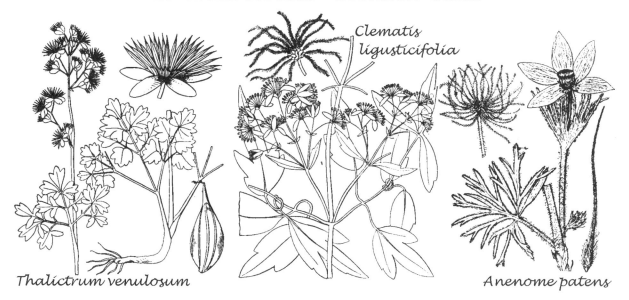

Clematis ligusticifolia

Thalictrum venulosum

Anenome patens

Buttercup Subfamily

The plants of the Buttercup Subfamily produce "achenes", which are dry seeds without seams.

Adonis— (-/1/1) Contains cardiac glycosides (Geller), used for enlarged or strained heart conditions (Kadans).

Anemone—Anemone, Pasque Flower (120/25/9) • Pasque flowers are among the first blossoms of spring. The plants can be used as an acrid poultice to irritate a closed wound to stimulate healing. The tincture is used to slow and strengthen pulse and respiration (Moore). The juice in the nose can purge out congestion (Culpeper). It is listed as diaphoretic and diuretic. Anemone contains depressant alkaloids and can be dangerous (Lust).

Clematis—Clematis, Sugarbowl, Virgin's Bower (300/35/4) • A tea of the plant acts as a vasoconstrictor on the brain-lining, but also as a dilator on the blood vessels. It is taken for migraine headaches (Moore, Sweet). The plant is used externally as a stimulating poultice (Kloss, Moore, Willard). It is listed as diaphoretic and diuretic (Lust).

Myosurus—Mousetail (-/5/2)

Ranunculus—Buttercup (400/81/29) • The seeds and greens of some species of Buttercup are edible with boiling (Kirk). The edibility depends on how acrid the plants are and how well this is removed through boiling. The plants are listed as diaphoretic and antispasmodic (Lust).

Thalictrum—Meadow Rue (120/21/5) • The leaves are edible raw or cooked. The root contains some berberine, like goldenseal (Willard). A tea of the root is used for colds (Murphey), and a poultice is used for rheumatism (Klein). Meadow rue is being studied as a possible cancer drug (Phillips).

Trautvetteria—False Bugbane (-/2/1) •

Ranunculus repens

Peony Subfamily

The Peony subfamily includes the cultivated varieties and one wild species in North America. The flowers are somewhat irregular in size or shape. Recent botanists have separated the Paeonia into its own family, based mostly on obscure characteristics. The fruits are leathery follicles (one-celled capsules that open along a single seam).

Paeonia—Peony (33/1/1) • Our native species, *P. brownii*, is found from British Columbia south to California and east to the Rocky Mountains. Native Americans drank a tea of the plant for lung troubles (Spellenberg).

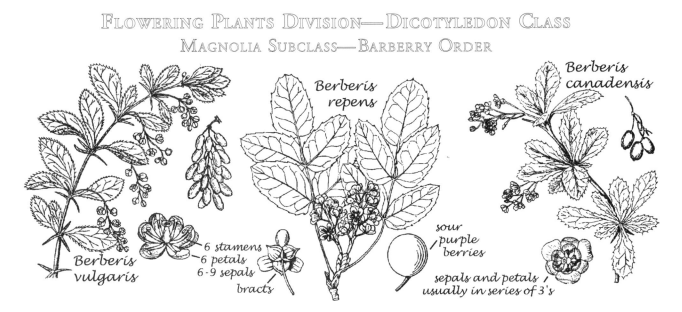

Berberis vulgaris

6 stamens
6 petals
6-9 sepals
bracts

Berberis repens

sour purple berries

sepals and petals usually in series of 3's

Berberis canadensis

Berberidaceae—Barberry Family

If you happen across an evergreen dicot plant with holly-like leaves and flower parts in multiples of 3 then it is likely a member of the Barberry family. The small yellow flowers are clustered together in racemes and mature into purplish, sour berries. Members of this genus may have 2 or 3 small bracts masquerading as sepals on the back of a flower, but otherwise there are 6-9 true sepals, 6 petals, and 6 stamens. The ovary is positioned superior and consists of 2-3 united carpels (syncarpous) forming a single chamber. The inner bark is a brilliant yellow, due to the presence of an intensely bitter **berberine alkaloid**.

Worldwide there are 9 genera in the family and 590 species. Our native genera are *Berberis* and *Mahonia*. *Berberis* has simple leaves while *Mahonia* has pinnate leaves, and there is some argument as to whether they belong in separate genera or should be grouped together. For the purposes of this book, I have treated them as a single genus. (Note the pinnate leaves in *B. repens* above.) The Mayapple family (*Podophyllaceae*) is sometimes included in the Barberry family.

Key Words
Evergreen dicot plants with floral parts in 3's
and bright yellow inner bark.

Berberis—Barberry, Oregon Grape, Algerita (520/-/4) • The various species of *Berberis* produce edible, but very sour berries. The shorter species seldom produce berries, but they are always a treat when you can find some, at least after you doctor them with enough sugar. The berries are excellent in jams and jellies, and provide their own pectin. The very young leaves are also said to be edible (Kallas).

Medicinally the yellow berberine alkaloid acts as a potent bitter stimulant and antiseptic/antibacterial. As a bitter substance, berberine is stimulating to the digestive tract, promoting gastric activity, bile production, liver cleansing, and acting as a laxative. By stimulating liver function it is considered a "blood purifier", useful for the venereal diseases, syphilis and gonorrhea, as well as premenstrual syndrome (Hart); it calms a person by facilitaing liver function. Chewing the leaves may help acne (Sweet). This is again the result of increased liver function.

Because berberine is so incredibly bitter it stimulates the entire body and not just the digestive system. It opens up the blood vessels (vasodilation) to lower blood pressure (Lust). Increased blood flow can stimulate involuntary muscles, and so the Flathead Indians used berberine to stimulate delivery of the placenta during childbirth (Hart).

Berberine is not a narcotic alkaloid, but it is reported to have a novocaine-like effect if you chew the root prior to dental work (Bigfoot). As an antiseptic, berberine has been used externally and internally. Externally it is a treatment for cuts and wounds. The roots are cleaned, crushed, and applied to the open injuries. Berberine is also useful to lower fevers and inflammation (Moore). Mixing barberries with licorice plants (*Glycyrizia spp.* of the Pea family) somehow negates the effects of the berberine (Fern). Any of the *Berberis* species are excellent substitutes for the overharvested and now endangered goldenseal (*Hydrastis*) of the Buttercup family.

Methoxyhydrocarpin or MHC, found in Colorado's Fremont barberry has proven useful against antibiotic-resistant bacteria. MHC prevents bacteria from pumping the antibiotics, including berberine, out of the cells (Wohlberg).

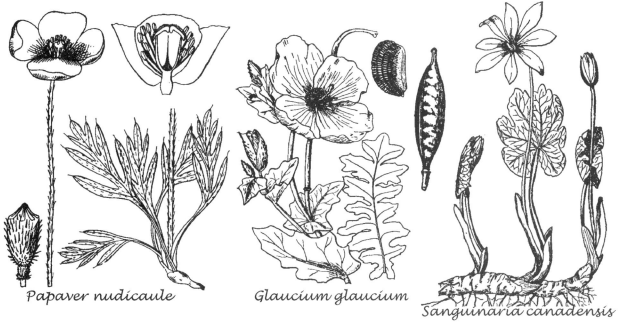

Papaver nudicaule   *Glaucium glaucium*   *Sanguinaria canadensis*

Papaveraceae—Poppy Family

Watch for members of the Poppy family in flower beds. The poppies have flowers that are regular and bisexual, with 2-3 separate sepals (united in *Eschscholzia*) and either 4, 8, or 12 separate petals, plus numerous stamens. The ovary is positioned superior and consists of 2 or more united carpels (syncarpous) forming a single chamber. It matures as a capsule containing many small seeds. The poppies are uncommon in the north, but quite abundant in the southwest. World-wide there are 26 genera and 200 species, including 13 genera in North America.

Many plants in the Poppy family contain *narcotic alkaloids* and an *acrid latex* sap. Opium is a narcotic alkaloid found in *Papaver somniferum*. Morphine, heroin, and codeine are derived from this poppy too. Narcotics depress the central nervous system, causing sedation and relief from the feeling of pain (analgesic). Be sure to read more about narcotic alkaloids in the Medicinal Properties section of this book.

Key Words: Petals in 4's with numerous stamens, and often milky sap.

Argemone—Prickly Poppy (15/15/1) • The seeds are edible like conventional poppy seed, but are cathartic in excess. The acrid plant juice is used for burning off warts. A tea of the leaves or seeds is mildly narcotic. It is used externally as an analgesic wash for sunburns, internally as a sedative and antispasmodic (Moore).

Eschscholzia—California Poppy (123/10/D) • The California poppy is often planted domestically in the north, but it grows wild in the southwest. It contains narcotic isoquinoline alkaloids. The tea is mildly sedative and analgesic, suitable even for children. Too much can result in a hang-over (Moore). The plant is said to be edible as a potherb (Sturtevant).

Glaucium— (-/1/1) *G. flavum* is reported to produce a sweet and edible oil (Sturtevant).

Papaver—Poppy (100/16/4) • The poppies include many ornamental flowers, plus *P. somniferum*, from which we derive opium, morphine, and heroin (Smith). The poppies have edible seeds useful for seasoning, but minute quantities of opium are present in some species. The flower petals can be boiled into a flavorful, but medicinal syrup—it is slightly narcotic with sedative, hallucinogenic, and vasodilator effects. The latex is also narcotic and the potency varies from one species to another (Fern).

Sanguinaria—Bloodroot (1/1/0) Bloodroot contains narcotic opium-like alkaloids (Fern) that depress the central nervous system; the plant or root acts as an expectorant in small doses, but is nauseating and emetic in larger amounts (Densmore). As a narcotic, the plant is sedative in effect and can be fatal in excess (Lust). Bloodroot is used as an anesthetic, and to dilate the blood vessels throughout the body, thereby improving circulation, helping the bronchials in an infection, and stimulating menstruation. This plant should only be administered by a qualified professional. The fresh or dried powdered root is used to treat skin eruptions, cuts, nose polyps, warts or slow healing sores. Bloodroot is used as an anti-plaque agent in Viadent toothpaste (Klein). The crushed root may be used as an insect repellent, but caution is advised, as the alkaloids may be absorbed through the skin. The root is also a source of red dye (Fern).

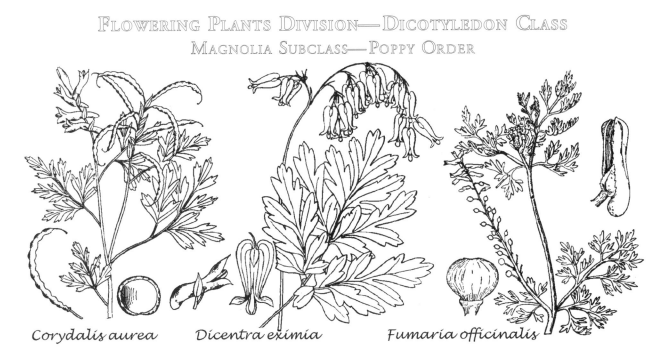

Corydalis aurea   Dicentra eximia   Fumaria officinalis

Fumariaceae—Bleeding-Heart Family

The delicate flowers of the Bleeding Heart or Fumitory family are always a delight to find. The flowers are irregular and bisexual with 2 scale-like sepals and 4 petals. The outer petals spread above the narrower inner petals. The flowers usually have 6 stamens in two groups of three on opposite sides of the pistil, but may have 4 stamens positioned opposite with the petals. The ovary is positioned superior and consists of 2 united carpels (bicarpellate) to form a single chamber. It matures as a capsule or a 1-seeded nut.

World-wide there are about 16 genera and some 450 species. Three genera below are native to North America and *Fumaria* was introduced. The Bleeding-Heart family is sometimes combined with the Poppy family, and shares at least some medicinal properties. Both families are rich in *alkaloids*, many with *narcotic* properties.

<u>Key Words</u>
Irregular dicot flowers with 2 sepals and 4 petals.

Adlumia—Mountain Fringe (-/1/0) *A. fungosa* grows in southeastern Canada south and west to Tennessee.

Corydalis— (280/13/2) The species of *Corydalis* contain narcotic alkaloids to varying degrees, especially in the roots. The narcotic properties are used in the conventional ways for their analgesic, sedative, antispasmodic, and hallucinogenic properties, and to slow the pulse and dilate the bronchials (Fern). Some species have been used to treat Parkinson's disease. These plants are potentially dangerous and should only be used by a trained professional (Lust).

Dicentra—Bleeding Heart, Dutchman's Breeches (17/9/1) • Bleeding heart contains narcotic isoquinoline alkaloids useful for nervous system disorders like paralysis and tremors and as an analgesic to relieve pains such as from a toothache (Moore). A poultice of the leaves is used as a muscle rub. A tea of the root is reportedly diaphoretic and diuretic in effect. The plant may cause dermatitis in some individuals (Fern).

Fumaria— Fumitory (50/1/1) The fresh plant may be used to curdle milk. The plant is afterwards removed; it reportedly acts as a preservative and imparts a tangy taste, while preventing a rancid flavor (Fern). The alkaloids in fumitory are used for their bitter taste to stimulate the digestive processes (Schauenberg).

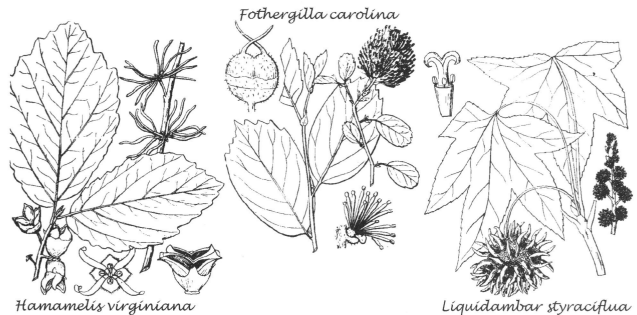

Fothergilla carolina

Hamamelis virginiana

Liquidambar styraciflua

Hamamelidaceae—Witch Hazel Family

The Witch Hazel family consists of a handful of trees and shrubs in the eastern half of the country, some of which are planted elsewhere as ornamentals. The flowers can be either bisexual or unisexual. There are 4 or 5 (sometimes 0) sepals, fused together at the base, and 4 or 5 (sometimes 0) separate petals, plus 4 or 5 stamens. The ovary is positioned inferior or rarely superior and consists of 2 united carpels (bicarpellate) with the partition walls present to make 2 chambers. It matures as a woody capsule that spreads open from the top, releasing 1 or 2 bony seeds from each cell.

The Witch Hazel family is closely related to the Sycamore family (*Platanaceae*), which grows only in the southern states. World-wide there are about 25 genera and 100 species in the Witch Hazel family. Our native genera are listed below. Only witch hazel grows in cold climates, the other genera are found in the deep south.

Hamamelis virginiana

<u>Key Words</u>
Trees and shrubs with
2-celled woody capsules and bony seeds.

Fothergilla— (4/3/0)

Hamamelis—Witch Hazel (8/2/0) The seeds are reported to be edible (Weiner), but there is some question about the validity of this claim (Fern). Medicinally, the leaves and bark contain tannic acid. Witch hazel has long been used as an astringent in the typical ways, internally for sore throat and diarrhea, externally for stings, minor burns, and hemorrhoids (Lust). Native Americans used a tea of the leaves as a lineament for athletes (Weiner).

Liquidambar—Sweet Gum (5/1/0) The sap of the tree may be used as chewing gum. The gum is used medicinally as a drawing poultice, also for sore throats. It is astringent and expectorant in effect (Fern, Moerman).

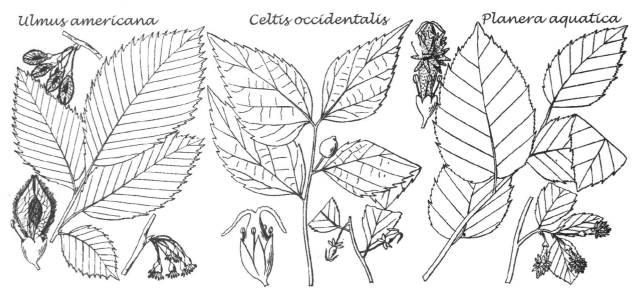

Ulmus americana   *Celtis occidentalis*   *Planera aquatica*

Ulmaceae—Elm Family

The Elm family consists of a handful of trees and shrubs in the eastern and southern parts of the country, some of which are planted elsewhere as ornamentals. The leaves are simple and alternate, but often a little bit asymmetrical at the base. The flowers are bisexual in the elms and unisexual in the other genera. There are 4 or 8 separate sepals, and 0 petals, plus 4 to 8 stamens. The ovary is positioned superior and consists of 2 united carpels (bicarpellate) forming a single chamber. It matures as a winged seed or a drupe (a fleshy fruit with a stony pit).

World-wide there are about 15 genera and 200 species in the Elm Family. Our native genera are listed below. Only the hackberry is found naturally in the west. Other cultivated genera from the family include *Aphananthe*, *Hemiptelea*, *Pteroceltis*, and *Zelkova*. The elm population has suffered greatly from Dutch Elm disease. Please use this resource only with deep consideration and ethic.

Key Words: Trees and shrubs with simple leaves asymmetrical at the base.

Celtis—Hackberry (70/5/D) • The hackberry is sometimes planted domestically in Montana; otherwise it is native to warmer parts of the continent. The berries are edible (Sturtevant, Moerman).

Planera—Water Elm (1/1/0) *P. abelica.* Southeastern.

Ulmus—Elm (20/7/2) • The leaves are edible raw or cooked (Fern). The bark may be dried and ground into flour; it is used in times of scarcity. The green fruits are also edible (Sturtevant).

The slippery elm, *Ulmus fulva*, is widely popular as a medicinal plant. The inner bark is highly mucilaginous and somewhat astringent. Other species may be more astringent and less mucilaginous. The elm is used especially as a soothing remedy, externally as an emollient for burns or internally as a demulcent for sore throats or other internal inflammations, including diarrhea (Lust). It is the kind of remedy that can be used for just about anything. A friend once gave me some in tea to take down a fever on an expedition. I recall that it was very effective.

The inner bark of the slippery elm can be used as a cordage material.

Ulmus fulva

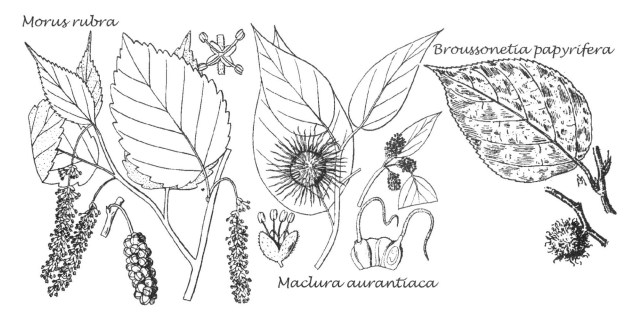

Morus rubra

Broussonetia papyrifera

Maclura aurantiaca

Moraceae—Mulberry Family

The Mulberry family consists of trees and shrubs with alternate leaves and milky latex sap. The flowers are small, usually in tight clusters. Botanically the flowers are unisexual with male and female flowers appearing either on the same or different trees. The male flowers have 4 (sometimes 0) sepals, 0 petals, and 4 stamens. Female flowers have 4 (sometimes 0) sepals and 0 petals. The ovary is positioned superior or inferior and consists of 2 united carpels (bicarpellate) but one is usually aborted, forming a single chamber.

The mulberry is a "multiple" of many small fruits (from many small flowers) clustered together. Likewise, the spiny fruit of the Osage Orange is considered a "false fruit", because it consists of multiple smaller fruits from separate flowers grown together to appear as a single fruit. Figs are highly unusual in that the flowers are borne in the hollow end of a branch, which later swells around the developing seeds to become the fruit, called a "syconium". Other members of the family produce a nut or a drupe (a fleshy fruit with a stony seed).

World-wide there are about 53 genera and 1400 species in the family, a thousand of which belong to the *Ficus* genus, including figs, the banyan tree, and the Indian rubber tree. The breadfruit and jackfruit belong to the genus *Artocarpus*. Other cultivated genera (mostly in the tropics) include *Antiaris*, *Brosimum*, *Cecropia*, *Chlorophora*, *Coudrania*, *Coussapoa*, *Dorstenia*, *Musanga*, and *Treculia*. Native North American genera include *Maclura* and *Morus*.

Key Words
Trees and shrubs with alternate leaves and milky sap.

Broussonetia—Paper Mulberry (7/1/0) The paper mulberry was introduced from Asia and has escaped cultivation in some areas (Benson).

Maclura—Osage Orange (12/1/0) Osage orange is valued as one of the premier woods for bow-making in this country, in spite of the fact that the wood is almost all knots.

Morus—Mulberry (12/3/0) • My family lived in Los Altos, California until I was twelve years old. We picked the leaves of the mulberry trees in the yard and fed them to silkworms we raised in the house. The berries of these trees are edible, and vary from sweet to acidic. The berries of some species are a significant food source in certaom parts of the world.

Medicinally, a tea of the bark is used as a laxative and to expel tapeworms. The milky juice and the unripe fruit may cause hallucinations, nervousness, and an upset stomach (Lust).

Cannabaceae—Hemp Family

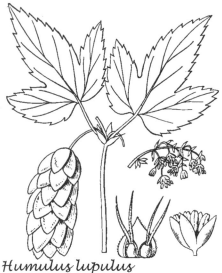

Humulus lupulus

The plants of the Hemp family may not have much in the way of showy flowers, but the family does claim one of the most recognized plants on earth: marijuana (*Cannabis sativa*).

Members of the Hemp family are "dioecious", meaning they produce the male and female flowers on separate plants. The male flowers grow in racemes or panicles, each flower with 5 sepals, 0 petals, and 5 stamens. Female flowers form dense clusters or spikes called strobiles; they have 5 sepals and 0 petals. The ovary is positioned superior and has only one carpel (unicarpellate). It matures as a dry seed called an "achene". This is a small family with only two genera and a total of 3 to 5 different species world-wide. It is sometimes included with the Mulberry family.

Marijuana is used medicinally to effect the nervous system as a pain-killer, antispasmodic, cough suppressant, etc. (Lust). Of course it is also euphorigenic and illegal to posses or use.

Whether or not recreational use of marijuana is physically or mentalling damaging remains debatable. Some people contend that marijuana is safe compared to truly dangerous substances like cigarettes or alcohol (Pendell). In other words, marijuana might be a step up for the people who are already living dead, with no vision or spark left in their lives, currently numbing themselves with alcohol and cigarettes. At least while they are on drugs they can feel like they are really going somewhere. Personally, I think it is a poor substitute or remedy for the shattered dreams of youth. Too many young people who started out with vision get derailed on drugs and think they are on the verge of something brilliant, at least while they are high.

Cannabis is also famous for its fiber. Most of our ropes and paper and much of our fabric was once made from hemp fibers. Out-lawing this plant eliminates an extremely valuable resource. Fortunately, French scientists have developed a variety of *Cannabis* with virtually no psychoactive properties. Perhaps one day it will again be grown as a useful resource.

Key Words
(*Humulus*) Vining plants with papery "cones".

Humulus—Hops (2/1/1) • The young leaves, shoots and roots may be cooked and eaten, and the seeds contain gamma-linolenic acid. The female flowers have a powdery appearance due to many small translucent-yellow glands; this appears to be the source of the bitter and antibacterial properties that are valued in beer making (Fern). Hops is also rich in pectin (Duke).

The primary use of hops is as a sedative. Stuffing a pillow with dried hops, or brewing a tea of the plant or flowers, will produce the sedative effects. The tea is a bitter tonic that stimulates digestive functions while acting as a general antispasmodic. Antibiotic properties must be tinctured out with alcohol (Moore). The plant is also diuretic. The poultice is used for inflammations, boils, tumors, etc. (Kloss). Hops increases milk flow in lactating women; a hormone in the plant may cause the effect. The fresh or dried flowers can be used as a poultice for swellings (Fern)

Hops vines are a source of fiber for cordage, but the quality is not very good if you just rip it off the stalk. Reportedly the stems need to be soaked over winter before separating the fibers. The fibers are also used in making paper (Fern).

Urticaceae—Stinging Nettle Family

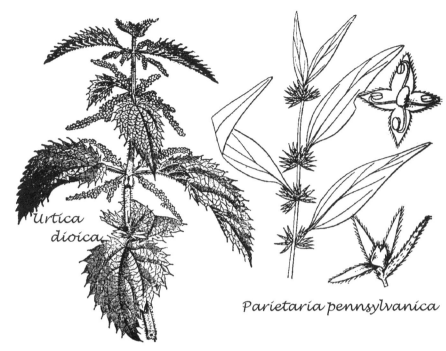

The Stinging Nettle family has a way of identifying itself for you! The hairs on the underside of nettle leaves function as hypodermic needles to inject formic acid into the skin when you come in contact with them. Three genera of the family have stinging hairs: *Urtica*, *Laportea*, and *Hesperocnide*, the last being a native of California.

Botanically the flowers are greenish or brownish, with 4 or 5 sepals, 0 petals, and 4-5 stamens. The ovary is positioned superior and has only one carpel (unicarpellate). It matures as a dry seed, called an "achene". World-wide there are 45 genera and 550 species. Six genera are found in North America. The Mulberry family is sometimes included in this family.

Urtica dioica

Parietaria pennsylvanica

Most species in the family are **edible** as potherbs. The plants have strong fibers for making **cordage**. The silkplant (*Boehmeria*) is said to have the longest fibers known in the Plant Kingdom, with a tensile strength eight times greater than cotton (Fern).

<u>**Key Words**</u>
Squarish stalks with opposite leaves and often stinging hairs. 0 petals.

Laportea—Wood Nettle (45/-/0) The young leaves are edible after cooking to destroy the stinging hairs. The fiber from the stems is up to 50 times stronger than cotton (Fern).

Parietaria—Pellitory (14/-/1) The young plant is edible raw or cooked (Sturtevant). The plant has both astringent and demulcent properties; it is used externally as a poultice for burns and wounds. A tea of the plant is taken internally for bladder stones and as a laxative. The whole plant may be crushed and used to clean windows or copperware (Fern).

Urtica—Stinging nettle (35/-/2) • Nettles have been used medicinally as a rubefacient to irritate rheumatic joints by whipping them with the plant (Coon), or by applying crushed leaves as a poultice (Lust) to stimulate healing activity in the area. Formic acid is easily destroyed by cooking, so the plant is a delicious potherb. Nettles are high in vitamins A, C, and D, and the minerals calcium, iron, phosphorus, potassium, sodium, silica, and albuminoids (Willard), and relatively high in protein. The plants are reportedly edible raw if properly crushed first (Kramer).

For obvious reasons you are wise to pick nettles with gloves or a shirt sleeve, etc., but it is also reasonably safe to pick them by hand, if you touch only the stems. Nettles can be easily dried and powdered for use as a flour additive and stew thickener. The plants may be dried in the sun, or bundled at the roots and hung inside to dry. When they are dry, simply use your hands to strip and powder the leaves. It is especially nice to take nettle powder along on winter camping trips when other greens are scarce. They should be harvested when young, before blooming. The plants may accumulate nitrates or form calcium carbonate cystoliths as they continue to age.

Medicinally, nettle tea is a good astringent, useful externally as a wash and hair cleanser, or internally for bleeding (Kloss). Nettles are diuretic, but may irritate the kidneys with prolonged use. The plant is also known to bind up immunoglobulin G, reducing sensitivity to food allergies (Willard).

The tea can be used to curdle milk for making cheese (Moore). The dead stalks make excellent cordage material and were used in Germany in World War I for weaving when cotton was inaccessible. (Coon).

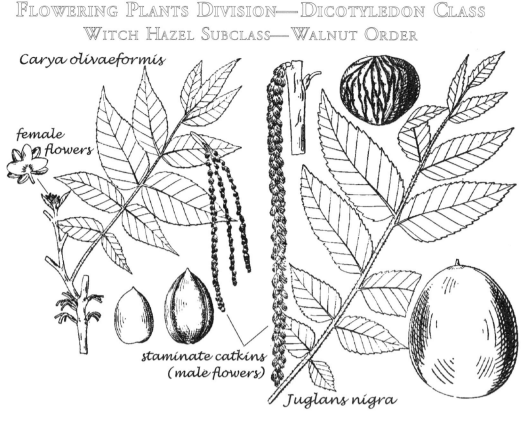

Carya olivaeformis

female flowers

staminate catkins
(male flowers)

Juglans nigra

Juglandaceae—Walnut Family

Members of the Walnut family are resinous, aromatic trees with alternate, pinnately compound leaves. Glandular dots beneath the leaves help to identify this family. The flowers are unisexual, with male and female flowers appearing on the same trees. The male flowers are born in catkins, with 3-6 (sometimes 0) sepals, 0 petals, and 3-40 stamens (sometimes 100). Female flowers have 4 sepals and 0 petals. The pistil is syncarpous with 2-3 carpels fused together to make a single-celled ovary, and matures a single hard-shelled nut enclosed in a husk. World-wide there are about 6 genera and 60 species, mostly walnuts. Our natives are listed below. Other cultivated genera include *Platycarya* and *Pterocarya*.

Key Words:
Aromatic trees with pinnate leaves and walnut-like fruits.

Carya—Pecan, Hickory, Bitternut, Pignut (27/10/0) The hickory and its related species are processed and used similarly to the walnuts, including that the trees may be tapped for syrup (Hall, Gilmore).

Juglans—Walnut, Butternut (40/4/D) There are about forty species of walnuts in the world, and they all produce edible nuts, but of varying quality. Walnuts are not native to Montana, but the black walnut is often planted domestically. Some friends and I collected black walnuts on an expedition in eastern Oregon where the trees escaped cultivation. We gathered them in the spring, so the husks had already rotted away. Compared to the English walnut, the black walnuts are mostly shell with only a little meat inside; the job of cracking the shells and picking out the meat with a sharp stick seems only marginally productive. I was able to extract about one cup of nut meat per hour of effort... but it sure was good!

One author recommends gathering the nuts in the fall and drying them before removing the husks. After husking the nuts should be crushed then slowly boiled in water. The oil and nut meats rise to the top, while the shells settle to the bottom. The oil and meats can be used separately, or blended together to make walnut butter. The trees can also be tapped for syrup in the springtime (Hall). (See the Maple family for additional information.)

Walnut husks are rich in tannins, especially useful for dye. The butternut makes a rich purple dye while the walnut gives a black dye. Boil the husks to extract the pigment (Hall). Medicinally, the leaves, bark, and husk are rich in tannic acid, with some bitter components; it is used mostly as an astringent, but also as vermifuge, internally to get rid of worms, externally for ringworm fungus. The green husk is rich in vitamin C (Schauenberg). Butternut bark contains a naphthaquinone laxative (Hobbs). (Read about the similar anthroquinone glycosides in the Medicinal Properties section of this book.)

Fagaceae—Beech Family

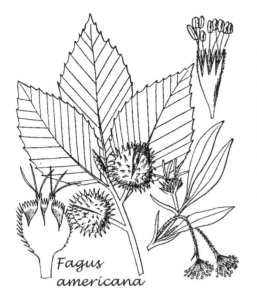

Fagus americana

Members of the Beech family are trees or shrubs, either deciduous or evergreen. The leaves are simple and alternate and often, but not always, lobed like the oak leaf shown below. The flowers are typically unisexual, with both male and female flowers appearing on the same plant (monoecious). The staminate (male) flowers have 4-6 sepals, 0 petals, and 4-40 stamens. The pistillate (female) flowers have 4-6 sepals and 0 petals. The ovary is positioned inferior and consists of 3 (sometimes 6) united carpels (syncarpous) forming a single chamber. Only one ovule is fertilized; it matures as a nut, usually attached to a scaly or spiny cap formed of numerous small, over-lapping bracts.

World-wide there are 8 genera and approximately 900 species in the family. Five genera are native to North America, including the chinquapin (*Chrysolepis*), tanbark oak (*Lithocarpus*) and the chestnut (*Castanea*), plus the genera below. Cork comes from the bark of the cork oak, *Quercus suber*. The members of this family contain varying amounts of *tannic acid*, making them astringent and diuretic.

Key Words
Trees or shrubs with single nuts attached to scaly or spiny caps.

Fagus—Beech (10/-/0) Beech leaves are edible raw or cooked as a potherb early in the spring. The seeds are rich in oil and high in protein, edible raw or cooked, but should not be eaten in large quantities due to an alkaloid in the outer covering (Schauenberg). The seeds may be dried and ground into flour. The roasted seed is used as a coffee substitute. The sprouted seeds are also edible and reportedly delicious. Oil from the seeds may be used in cooking and salad dressings, or in lamps (Fern).

Quercus—Oak (450/-/1) • The oaks are common across most states, but are rare here in Montana. There is only one species of shrub oak in a small portion of south-central Montana. Another species, the bur oak, is a large tree planted domestically in many Montana towns.

Acorns are edible and highly nutritious, rich in carbohydrates, oil and protein, but they also contain the astringent tannic acid and some bitters. The tannin content varies widely between the species, making some palatable raw, and others unpalatable, including Montana's bur oak, even after extensive leaching.

The acorns should be cracked open, and the nuts removed, then ground into flour. It may be possible to leach the whole nuts, after shelling, but this would take longer to remove the tannin. The nuts or flour can be leached by a couple methods. It can be placed in a cloth bag and soaked in a stream. The tannic acid will wash out over a period of time. Alternately, the flour can be boiled in several changes of water. Dark water indicates high concentrations of tannin. The water is changed until it remains clear. Another approach is to leave the tannic acid in the acorns, but to neutralize it by adding gelatin or milk, or some other protein to the flour to bind the acid.

Quercus macrocarpa

Medicinally the oaks are astringent throughout, due to the tannin. The bark also contains quercin, a compound similar to salicin (like aspirin). The astringency is used internally for gum inflammations, sore throat and diarrhea. Externally it is used for first and second degree burns. The tannin binds the proteins and amino acids, sealing off the burns from weeping and from bacterial infection. The leaves can be chewed into a mash for use as an astringent poultice (Moore).

Oak galls also have a high tannin content, as much as 60-70% in the galls of *Q. lusitanica* (plus 2-4 % gallic acid) The galls were formerly collected and used as dye (Pammel)

55

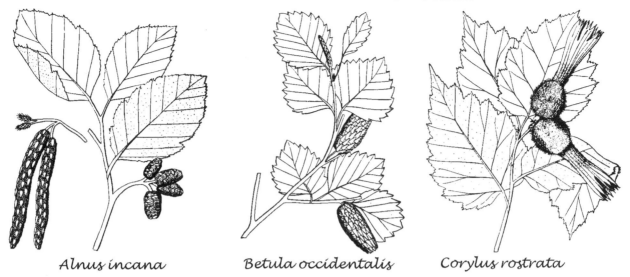

Alnus incana   *Betula occidentalis*   *Corylus rostrata*

Betulaceae (Cupuliferae)—Birch Family

The Birch family includes deciduous trees and shrubs with simple, toothed, alternate leaves. Male and female catkins form separately on the same bush. Staminate (male) catkins have small flowers with 0 or 4 sepals, 0 petals, and 2-20 stamens. Pistilate (female) catkins also have numerous small flowers, each with 0 sepals and 0 petals. The ovary is positioned inferior (some cannot be determined) and consists of 2 united carpels (bicarpellate) forming a single chamber. It matures as a nut or winged seed.

World-wide there are 6 genera and approximately 150 species in this family, including filberts (also called hazelnuts) of the genus *Corylus*, which produce *edible* nuts. (Note that the witch-hazel belongs to the family *Hamamelidaceae*.) Members of the Birch family contain varying amounts of *tannic acid*, making them somewhat astringent and diuretic. North American genera are listed below.

Key Words: Trees or shrubs with cone-like catkins or nuts and attached bracts.

Birch Subfamily

Alnus—Alder (30/-/2) • Alders are very astringent, and the bark is the most potent. The live inner bark from our local alders quickly turns to a flaming orange-brown color when exposed to air. The color is from the tannic acid. It is a brilliant and permanent dye. Some Native Americans even dyed their hair with it! Other species of alder may produce darker colors. Medicinally, the alder can be used as a potent astringent for wounds, diarrhea and so forth. Some species produce anti-tumor properties similar to the birches. It may be possible to make syrup from the sap of large alders.

Betula—Birch (40/-/3) • A tea of the leaves or twigs can be used externally as an astringent wash, or internally for diarrhea or boils (Lust). A tea of the twigs is also somewhat anthlementic (Kloss).

      The trees can be tapped for syrup like maple trees in the early spring. The sap is about 50-60 parts water to 1 part syrup, so it must be boiled down extensively to get the syrup. (See the Maple Family for more information.) The birches also contain some amount of methyl salicylate oil (like willow and aspirin), making them both diaphoretic and analgesic. The bark and twigs are chopped, then simmered overnight and distilled; it is commonly substituted for wintergreen oil (Coon). A strong tea of bark or leaves can be used externally as a wash for poison ivy or acne, or internally as a mild sedative (Brown). The bark can be boiled and then folded into a variety of useful containers. A compound called betulinic acid, derived from the bark, is being tested on some types of skin cancer.

Hazelnut Subfamily

Carpinus—American Hornbeam, Blue Beech (26/-/0) The seed is reportedly edible in emergencies. The leaves are astringent, used in conventional ways (Fern).

Corylus—Hazelnut, Filbert (17/-/0) The nuts of all species are edible raw or cooked. The nuts are reportedly sweet and comprised of up to 65% oil. The nut is sweetest during the "milk" stage, prior to maturity. Medicinally, the oil from the nut is said to be a gentle remedy for pinworm and threadworm infections in babies and small children. The leaves and bark are astringent. The inner bark of at least some species is fibrous, suitable for making cordage or paper. The nut oil can be used to polish and oil wood. The root or inner bark of one species is known to yield a blue dye (Fern).

Ostrya—Ironwood, Hop-Hornbeam (5/-/0) A tea of the bark is taken for intermittant fevers and nervousness (Hutchins).

Cactaceae—Cactus Family

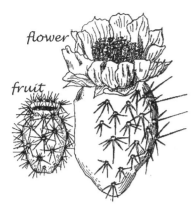

flower

fruit

If you find a thick, succulent plant with clusters of spines it is certainly a member of the Cactus family. The regular, bisexual flowers are showy with numerous sepals, petals, and stamens. The ovary is positioned inferior and consists of 2 or more united carpels (syncarpous) forming a single chamber. It matures as a pulpy "berry" with numerous seeds and usually spines. The cacti originated in the New World. World-wide there are now about 125 genera and more than 2,000 species. Sixteen genera are found in North America. Some well known members of this family include peyote (*Lophophora Williamsii*), saguaro (*Carnegiea* or *Cereus*), Christmas cactus (*Zygocactus*), and the barrel cactus (*Ferocactus*). The spines of some species were once used as phonograph needles (J. Smith).

Key Words
Succulent desert plants with spines. Flower parts numerous.

Coryphantha—(*Mammillaria*) Pin Cushion Cactus (300/-/2) • Pin cushion cactus is rare in Montana. The plant and fruit is edible raw or cooked (Olsen).

Echinocereus—Hedgehog Cactus (70/-/0) • Hedgehog cactus grows in the southwest. It is easy to collect and peel. It can be used as a poultice for cuts and burns, or eaten raw or cooked. It is rare and should be used sparingly.

Opuntia—Prickly Pear, Cholla (200/-/2) • A large species of prickly pear is still a common food in Mexico. The spiny fruits and cactus pads are both edible. Here in Montana the prickly pears are small and difficult to process. I struggled for years to figure out how to safely get into the cactus flesh. The big spines burn right off, but the little hair-like spines are the real problem and the flame just does not reach them. I tried many times to skin all sides of them with a knife, but typically ended up with little more than prickled fingers for my efforts.

Archaeological studies in the southwest revealed that the Indians ate many of the prickly hairs with their cacti. Remarkably, this is not such a bad experience as you might imagine! Remove as many hairs as you can, and the few that are left will stick to your lips and in the roof of your mouth. The irritation goes away after a few days. You might grow used to it if you were eating cacti every day!

Finally my friend Jack Fee discovered the obvious way to get past all the spines to the flesh inside. First incinerate the big spines over the fire. Be careful to avoid cooking the cactus pad; they are much better raw. Next, make one slice lengthwise down the middle of the cactus. Open the two halves and scrape out the mucilaginous green flesh with a spoon. The pads are okay raw and acceptable when cooked, but are very good with just a little sugar. Also, prickly pear flesh serves as a sort of slimy "gelatin". You can make a primitive "jelly" by adding the flesh to a pot of berries and sugar.

The seeds are edible, just very hard. The method I have found for processing them is to roast the dry seed pods with hot coals. This burns off the spines and some of the pods without scorching the seeds inside. Crush up the remaining pods and winnow out the waste, leaving just the seeds. The seeds are hard enough to break your teeth and need to be ground into meal. I have used a commercial flour mill; I think they could be difficult to crush with rocks. Perhaps boiling first would help.

Opuntia spp.

Medicinally the pads are very similar to *Aloe vera*, and like *Aloe*, an *Opuntia* poultice osmotically draws out waste material from bruised, burned or other injured tissues, while also soothing those tissues with its mucilaginous property (Moore). This mucilage is a complex sugar called a mucopolysaccharide. A similar mucopolysaccharide forms a "hydrogel" between your body's cells. This gel can dry out or break down after an injury, especially from a burn or sunburn. Your body will absorb the mucilage out of the cactus pad to strengthen your own mucopolysaccharide gel. Wipe a cactus pad over the burn and you will feel how quickly the mucilage is absorbed into the skin. Keep rubbing in fresh mucilage and you can recover many other-wise serious burns.

Prickly pear has a hypoglycemic effect for adult-onset diabetes. The effective doses averaged 4 ounces of juice per day. Please refer to Michael Moore's *Medicinal Plants of the Desert and Canyon West* for more information. Prickly pear juice is also used as a mordant for setting some dyes (Hart).

Caryophyllaceae—Pink Family

The next time you see a carnation or pink (*Dianthus*), stop and examine the vegetation and the flower. The coarse, durable stem and leaves are characteristic of this family. The leaves are usually positioned opposite on the stems, but are sometimes whorled. Members of the Pink family have regular, bisexual flowers with 5 sepals (rarely 4). The sepals can be united or separate. There are 5 separate petals (rarely 4, or sometimes numerous in domestic varieties). The petals are often split at the ends. There are 5 or 10 stamens (rarely 3 or 4), appearing in 1 or 2 whorls. The ovary is positioned superior and consists of 2-5 (rarely 1) united carpels (syncarpous) forming a single chamber. (*Silene* is apocarpous.) The ovary matures as a dry capsule with numerous seeds and opens by valves at the top. World-wide there are about 80 genera and 2000 species. About 20 genera are found in North America.

Baby's breath and chickweed are well-known members. Many species of the family contain at least a small amount of *saponin*, most notably the soapwort plant (*Saponaria*). Plants with a significant saponin content can be mashed in water and used as a soap substitute or added to a pool or slow moving stream as fish poison to stupefy the fish so they will float to the surface. Please read more about saponin under the Glycosides heading of the Medicinal Properties section of this book. Several plants in the Pink family have *edible* greens or seeds.

Key Words
Coarse plants with split petal-ends and flower parts in 5's.

Achyronychia—(-/1/0) *A. cooperi* is found in the deserts of California and Arizona.

Agrostema—Corn Cockle (1/1/1) *A. githago* was introduced from Europe. The plant and especially the seeds contain saponin. People and livestock have been poisoned when large quantities (40%+) of *Agrostema* seed have been mixed in feeds and flour (Pammel)

Arenaria—Sandwort (160/50/12) • The plant is boiled as a vegetable or fermented like sauerkraut (Sturtevant). A tea of the plant has diuretic properties (Kadans); it is also used as an eye wash (Murphey).

Cerastium— Field Chickweed (100/25/5) • Field Chickweed is less succulent than *Stellaria*, but still very edible.

Dianthus—Carnation, Pink, Sweet Williams (300/4/2) •

Gypsophila—Baby's Breath (126/-/1) A species of baby's breath from Spain is known to contain saponin and a sapotoxin (Pammel).

Lychnis—Cockle (10/15/5) • The plant contains some amount of saponin (Pammel), especially in the root (Fern).

Paronychia—Nailwort (40/-/1)

Sagina—Pearlwort (30/10/1)

Saponaria—Soapwort, Bouncing Bet (30/1/1) • As the Latin and common names suggest, *Saponaria* contains saponin and can be crushed in water for use as a soap substitute. The plant is another import from Europe, now considered a noxious weed in some areas. I love the sweet, sweet smell of the flowers. A tea of the root is used as an expectorant, purgative and diuretic (Lust). As a diuretic it is used for jaundice, gout, rheumatism, and venereal diseases. It is also used externally as a wash for skin diseases (Coon).

Silene—Moss Campion (400/50/13) • At least some species of moss campion are edible as a potherb (Kirk, Willard), although many species may be too dry and woody to eat. Medicinally, *S. stellata* and *S. virginica* have been used to expel worms (Coon). *Silene acaucis* grows on the dry, wind-swept ridge-lines of the foothills behind my house. They bloom mostly in May and early June, but solitary blossoms can sometimes be found even in December and January.

Spergula—Spurry (5/2/1) The seeds are edible; they have been harvested in times of scarcity (Sturtevant).

Spergularia—Sand Spurry (20/12/2)

Stellaria—Chickweed (100/30/14) • The common chickweed, *S. media*, is an import from Europe. Sometimes the green plants can be found growing in the midst of winter in the snow-free space underneath the trees. The whole plant is edible and delicious as a salad green or potherb. Chickweed haa demulcent, diuretic, laxative and mildly anti-inflammatory properties. The poultice or tincture is used externally to reduce swellings from sprains or arthritis (Moore), or to sooth minor burns and itchy, dry skin (Tilford). It contains at least some saponin (Densmore).

Vaccaria—Cow Cockle (-/1/1) *V. segetalis* was introduced from Europe. It is found across much of North America.

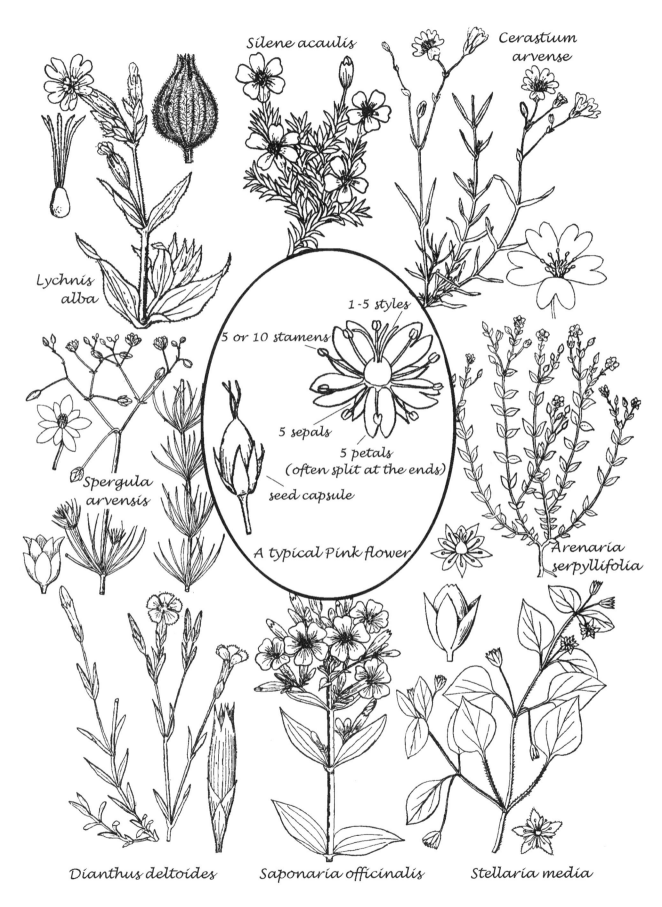

Silene acaulis

Cerastium arvense

Lychnis alba

Spergula arvensis

1-5 styles

5 or 10 stamens

5 sepals

5 petals
(often split at the ends)

seed capsule

A typical Pink flower

Arenaria serpyllifolia

Dianthus deltoides

Saponaria officinalis

Stellaria media

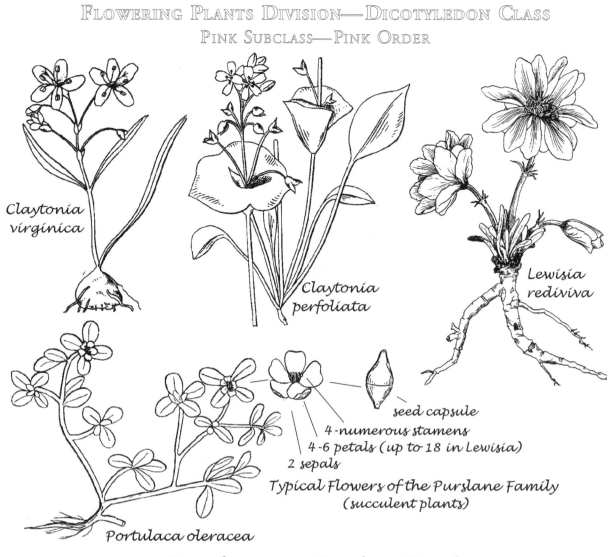

Claytonia virginica

Claytonia perfoliata

Lewisia rediviva

seed capsule
4-numerous stamens
4-6 petals (up to 18 in Lewisia)
2 sepals

Typical Flowers of the Purslane Family
(succulent plants)

Portulaca oleracea

Portulacaceae—Purslane Family

If you do much gardening then you may have met one member of this family already. Purslane is a succulent reddish-green plant found growing flat on the ground with fat stems and small, fat leaves. One plant can produce as many as 250,000 seeds from its tiny flowers, so if they are in your garden then you had better start pulling them now!

The plants of this family are succulent herbs with regular, bisexual flowers. There are usually 2 sepals and 4-6 petals, but a few species have 2-3 petals, and the bitterroot (*Lewisia*) has up to 18 petals. There may be an equal or double number of stamens as petals, or they may be numerous. The ovary is positioned superior or half-inferior and consists of 2-8 united carpels (syncarpous) forming a single chamber. It matures as a capsule that opens along three seams, or by a cap-like top. Many members of this family are particularly adapted to dry areas with intense sunlight. World-wide there are about 19 genera and 580 species. Nine genera are native to North America, as listed below. The bitterroot (*Lewisia*) is the state flower of Montana.

Many plants in the family contain some amount of *oxalic acid*, resulting in a mild lemon-like taste. Most plants in the family are *edible*, except that excess consumption of oxalic acid can block the body's ability to absorb calcium. Read about Oxalic Acid in the Medicinal Properties section of this book for additional information.

Key Words
Succulent plants growing in intense sunlight. 2 sepals.

Calandrinia—Red Maids (-/4/0) Red maids are found in the Pacific Coast states.
Calyptridium— (-/7/0) *Calyptridium* grows in Oregon, Idaho, Utah, Nevada, and California.
Claytonia—Spring Beauty (20/13/6) • The small, potato-like roots are edible raw or cooked. I can harvest about a cup of roots per hour of work, and it is very much worth the effort. Cleaning the roots takes another 10 minutes. Cooked spring beauty roots taste as good or better than buttery "new potatoes". Some authors recommend peeling the roots,

but I find that unnecessary. The whole plant is good as a salad or potherb. The spring beauty was a favored crop of the Montana Indians (Hart).

Lewisia—Bitterroot (15/15/4) • Bitterroot is the state flower of Montana, and it is legal to collect it. Be sure to harvest only in areas of extreme abundance. The starchy roots are edible. Kirk says to peel the roots or rub them vigorously between the hands to remove the bitter bark, or to boil the bitterness out. Sweet says to boil them and then peel them.

Bitterroot has a well-known history as one of Montana's premiere native food crops. In an experiment, I collected over a gallon of the whole plants in a one-hour harvest in May. Trimming away the vegetation left approximately 1.5 quarts of roots. Peeling off the bitter bark took another eight hours! The peeled roots cook up nicely in a stew. They are starchy, gelatinous, and filling. However, it is important to remove all of the red bark. Even a little bit will make the whole stew bitter beyond edibility.

Since that experience, I've heard that the Flathead Indians monitor the bitterroot crop each spring to see when the bark slips easily off the root, usually late April or early May. Then they have a big harvesting day to collect the year's supply. I've also stumbled across a few plants at just the right time, and yes the bark slides right off. I'll have to try another controlled study at just the right time.

Montia—Miner's Lettuce (50/18/2) • *Montia* is sometimes combined with the *Claytonia* genus. They do not have starchy roots, but they are succulent and tasty as a salad green or potherb. Medicinally, the tea may be used as a laxative (Sweet). The common name "miner's lettuce" is confusing, because the same name was given to many different wild plants that were eaten by early miners.

Montiastrum— (2/2/2) Like the miner's lettuce, this genus was also previously part of the *Claytonia* genus.

Portulaca—Purslane (100/11/1) • Originally from India, the purslane is uncommon in Montana, except in some gardens. It is more prolific further south. The whole plant is quite edible raw or cooked. Purslane is surprisingly high in carbohydrates (Harrington, Storer), as well as proteins, omega 3 fatty acids, antioxidants and vitamin E. However, it also contains oxalic acid which blocks the absorption of calcium in the digestive system (Gillaspy). Hall says that the plants can be picked and dried, which causes them to use stored moisture to finish developing the seed pods. The dried plants are beaten on a tarp and the seeds winnowed out for use as flour.

Sprague—Pussypaws (1/1/1)

Talinum—Flame Flower (-/16/0) Flame flower grows in the southwest.

Nyctaginaceae—Four-O'clock Family

The Four-O'Clock family is mostly native to the tropics, with only a handful of plants in the northern latitudes. The funnel-shaped flowers are usually bisexual with 4 or 5 united sepals and no true petals, although the sepals are colored like petals. There may be sepal-like bracts at the base of the flower. There are 3-7 stamens. The ovary is positioned superior and consists of 1 carpel (unicarpellate). It matures as a dry seed (an achene). The sepals persist as the ovary matures.

World-wide there are 30 genera and 300 species, a few of which are used as ornamentals, including *Bougainvillea*. Fifteen genera are native to North America, mostly in the south and southwest. The flowers of *Mirabilis* bloom late in the day, hence the family name.

Abronia
fragrans

Key Words
Tubular flowers with 4-5 colored sepals and 0 petals.

Abronia—Sand Verbena (50/23/2) The roots of three species are known to be edible; with some specimens reportedly large and sweet (Fern). Another species was used by the Ute as a remedy for stomach and bowel troubles. The tea is also reported to be diuretic (Murphey).

Boerhavia—Spiderling (-/20/0) Among the species listed, the leaves are edible (Zomlefer), as are the cooked seeds and roots. The roots are rich in carbohydrate and protein, but may have a woody texture. The roots contain an alkaloid that causes a rise in blood pressure (Fern).

Mirabilis—Four O'clock (60/35/3) Some four o'clocks have large roots rich in carbohydrates and proteins, but they may contain mildly narcotic properties. The mashed root is used as a local analgesic. Taken internally, the root raises blood sugar levels, acting as a temporary stimulant and apetite depressant. Larger doses lead to a feeling of well-being and hyperactivity followed by slurred speach and befuddlement. It also has a purgative and gas-producing effect (Moore).

Chenopodiaceae—Goosefoot Family

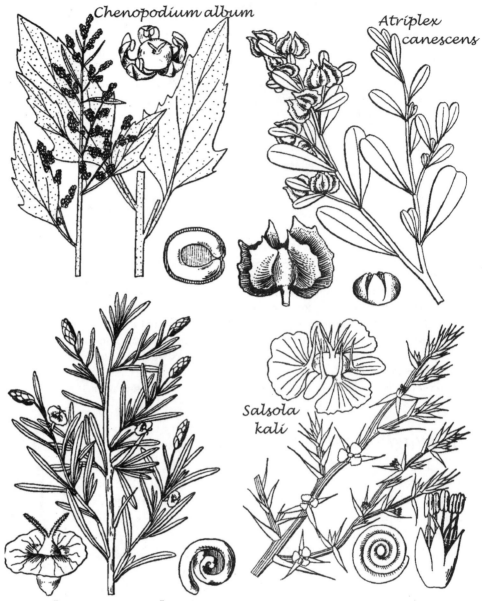

Chenopodium album

Atriplex canescens

Salsola kali

Sarcobatus vermiculatus

Look closely at a beet, chard, or spinach plant the next time you see one going to seed in the garden. You might notice little green "globs" forming along an upright stalk, sometimes colored with specks of yellow, the sign of pollen and stamens... yes these globs are true flowers! If you find a weedy plant lacking obvious flowers, and forming globby or poky seeds along the stems, it is likely you have a species from this family.

If you were to examine the flowers of a Goosefoot plant under a microscope you would see 2-5 (usually 5) sepals, often united, and no petals. There are an equal number of stamens as sepals. The ovary is positioned superior (half inferior in *Beta*) and consists of 2 (rarely 3-5) united carpels (syncarpous) forming a single chamber. It matures as a nutlet.

World-wide there are 102 genera and 1500 species. The 17 genera listed here are native to North America, mostly in the west. Domestic chard and beets belong to this family; both were bred from *Beta vulgaris,* originally from the coast of France. Spinach belongs to the genus *Spinacia*. Sugar beets are grown in parts of Montana and processed for sugar. Quinoa seed is sold as a hot cereal at many health food stores; it comes from a species of *Chenopodium*. Note: members of the Ragweed tribe of the Aster family could be mistaken as Goosefoots.

Most plants in this family are *edible* in salads or as potherbs, and are rich in calcium and other minerals. However, they are largely adapted to disturbed, salty, or alkaline soils, and are prone to accumulating both selenium and nitrogen. The nitrogen often appears in the plants as *oxalates*. Ironically, oxalates can inhibit the body's ability to absorb calcium and should not be consumed for extended periods of time. Many species from the Goosefoot family accumulate salts from the soil. The plants can be utilized as *salt substitutes*, either whole or burned and the ashes used. The seeds of most species are also edible. Saponins are also common in the family.

Key Words
Weedy plants with "globby or poky flowers", found in disturbed or alkaline soils. No petals.

Edible and Medicinal Properties of the Goosefoot Family Plants

Allenrolfea— (-/-/0) • *Allenrolfea* is found in desert alkaline environments, including Death Valley, California.

Atriplex—Saltbush (150/-/10) • The leaves are used as a potherb. The seeds can be harvested and ground into meal. Note that the plant may absorb selenium (Sweet). Atriplex can also accumulate enough salt from the soil to flavor food (Harrington). Pinole is a southwestern drink made with the parched, ground seeds plus sugar and water (Bigfoot). Medicinally, a poultice of the leaves can be used for bee stings, and a tea of the root is taken for colds.

Axyria—(-/-/1)

Bassia—Summer Cypress (-/-/1) The young leaves or seeds of one species are known to be edible, but only in moderate quantities since the plant contains some saponin. The plant is grown in Korea and made into brooms (Fern).

Ceratoides (Eurotia)—Winterfat (8/-/1) As the common name implies, winterfat is an important winter range plant.

Chenopodium—Goosefoot, Lamb's Quarters, Strawberry Goosefoot (200/-/11) • Lamb's quarters got its popular name from its habit of growing in disturbed manure rich soils like barnyards. The Latin "*Cheno-podium*" means "goose-foot", in reference to the shape of the leaves. *C. album* was introduced from Europe. It is commonly found in gardens. Goosefoot is a delicous salad green or potherb, and highly nutritious. It contains more calcium than any other plant ever analyzed, plus lots of riboflavin, vitamins A and C, and protein (Kallas). The seeds are also easy to gather and highly nutritious.

Most seed crops need to be winnowed to separate the seeds from the chaff, because the chaff is undigestible cellulose. Not so with the goosefoot. The plant is quite edible and delicious, and the chaff that comes off with the seeds is just dried greens—extra nutrition. You can rub the seeds between your palms to separate the chaff if you want to winnow it out for a more refined product, but is not necessary. One hour of hand-stripping the seeds from the dead stalks in September yielded slightly over a gallon of seeds.

Archaeologists have recently discovered that the Indians were making extensive use of goosefoot seeds some 9,400 years ago in this area. The Indians used the slimleaf goosefoot which has a remarkably bitter seed. I finally threw out my harvest of slimleaf goosefoot seeds; it was just too over-powering for me.

C. capitatum, sometimes called "strawberry blite", is strikingly unique from other goosefoots because it develops a bright red berry around its seeds. They are bland and uninteresting compared to "real" berries, but easy to gather and highly nutritious. I gathered 3 1/2 quarts of berries in one hour. Lamb's quarters contain some oxalic acid (Willard).

Note: epazote or wormseed (*C. ambrosioides*) is found mostly in the southwestern states and Mexico. The seeds contain a potent and bitter oil used as an anthelmentic to kill intestinal parasites. Excess consumption could be toxic (Moore).

Corispermum—Bugseed (-/-/2)

Cycloloma—Ringwing (-/-/1) The seeds are edible (Kirk).

Grayia—Hop Sage (-/-/1)

Halogeton— (3/-/1) Halogeton contains an oxalate that may poison sheep (Booth).

Kochia—Summer Cypress (80/-/2) The young shoots may be eaten as a potherb. The seeds are edible (Kirk).

Monolepis—Poverty Weed (-/-/1) The plant is edible as a potherb (Harrington).

Salicornia—Pickleweed, Glasswort (30/-/1) The plant is edible as a salad, pickle, or potherb (Kirk). It is high in salt and can be added to stews to provide salt flavoring (Olsen). *Salicornia* and several other salty plants were used in early glass-making. The plants were dried then burned in a heap. The ashes were added to sand for crude glass-making, or leached with lime water to make caustic soda. The moisture was then evaporated away to leave crystals of mostly pure sodium hydroxide, and this was used for making finer glass (Mabey).

Salsola—Russian Thistle (100/-/2) • The plant is edible as a potherb. The seeds are also edible (Harrington). *Salsola* is often high in salt, used similarly to *Salicornia*, above.

Sarcobatus—Greasewood (2/-/1) • The tender young twigs are edible with several hours of boiling (Kirk).

Suaeda—Seepweed (-/-/3) The plant is edible as potherb; it has a salty flavor. The seeds are also edible. A black dye can be made by soaking masses of the plant (Kirk).

Suckleya— (-/-/1) The plant contains a poisonous cyanogenetic substance that can form hydrocyanic or prussic acid in the digestive system (Harrington). Similar cyanide compounds in other plants are typically destroyed by cooking. It is probable that would be the case here as well, but I do not have a means to confirm that.

Amaranthaceae—Amaranth Family

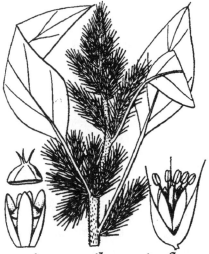

Amaranthus retroflexus

If you have ever weeded a garden then you have probably met a member of this family. The Amaranth family is large with 60-65 genera and 900 species world-wide, mostly in the tropics. Of these 12 genera occur in the states, and most of them in the warm and moist southeast portion of the country. Only the genus *Amaranthus* is widespread in the northern latitudes. One of the tumbleweeds is a species of *Amaranthus*. Other tumbleweeds are found in the Goosefoot and Mustard families.

Members of the Amaranth genus are annual weeds with alternate leaves and typically red stems. If you were to look at a specimen under a microscope you would find 3 scale-like bracts, often colored, enclosing the flowers. There are 2-5 sepals, 0 petals, and the same number of stamens as sepals. The ovary is positioned superior and consists of 2-3 united carpels (syncarpous), forming a single chamber. It matures as a lidded capsule, called a "pyxis", with only one seed per flower. Just watch for the weedy plants with red stems that develop poky seed clusters around the upright stalks. Rub the seed cluster between your palms and blow away the chaff and you will see the shiny black seeds, often with red and pale seeds mixed in.

The Amaranth and Goosefoot families are closely related and share some similar properties. Members from both families are adapted to disturbed soils. The plants are mostly *edible* and rich in calcium, although they may also absorb nitrates from the soil and form *oxalate crystals* in the leaves.

Key Words(Amaranthus spp.)
Weedy plants with red stems, poky flowers, and shiny black, red, and pale seeds. No petals.

Amaranthus—Amaranth, Pigweed (50/-/7) • Amaranth is sometimes called pigweed because certain species become prolific in the disturbed, manure rich soil of barnyards and pig pens. However, several other plants are called pigweeds as well, so amaranth is clearly the better name.

Amaranth leaves and tender stem tips are edible as a salad or potherb and rank among the most nutritious wild greens there are, especially high in iron, calcium, protein and vitamin C. Amaranth grown in manure-rich soil or drought conditions may accumulate nitrates (Kallas).

One species of amaranth (*A. caudatus*) was once grown extensively as a crop by the Aztec Indians of Mexico. It has been making a comeback in recent years, so you can now buy amaranth seed or products made with the flour at most health food stores. Our species of amaranth are most often found as prolific garden weeds. They are just as good as the commercial variety. I cut the whole, dead stalks in the fall and place them on a tarp, then beat the seeds out with a stick. Sometimes the plants need to dry a little more to release all their seeds. I use a gold pan as a winnowing tray to winnow out the trash. An hour of picking, fifteen minutes of beating, and a half hour of winnowing yields close to a gallon of the seeds at the peak of the season.

Amaranth seeds can be boiled into a good hot cereal. The seeds are small and hard enough to be difficult to digest, so cook them for at least an hour to get them to swell and split. Parching the seeds prior to cooking may make the final product easier to digest. The seeds can be parched by placing the gold pan on the coals and stirring the seeds. You might also experiment with sprouting the seeds. The young, tender leaves and stems are also edible raw or as a potherb (Tilford). Medicinally, the plants are useful as a mild astringent, internally and externally (Brown, Willard).

Polygonaceae—Buckwheat Family

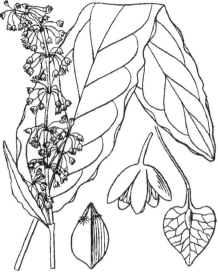

Rumex crispus

The Buckwheats have small flowers in clusters, with flower parts usually in multiples of three, often producing a three-sided (triangular) seed. They have simple, toothless leaves, and often swollen joints, or nodes, on the stem. The Latin "Polygonum" literally means "many knees", and refers to these swollen nodes of the leaf stems. There are 3-6 sepals, sometimes colored like petals, but no true petals, and 4-9 stamens. The ovary is positioned superior and consists of 3 (rarely 2 or 4) united carpels (syncarpous), forming a single chamber. It matures as a dry seed, usually brown or black and triangular in shape, sometimes with wings.

World-wide there are about 40 genera and 800 species, including 15 genera in North America. Sour juice, from *oxalic acid*, is common in this family. Rhubarb, buckwheat, and some of the sorrels are cultivated as food plants. Several plants in this family are known to be high in calcium, potassium, and iron. However, over-consumption of plants containing oxalic acid can inhibit the body's ability to absorb calcium. Many plants of this family also contain *tannic acid*, and are thus highly astringent.

<u>Key Words</u>: Small flowers with colored sepals, no petals and often triangular seeds.

Eriogonum—Wild Buckwheat (200/180/15) • The leaves are edible as a potherb. The seeds are ground into meal or flour (Olsen). The buckwheats are astringent plants, useful internally and externally (Sweet).

Fagopyrum—Buckwheat (2/2/1) The *Eriogonums* (above) are also called "buckwheat", but the commercial crop comes from *Fagopyrum*. It is planted as a "cereal" grain. The plant is rich in flavanoids (Schauenberg).

Oxyria—Mountain Sorrel (1/1/1) • Mountain sorrel is edible as a salad or potherb. It contains oxalic acid (Willard).

Polygonum—Smartweed, Knotweed, Bistort (200/70/23) • The leaves and shoots of the *Polygonums* are edible in the spring before becoming too astringent (Angier). *P. bistortes* is the bistort; the roots are quite astringent, useful internally and externally (Willard). Surprisingly, they are also quite edible and taste like nuts when cooked. Cooking may somehow destroy the astringency, I don't know. I can collect approximately 1 cup of roots per hour with a digging stick. The seeds are also edible. I sometimes snack on the whole flowers.

Rheum—Common Rhubarb (40/-/1) • Rhubarb is often found growing wild beside the remains of old cabins. The chopped stems make great pies, but the leaves contain toxic levels of calcium oxalate. The root also contains anthraquinone glycosides with laxative properties, plus tannic acid (Schauenberg).

Rumex—Dock, Sorrel, Canagrie (200/-/10) • The docks and sorrels are all edible to varying degees. The sorrels have a lemony taste due to the oxalic acid. I enjoy these in salads. The docks are often unpalatable due to excessive levels of oxalic and/or tannic acid. Cooking them as a ptherb and changing the water once or twice may tame them sufficiently. The seeds are said to be edible, but require leaching to take away their astringent nature. The roots are even more astringent. Anthraquinone glycosides with purgative properties appear in numerous species of *Rumex* (Geller, Schauenerg). The leaves of *R. hymenosepalus* may be toxic (Bigfoot), probably due to oxalates.

Eriogonum flavum

Polygonum persicaria

Oxyria digyna

Hypericum perforatum

Hypericaceae—St. Johnswort Family

If you've been troubled by depression then you may be delighted to learn about the St. Johnswort family. St. Johnswort has become a well-known and effective herbal alternative to Prozak and other antidepressants. These are perennial herbs with simple, opposite leaves. The leaves are often covered with dark glands or clear dots. The petals are usually yellow, but may be tinged with red or orange spots. At least one species has pink blossoms. The flowers are regular and bisexual with 4-5 sepals, 4-5 petals, and 10 or more stamens. The ovary is positioned superior and consists of 3-5 united carpels (syncarpous) with the partition walls present, forming an equal numberof chambers. It matures as a capsule.

World-wide there are at least 3 genera and 356 species in the family, mostly of *Hypericum*. *Hypericaceae* is often considered a subfamily of the larger *Clusiaceae* (also known as *Guttiferae*).

Key Words
Yellow flowers with parts in 4's or 5's. Opposite leaves with clear dots.

Ascyrum—St. Peterswort, St. Andrews Cross (5/5/0) These flowers are found in the eastern and southern states.

Crookea— (1/1/0) *Crookea* has two narrow petals and two broad petals. It is found in Georgia and Florida.

Hypericum—St. John's Wort (350/25/4) The leaves are edible as salad (Sweet), and the plants were dried by Native Americans and used a meal (Hutchins). A tea of the plant is antispasmodic, nervine, expectorant, astringent and diuretic. It is used for nervous conditions such as insomnia and bed-wetting (Lust). A pigment in the leaves and flower dots, called hypercin, is used as an antidepressant altnative to Prozak. St. John's Wort has been demonstrated to significantly increase the healing of burns. Internal use of the plant may cause temporary sensitivity to intense sunlight (Klein).

    H. perforatum, illustrated here, is an import from Europe and an invasive weed in this continent. It is being planted as a crop in some places and sprayed as a weed in others. Native plants are threated by habitat loss due to plants like this. It would make a lot more sense to stop both the spraying and the planting of St. Johnswort in favor of intensive wildcrafting to control its population, with subsidies if necessary.

Hypericum perforatum

MS.

Tilia heterophylla

Tiliaceae—Basswood Family

The members of the Basswood family are mostly trees and shrubs with simple, alternate leaves, but there are some smaller plants n the family, including jute. The flowers are regular and bisexual. There are usually 5 (sometimes 3 or 4) sepals separate, or sometimes joined at the base, with an equal number of petals (sometimes 0), plus numrous stamens. The ovary is positioned superior and consists of 2-10 united carpels (syncarpous), with the partition walls present, forming an equal number of chambers. It matures as a berry, capsule or sometimes a "schizocarp", meaning a dry fruit that splits apart into one-seeded sections.

The Basswood family is relatively large with about 50 genera world-wide and 450 species, but most are native to the tropics. Our native genera are listed below. *Sparmannia, Entelea,* and *Lueea* are common ornamentals planted in tropical climates. Basswood tree can be distinguished from other trees by the slender leaf-like bract that supports the flower cluster.

Key Words (Basswood tree)
Trees with flower/berry cluster from a slender leaf-like bract.

Corchorus—Jute (40/3/0) A few species of jute have been commercially grown for their fibers. These and other species have also been cultivated in gardens for use as a potherb (Sturtevant). Medicinally, jute greens function as a digestive stimulant. The seeds of some species may contain a cardiac glycoside (Fern).

Tilia—Basswood, Linden Tree (50/-/D) • Linden trees are native to the eastern forests, but are sometimes planted domestically in Montana. Reportedly the fruit and flowers of the linden tree can be ground together to produce a chocolate flavor. There were attempts long ago to commercialize the chocolate substitute, but it was too perishable for shipping and storage. The tree may be tapped for syrup (Sturtevant) (see Maple family for more information). The young leaves are somewhat mucilaginous and edible raw. The flowers are also edible, but caution is advised, as narcotics may develop in the older flowers (Fern).

Medicinally, a tea of the inner bark is soothing for burns. A tea of the dried flowers is expectorant, sedative, and diaphoretic i effect (Fern).

Linden provides a quality cordage material. Cut long strips of bark from the tree (please use some ethics here) and soak them in water for at least a week to separate the inner and outer bark. The inner bark can be split into narrower strips with the ad of a fingernail. The material can be made into cordage at this point, or for extra strength you can boil the fibers in a mix of ashes and water for about twenty-four hours (Jaeger).

Triumfetta—Burweed (-/2/0) Burweeds grow in Florida. At least one species produces cordage material similar to jute (Benson).

Tilia americana

Malvaceae—Mallow Family

If you have seen a holyhock or hibiscus flower, then you have seen the Mallow family. The mallows have a distinct, funnel-shaped flower. The flowers are regular, with 3-5 partially united sepals and 5 separate petals, often surrounded by several bracts. There are numerous stamens united to form a distinctive column around the pistil. The ovary is positioned superior and consists of 5 or more united carpels (syncarpous), with the partition walls present, forming an equal number of chambers (rarely unicarpellate). It matures as a capsule, a schizocarp (the round "cheeses", as high-lighted in the picture), or rarely as a winged seed or berry. Mallow leaves are alternate, usually lobed or palmately veined.

World-wide there are about 85 genera and 1500 species, including 27 genera in North America. Hollyhock, hibiscus, and cotton are members of this family. Okra is the edible fruit of a variety of hibiscus. Marshmallows were originally derived from *Althaea officinalis*. Our species of *Malva* can be used similarly (Hall). The root or seeds are covered with water and boiled until half the liquid is gone. Then the liquid is beaten into a froth, and sugar is added. It should make something resembling whipped cream. The plants contain natural gums calledmucilage, pectin, and asparagin, which gives them their slimy, mucilaginous characteristic; it is the presence of these gums that creates the marshmallow effect. The members of the Mallow family are mostly *edible* as a salad greens and potherbs, although not very commonly used, probably due to their slimy consistency. The flowers and seeds are also edible.

Medicinally, the mallows tend to be *mucilaginous* like aloe vera or cactus. This slimy characteristic makes them useful externally as an emollient for soothing sunburns and other inflamed skin conditions, and internally as a demulcent and expectorant for soothing sore throats. The mallows may be mildly astringent, which increases their effectiveness for these uses.

Key Words
Mucilaginous plants and flowers with numerous stamens fused into a central column.

Abutilon—Indian Mallow (150/-/1) *A. indicus* is a source of fibers (Pammel). The flowers of two foreign species are known to be edible (Sturtevant) however, our *A. theophrasti* has a strong odor and may be poisonous (Pammel).

Althaea—Hollyhock, Wild Hollyhock (75/-/2) • The leaves are edible as a salad green or potherb. Medicinally, these plants are listed as demulcent, diuretic, emollient (Lust). The tea is used for lower urinary tract infections. A hot drawing poultice of the powdered root or leaves speeds up the white blood cell activity in an infected wound (Moore). Holly-hocks make acceptable cordage material in the winter when the dead stalks have lain in the snow long enough for the outer layer to moisten and separate.

Hibiscus— (200/19/1) • The various species of hibiscus are generally mucilaginous, emollient and demulcent; some are mildly astringent and diuretic (Lust). The flowers of some species of hibiscus are commonly used in commercial herbal teas. They are rich in citric, malic, and tartaric acids (Schauenberg). One species of hibiscus is called kenaf. It is being grown as a fiber crop for making paper.

Gossypium—Cotton (20+/-/0) The seeds of cotton are mucilaginous and oily. The oil from the seeds is sometimes used in cooking. A tea from the bark of the root has been used as a stimulant for menstruation, contractions during birth, and abortions. Cotton is the only member of this family with documented poisonous properties (Pammel). Do not use without medical supervision (Lust).

Iliamna—Globe Mallow (-/7/1)

Malva—Mallow, Cheeseweed (30/8/6) • *M. neglecta* was imported from Europe. It is edible as a salad green or potherb, and it is a good stew thickener. The "cheeses" are a popular snack found in the lawn and garden. The poultice helps to break down and remove damaged tissues while increasing white blood cell activity in the area (Moore). A tea of the plant is astringent, demulcent, emollient, and expectorant, useful for sore throat, bronchitis, etc. (Lust). Mallows are rich in calcium and iron.

Sidalcea—Checker Mallow (25/25/2)

Sphaeralcea—Globe Mallow (60/22/2) • The plant and root is mucilaginous and soothing (Bigfoot). The tea is used for lower urinary tract infections. (Moore). A paste of the plant was applied by some Native American medicine men to temporarily protect their hands when they reached in boiling water to demonstrate their powers (Weiner).

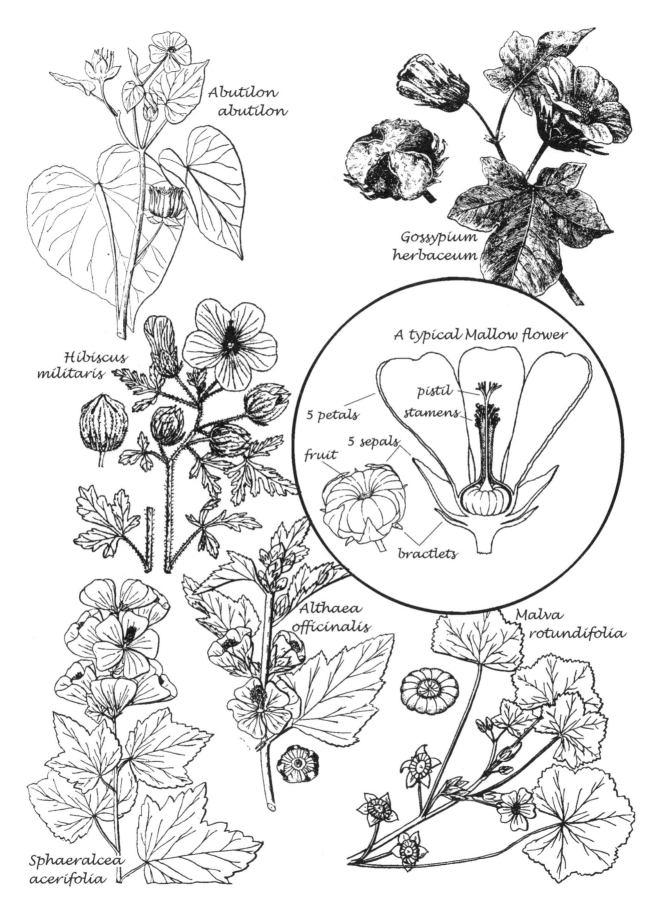

Abutilon
abutilon

Gossypium
herbaceum

Hibiscus
militaris

A typical Mallow flower

5 petals

pistil
stamens

5 sepals
fruit

bractlets

Althaea
officinalis

Malva
rotundifolia

Sphaeralcea
acerifolia

69

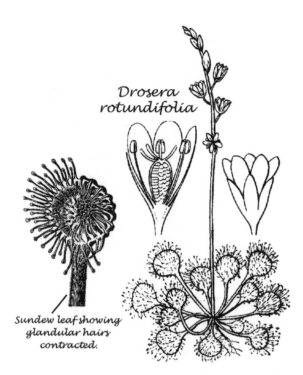

Drosera rotundifolia

Sundew leaf showing glandular hairs contracted.

Droseraceae—Sundew Family

The Sundews are rare plants in moist forests that catch and consume insects. The basal leaves are hairy and covered with a sticky substance used to catch their prey. Botanically there are 5 sepals united at the base and 5 separate petals, plus 5 stamens. The ovary is positioned superior and consists of 2, 3, or 5 united carpels (syncarpous) forming a single chamber It matures as a capsule with several to many seeds per carpel.

World-wide there are 4 genera and 105 species. Our natives are listed below. Genera native to the old world include *Drosophyllum* and *Aldrovanda*. The closely related Pitcher Plant family, *Sarraceniaceae*, includes other insectivorus plants such as the pitcher plant (*Sarracenia*) and cobra lily (*Darlingtonia*). A third family of insectivorus plants is the distant Bladderwort family, *Lentibulariaceae*.

Key Words
**Insectivorous forest plants
with sticky leaves.**

Dionaea—Venus Fly Trap (1/1/0) The Venus fly trap grows wild in the Carolinas.

Drosera—Sundew (90/8/2) The juice of the plant is acrid; it has been used to remove warts and even freckles, but it can raise a blister on the skin (Willard). For tea the plant is usually boiled, instead of steeped. These plants are antispasmodic, expectorant, and antibiotic. An alcohol tincture may be required to extract the antibiotic properties. Caution is advised with this plant. Larger doses can irritate your system (Lust). The leaves may contain cyanide (Pammel).

Dionaea leaves & traps

Violaceae—Violet Family

Violets have a distinctive, slightly irregular flower. The pansy and Johnny-Jump-Ups are members of the *Viola* genus; if you have seen them, then you will recognize other flowers of this group.

Botanically, the violets are perennial plants with simple leaves, either alternate or basal. The nodding flowers have 5 sepals and 5 petals, with the lower petal being larger than the side and top petal pairs. The 5 stamens are alternate with the petals. The ovary is positioned superior and consists of 3 united carpels (syncarpous) forming a single chamber. It matures as an explosive 3-valved capsule. World-wide there are 16 genera and

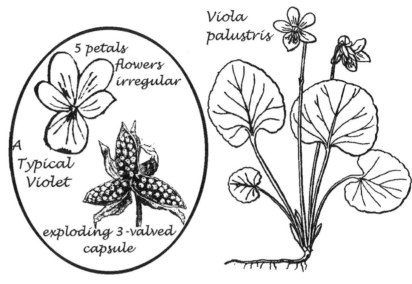

850 species. The genera listed below are found in North America. Note that the African violet is not a member of this family. It belongs to the family *Gesneriaceae*.

Key Words
Slightly irregular pansy-like flowers.

Hybanthus—Green Violet (80/2/0)

Viola—Violet, Pansy (450/60/13) • All of our species of Viola are edible as a salad or potherb, some are better than others. Violets make an excellent tea. They are high in vitamins A and C (Willard). As a child, I collected blue violets with my grandmother every summer. We dried them for winter tea; it is still one of my favorites.

Violet leaves contain varying amounts of saponin. Medicinally they are diuretic, expectorant, alterative, and mildly laxative. The yellow violets are more laxative than others. Violets are sometimes used in cancer cases as "blood purifiers" to aid the liver in eliminating waste from the blood, so there is no junk to feed to cancer cells (Willard). Violets can also be used externally as a poultice on cancer (Kloss). Violets are mildly astringent, as well as mucilaginous and thus useful for treating ulcers (Kloss). The roots of some species contain saponins and alkaloids useful for expectorant and emetic properties (Zomlefer).

Loasaceae—Loasa Family

Mentzelia decapetala

The plants of the Loasa family have mostly rough vegetation with rough, hooked, or even stinging hairs. North American members of the family have regular flowers, often 2-4 inches in diameter, typically with 5 sepals (sometimes 4) and 5 petals (sometimes 4 or 10), and numerous stamens—as many as 200! The ovary is positioned inferior and consists of 4-7 (rarely 3 or 8) united carpels (syncarpous), forming a single chamber. It matures as a capsule with numerous seeds (only 1 seed in *Petalonyx*).

In *Mentzelia laevicaulis* the outer ring of stamens can be flat, wide, and missing the anthers, so they look like petals. In some specimens from southern California the sepals, petals and styles even resemble leaves.

World-wide there are 15 genera and 250 species, mostly in South America and the southern parts of North America, but 4 genera are found in the north, as listed below. Many species of the family have stinging hairs.

Key Words
**Coarse, hairy, dry-land plants
with numerous stamens and a large ovary.**

Cevallia— (-/1/0) Cevallia is found from Arizona to Texas.

Eucnide— Rock Nettle (-/2/0)Rock nettle is found in the desert southwest.

Mentzelia—Blazing star (-/53/5) • The seeds can be parched or roasted and ground into a flour, for use as mush or bread (Olsen). Reportedly they could be used to thicken gravy (Murphey).

  Medicinally, a tea of the plant may be beneficial for hardened arteries, if taken over a long period of time (Bigfoot). The seeds were used in burn dressings by Native Americans. The leaves were used as an aid for toothache (Moerman).

Petalonyx—Sand Paper Plant (-/-/0) The sand paper plant is a native of the desert southwest.

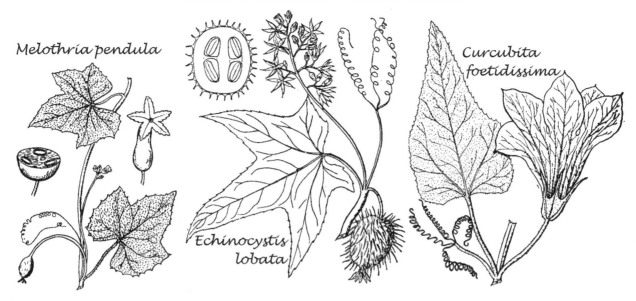

Melothria pendula

Echinocystis lobata

Curcubita foetidissima

Cucurbitaceae—Gourd Family

The Gourd family is as easy to recognize as pumpkins and squash. Look closely at one of these flowers and you will know the family. Male and female parts are borne on separate funnel-shaped flowers. There are 5 separate sepals and 5 united petals (rarely 6 of each). The 5 stamens (sometimes 3) of the male flower are often twisted together. In the pistillate (female) flower, the ovary is positioned inferior and consists of 3 united carpels (sometimes 4, as in *Echinocystis* pictured above) with the partition walls present, forming an equal number of chambers (You will see the pattern when you cut across a zucchini or other fruit.) The plants form prostrate or climbing vines.

World-wide there are 100 genera and 850 species, including 14 genera in North America. Pumpkins, squash, zucchini and gourds belong to the *Cucurbita* genus of this family. Muskmelon, cantaloupe, honeydew, and cucumbers belong to *Cucumis*. Other family members include watermelons (*Citrullus*), chayote (*Sechium*), and the *Luffa* vegetable sponge. Pumpkin seeds contain alkaloids capable of arresting cell division, useful for certain types of cancer (Schauenberg). **WARNING:** Some genera contain toxic alkaloids.

Key Words
Vining plants with tendrils. Funnel-shaped flowers forming large 3- or 4-celled fruits.

Bryonia—Bryonia (-/-/1) The whole plant is poisonous. The root is used in minute quantities as an irritating stimulant. Externally it may be used to irritate sore muscles or joints (a rubefaceint) to stimulate healing. Internally, it functions as an irritating expectorant, beneficial for congested lungs, or as an irritating purgative-cathartic to clear out the digestive tract. Toxicity varies between species, but an overdose may lead to severe diarrhea, vomiting and death within a few hours (Fern). This plant is not for amateurs.

Cucurbita—Wild Gourd, Pumpkins, Squash, etc. (20/4/D) • The raw seeds of pumpkins and other species contain cucurbitin acid, a popular treatment for internal parasites. The concentration is extremely variable within the genus, even among the many varieties of pumpkins (Tyler). The wild gourds, *C. foetidissima* and *C. digitata*, are not native to Montana, but I have successfully planted seeds brought from Arizona and southern Colorado. So far the plants have never put on fruit, apparently due to the short growing season in Montana, but surprisingly, the plants are biennial and prosper in spite of our extreme winters. The massive root of these contain large amounts of saponin. It can be chopped and used for soap or fish poison. The seeds are edible after complete drying and roasting. The plant and the gourd flesh has a strongly laxative effect (Bigfoot), possibly due to the saponins.

Echinocystis—Wild Cucumber (25/1/1) • *Echinocystis* is an uncommon plant in Montana. I've found only one small patch so far. The seeds were reportedly roasted and eaten for kidney trouble (Murphey). The root has analgesic properties. It may be pulverized and used as a poultice for headaches, or brewed as a bitter tea and taken internally (Fern).

Marah—Wild Cucumber (7/6/0) The fruits and seeds of the plants appear to contain saponins and narcotic alkaloids. The whole fruits can be crushed and used to stun fish, but with variable results. At least one death is attributed to this plant. The man made a tea of the seeds, possibly for its narcotic effect (Nyerges).

Salicaceae—Willow Family

It would be hard to miss the Willow family. You can usually find one or another of willows, aspens, cottonwoods or poplars along any stream, lake, or mountain meadow. Botanically, the Willow family consists of bushes and trees with simple, alternate leaves. The flowers are unisexual with male and female flowers appearing in catkins on separate plants. The sepals are greatly reduced or absent, and there are no petals. Male flowers have 2 or more stamens. In the pistillate (female) flower, the ovary is positioned superior and consists of 2-4 united carpels (syncarpous) forming a single chamber. It matures as a capsule, usually with silky "cotton" to help transport the seeds by air. World-wide there are 2-3 genera and 350-500 species.

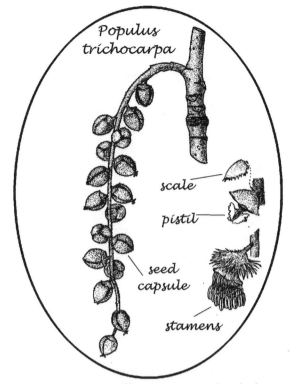

Populus trichocarpa

scale

pistil

seed
capsule

stamens

Medicinally, the willow family is analgesic, anti-inflammatory, astringent and diuretic. The members of this family contains varying amounts of the ***simple phenol glycosides*** populin, salicin, and methyl salicylate from which the common aspirin was originally derived. These properties are strongest in the inner bark, but are also present in the leaves. Like aspirin, the willow family is used for fevers, headaches, arthritis, and other inflammations, particularly in the urinary tract. Unfortunately, the presence of tannic acid in the bark makes it difficult to ingest enough salicin to affect a common headache. A strong tea of the leaves might prove more effective, without the bad taste. A strip of the bark can be tied over a cut to serve as the band-aid and as an astringent-antiseptic. Members of the willow family may also expel worms (Hart).

Recent studies have indicated that when used as a long-term tonic the common aspirin can greatly reduce a person's risk of heart disease or colon cancer in later life. Willow tea may or may not have the same potential—more research needs to be done in this area. Like asprin, large quantities of willow can irritate the stomach lining.

<u>Key Words</u>
Trees and bushes with alternate leaves in moist soil. Catkins form many small capsules.

Populus—Poplar, Cottonwood, Aspen (40/-/7) • Aphids sometimes produce an edible honeydew that can be scraped or boiled off the leaves and buds and eaten (Olsen). The inner bark and sap of the cottonwood is reportedly sweet early in the spring and was eaten by the Indians.

    Medicinally, the buds are diaphoretic, expectorant, and diuretic (Lust). The leaves were used as a poultice (Hart). Cottonwood and aspen leaf buds contain a sticky, aromatic resin that can be collected early in the spring and used in an oil-based ointment for burns and skin irritations. It is popularly known as "Balm of Gilead". The buds are soaked in olive oil for a week to extract constituents (Moore).

Salix—Willow (300+/-/28) • Willow is a commonly known wilderness medicine due to its aspirin-like qualities. It is used for headaches, fevers, hay fever, neuralgia, and inflammations of the joints. Some of the salicylic acid is excreted in the urine, making it useful as an analgesic to the urethra and bladder (Moore).

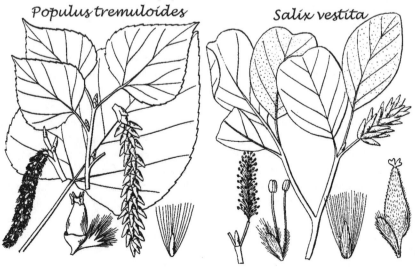

Populus tremuloides

Salix vestita

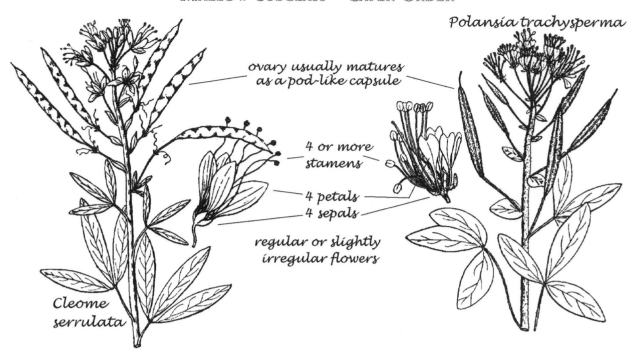

Polansia trachysperma

ovary usually matures
as a pod-like capsule

4 or more
stamens

4 petals

4 sepals

regular or slightly
irregular flowers

*Cleome
serrulata*

Capparaceae—Caper Family

Plants of the Caper family have regular or slightly irregular, bisexual flowers with 4 sepals, 4 petals, and 4 to numerous stamens. The ovary is positioned superior and consists of 2 united carpels (bicarpellate) forming a single chamber. It matures as a capsule (sometimes a berry) with 1 or more kidney-shaped seeds. Our members of this family are annual herbs with alternate, clover-like leaves.

World-wide there are 46 genera and 800 species. North American genera are listed below. Many species are adapted to desert or tropical conditions. Only *Cleome* and *Polanisia* are widespread across the continent. A species of *Capparis* supplies the capers used in cooking. The Caper family is closely related to the Mustard family.

<u>Key Words</u>
Pea-like plants with flower parts in 4's and mustard-like pods.

Atamisquea— (-/-/0) The plant is found along the southern border of Arizona.

Capparis—Jamaica Caper Tree (350/-/0) The tree grows on the Florida peninsula.

Cleome—Bee Plant (200/12/2) • The young shoots and leaves can be used as a potherb, boiled in two or three changes of water. The seeds are edible. Indians boiled the plant down for an extended time to produce a dark paint (Harrington). Medicinally, the tea is reported to be taken for a fever (Murphey).

Cleomella—Stinkweed (20/11/0) Stinkweed is native to the desert southwest.

Isomeris—California bladderpod (1/1/0) *I. arborea* is also known as *Cleome isomeris*; it is a native of southern California.

Polanisia—Clammy Weed (-/8/1)

Oxystylis—Spiny Caper (-/1/0) The spiny caper is found in southeastern California and adjacent Nevada.

Wislizenia—Jackass Clover (10/1/0) Jackass Clover is a native of the southwest.

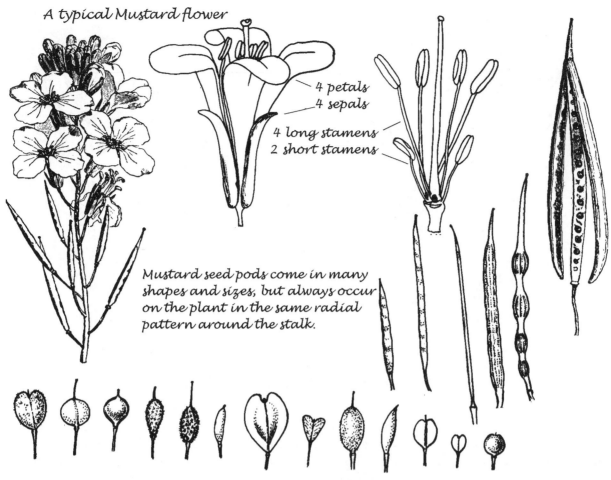

A typical Mustard flower

4 petals
4 sepals

4 long stamens
2 short stamens

Mustard seed pods come in many shapes and sizes, but always occur on the plant in the same radial pattern around the stalk.

Brassicaceae (Cruciferae)—Mustard Family

Mustards are easy to recognize. There are typically 4 petals arranged like either the letters "X" or "H". The petals may be deeply split, making them appear as eight petals. Mustard seed pods come in many shapes and sizes, but they are always form a raceme on the flower stalk, which looks something like a spiral staircase for the little people (see illustrations). The crushed leaves usually smell something like mustard. Another pattern of the mustards is that they are typically weedy annuals that inhabit disturbed, barren soils. Mustards have 4 sepals, 4 petals, and 6 stamens (2 short, 4 long). The ovary is positioned superior and consists of 2 united carpels (bicarpellate) forming a single chamber. It matures as a silicle or silique, meaning a pod where the outside walls fall away leaving the translucent interior partion intact. Look for it on dried specimens. World-wide there are 375 genera and 3200 species. About 55 genera are found in North America.

Domesticated mustards include horseradish (*Armoracia*), water cress (*Nasturtium*), radish (*Raphanus*), turnip and mustard (*Brassica*). Commerical mustards are usually made from the seeds of the black mustard (*B. nigra*) mixed with viniger. Interestingly, six of our common vegetables—cabbage, cauliflower, kohlrabi, Brussels sprouts, broccoli, and kale—were all bred from a single species, *Brassica oleracea*. Plant breeders developed the starch-storage abilities of different parts of the plant to come up with each unique vegetable. Also, canola oil comes from the seed of a species of *Brassica*. The horseradish has been humanly propagated with pieces of the root for so long that it no longer produces viable seed. Many wild members of this family are *edible* in moderate quantities, and the seeds are often used as a mustard-like spice.

Medicinally the plants of the mustard family contain varying concentrations of *sulfur glycosides*, strongest in *Brassica*, *Raphanus*, and *Amoracia*. In small amounts mustards are somewhat bitter and stimulating to digestion. In larger amounts they tend to be *acrid* and irritating. Several of them are acrid enough to blister the skin with prolonged contact. This acrid quality is often used as irritating poultices to stimulate healing. A "mustard plaster", for instance, can be placed on the chest to penetrate the skin and irritate the lungs; this stimulates coughing of phlegm from the lungs. Read more about sulfur glycosides in the Medicinal Properties section of this book.

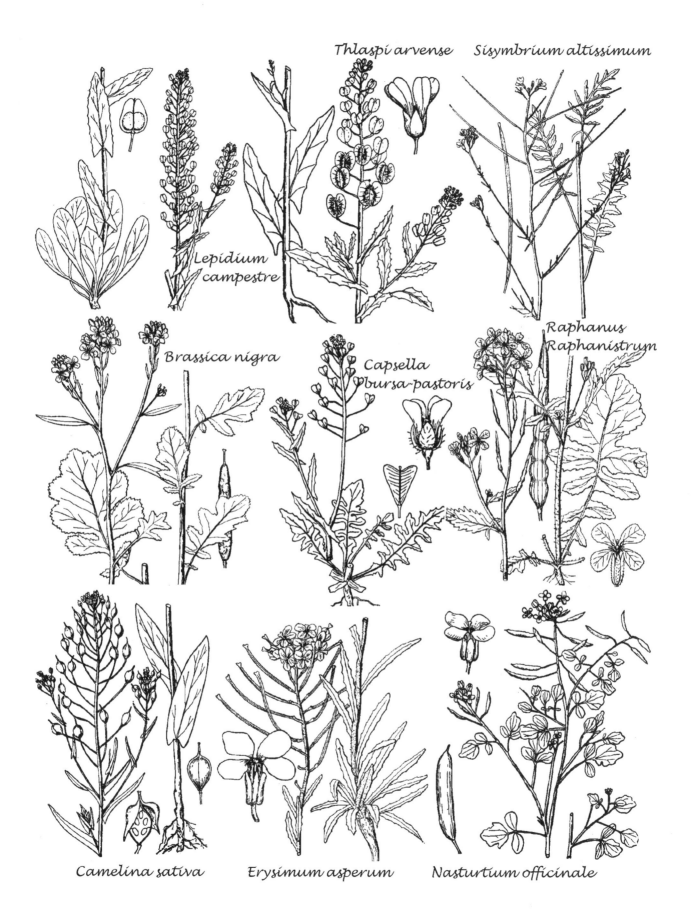

Thlaspi arvense

Sisymbrium altissimum

Lepidium campestre

Brassica nigra

Capsella bursa-pastoris

Raphanus Raphanistrum

Camelina sativa

Erysimum asperum

Nasturtium officinale

Key Words for the Mustard Family
4 petals and 6 stamens: 4 tall and 2 short

Edible and Medicinal Properties of Mustard Family plants

Alyssum— (100/4/2) • Alyssum is a common garden flower. It is edible.

Arabis—Rock Cress (120/70/15) • The flowers and basal leaves are edible. The stem leaves may be too bitter (Angier).

Barbarea—Wintercress (12/3/1) The leaves can be used as a salad or potherb (Hall).

Brassica—Mustard (50/10/5) • The leaves can be used as a salad or potherb. The seeds can be used for seasoning. Medicinally, the seeds can be ground into a powder and mixed with flour and water to make a mustard plaster (Hall). The mustard poultice is an irritant, stimulating activity underneath the skin. Prolonged contact can cause serious inflammation (Lust). Members of this genus contain sulfur glycosides (Geller).

Camelina—False flax (-/-/2) The plant is sometimes grown for the fibers of the stalk and for the oil in the seeds (Sturtevant).

Capsella—Shepherd's Purse (5/-/1) • The seeds are used for seasoning (Hall) or cooked and ground into meal (Olsen). The root is a substitute for ginger (Harrington). The seeds dumped in still water will kill mosquito larvae (Willard).

      Medicinally, *Capsella* is astringent and diuretic; it is especially known as a potent vasoconstrictor and coagulant. The tea can be used internally or externally to stop bleeding; it is commonly used for women's mid-cycle bleeding. It may also equalize blood pressure (Willard), but it can have inconsistent effects, causing either vasodilation or hypertension. As an astringent and diuretic, *Capsella* is good for the urinary tract and bladder, and it stimulates phosphate recycling in the kidneys. Also given during birth to stimulate uterine contractions (Moore). It is a remedy for diarrhea (Kloss).

Cardamine—Bittercress (160/45/5) The whole plant is edible as a salad or potherb. The root is hot like horseradish.

Chorispora (1/1/1) Introduced from Asia. The plant is edible (Sturtevant).

Descurainia—Tansy Mustard (46/-/3) • The plant can be used as a potherb, boil in 2 or 3 changes of water. The seeds can be used as meal (Harrington).

Eruca—Rocket Salad (1/1/1) *E. sativa* is an import from Europe. The plant is edible as a salad green (Sturtevant).

Erysimum—Wall Flower (80/25/4) • The plant, mashed with water was applied to prevent sunburn (Weiner).

Isatis—Dyer's Woad (30/-/1) *I. tinctoria* was introduced from Europe and cultivated as a source of blue dye. It is considered an invasive weed across much of the west.

Lepidium—Pepperweed (130/-/1) Pepperweed is edible in a salad or as a potherb (Duke). The freshly bruised plant has been used as a treatment for poison ivy (Vogel).

Nasturtium—Watercress (50/-/1) • Watercress came from Europe. It is now widespread and one of our few greens of winter. It can be found growing in the water near springs. Rice cooked with watercress is one of my favorite meals on camping trips. Watercress is rich in vitamin C, iron, and iodine (Lust).

      Medicinally, watercress is mild, but diuretic and stimulant. Prolonged use may lead to kidney problems, and consumption is not advised during pregnancy (Lust). Note that the common garden nasturtium is *Tropaeolum majus* of the family *Tropaeolaceae*.

Physaria—Twin Pod (-/14/3) Native Americans used the plant as a cure for sore throat (A. Brown, Murphey).

Rorippa—Yellowcress (-/20/7) • The plants are edible.

Sisymbrium—Tumble Mustard (80/-/4) • The plant can be used as a potherb. The seeds can be gathered and used for meal or seasoning (Harrington). Medicinally, tumble mustards are used similarly to the *Brassicas* (Lust).

Stanleya—Prince's Plume (6/6/2) • The fresh plant has an emetic effect, but is reportedly safe to eat after boiling in several changes of water (Murphey). The plant requires selenium in the soil for proper growth, and is used as an indicator of this mineral.

Thlaspi—Pennycress (60/6/2) • The plant can be used as a salad green or potherb in moderate amounts.

Other selected genera of the Mustard family:

Arabidopsis—Mouse-Ear Cress (-/2/1) … *Berteroa*—False Alyssum (-/-/1) … *Cardaria*—Whitetop (-/-/2) • … *Conringia*—Hare's Ear Mustard (-/-/1) … *Draba*—Whitlow Grass (270/90/18) … *Erucastrum*— (-/-/1) … *Halimolobos*— (-/-/1) … *Hesperis*—Rocket (24/1/1) • … *Lesquerella*—Bladderpod (-/54/3) • … *Smelowskia*— (-/5/1) … *Subularia*—Awlwort (-/-/1) … *Thelypodium*— (-/21/2)

Ericaceae—Heath Family

The Heath family is as exciting to know as blueberries and huckleberries. Many of the plants have evergreen leaves that can be seen whenever the snow melts away in winter. The bisexual and regular or nearly regular flowers have 4 or 5 sometimes united sepals and 4 or 5 petals, usually united in a bell shape and white or red in color. Expect to find either the same number, or twice as many stamens as petals. The ovary is positioned superior or inferior and consists of 4-10 (rarely 2-3) united carpels (syncarpous) with the partition walls present, forming an equal number of chambers. It matures as a capsule, a berry, or rarely as a drupe, meaning a fleshy fruit with a stony pit. When you have identified a plant as a member of the Heath family you can read about each of the subfamilies to find which group your specimen belongs with.

Most plants of the Heath family inhabit acid soil, or bogs. Worldwide there are at least 50 genera, representing more than 1350 species. About 25 genera are native to North America.

<u>Key Words</u>
Mostly red or white bell-shaped flowers with parts in 4's or 5's, often with evergreen leaves.

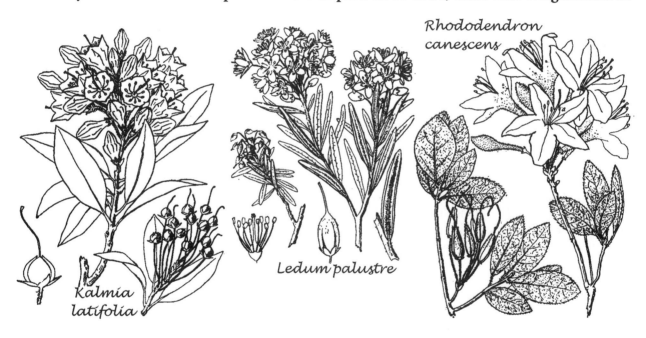

Rhododendron canescens

Kalmia latifolia

Ledum palustre

Rhododendron Subfamily

Plants of the Rhododendron Subfamily have leaf buds that can be seen in winter. The flowers have an ovary positioned superior that matures as a capsule; the capsule splits open along the partitions of the ovary. The seeds are usually winged. Most plants of this subfamily are poisonous to varying degrees.

Kalmia—Swamp Laurel (6/2/1) Swamp Laurel contains a substance called andromedotoxin (Craighead), used in small doses as a sedative and for neuralgia. Native Americans drank a tea of the leaves to commit suicide (Lust). In other words, don't mess with it!

Ledum—Labrador Tea (5/-/1) • Labrador tea contains the volatile oil ledol or ledum, a mildly narcotic substance with the potential to cause abortions, heart palpitations, drowsiness, or temporary paralysis if used in excess. However, the substance is not readily soluble in water, and the plant has a long history of use as an aromatic, mildly bitter tea, drunk either hot or cold (Moore). Medicinally the tea is antispasmodic, diuretic, diaphoretic and expectorant (Lust).

Menziesia—False Huckleberry (-/-/1) • The fruits are edible (Fern).

Rhododendron—Azalea, Rhododendron (1300/-/1) • The flowers are sometimes made into jelly, but may have an intoxicating effect (Sturtevant). I do not advise trying this, because Rhododendrons are known to contain the andromedotoxin, like that found in *Kalmia*, above. Its use can lead to paralysis and heart failure (Klein).

Phyllodoce—Mountain Heather (10/42) •

Gaultheria procumbens

Vaccinium ovalifolium

Arctostaphylos uva-ursi

Blueberry Subfamily

Members of the Blueberry subfamily also have leaf buds that can be seen in winter. The flower petals are united in an urn or bell shape. The ovary is positioned inferior and matures into a berry (sometimes a capsule). Most members of this subfamily produce edible fruits.

Arbutus—Madrone (20/-/0) The berries are edible, but hardly exciting. Medicinally, the plant contains simple phenol glycosides and tannic acid similar to *Arctostaphylos* (Moore).

Arctostaphylos—Kinikinnick, Bearberry, Manzanita (70/-/3) • This genus includes the manzanita bushes that are common in the southwest. The mealy berries of all manzanitas are edible. The plants are rich in the astringent tannic and gallic acids and the simple phenol glycosides arbutin, and ericolin (Schauenberg). In the presence of bacteria and alkaline urine, the phenols are hydrolized (see Glycosides for more information) in the bladder into the disinfectant hydroquinone, useful for urinary tract ulcerations and inflammation and as a solvent for calcium stones in the urinary tract. In cases of acid urine, sodium bicarbonate must be taken with the herbs to activate the reaction.

> The high tannin content makes the plants useful for a sitz bath after childbirth. The plants can be used in hide-tanning. You can even "tan" the bottoms of your feet—to prevent blisters—by soaking them in a tea the night before hiking (Willard). (Please read about Tannic Acid for more information.)

Gaultheria—Salal, Wintergreen (150/6/2) • Salal is abundant in the Pacific northwest. The berries are edible and tasty. The leaves are astringent, used externally for burns, internally for sore throat and coughs. It has carminative properties, meaning it helps to dispel gas and will relieve heartburn caused by gas (Willard). The leaves contain the phenolic glycoside methyl salicylate, and like willow it can be used as aspirin (Brown, Hall, Lust). *Gaultheria procumbens*, from the eastern U.S. was the original source of wintergreen oil, a volatile oil and spice later extracted from the twigs of black birch, and finally produced synthetically (Hall). Other species may have similar properties (Harrington).

Oxydendrum—Sourwood (1/1/0)

Vaccinium—Blueberry, Huckleberry, Cranberry, Bilberry, Lignonberry (200/-/8) • In the Tobacco Root Mountains behind my house there are very few of the purple huckleberries, but lots of the smaller, red "wortle berries", which I call "dwarf huckleberries". These are just as tasty as any other berries of this group, but much more tedious to pick. A one-hour study of hand-picking produced one cup of berries. That was an exercise in both patience and abstinence! The use of a comb to strip the berries from the plants seems to speed up the harvesting a little.

> Medicinally the plants and berries are mildy astringent, diuretic, and sometimes act as vasoconstrictors. The berries or a tea of the plant are thus useful against diarrhea (Willard). The leaves also contain quinic acid, which may inhibit the formation of uric acid. Excessive uric acid in the urine can lead to both gout and formation of kidney stones. A cup or two of leaf tea every day can lower the sugar level in both the blood and urine (Moore). The berries and plants alike are rich in flavanoids, which are consumed for their anti-oxidant effects. Bilberries benefit night vision by increasing the number of "purple" receptor rods in the eyes (Klein). Some species contain simple phenols, similar to *Arctostaphylos*.

Heath Subfamily

Plants of the Heath Subfamily do not have leaf buds present in winter. The petals are usually, but not always united to form an urn or bell shape.

Cassiope—Heather (12/5/2)

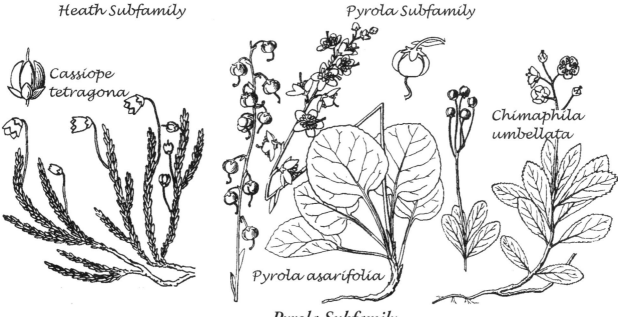

Heath Subfamily

Cassiope tetragona

Pyrola Subfamily

Pyrola asarifolia

Chimaphila umbellata

Pyrola Subfamily

Members of the Pyrola Subfamily have evergreen leaves. There are 4 or 5 separate sepals and 4 or 5 separate petals. There are usually 10 stamens (sometimes 8), and an ovary positioned superior, comprised of 4 or 5 united cells, forming a capsule.

Chimaphila—Pipsissewa (4/3/2) • The leaves are edible (Willard), but tough and astringent. A tea of the leaves is astringent, diuretic, and diaphoretic, useful internally and externally (Lust). It is basically identical to *Pyrola* (Moore). Pipsissewa is being over harvested in many areas as an ingredient for soft drinks.

Pyrola—Wintergreen, Pyrola (40/12/8) • Pyrola contains tannic acid and simple phenol glycosides, especially useful as a diuretic for the kidneys and urinary tract infections (Schauenberg), also helpful for sore throats. Externally the plant is used to stop bleeding and to heal bruises and insect bites. Its antispasmodic properties makes the plant useful for nervous disorders, such as epilepsy. The chewed roots were used as throat lozenges (Willard).

Indian Pipe Subfamily

The Indian Pipe Subfamily includes plants that are parasitic on the roots of other plants. The plants lack chlorophyll, so they are not green, but often white, yellow, brownish, or even candy-striped red and white. There are 2-6 sepals, 3-6 petals, sometimes united, and 6-12 stamens. The ovary is comprised of 4-6 united cells, and matures into a capsule.

Monotropa uniflora

Allotropa—Candystick (1/1/1) *A. virgata* is mostly found in Pacific Coast states.

Monotropa—Indian Pipe (3/3/2) A tea of the root is antispasmodic, nervine, and sedative (Lust), suggesting the possible presence of alkaloids.

Pterospora—Pine Drops (1/11) • *P. andromedea*, a tea of the stems and berries was used by the Cheyenne to prevent bleeding from the nose and lungs (Vogel).

Sarcodes—Snow Plant (1/1/0) *S. sanguinea* is found in the mountains of the Pacific Coast states and Nevada.

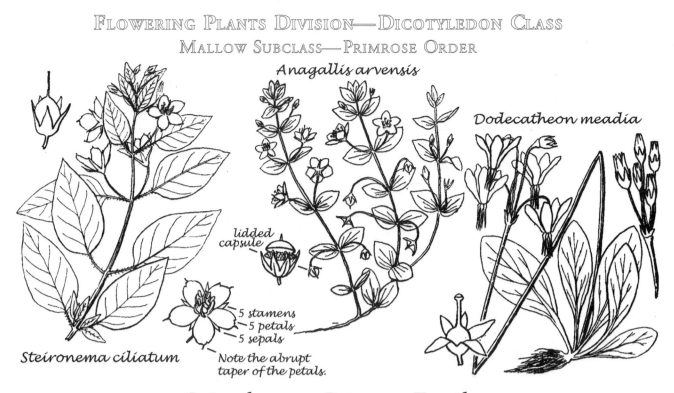

Anagallis arvensis

Dodecatheon meadia

lidded capsule

5 stamens
5 petals
5 sepals

Steironema ciliatum

Note the abrupt taper of the petals.

Primulaceae—Primrose Family

If you have a primrose or cyclamen at home, stop and look at it now. If not, then be sure to look for these plants at your local florist. The plants have basal, whorled, or opposite leaves. The flowers are regular and bisexual, usually with 5 (rarely 4-9) sepals, and a similar number of petals and stamens. The petals may be united (often at the base) or separate. The ovary is positioned superior or partly-inferior and consists of 5 united carpels (syncarpous) forming a single chamber. It matures as a capsule with 1 to numerous seeds. In some species the capsule is "circumscissile", meaning the capsule has a "lid" like a pot. Two patterns are especially helpful to distinguish the Primroses. First, notice the way the petals are fat in the middle then suddenly taper to a point in *Steironema* and *Anagallis* above. Second, the stamens are aligned in the middle of each petal, instead of in between them. World-wide there are about 28 genera and 800 species, including 11 genera in North America. The Primrose family is not related to the Evening Primrose family (*Onagraceae*). The common names are misleading.

Key Words: **Parts in 5's. Petals with pointy tips. Stamens aligned at the middle of the petals.**

Androsace—Rock Jasmine (100/7/4) • A tea of the plant was taken for birth injuries and postpartum bleeding, or taken cold for internal pain (Moerman).

Anagallis—Pimpernel (40/1/1) *A. arvensis* was ntroduced from Europe. Some species of pimpernel are used in salads, but otherwise the plants are diaphoretic, expectorant, diuretic, and purgative. Small doses cause sweating and increased kidney activity. Larger doses act on the central nervous system and the brain, leading to trembling, watery stools and excessive urination (Lust). The plants contain some saponin; it is used for fishing in India (Schauenberg).

Centunculus— (-/-/1) A tea of the plant was used by California Indians for venereal disease where there was failure of the urinary tract (Moerman).

Cyclamen — (20/D/D) • *Cyclamen* is a popular house plant. It contains a potent from of saponin (Schauenberg). It is reported to be extremely purgative (laxative). A tea of the dried bulb is used for colds, congestion, gas, and worms. The toxic dosage is very small, so it should not be used without medical supervision (Lust).

Dodecatheon—Shooting Star (15/15/3) • The whole plant is edible as a salad or potherb (Willard). Shooting star is mildly astringent. I like to pick the flowers and present them to whomever I am with. Then I gobble them down! Medicinally, a tea of the root or plant was used as a wash for sore eyes or gargled by children for canker sores (Moerman).

Glaux— (1/1/1) *G. maritima*, the young shoots and cooked roots are edible. Roots have a sedative quality (Fern, Moerman).

Lysimachia—Loosestrife (200/16/1) The cooked leaves are edible. Various species are largely astringent with some diaphoretic and emetic properties. The live plant is reported to repel gnats and flies, or can be burned as a smudge (Fern).

Primula—Primrose (540/20/2) The flowers or young leaves are edible and can often be found in winter. Some species contain saponins and salicin. The saponins have an expectorant effect, while the salicin is a pain reliever like aspirin. The plants are also mildly sedative (Fern). Some people are allergic to primrose (Lust).

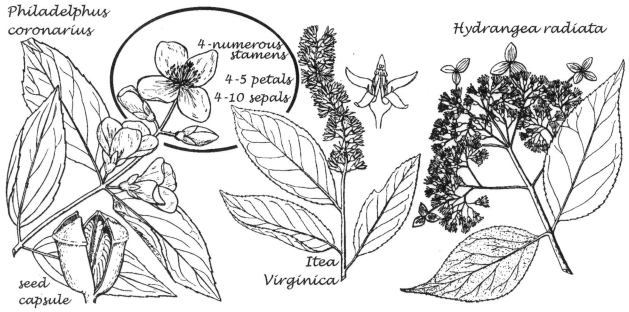

Hydrangeaceae—Hydrangea Family

The Hydrangea family includes mostly bushes with showy flowers and parts in multiples of four. The leaves are mostly opposite, but there are some with alternate leaves. The flowers are bisexual and regular. There are 4-10 united sepals and 4-5 (rarely 10) separate petals, plus 4-numerous stamens. The ovary is positioned inferior and consists of 2-5 united carpels (syncarpous) with the partition walls present, forming an equal number of chambers. It matures as a capsule containing numerous seeds. World-wide there are 17 genera and 250 species, including 9 genera in North America. The *Hydrangea* is often planted domestically in the warmer states. The cluster of showy flowers are sterile. The fertile flowers are smaller and shorter, appearing in the middle of the group.

<u>Key Words</u>
Bushes with opposite leaves and showy flowers with parts in 4's or 5's.

Carpenteria—Tree Anenome (1/1/0) *C. californica* is found in California.

Deutzia—(60/D/D) *Deutzia* is planted as an ornamental.

Hydrangea—Hydrangea (23/-/0) • The fresh leaves contain a cyanide, but some species are dried and powdered for use as a tea sweetener. Medicinally, the roots are emetic and cathartic, diaphoretic, diuretic, and anthelmintic. The plant might contain an antimalarial alkaloid (Fern).

Itea—Sweet Spire (20/-/0)

Jamesia—Jamesia (0) The seeds were sometimes eaten raw by southwestern Indians (Moerman).

Philadelphus—Mock Orange, Syringa (71/-/1) • The common name "syringa" is misleading, since that is also the Latin name of the unrelated lilac. The fruits of one species of Philadelphus were eaten by the Indians. The leaves were used as a poultice for a variety of sores. The leaves and flowers contain saponin and were crushed in water for use as soap. (Moerman). The soap reportedly removes dirt, but not oils (Fern).

Whipplea—Yerba de Selva (1/1/0) Yerba de Selva is a native of the Pacific Coast states.

Grossulariaceae—Gooseberry Family

I remember as a child when I went with Mom and Dad down in the field by Grandma's house to collect gooseberries. We placed tarps under the bushes and beat the berries out with a stick. At home Mom floated away the leaves and made delicious gooseberry pie and jam.

The gooseberries and currants have regular, bisexual flowers, usually about 1/4 in diameter. The blossoms are yellow, white, greenish, or sometimes red. The flowers have 5 united sepals and 5 separate petals (rarely 4 of each). There are 5 stamens, alternate with the petals. The ovary is positioned either superior or inferior and consists of 2 united carpels (bicarpellate) forming a single chamber. It matures as a berry with several to numerous seeds.

Once you become familiar with these shrubs, you will recognize them by their distinctive leaves alone. Note that ninebark (*Physocarpus*) of the Rose Family has very similar leaves. World-wide there is only 1 genus consisting of 150 species of gooseberries and currants.

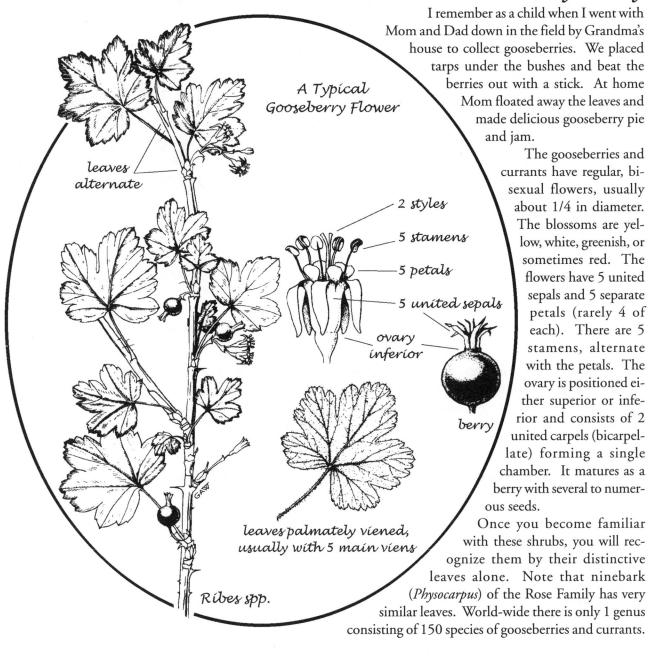

A Typical Gooseberry Flower

leaves alternate

2 styles
5 stamens
5 petals
5 united sepals
ovary inferior

berry

leaves palmately viened, usually with 5 main viens

Ribes spp.

Key Words
Bushes with palmate leaves. Translucent berries with attached sepals..

Ribes—Currants, Gooseberries (150/-/11) • The berries of all currants and gooseberries are edible, but a few are extremely rank in odor and flavor. In my timed studies I have been able to pick a quart of gooseberries per hour by hand and three quarts per hour by beating the berries off with a stick onto a tarp. The berries are easily separated from the twigs and leaves with a hose and a bucket. The good berries sink to the bottom and the junk floats to the top.

Medicinally the leaves, bark and roots are largely diaphoretic, astringent and diuretic, often used to bring down fevers. The jelly can be used as a demulcent, useful for sore throats or burns. A Russian study has shown that unripe gooseberries can prevent degeneration of body cells, which may stave off illness and aging. The green berries also counteract the effect of spoiled foods and help to remove toxins from the body. Black currant seeds contain omega 3 and omega 6 essential fatty acids, similar to evening primrose (*Oenothera*) (Willard, Tilford). I often find gooseberry bushes still loaded with shriveled berries in mid-winter. I crave them that time of year, and I feel their revitalizing effect on my body.

Crassulaceae—Stonecrop Family

Sedum stenopetalum

Sedum roseum

If you've ever seen the hen-and-chicks plant (*Sempervivum*), illustrated below, then you have met a member of the Stonecrop family already. These are fleshy, succulent herbs with regular, bisexual flowers. There are typically 4-5 (sometimes 30) sepals and an equal number of petals. There may be as many or double the number of stamens as petals. The ovary is positioned superior and consists of 3 or more carpels wholly separate (apocarpous) or united only at the base, each producing 1 dry seed.

World-wide there are 35 genera and 1500 species, including 9 genera in North America. Many are cultivated as ornamentals, including: *Aeonium, Cotyledon, Crassula, Dudleya, Echeveria, Kalanchoe, Sedum* and *Sempervivum*.

<u>Key Words</u>
Small succulents with 3 or more simple pistils.

Dudleya—(-/-/0) *Dudleya* is native to Arizona, California and Baja California.

Echeveria—Desert Savior, Bluff Lettuce (100/35/0) Desert savior is found in the southwestern states.

Sedum—Stonecrop (500/46/6) • The plants are edible as a salad or potherb. Medicinally, the plants are mucilaginous and mildly astringent, useful for minor burns, insect bites and skin irritations (Tilford). It is a safe laxative for children (Moerman).

    A European species, *Sedum acre*, is strongly acrid and may cause blistering. It also contains alkaloids; the plant has been used medicinally for hypertension and epilepsy (Schauenberg).

Tillaea—Pigmy Weed (-/-/2).

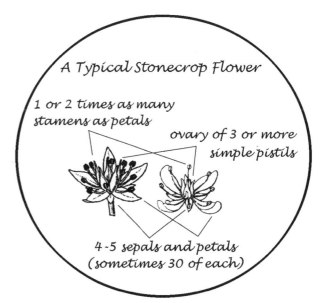

A Typical Stonecrop Flower

1 or 2 times as many stamens as petals

ovary of 3 or more simple pistils

4-5 sepals and petals (sometimes 30 of each)

Sempervivum assimile

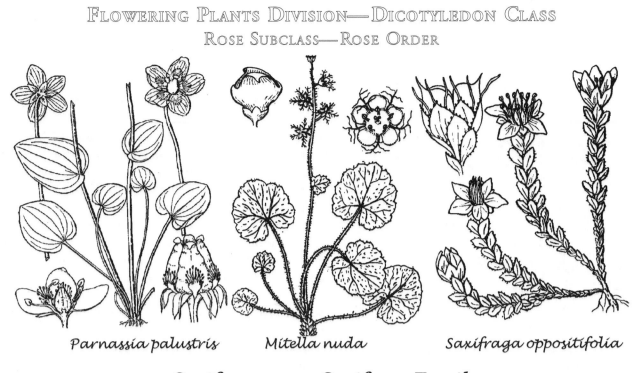

Parnassia palustris   Mitella nuda   Saxifraga oppositifolia

Saxifragaceae—Saxifrage Family

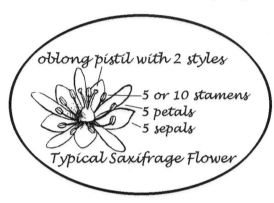

oblong pistil with 2 styles

5 or 10 stamens
5 petals
5 sepals

Typical Saxifrage Flower

The flowers of the Saxifrage family are typically small, often less than 1/4 inch in diameter, with a few eye-catching individuals approaching 1/2 an inch. The flowers are regular and bisexual, usually with 5 sepals and 5 petals (rarely none). There are 5 or 10 stamens. The ovary is usually positioned superior with 2 united carpels (rarely 5) forming a single oblong chamber. This oblong-shaped ovary is one of the better keys to identifying this family. The ovary matures as a capsule with a few or numerous seeds per carpel. World-wide there are about 30 genera, representing 580 species. Twenty genera are found in North America.

Key Words: **Small plants with small flowers, parts in 5', plus an oblong pistil with 2 styles.**

Boykinia— (-/6/1) Drink a tea of the dried plant for lung hemorrhages or tuberculosis (Moerman).

Conimitella— (-/-/1)

Chrysosplenium—Water Carpet (55/6/1) 0 petals. The plant is edible as a salad green (Sturtevant).

Heuchera—Alumroot (50/40/4) • The leaves are edible as a potherb, but may be mildly astringent (Willard) Medicinally, the root contains up to 20% tannin (Tilford), for a very potent astringent, hence the common name "alumroot". For more information just read the section on tannic acid in the Medicinal Properties section of this book.

Leptarrhena— (1/1/1) *L. pyrolifolia*, a tea of the plant is taken for the flu. A poultice is used on wounds and sores (Moerman).

Lithophragma—Woodland star (-/12/4) • The root of a California species was chewed by the Indians for colds or stomach aches (Moerman).

Mitella—Miterwort (15/10/6) A tea of the plant was used medicinally by the Indians as powerful laxative to purge the system, or as an emetic to cause vomiting, also as drops for sore eyes. The crushed leaves were wrapped in cloth and placed in the ears for ear aches (Moerman).

Parnassia— (-/11/4) • A tea of the powdered leaves was given to babies for stomach aches (Moerman).

Saxifraga—Saxifrage (350/70/19) • Brook saxifrage is very common along streams at high elevations; it is easy to gather in quantity for use as a salad or potherb. It is pretty much tasteless, which makes it useful for taming other more bitter herbs in a salad. Other species of saxifrage also appear to be edible and rich in vitamin C.

Suksdorfia— (-/2/2)

Telesonix— (1/1/1) *T. jamesii* is found from Nevada to Colorado, north to Idaho and South Dakota.

Tiarella—False Miterwort (6/5/2) Native Americans used a tea of the roots for diarrhea in children. The fresh leaves were chewed as a cough medicine (Moerman).

Rosaceae—Rose Family

If you have ever stuck your nose into an apple, rose, strawberry or cherry blossom, then you know the Rose family. Like many families of plants, the Rose family has regular flowers with 5 sepals and 5 petals, yet there is also something distinct about flowers in the Rose family. One thing that helps these flowers stand out is the numerous stamens: the flowers have a minimum of 5 stamens, but often many more, usually in multiples of five. In most cases you can recognize the Rose Family based solely on the sepals, petals and stamens. Domestic roses have additional petals that were bred from the stamens.

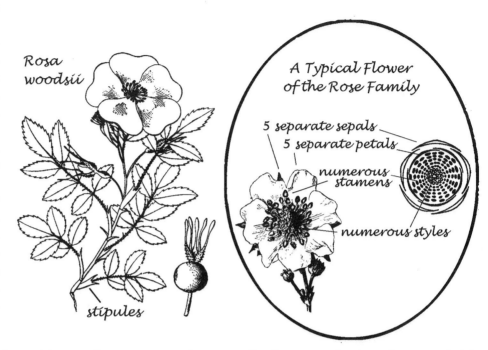

Most flowers of the Rose family have several to numerous simple pistils (apocarpous), or they may be united at the base, with the styles still separate, to make a single compound pistil (syncarpous) with numerous styles. Members of the Plum subfamily have a single simple pistil (unicarpellate).

Note that the juicy "fruit" of the strawberry is actually the swollen receptical beneath the pistils. Botanically speaking, the "fruit" is only the dry seed—the remains of the pistil or ovary—on the strawberry's surface. The raspberry is different, where the ovary of each simple pistil has swollen to create an "aggregate fruit" covering the domed receptical. The fleshy rose "hip" looks much like the service berry and other fruits of the Apple subfamily, but the rose hip is formed from the swollen receptical where the flower parts are attached, while the fruits of the Apple subfamily are the swollen ovaries.

The only problem with identifying the Rose family is that a few species of the Rose subfamily strongly resemble Buttercups with their numerous stamens and numerous simple pistils attached to a cone-like receptical. But it is easy to tell the difference between the two. All of the Roses (except Spiraeas) have stipules, while none of the Buttercups do. Stipules are small, leaf-like growths at the base of the leaf stems (see illustration). Another useful pattern of the Rose family is that many (not all) of the plants have oval, serrated leaves or leaflets.

World-wide there are about 100 genera and 3000 species. About fifty genera are found in North America. Be sure to familiarize yourself with each of the subfamilies to better understand the range of possibilities within the family. When you have a specimen in hand then you can read again through each of the subfamilies to narrow down the choices for idenfication.

The fruits of the Rose family are *edible* but somewhat laxative, while the rest of the vegetation is usually astringent, due to the presence of *tannic acid*. It is strongest in the roots, followed by the bark or stems, and the leaves. A few species have mildly mucilaginous properties. This can help balance out the drying effect of the astringents when used to stop diarrhea. *Cyanide* compounds are found especially in the leaves and fruits of the Plum subfamily, but may appear in the seeds or wilted leaves of a few other species too. It is easily destroyed by heat and/or oxygen.

Key Words
5 sepals and 5 petals with usually numerous stamens. Oval, serrated leaves.

Rubus strigosus

Frageria virginiana

Potentilla anserina

Rose Subfamily

Most flowers of the Rose subfamily have a slightly domed receptical in the center where numerous simple pistils are attached. Some genera, especially *Geum* and *Potentilla,* may be confused with the Buttercups. See the previous page for notes on the strawberry, raspberry and rose fruits. Other genera produce dry seeds (achenes).

Agrimonia—Agrimony (-/8/1) Agrimony is astringent and diuretic, containing malic and tannic acid (Moore, Lust).

Alchemilla—Lady's Mantle (-/-/1) The plant is astringent, useful internally and externally (Lust)

Dryas—Dryad (-/3/3) The alpine species of this plant is one of few species outside the pea family that are capable of fixing nitrogen in the soil (Craighead). The astringent leaves are used in tea (Sturtevant).

Cercocarpus—Mountain Mahogany (10/-/2) • Mountain mahogany is apparently astringent, yet laxative (Moore). It contains some hydrocyanic acid (Phillips).

Geum—Avens (56/18/6) • The root of *G. rivale* can be boiled and sugar added for a "chocolate substitute" (Hall). *Geum* contains tannic acid, and bitters, and releases volatile oils with hydrolysis (Schauenberg).

Frageria—Strawberry (20+/8/2) • Most wild strawberries are really packed with flavor, although some east coast varieties are nearly flavorless. Strawberry patches in my area yield only about a cup of berries per hour of harvesting, but one year I found a patch that yielded several times that, although I did not do a timed study. I just stuffed them in my mouth as quickly as I could! When I am camping I like to use the strawberries to make "ashcake pies". Strawberry leaves are mildly astringent and mucilaginous.

Horkelia—Pink Root (-/20/1) The root of at least one species has a pink sap. A tea of the root is taken as a "tonic" (Murphey).

Ivesia— (-/20/1)

Kelseya— (-/-/1)

Luetkea—Partridge Foot (-/1/1) *L. pectinata* is found from Alaska south to California and east to the Rockies.

Potentilla—Cinquefoil (300/120/26) • All potentillas are astringent; the roots of some contain up to 20% tannin. Some bitter principles are also present (Densmore, Schauenberg).

Purshia—Bitterbrush (2/2/1) • The seeds are collected and stored in quantity by mice (Craighead).

Rosa—Rose (100/-/5) • The nicest thing about rose hips is that they stay on the bushes for most of the winter. In a timed study I picked 3 quarts in one hour. I grew up eating the fruits and drinking the tea. I thought maybe I could mash them into a cereal, but none of my concoctions were palatable; the best way to eat them seems to be one at a time, as you find them. They are very seedy, but the seeds are nutritious too and should be eaten. The vegetation is astringent, diuretic (Willard), and mildly mucilaginous (Geller).

Rubus—Raspberry, Blackberry, Salmon Berry, Thimble Berry (700/-/6) • Wild raspberries contain citric and malic acids (Densmore). I can pick approximately 1 quart of berries per hour. Thimble berries, however, are so sporadic that you are lucky to find 10 ripe ones in fifty feet. Either are delicious as is, or dried and stored. The vegetation is mildly astringent and diuretic, generally recommended during pregnancies (Willard). It is also mildly mucilaginous (Geller). It is used for diarrhea (Lust). Note: the wilted vegetation may produce cyanide (Tilford).

Sanguisorba—Burnet (30/8/1) • A tea of the root is highly astringent, used for diarrhea, hemorrhaging and varicose veins (Lust). (4 petal-like sepals. 0 petals. 2-12 stamens. 1-3 pistils.)

Sibbaldia— (-/1/1) *S. procumbens* is an arctic plant, also found in the higher elevations in the states.

Spirea Subfamily

If you find a member of the Rose family with dense, "foamy" clusters of small, white or pink flowers then it is probably a member of the Spirea subfamily. Look close and you will see that the flowers typically have 2-5 simple pistils (sometimes 1-12) which may be partially fused at the base. Another distinguishing feature of this group is that none of the plants have stipules on the leaves. Stipules are small, leaf-like growths at the base of the leaf stems. The Spireas are the only members of the Rose family without stipules. Fruits of this group include capsules, follicles (dry fruits that split along one seam), or sometimes achenes (dry seeds).

Aruncus—Goat's Beard (3/2/0)
Chamaebatiaria—Desert Sweet (-/-/0)
Chamaerhodes— (-/-/1)
Gillenia—Indian Physic (2/2/0)
Holodiscus—Ocean Spray (8/-/1) • The small, dry fruits were reportedly eaten by Indians (Craighead). Medicinally it is astringent and diuretic (Willard).
Petrophyton—Rock Mat (-/3/1)
Physocarpus—Ninebark (10/-/2) • The palmate leaves look similar to the Gooseberry family.
Spiraea—Meadowsweet (100/-/3) • Meadowsweet is astringent, diuretic, and it contains methyl salicylate (similar to aspirin or willow), used especially for arthritis, rheumatism and infections of the urinary tract (Schauenberg). Meadowsweet is becoming a popular herb because the salicylate content is much more reliable from plant to plant than willows or poplars. It also tastes better!
Vauquelinia—Arizona Rosewood (-/-/0)

*Spirea
salicifolia*

Plum Subfamily

Plums, cherries, apricots, peaches, nectarines and almonds are all included in the *Prunus* genus. (Sometimes they are split into separate "subgenera".) Next time you see one of these fleshy fruits, notice the "seam" down one side, and the almond-like pit in the middle; those are the obvious marks of the *Prunus* genus.

Prunus—Cherries, Plums (200/-/4) • Wild plums grow naturally in eastern Montana, and they are often planted domestically in western Montana. I wish they grew wild in my area because they are so big and easy to gather, compared to other wild fruits. They are already plenty sweet, but mashing and drying sweetens them even more, and the natural sugars visibly crystallize in the flesh.

*Prunus
virginiana*

Chokecherries are the main wild crop we get from this genus in Montana. I always thought they were nearly useless, because the only processing method I knew of was to boil out the juice and throw the pulp away. As a "survivalist" I like real, solid food, and the juice was never quite good enough. Then an Indian lady showed me the native way of processing them. You put the fresh berries on a metate stone and mash them up, pits and all, then dry them. The nut inside the pit has an almond-like aroma. This is no coincidence, since the almond is in this genus. Anyway, the combination cherry-almond odor is richly intoxicating to work with, when mashing them on a rock. Like most of the other members of this genus, chokecherry pits contain a form of cyanide, but cyanide is very unstable and easily destroyed by heat, sunlight and oxygen. Mashing and drying the chokecherries renders them safe to eat. The pit shells are crunchy, but not nearly as obtrusive as you might think. I cook up the fresh mash and use it as a filling in "chokecherry ashcake turn-overs", and the dried mash I just use as trail mix. I can hand-pick 1 gallon of cherries per hour, which take another 40 minutes to mash with a rock.

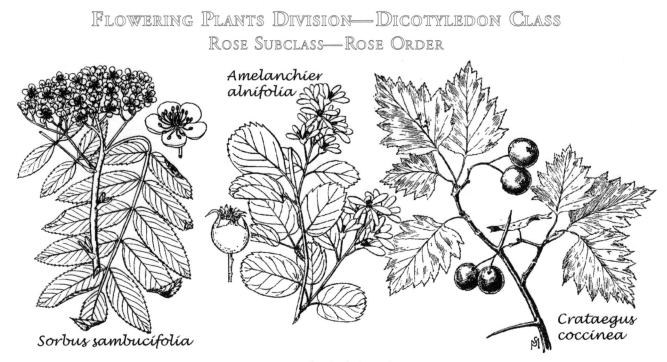

Amelanchier alnifolia

Sorbus sambucifolia

Crataegus coccinea

Apple Subfamily

If you find a member of the Rose family with fleshy fruits and a five-pointed star on the bottom then it belongs to the Apple subfamily. The only other fleshy fruit of the Rose family with a five-pointed star is the rose itself. The star is formed from the sepals left over from the flowering stage. (The ovary is positioned inferior in the Apple subfamily. It is partly or wholly superior in other members of the Rose family.) All fruits of the Apple subfamily are edible, though some, like the mountain ash (*Sorbus*) are highly sour-astringent. Other cultivated members of the Apple subfamily include the apple (*Malus*), pear (*Pyrus*), quince (*Cydonia*), loquat (*Eriobotrya*), Christmasberry (*Photinia*) and *Pyracantha*. The fruits of most of these plants are sweeter after a frost.

Aronia—Chokeberry (3/3/0) The fruits are edible, but usually require a frost to sweeten them (Fern).

Amelanchier—Service Berry (20/-/2) • Many wild berries are all juice, but service berries are both juicy and fleshy. They are some of my favorite berries, and I can easily eat a quart of them on site when I find a good thicket of them. Unfortunately, there are not too many of them immediately in my area—I have to travel 60 miles to get to the nearest worthwhile patch. However, in a good patch I can easily pick 2 to 4 quarts of berries per hour. Medicinally, the berries may be laxative; otherwise the leaves and bark are astringent (Willard).

Cotoneaster—(95/D/D) • Cotoneaster has small, purplish edible berries. It is an import from Russia, commonly planted as an ornamental in towns.

Crataegus—Hawthorn (200/-/4) • Hawthorns produce an abundance of fruit well worth harvesting. All hawthorn berries are edible, black, blue, red, or yellow. The blue-black ones tend to be pulpy and delicious, whereas the red ones are more seedy and astringent.

Medicinally, the leaves,flowers and fruit are rich in flavonoids especially beneficial to the heart. Hawthorn is used to normalize arrhythmia, high or low blood pressure, and to reduce blood clots. It makes the blood vessels more flexible, reducing vascular resistance so the heart doesn't have to pump so hard. (Klein).

Sorbus—Mountain Ash (100/-/2) • Mountain ash is uncommon in the wild in Montana. It is mostly planted as an ornamental in towns. The berries are mealy and initially sour; they require a good frost to sweeten them. They are easy to gather in abundance. The vegetation is astringent, diuretic, and contains cyanide (Willard). One of the sugars found in the berries is given intravenously for cases of glaucoma to reduce pressure on the eyeball (Lust).

Fabaceae (Leguminosae, Papilionoideae)—Pea Family

Key Words: "banner, wings, and keel". Pea-like pods and often pinnate leaves.

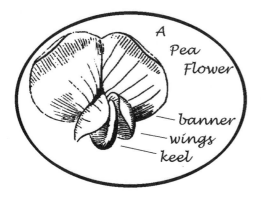

A Pea Flower
banner
wings
keel

If you have seen a pea or bean blossom in the garden, then you will be able to recognize members of this family. There are 5 united sepals. The five petals form a distinctive "banner, wings, and keel", as shown in the illustration. There are usually 10 stamens. The parts are positioned perigynous. The pistil has a unicarpellate (single-celled) ovary. It matures as a pea-like pod with several seeds.

Identifying the banner, wings, and keel is sufficient to recognize all the Peas across the northern latitudes, which belong to the **Pea Subfamily**. When you have identified a plant as a member of the Pea subfamily, just read the descriptions of each tribe to find which tribe your specimen is most related to.

As you move south you will encounter Peas from two additional subfamilies, the **Mimosa Subfamily** and the **Senna Subfamily**. Both of these subfamilies include mostly trees and shrubs, but also a few herbs. Their flowers are significantly different from the flowers of the Pea Subfamily. However, most of these trees have pinnate leaves, as shown below, and distinctive pea-like pods that open along two seams. Once you recognise a plant as a member of the Pea family by these characterisics, then read more about each of the subfamilies to narrow down the identity. Remember, if the flowers have a distinctive banner, wings, and keel, then it is a member of the Pea Subfamily.

The Pea family includes herbs, shrubs and trees with distinct pea-like pods and often pinnate leaves.

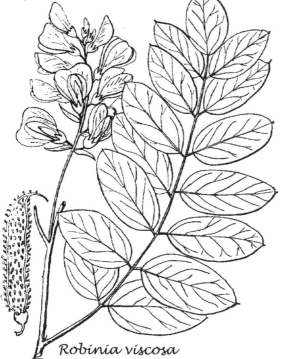

Robinia viscosa

World-wide there are 600 genera and 13,000 species in the Pea family, including peas, beans, and peanuts. This is the third largest family of plants after the Orchid and Aster families. Most of the plants of this family form a symbiotic relationship with bacteria in the soil. The bacteria take in nitrogen from the atmosphere and feed it to the plants. Just look for little bumps, often pinkish, on the roots. The nitrogen is "fixed" in the soil when the vegetation decomposes.

Overall, the plants of the Pea family range from being *barely edible* to *barely poisonous*. Some species do contain toxic alkaloids, especially in the seed coats. Many people are familiar with the story of Christopher McCandless who trekked into the Alaska wilderness in 1992 and was found dead four months later. He had been eating the roots of *Hedysarum alpinum*, and assumed the seeds were edible too, so he gathered and ate a large quantity of them over a two-week period. The seeds, however, contained the same toxic alkaloid found in locoweed (*Astragalus*), which inhibits an enzyme necessary for metabolism in mammals. It is now believed that McCandless was still eating, but starved to death because his body was unable to utilize the food (Krakauer). Even the common garden pea can lead to depression and nervous disorders with excess consumption.

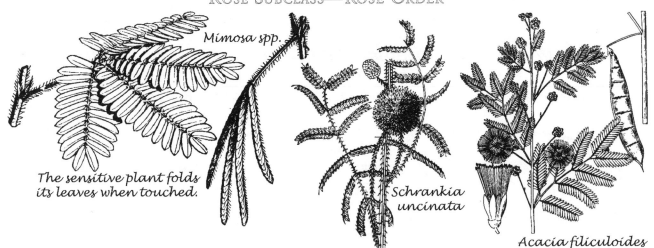

Mimosa spp.

The sensitive plant folds
its leaves when touched.

*Schrankia
uncinata*

Acacia filiculoides

Mimosa Subfamily

The Mimosa subfamily consists of mostly trees and shrubs, plus a few herbs. The leaves are alternate and usually distinctively bi-pinnate (see the leaf terms illustrated below). There are 5 united sepals, 5 separate petals, and sometimes 4, or more often 10 to numerous stamens. These are usually small flowers in dense clusters with long stamens radiating out. The filaments (the stamen stems) are often brightly colored. There are about 40 genera and 2000 species in mostly tropical regions. Some North American genera include:

Acacia—Acacia (700+/-/0) The *Acacias* produces gum arabic, used in many sore throat, cough and diarrhea formulas. The seeds of many species have been used as food (Sturtevant).

Desmanthus—Prairie Mimosa (40/-/0)

Prosopis—Mesquite, Screw Bean (35/-/0) The pods and seeds were pounded, cooked and eaten. The flowers are also edible (Harrington).

Schrankia—Sensitive Briar (30/-/0)

Senna Subfamily

The Senna subfamily includes mostly trees and shrubs (rarely herbs) with showy, slightly irregular flowers. The leaves may be either simple, pinnate, or bi-pinnate. Some North American genera include:

Cassia—Senna (500/-/0) Many species of senna are found across the southern and eastern states. All are strongly laxative.

Cercis—Redbud, Judas Tree (7/-/0) The flowers and pods have been used in salads (Sturtevant).

Gleditsia—Honey Locust (15/-/D) Sugar has been extracted from the sweet, pulpy seed pods (Sturtevant).

Gymnocladus—Kentucky Coffee Bean Tree (2/-/0) The pods are edible. Seeds are used as a coffee substitute (Sturtevant).

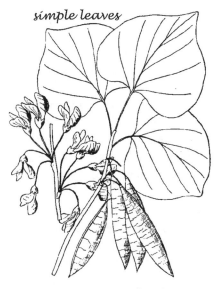

simple leaves

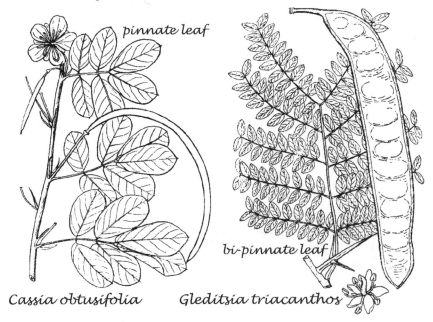

pinnate leaf

bi-pinnate leaf

Cercis canadenis

Cassia obtusifolia

Gleditsia triacanthos

Pea Subfamily

The Pea Subfamily includes all members of the Pea Family with a distinctive "banneer, wings, and keel". The Pea Subfamily consists mostly of herbs, but also includes a few shrubs or trees. When you've identified a plant as a member of this Subfamily, then read about each of the tribes that follow to see which group yours belongs to.

Golden Pea Tribe

The plants of the Golden Pea tribe could easily be mistaken for lupine of the Broom Tribe, but lupine has a palmate leaf while members of the Golden Pea tribe have trifoliate (3-parted) leaves.

Baptisia—Wild Indigo (30/25/0)
Thermopsis—Golden Pea (20/9/2) • May be poisonous to livestock.

Thermopsis rhombifolia

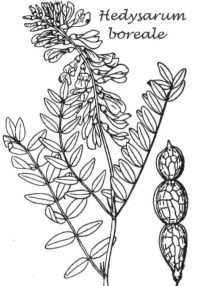

Hedysarum boreale

Hedysarum Tribe

Members of the Hedysarum tribe have either trifoliate (3-parted) or pinnate leaves, but no tendrils. The distinctive feature of these plants is that the pods on most species are deeply constricted between the seeds (see *Hedysarum boreale* on this page). A few are not constricted, but the pods still tend to break apart transversely (cross-wise instead of lengthwise). The peanut (*Arachis*) belongs to this group. It blooms above ground, then buries the developing seed pods (the peanuts) into the soil.

Coronill—Crown Vetch (25/1/1) *C. varia* is introduced from Eurasia. The plant may contain cardia glycosids. A British species is considered highly toxic, so all species should be suspect (Fern).
Desmodium—Tick Trefoil (200/-/0)
Hedysarum—Sweet vetch (-/8/4)

The roots of some species are known to be edible (Willard), but others are believed to be poisonous. The seeds contain the same alkaloid as *Astragalus* (Krakauer).

Lespedeza—Bush Clover (100/20/0)

Broom Tribe

The Broom tribe includes mostly shrubs, sometimes with spines. The leaves may be either simple, trifoliate, or palmate (*Lupinus*), but not pinnate (refer to the leaf glossary in the back of the book).

Crotalaria—Rattle Box (500/13/0)
Cytisus—Scotch Broom (60/-/0) Scotch broom was introduced from Europe. It is now found along the Atlantic andPacific coast states. *C. scoparius* contains the alkaloid sparteine, which slows the heart and stimulates uterine contrations (Tyler).
Genista—Broom (90/-/0)
Lupinus—Lupine (200/150/10) • The root and seeds of some species may be edible after cooking, but some are known to contain poisonous alkaloids (Harrington). More research needs to be done in this area.
Spartium—Spanish Broom (1/1/0)
Ulex—Gorse (15/-/0)

Lupinus perennis

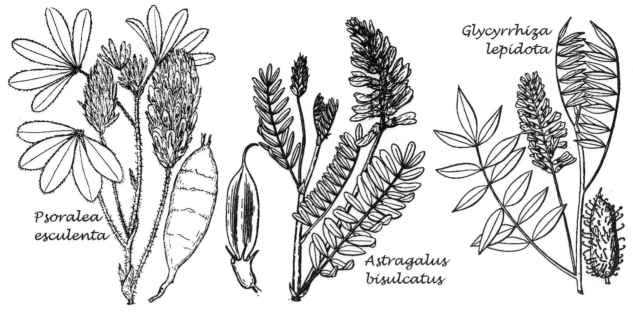

Psoralea esculenta

Astragalus bisulcatus

Glycyrrhiza lepidota

Licorice Tribe

Except for *Psoralea* shown above, most species of the Licorice Tribe have pinnate leaves. None of the plants have tendrils like the Pea tribe, or deeply constricted pods like the Broom tribe. Note that the Licorice tribe includes the locust or black locust tree (*Robinia*). The honey-locust (*Gleditsia*) belongs to the Senna Subfamily.

Amorpha—False Indigo, Lead Plant (20/20/1)

Astragalus—Locoweed, Vetch, Ground Plum (1600/375/43) • The pods of *A. succulentus* are swollen and plum-like, easy to distinguish from other members of this genus. The whole pods are edible when young, and the "peas" are still good, even when the pod becomes tough. Members of this genus are known accumulators of selenium from the soil, and some contain poisonous alkaloids. All except for the above should be avoided by amateurs. Medicinally, *A. americanus* may be chemically similar to a popular Chinese herb of this genus (Willard). Several species of *Astragalus* produce a gum called tragacanth, used to stabilize medicinal preparations, to keep them from separating into the solid and liquid parts (Klein).

Caragana—Caragana (-/-/D) • The flowers, seeds, and young pods are edible, but should probably be cooked. Some species have fibrous bark or flexible twigs that may be used for crdage (Fern)

Dalea—Prairie Clover, Indigo Bush (25030/4) The root is edible raw and sweet. The fresh plant is emetic, but a beverage tea can be made from the dried leaves (Fern).

Glycyrrhiza—Licorice Root (15/1/1) A European species, *G. glabra*, was the original source of licorice flavor. Chop and boil the root in hot water to extract the flavor. Our native species can be used similarly, but they don't taste like licorice. Also, the root can be roasted, pounded to remove the fibers, then eaten. Licorice usually has small, woody roots, but I have seen a few large ones sticking out of the soil along river banks. Most licorice candies are artificially flavored.

Medicinally, licorice root contains chemicals similar to the human adrenal hormone; it is used to regulate women's hormones for PMS and menstrual cramps (Willard). It can stimulate higher levels of adrenocorticsteriods and estrogen (Moore). Licorice root has an anti-inflammatory effect that mimics cortisone in the body, but without the side effects of steroid drugs. In studies of cough suppression medicines, licorice root was as effective as codeine, a narcotic drug often added to commercial cough remedies (Tilford). Note: When taken over an extended period licorice can cause the body to excrete more potassium and retain sodium (Hobbs), leading to water retention and elevated blood pressure. People have been hospitalized after consuming too much licorice (Tyler).

Oxytropis—Pointloc, Vetch (200+/36/11) Several species contain toxic alkaloids.

Petalostemon—Prairie Clover (40/27/2)

Psoralea—Breadroot, Scurf Pea (150/40/5) • There are many species of *Psoralea* across the U.S., and all apparently have edible roots (Sturtevant). *P. esculenta* is abundant in eastern Montana. The starchy root is dug in the spring when the ground is moist. The bark is peeled off and the root is eaten raw or cooked. It is a first-class food plant where it is available. Caution is advised, however, as it is somewhat similar to *Lupinus* in appearance. The seed-coat contains the lactone glycoside coumarin.

Robinia—Locust Tree (20/-/1) Locust seeds are acidic and high in oil, but edible after thorough boiling (Sturtevant).

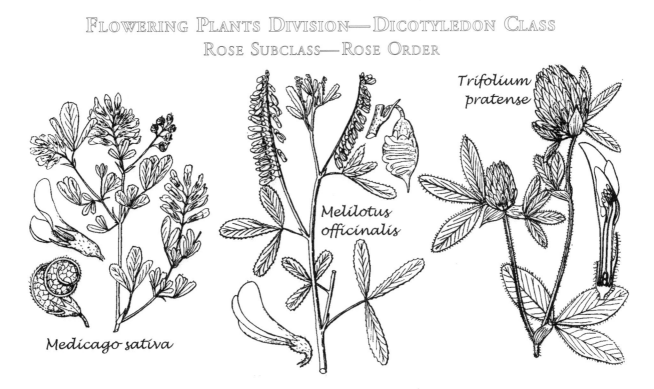

Trifolium pratense

Melilotus officinalis

Medicago sativa

Clover Tribe

The distinctive characteristic of the Clover Tribe is the trifoliate (three-part) leaves. Trifoliate leaves are common in many tribes of the the Pea subfamily, but in this case the leaves really look like clover leaves. Also, the flowers of these specimens are smaller than most other blossoms in the family.

Medicago—Alfalfa, Black Medic (110/-/4) • Alfalfa is an introduced crop plnt from the Middle East. The mature plant has deep roots (i.e. 60 feet) and accumulates many mineral nutrients. It contains calcium, chlorine, iron, magnesium, phosphorus, potassium, silica, sodium and trace minerals, plus significant quantities of the vitamins A, B1, B6, B12, C, E, K1, and P. Alfalfa also contains dozens of amino acids, making the plants high in protein. A tea of the plant or a few of the leaves in salad is used as a highly nutritional health tonic. Tonics like his are useful for helping the body deal with chronic ailments, such as arthritis, rheumatism and ulcers. Alfalfa also contains coumarins, mildly useful for lowering cholesterol, except that coumarins are destructive to red blood cells and interfere with the utilization of vitamin E. This is believed to be one of the causes of bloatin farm animals. Please note that alfalfa *sprouts* contain a toxic substance called canvanine, which can lead to scarred lesions on the face and scalp with excessive use.

Melilotus—Sweet Clover (25/6/3) • Sweet clover is used externally as an astringent, and internally as a diuretic. A concentrated dose is sometimes administered as an anticoagulant to break up blood clots. Excessive use may lead to symptoms of poisoning (Lust). The "sweet" odor of these plants is due to the presence of coumarin. Coumarin can break down into toxins if it is allowed to spoil (as in moldy hay); the toxins reduce the prothrombin content of the blood and prevent the blood from clotting in a wound (Craighead).

Trifolium—Clover (300/95/20) • The whole plants are edible as a salad or potherb, but are minimally digestible and may cause bloating. Soaking them in salt water apparently counteracts this effect (Kirk). Red clover seems to be more edible than other species. Clover seeds are also edible (Olsen).

Medicinally, red clover is a diuretic and expectorant (Willard). A tea of the flowers isused to stimulate liver and gall bladder activity (Lust). Red clover contains some coumarins, saponins, and flavonoids (Hobbs).

Trefoil Tribe

Members of the Trefoil tribe have trifoliate (3-parted) or pinnate leaves, sometimes with stipules at the base of the leaves.

Lotus—Bird's Foot Trefoil (150/60/3) The fresh plant can produce cyanide and may be toxic raw. The young seed pods may be cooked and eaten. The plant has carminative, antispasmodic and hypoglycemic properties. It is also used as a poultice for skin inflammations (Fern).

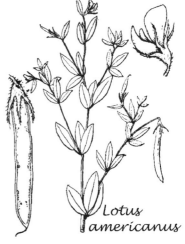

Lotus americanus

Pea Tribe

The plants of the Pea Tribe can be distinguished by their pinnate leaves and tendrils. This tribe includes the chick pea and garbanzo bean (*Cicer*), the sweet pea (*Lathyrus*), lentils (*Lens*), and the garden pea (*Pisum*). The seeds of many species of this tribe, including the garden pea, can cause nervous disorders if consumed in excess. Most poisonings occur in hot climates.

Lathyrus—Sweet Pea (130/45/6) • A few species are edible in moderation, but may cause nervous disorders if eaten excessively over an extended period of time. Other species are toxic. (Kirk).

Vicia—Vetch (150+/30/5) The seeds and young stems are edible (Craighead). The plants may contain cyanide (Phillips).

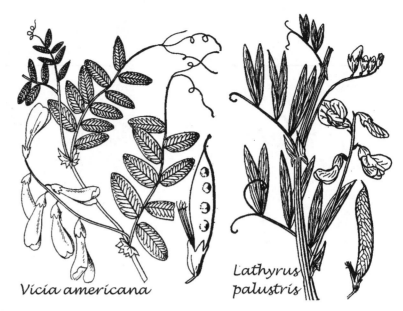

Vicia americana

Lathyrus palustris

Bean Tribe

Most species of the Bean Tribe are twining plants that climb by growing their vine-like stems around poles or other objects. The leaves are usually three-pated. This tribe includes many common beans (*Phaseolus*), the soybean (*Glycine*), plus cow peas and black-eyed peas (*Vigna*).

Amphicarpa—Hog Peanut (-/1/0) Hog Peanut is native to the southeastern U.S. The pods are edible (Sturtevant, Hal).

Apios—Ground Nut (8/2/0) Ground nut is a native of the eastern states. The starchy tubers form on the roots much like beads on a string. They are edible raw, and reportedly taste "like Idaho potatoes" when cooked (Kallas).

Erythrina—Coral Tree (104/1/0) *E. herbacea* can be found from Texas to North Carolina.

Galactea—Milk Pea (-/17/0)

Pueraria—Kudzu (15/1/0) The kudzu vine is an introduced weed from Asia. It is common across the south-eastern states, where it can engulf trees and sometimes kill them by taking all the light. The tubers can be added to stews, or pounded into flur. The young leaves, shoots, and blossoms are all edible as potherbs. The roots are high in flavanoids (Duke).

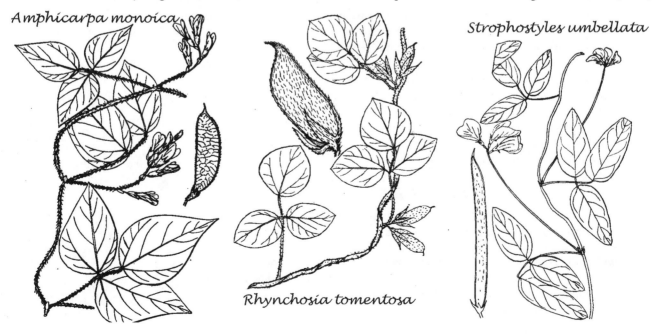

Amphicarpa monoica

Strophostyles umbellata

Rhynchosia tomentosa

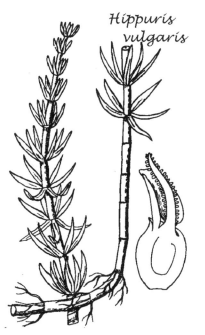

Hippuris vulgaris

Hippuridaceae—Mare's tail Family

If you find a mass of plants floating in the watr with whorled leaves it is likely a member of this family—in fact it may be *the* member of this family. World-wide there is only 1 genus (*Hippuris*), and botanists disagree on how many species are included in that. There could be 3 separate species, or they might all be varieties of the single species *Hippuris vulgaris*.

Hippuris has a greenish flower without petals. The sepals are fused together and not individually distinguishable. There is only 1 stamen. The ovary is positioned inferior, consisting of one carpel (unicarpellate). It matures as a nut-like seed.

There are at least two othr dicot plants which may initially be confused with mare's tail. One is a buttercup, *Ranunculus aquatilus*, with its submerged, finely divided leaves. However, the leaves are not whorled, and it has a distinctive buttercup flower. The other plant is water milfoil from the closely related Water Milfoil family (*Haloragaceae*), not covered in this text. Water milfoil has weak floating stems while mare's tail has stiff, upright stems. Several monocot families include submerged aquatic plants as well.

Key Words
Aquatic plants with whorled leaves and greenish flowers.

Hippuris—Mare's Tail (1/1/1) • Mare's tail is edible as a potherb any time of year (Harrington). Reportedly, the plants are best harvested between fall and spring, and even the browned, over-wintered stems can be eaten. Alaska natives once stored mare's tail in big piles to eat in winter.

Medicinally, the juice of the plant is used internally or externally as a "vulnerary" (Fern), meaning the plant aids the healing process, without specifying how.

Lythraceae—Loosestrife Family

Members of the Loosestrife family have regular, bisexual flowers with 4, 6, or 8 sepals and a like number of petals (sometimes absent). There are typically twice as many stamens as petals, forming two circles of different lengths. The ovary is positioned inferior to partly superior (notice the floral cup or "hypanthium"). It consists of 2-6 carpels (syncarpous) with the partition walls present, forming an equal number of chambers. It matures as a capsule with several to numerous seeds.

Most plants in this family are adapted to damp soils. World-wide there are 25 genera and 550 species. Seven genera are native to North America.

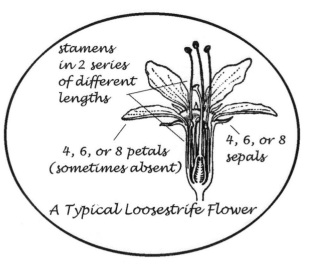

stamens in 2 series of different lengths

4, 6, or 8 petals (sometimes absent)

4, 6, or 8 sepals

A Typical Loosestrife Flower

Tannins and *alkaloids* are common in this family (Zomlefer). Purple loosestrife (*Lythrum salicaria*) pictured below, was introduced from Europe and Asia. Its square stems and opposite leaves may mislead you to think that it is a member of the Mint family, until you examine the flowers. Purple loosestrife propagates quickly via spreading roots and prolific seed production. It has taken over swamps from coast-to-coast, altering the ecology and reducing habitat for native species. Any small or isolated patches should be reported to the land owner or public agency in charge of the land.

Key Words
Twice the stamens as petals, in 2 series short and tall.

Ammannia— (-/-/1) The seeds are edible (Moerman).

Cuphea—Cigar Flower (200/6/0) Cigar flower is found in the southern and eastern states.

Decodon—Swamp-Loosestrife (1/1/0) *D. verticillatus* is found in the eastern third of the continent.

Lythrum—Loosestrife (30/11/2) • The cooked leaves are edible and rich in calcium. Medicinally, the plant is highly astringent, 12% by content in the leaves, and slightly more or less in other parts of the plant. A tea of the plant is used internally in the expected ways, for diarrhea, excessive menstruation, and internal bleeding, etc. Externally, the tea is used as a wash for wounds, etc. The dried, powdered plant is used to stop bleeding (Fern, Lust).

Rotala— (-/-/1)

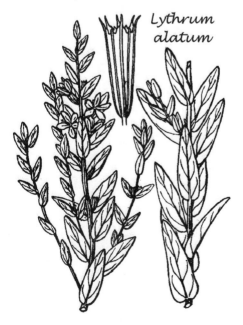

Lythrum alatum

Lythrum salicaria

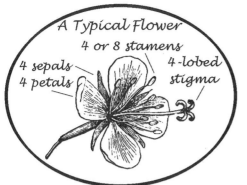

A Typical Flower
4 or 8 stamens
4 sepals
4 petals
4-lobed stigma

Onagraceae—Evening Primrose Family

The delicate flowers of this family have regular, bisexual flowers with 4 sepals and 4 petals (rarely 2, 3, or 5 of each). There are an equal number or twice as many stamens as petals. The ovary is positioned inferior, within a floral cup (hypanthium). The ovary consists of 4 (rarely 2 or 5) united carpels (syncarpous) with the partition walls present, forming an equal number of chambers. The stigma is a distinctive feature of many species, with as many lobes as there are carpels in the ovary (usually 4, as illustrated). The ovary matures as a capsule with many seeds, or sometimes as a berry or drupe (a fleshy fruit with a stony pit). World-wide there are 20 genera and 650 species, including 12 genera in North America. The *Fuchsia* is part of this family. The plants of this family are mostly *edible*, with *astringent*, *mucilaginous* and antispasmodic properties.

Key Words: Flower parts usually in 4's, including a 4-lobed stigma.

Boisduvalia— (-/6/2) The seeds are edible and high oil. They are shaken into a basket and then parched (Sweet).

Camissonia—Evening Primrose (55/-/0)

Circaeae—Enchanter's Nightshade (7/3/1)

Clarkia— (30/30/2) • The seeds are edible (Sweet).

Epilobium—Fireweed (200/40/10) • The pith of the plant is edible and sweet (Angier). The young leaves and shoots are edible as a potherb and mildly mucilaginous, but also bitter and astringent. A strong tea is used as a mild laxative and to settle the stomach (Tilford). Fireweed is useful internally for sore throat and ulcer, and externally for burns and other skin irritations. The flowers were reportedly rubbed on rawhide for water-proofing, and the powdered core of the plant will somehow help protect the hands and face from thecold. It prevents the stinging sensation when rewarming the skin (Willard).

Gaura— (-/21/2) •

Gayophytum—Ground Smoke (-/-/3)

Oenothera—Evening Primrose (80/80/12) • The seeds are edible (Olsen), although they seem quite astringent. The carrot-like tap root, especially *O. iennis*, is edible cooked. Collect the roots of the first year plant in the fall or early spring. The roots have a biting flavor which may be minimized by boiling in several changes of water. The young leaves and shoots are edible as a salad or potherb (Harrington).

   Medicinally, the plant contains mucilage and tannins (Lust), useful in the expected ways. The seeds are more popularly known, as they contain tryptophan, potassium nitrate, and the essential oils linoleic and gamma-linoleic acid, useful for lowering cholesterol (Klein). Gamma-linoleic acid has a regulatory effect on systemic fatty acid imbalances and metabolism in the liver (Tilford). Tryptophan is commonly used as an over-the-counter sedative. The sprouts also contain alpha-linoleic acid (Duke). (See also Tyler.)

Oenothera biennis

seed capsule

Epilobium angustifolium

Gaura coccinea

Shepherdia argenta

Elaeagnus argentea

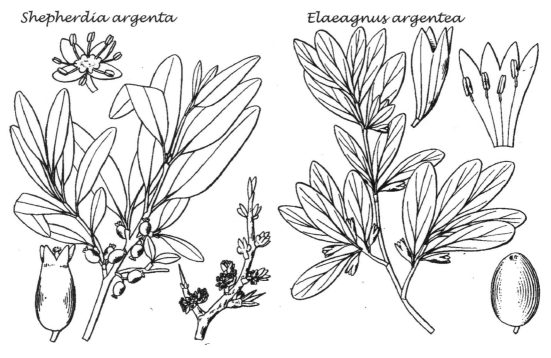

Elaeagnaceae—Oleaster Family

The Oleaster family consists of occasionally thorny shrubs and trees with alternate or opposite leaves, often silvery in appearance due to the presence of minute hairs. Some species have small orange dots under the leaves. Several members of this family especially prosper in valley bottoms where the soil surface remains dry, but the water table is not far below.

The flowers are regular and mostly bisexual, but sometimes "dioecious" with male and female flowers appearing on separate plants. There are 4 united sepals but 0 petals. There are 4 stamens in *Elaeagnus* and 8 in *Shepherdia*. The ovary is positioned partly or wholly inferior, consisting of one carpel (unicarpellate). The fruit looks like a drupe (a berry with a stony seed), but in this case the ovary matures as an achene (dry seed), and the fleshy fruit is really the swollen calyx (the sepals). The gray or red-orange fruits will help to identify this family. World-wide there are 3 genera and 50 species, all native to the northern hemisphere.

<u>Key Words</u>
Shrubs or trees often with silvery leaves and gray or red-orange fruits.

Elaeagnus—Russian Olive, Oleaster, Silverberry (-/-/2) • Gray fruits. The Russian olive, *E. angustifolia*, is an introduced tree with big thorns. It is especially tolerant of drought and alkaline soil. It is cultivated in many areas, but often naturalized in the countryside, sometimes becoming invasive. The fruits are astringent, but edible. They can be dried and powered and are used in bread in Arabia (Duke). Our native species, *E. commutata*, also produces edible fruit. It has no thorns. The inner bark was used extensively for cordage material by northwest coast Indians (Turner).

Hippophae—Seaberry (-/-/D) *H. rhamnoides* is an introduced ornamental from Russia with large yellow, edible fruits.

Shepherdia—Buffaloberry (-/-/2) • Red-orange fruits. Buffalo berries ripen in late July, but frequently remain on the bushes all through the winter. The fresh berries are quite astringent, and they will really pucker your mouth. Picking them after a hard freeze helps sweeten them. I like the berries dried whole; they sweeten up quite a bit that way. On a good bush I can hand-pick a quart or more of berries per hour. My daughter and I collected a couple gallons of berries in about half an hour with the use of a baseball bat to beat the berries out on to a tarp. That made a lot of good syrup!

All of the buffaloberries have some saponin content, but *S. canadensis* has a lot. The fresh berries taste awful. However, the saponin allows the berries to be whipped into a froth; mixed with sugar it is called "Indian ice-cream", and it is reported to be quite good. The crushed berries may be useful as a soap substitute.

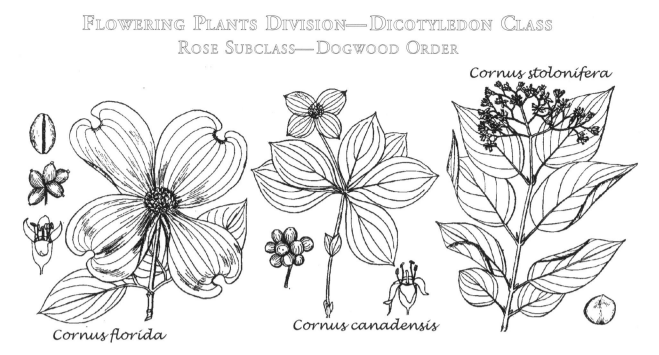

Cornus stolonifera

Cornus canadensis

Cornus florida

Cornaceae—Dogwood Family

The Dogwood family consists of 12 genera and 100 species around the world, but only the dogwood genus (*Cornus*) is native to North America. The dogwoods are trees, shrubs, or woody plants with opposite or apparently whorled leaves. Only *Cornus alternifolia* has alternate leaves. The big showy flowers of some dogwoods are illusionary. The showy, whitish "petals" are really bracts, while the true flowers are much smaller and clustered together in the center. There are usually 4 of these petal-like bracts, but the number may be variable. The flowers are regular and usually, but not always bisexual, with 4 or 5 (rarely 0) small sepals, and a similar number of usually white petals. There are 4 or 5 stamens. The ovary is positioned inferior, consisting of 2 (sometimes 1, 3, or 4) united carpels (syncarpous) with the partition walls present, forming an equal number of chambers. It matures as a berry, or sometimes a "drupe", a fleshy fruit with a stoney pit in the middle. Other cultivated genera from the family include *Aucuba, Corokia, Curtisia, Griselinia,* and *Helwingia*.

Key Words
Trees, shrubs or woody plants with opposite or whorled leaves, showy bracts and fleshy fruits.

Cornus—Dogwood, Bunchberry (45/-/2) • The red, white, and black berries of at least eight species are known to be edible, although some are very bitter or acid tasting (Sturtevant). The berries may be strongly laxative in excess. Cooking may be required to render some varities more edible. The berries may reduce the potency of some poisons when ingested or applied as a poultice (Willard).

The dogwoods contain varying amounts of cornic acid and the alkaloid cornine, mostly in the bark and/or the inner bark. It has a mildly narcotic and analgesic effect, especially helpful for individuals who have a negative reaction to salicylates like willow or asprin. The bark is also quite astringent, which further helps to draw down inflammed tissues. (Moore, Willard).

The aromatic greenish inner bark of the red osier dogwood (*C. stolonifera*) was often added to smoking mixtures. It should be used in moderation due to its narcotic effect. (Harrington, Willard).

Cornus alternifolia

101

Commandra umbellata

Santalaceae—Sandalwood Fmily

Th plants of the Sandawood family have regular flowers, either bisexual or unisexual, with 4 or 5 sepals, 0 petals, and the same number of stamens as sepals, aligned with the petals. The ovary is positioned partly or wholly inferior and consists of 3-5 (sometimes 2) united carpels forming a single chamber. It matures as a dry seed or a berry with a stony seed. World-wide there are 30 genera and 400 species. Five genera are found in North America, as listed below.

Comandra is the most common plant of this family, with small pink or greenish flowers. It is parasitic, often attached to the roots of sagebrush.

Key Words
Grayish plants with greenish or pink flowers. 0 petals.

Buckleya— (-/-/0)
Comandra—Bastard Toadflax (-/-/1) • The common name "bastard toadflax" is misleading since there is a flower in the Figwort family called "butter and eggs toadflax". The berries are edible. A tea of the plant was used for canker sores by the Native Americans (Moerman).
Geocaulon— (-/-/0)
Nestronia— (-/-/0)
Pyrularia—Buffalo Nut (-/-/0)

Viscaceae/Loranthaceae—Mistletoe Family

We are often repulsed by anything that is parasitic, but this is not the case with the mistletoe. You have probably seen it at Christmas time—maybe you have even gotten a kiss underneath it! The European mistletoe is *Viscum* while the American mistletoe is *Phoradendron*. It has poisonous berries. I remember selling it with the boy scouts as a fund-raiser. I knew that it hung from the branches of the trees it fed on, and I always wanted to see it that way—instead of in a box.

Mistletoe is surprisingly common, but most of the species are small and inconspicuous, particularly in the northern states. Botanically, the small flowers may be bisexual or not, with 2-5 sepals (usually 3), 0 petals, and the same number of stamens as sepals. The ovary is positioned inferior, consisting of 3 or 4 united carpels (syncarpous), forming a single chamber. The fruit is a berry or a drupe (a fleshy fruit with a stony pit). World-wide there are 11 genera and 450 species, including 2 genera in North America.

Mistletoes take water and inorganic nutrients from the host trees, but produce their own sugars through photosynthesis. They can absorb toxins from the host trees (Tyler).

Phoradendron flavescens

Key Words
Green plants with berries. Parasitic on trees.

Arceuthobium—Dwarf Mistletoe (15/-/4) • Native Americans drank a tea of the plant for tuberculosis and lung or mouth hemorrhages (Moerman).
Phoradendron—American Mistletoe (300/-/0) American mistletoe contains the alkaloid acetylcholine (Moore). It has been prescribed for epilepsy, stroke, and tuberculosis (Klein). A tea of the plant or the raw leaves has the effect of a strong vasoconstrictor and thus raises blood pressure. It has been used to stimulate contractions during childbirth, but the effects vary significantly from one person to the next and could be dangerous (Moore).

Euphorbiaceae—Spurge Family

If you have seen a Poinsettia at Christmas time then you have met a member of the Spurge family. The colorful bracts are common in the family. North American members of the Spurge family are succulent plants with milky juice and simple, but varied leaves. The non-showy flowers are mostly regular and unisexual, with staminate (male) and pistillate (female) flowers appearing separately on the same plant. (The male flowers may be immediately surrounding the female flowers.) There are 0 or 5 sepals and petals, plus 5, 10, or numerous stamens (up to 1000!) The ovary is positioned superior, and consists of 3 (sometimes 2 or 4) united carpels (syncarpous) with the partition walls usually present, forming an equal number of chambers. It matures as a capsule with one seed per cell. The colorful bracts may be mistaken for sepals or petals.

Euphorbia esula

World-wide there are 290 genera and 7,500 species. It is the fourth or fifth largest family of plants. About 25 genera are found in North America. The Poinsettia (*Euphorbia*), Croton (*Codiaeum*), and Crown-of-Thorns are ornamental plants from this family. The *Hevea* tree provides rubber. Castor oil comes from *Ricinus communis*. *Aleurites* is the source for tung oil. Tapioca (i.e.: tapioca pudding) is made from the starchy roots of *Manihot*. The Mexican jumping bean (*Sebastiana*) is another member of the family; the "jumping" is caused by the rapid movements of a moth larvae inside the seed. Most members of this family contain an **acrid latex** (which is made into rubber) with poisonous **alkaloids**. Saponins are also common in the family.

<u>Key Words</u>: Plants often with colored bracts and milky juice.

Eremocarpus—Turkey Mullein (-/-/0) Turkey Mullein was used by Native Americans to poison fish (Nyerges).

Euphorbia—Spurge, Poinsettia (1600/-/11) • The spurges contain an acrid latex sap which may cause a rash when the sap on the skin is exposed to sunlight. The sap is considered carcnogenic if it is handled a lot (Fern). The whole plant contains the latex but it is most concentrated in the roots. The acrid sap is useful xternally on warts, or internally to irritate and open up the body—functioning as an emetic, anthelmintic, vaodilator, and potentially violet purgative. A European species is considered to toxic for medicinal use (Fern). Large doses have a depressant effect on the heart and can be fatal to people (Lust). Spurges are considered noxious weeds, but can be controlled with sheep and goats. They relish them.

Ricinus—Castor Bean (D) The castor bean is cultivated as a ol crop in warm parts of the country. The plant and seeds are highly poisonous, but the toxin is water solubleand is separated out when the oil is pressed from the seeds. The seeds contain 35-55% oil.

Ricinus communis

Medicinally, castor oil is well known as a potent laxative; the oil literally lubricates the bowels to facilitate movement. The leaves are used as a poultice for headaches and on boils. A tea of the leaves and roots is taken internally as an expectorant.

Castor oil is used as an industrial lubricant, and as an ingredient in soaps, polishes, paints, varnishes, and fly paper. The living plant is said to repel flies and mosquitoes. The stem is a source of fiber (Fern).

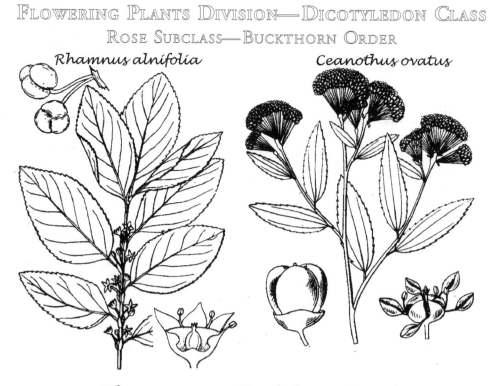

Rhamnus alnifolia

Ceanothus ovatus

Rhamnaceae—Buckthorn Family

If you find a dicot shrub or small tree with visibly 3-parted berries or capsules, then it is likely a member of the Buckthorn family. These shrubs have simple, alternate or opposite leaves. The small, white or greenish flowers are mostly regular and usually, but not always bisexual, typically forming in showy clusters. There are 4-5 sepals, petals, and stamens. Sometimes the petals are absent. The stamens are alternate with the sepals and opposite the petals. The parts are positioned perigynous (in the middle of the ovary). The ovary consists of 3 (sometimes 2 or 4) united carpels (syncarpous) with the partition walls present, forming an equal number of chambers. It matures as a berry or capsule with 1 (rarely 2) seeds per cell. The sections of the ovary are readily visible on the surface.

World-wide there are 58 genera and 900 species. Ten genera are found in North America, including *Berchemia*, *Colubrina*, *Condalia*, *Gouania*, *Krugiodendron*, *Reynosia*, *Sageretia*, and *Ziziphus*, plus the genera below.

<u>Key Words</u>
Small trees or shrubs with visibly 3-parted berries or capsules.

Ceanothus—Buckbrush, Red Root (80/30+/3) The flowers and berries of red root contain saponin and can be used for soap (Craighead). The leaves are a popular tea. The root can be used for a red dye (Hall). The root contains many acids, including tannin, and is thus an astringent, used in the conventional ways for inflamed tonsils, sore throat, nosebleeds, menstrual hemorrhage, etc.. Additionally, the root somehow stimulates "electrical repelling" between the blood vessels and the red blood cells. Increasing the blood charge helps keep the redblood cells flowing without clumping up. The enhanced flow is especially beneficial for headaches triggered by a heavy dinner, when fats flood into the blood stream. Increasing the blood charge also facilitates a better exchange between the blood vessels and the lymph nodes to expedite the break down and removal of wastes. Red root helps to "tone" or improve and strengthen the lymph tissues. It is beneficial to "healthy people under stress", but it is not a heroic her b to treat sick people. For more information on this fascinating herb please refer to Michael Moore's *Medicinal Plants of the Pacific West.*

Rhamnus—Buckthorn, Cascara Sagrada (155/-/3) • The berries of many species found in North America are reported to be edible (Sturtevant), but may contain laxative properties (Schauenberg). *Rhamnus* bark contains anthroquinone glycosides which is used as a powerful laxative that does not result in dependency (Willard). It is available commercially, the total trade consumes 1-3 million pounds each year. It is recommended that the bark be aged for a year (Hall) or baked at 212° for ten minutes (Bigfoot) before use. The fresh bark can cause severe diarrhea and vomiting. Native Americans sometimes used it as an emetic to expel ingested poisons (Tilford).

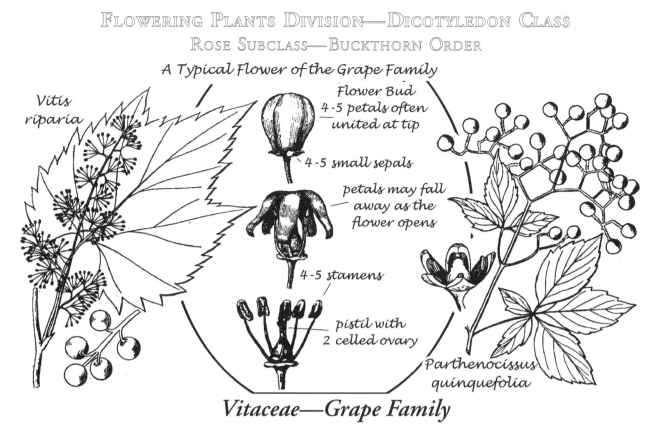

Vitaceae—Grape Family

If you can recognize a grape, then you can identify the members of this family with their climbing vines and tendrils and the distinctive clusters of berries. The leaves are alternate, forming opposite from the tendrils and flowers. Flowers are regular and may be bisexual or unisexual, with 4 or 5 sepals and petals and 4 or 5 stamens. The ovary is positioned superior. It consists of 2 (rarely 3-6) united carpels (syncarpous) with the partition walls present, forming an equal number of chambers. It matures as a berry with 1-2 seeds per cell. World-wide there 12 genera and 700 species, including 4 genera in North America, as listed below. Most members of the Grape family have *edible* leaves, stems, sap, and berries. The vegetation is often mildly *astringent*.

<u>Key Words</u>
Vining plants with tendrils and berries.

Ampelopsis—Blueberry Climber (20/-/0) The berries of the various species of *Ampelopsis* are reported to be edible raw or cooked, but poor in taste. The stems, leaves, and leaf buds of at least one species are edible (Fern).

Cissus—Grape Ivy (350/-/0) A tea of the plant was used by the Indians as a liver aid for yellow jaundice. Cordage can be made from the vines (Moerman).

Parthenocissus—Virginia Creeper (15/-/D) • Virginia creeper grows wildly across much of the U.S., but only domestically in Montana. The berries are edible, but not very flavorful. The sap of at least one species is reportedly sweet. The peeled, boiled stalks are also edible (Fern). The bark and twigs have astringent and expectorant properties, often used as a tea for colds.

Vitis—Wild & Domestic Grapes (50/-/1) • Wild grapes are used similarly to domestic grapes. In Montana they are prolific around the Crow Reservation, but not really anywhere else. I have not been at the right place at the right time to try a ripe grape,but I did once find some raisins still clinging to the vines in mid-winter. We have a wild grape vine growing in our greenhouse, but it hasn't produced fruit. Our kids especially like to eat the mildly tart leaves.

    Medicinally, a tea of the leaves is reported to be helpful for the pancreas, heart, and circulation. The leaves can be used as a poultice for blisters on the feet (Bigfoot). Grape seed extract from the seeds of *V. vinifera*, grown in Italy and France, contains high concentrations of powerful antioxidants called "gallic esters of proanthocyanidins". Their ability to fight free radicals is reportedly 20 times stronger than vitamin C and 50 times stronger than vitamin E. The extract is a popular herbal supplement also taken to maintain capillary integrity. It is especially helpful to bring increased blood flow to strained eyes from too many hours staring at a computer. The same antioxidant is found in the park of some species of pine (Amrion).

Aesculaceae (Hippocastanaceae)—Buckeye Family

It would be difficult to pass by the buckeye tree when the fruits are ripe and falling to the ground, without stopping to investigate. It is hard to miss the large seeds with the distinctive "eye". The Buckeye or Horse Chestnut family includes trees and shrubs with opposite, palmately compound leaves and very distinctive nut-like seeds.

The flowers are bisexual and slightly irregular, with 5 united sepals and 4 or 5 separate petals. There are 4 to 9 stamens in two rings around the pistil. The ovary is positioned superior, consisting of 3 united carpels (syncarpous or tricarpellate), but only one carpel develops into a fruit, usually containing one or a few large, nut-like seeds, white inside with a hard, leathery "peel" on the outside, often as large as a walnut. There is usually a small, circular patch, like an "eye" on the seeds.

World-wide there are only 2 genera and about 15 species. Only the buckeye grows in the states. The genus *Billia* is found in South America and Mexico.

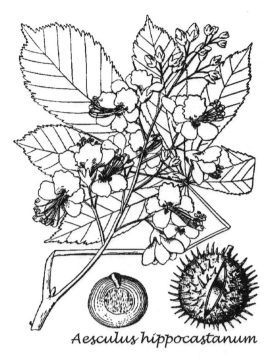

Aesculus hippocastanum

Key Words
Trees with opposite palmate leaves and large seeds with an "eye"

Aesculus—Buckeye, Horse Chestnut (13/-/D) • The buckeye is not native to Montana, but sometimes it is planted domestically here. The species I have experimented with have big nut-like seeds the size of walnuts and larger, and they are rich in saponins. I put slices of a fresh seed in the blender and used the resulting soap in the washing machine. I think it is one of the easier sources for saponins. Buckeyes can be used for fish poison (Weiner).

Despite the high saponin content, buckeyes are somewhat edible. The seeds must be crushed and the bitterness leached away by soaking in cold water (Sturtevant). Probably it is more of a survival food than a real staple. Caution is advised, as there are reports of poisonings from consuming the green seed casings (Schauenberg). Roasting apparently renders them safe (Lust).

Medicinally, in addition to the saponins, there is some tannin and coumarin glycosides in the seeds. An extract of the seeds increases blood circulation, in this case apparently helpful to stimulate digestion (Schauenberg).

Aesculus hippocastanum

106

Aceraceae—Maple Family

Most anyone recognizes the familiar maple leaf, common to almost all maples and symbol on the Canadian flag. Only the box elder (*Acer negundo*) has a different style leaf. Many people will also remember picking up the winged seeds as children and making "helicopters" with them.

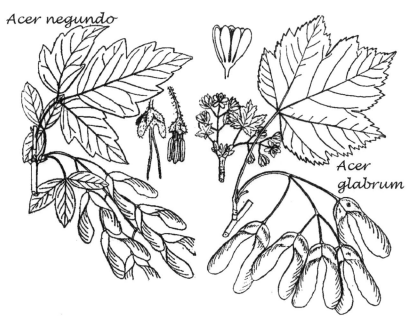

Acer negundo

Acer glabrum

If you were to examine the flowers in the springtime you would find 4 or 5 separate sepals, and 4 or 5 separate petals (sometimes 0). The flowers are typically, but not always unisexual, with male and female parts appearing in separate blossoms, often on separate trees. Male flowers have 4-10 stamens. On female flowers the ovary is positioned superior and consists of 2 united carpels (bicarpellate) with the partition walls usually present. The ovary matures into two winged seeds. The Maple family is sometimes included within *Sapindaceae*. World-wide there are 2 genera and about 200 species. The genera *Dipteronia* is native to China. Note that the ash (*Fraxinus*) of the Olive family has somewhat similar seeds.

Key Words
Trees with opposite leaves and winged seeds in pairs.

Acer—Maple, Box Elder (200/-/3) • The maple of commercial syrup production is *Acer saccharum*, but all other maples can be tapped for syrup as well, with varying results.

The box elder was once used extensively for syrup production where sugar maples were not available (Harrington). They grow wild in eastern Montana, but only domestically in western Montana. I put 2 taps in my neighbor's tree in mid March (late in the season) and collected about 6 gallons of sap in 3 weeks. This boiled down to 1.5 cups of thick, rich syrup—a real treat.

The sap "runs" in the trees on warm days from January to May, depending on where you are located. To collect the sap simply drill a hole 1 inch in diameter and 3 inches long into the trunk of the tree, about 2 feet above the ground and on the South side. I use a short length of 3/4" PVC pipe for a spout. The hole should be drilled in at a slight upward angle, and the spout tapped only part way in. A notch can be made into the top of the PVC pipe to hold the wire handle of a bucket, or you can use sheetrock screws to attach the bucket or its handle to the tree trunk. A large tree (16+ inches in diameter) can have more than one tap. The sap is mostly water, so it is boiled down to remove at least 30 parts of water to get 1 part pure maple syrup. The sap is high in B vitamins, calcium, phosphorus, and enzymes (Angier).

The *wild* maples of my area are more like bushes than trees, with a maximum trunk diameter of about 3". For these small trees we found the best method is to drill a 1/4" hole an inch into the tree, at an angle. Make two slashes in the bark, forming a "V" down to the hole. (Do not slash all the way around the tree—that will kill it.) Pound a stick into the hole, and the sap will run out and drip off the end of the stick. I take along a battery-powered drill and use a sheetrock screw to attach a plastic bucket below the spigot. In our area the sap flows from March to May. The small trees only produce a pint of sap per day, and the syrup content seemed low. It took me a month to get a pint of syrup from 8 trees. It was not particularly economical, but it sure was good. Please note that there is a risk of causing damage to any trees less than 12" in diameter. The inner bark and seeds of the maples are also reported to be edible (Angier).

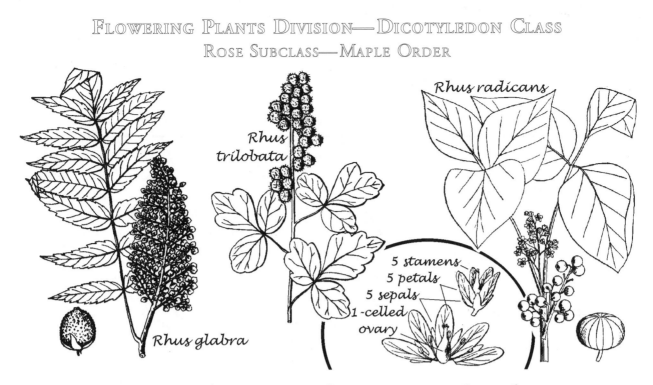

Anacardiaceae—Cashew or Sumac Family

If you have ever had a rash from poison ivy, then you have met the Sumac family. This family is a mixed bag of mostly trees and shrubs, including the cashew (*Anacardium*), mango (*Mangifera*), pistachio (*Pistacia*), zebrawood (*Astronium*) and sumac (*Rhus*). **Poison oak, poison ivy, and poison sumac** are usually included in the *Rhus* genus, but are separated by some into the *Toxicodendron* genus. Most members of the family are found in warmer climates, and the description here applies only to the *Rhus* genus. The flowers are regular and either bisexual or unisexual, typically with 5 sepals united at the base and 5 petals. There are usually 5 stamens, but sometimes 10. The ovary is positioned superior and consists of 3 united carpels (syncarpous or tricarpellate), but only one carpel develops into a fruit, forming a "drupe", meaning a berry with a stony seed. The berries of most *Rhus* species are bright orange, but poison ivy has white berries.

World-wide there are 79 genera and 600 species, including 7 genera in North America. Several members of the family produce oils, resins, an lacquers. Given te potency of these compunds it is not too surrising that there are ome poisonous species in the family. Genera of the Cashew family that are found in the southern states include the smoke tree *(Cotinus)* and the Peruvian pepper tree *(Schinus)*. The poison tree *(Metopium)*, American hog plum *(Spondias)*, and mango are found south Florida. The pistachio grows in southern Texas.

<u>Key Words (Rhus spp.):</u> Shrubs with 3-lobed or pinnate leaves and 1-seeded red or white berries.

Rhus trilobata, glabra—Lemon-berry Sumac, Staghorn Sumac • The bright red berries are high in calcium and potassium malates, and the leaves and bark contain gallic and tannic acid (Moore, Densmore). The berries can be infused into cold water to make a good lemonade-type drink.

    The leaves and bark are astringent (the berries less so), used in typical ways: sore throat, diarrhea, etc., with particular reference to cold sores (Moore). The leaf tea is recommended for asthma (Willard).

Rhus radicans—Poison Ivy • Poison ivy contains a non-volatile phenol-type oil, called "3-n-pentadecylcatechol" or more commonly "urshiol". Urushiol gives the leaves a shny, waxy appearance and i the agent that causes dermatiis. Not everyone is susceptible to poison ivy, and the potency does change throughout the year (Harrington) usually becoming stronger with age. In any case you should avoid all contact with the plant. Eating the white berries is extremely dangerous. It can cause your throat to swell shut. Burning the plant can release toxic smoke.

    Poison ivy was once used externally to treat the symptoms of herpes (Weiner).

    Peter Bigfoot wrote that he was allergic to poison ivy until he saw a deer browsing on the foliage in the spring-time when it is sweet, and he started eating it too. The poisonous oil may be dilute enough at that time of year to mildly stimulate the immune system without causing an adverse reaction. Author Verrill also mentions the leaves and berries as edible. I should emphasize that this practice could be extremely dangerous. The effects would certainly vary from one individual to another and a toxic reaction could cause your throat to swell shut—with fatal results.

Zygophyllaceae—Caltrop Family

Many people in the southern states know at least one member of the Caltrop family, the puncture vine, by the thorns pulled from their bicycle tires and shoes.

Members of the Caltrop family have opposite, pinnate leaves. They are usually herbs or shrubs, but some are trees. The Caltrops are largely adapted to desert conditions; they are rare in the northern latitudes.

A typical flower from this family is regular and bisexual, with 5 sepals and 5 petals (rarely 4 of each), and either 5, 10, or 15 stamens. The ovary is positioned superior. It consists of 5 united carpels (syncarpous) with the partition walls present, form-

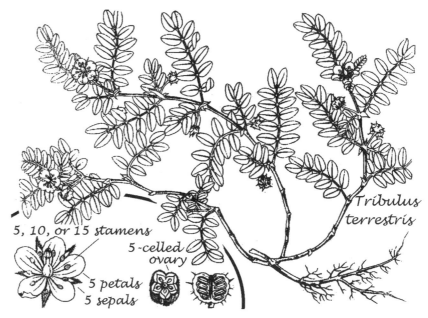

ing an equal number of chambers. It matures as a capsule with 2 or more seeds per cell, or rarely a s a drupe (a fleshy fruit with a stoney pit). World-wide there are about 30 genera and 250 species. North American genera are listed below.

Key Words
Desert plants with parts in 5's, and opposite, pinnate leaves.

Fagonia—(-/1/0) *F. californica* is found in the desert southwest.

Guaiacum—Lignum Vitae (6/-/0) A native of the Florida Keys.

Kallstroemia—Arizona "Poppy" (-/7/0) *Kallstroemia* is a native of the desert southwest. The plant is astringent. A tea of the plant is used externally as an eyewash and internally for diarrhea or excess menstruation (Moore).

Larrea—Chaparral, Creosote Bush (5/-/0) • Chaparral is a native of the desert southwest. Some individual plants are more than 10,000 years old. Chaparral has a sticky resin containing a potent antioxidant called nordihydroguaiaretic acid, or NDGA. It is especially effective at preserving fats and oils. The substance inhibits cellular metabolism. For many years it was thought to inhibit cancer, but new studies indicate that it can also stimulate it. Chaparral is used as an antiseptic for cuts and wounds, as an anti-oxidant, and to treat liver and blood disorders (Bigfoot, Hutchins, Moore). A tea of the plant is strong and repulsive to many people. Renee and I thought it tasted as if it were made from an old garden hose! Herbal use (or abuse) of chaparral has led to some cases of liver damage in recent years (Tilford). When NDGA was fed to mosquitoes it lengthed the average lifespan from 29 to 45 days (Tyler).

Peganum—Syrian Rue, African Rue (5/2/0) Syrian rue is an introduced weed from southwes Asia. It is now common in parts of Nevada and New Mexic. It is reported to have an awful taste. A tea of the plant or tincture of the seeds is used for many skin conditions and also to strengthen the heart while decreasing blood pressure (Moore). The seeds contain psychoactve alkaloids (Smith).

Tribulus—Puncture Vine (20/2/1) • Puncture vine is an introduced weed. The young shoots, leaves and seed capsules may be cooked and eaten, but it is considered an emergency food only. Medicinally, the seeds or leaves can be used in tea to reduce blood cholesterol and improve heart function. The tea is also used as a diuretic to dissolve urate deposits and therefore relieve pain in arthritis, but excess dosage can harm the kidneys (Bigfoot, Moore).

Zygophyullum—Bean Caper (-/-/1) The seeds and flowers of some species are usd as a pepper-like spice (Sturtevant).

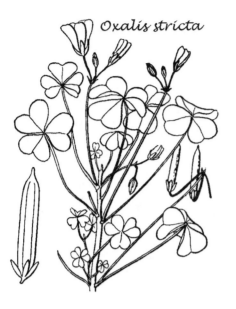

Oxalis stricta

Oxalidaceae—Wood Sorrel Family

If you celebrate St. Patrick's day, then you will like the Wood Sorrel Family. Woodsorrel is also called "shamrocks", and the little green leaves (or cut outs like them) are seen everywhere when the Irish spirit is in the air. Some species of clover (*Trifolium*) from the Pea family are also known as shamrocks. Woodsorrel could easily be mistaken for clover with its three-parted leaves.

The solitary flowers are regular and bisexual with 5 sepals, 5 petals, and 10 stamens. The length of the stamens may vary. The ovary is positioned superior. It consists of 5 united carpels (syncarpous) with the partition walls present, forming an equal number of chambers. There are separate styles for each carpel. It matures as an explosive capsule. These are delicate plants full of acidic, *oxalate* juice. Worldwide there are 8 genera and 950 species. Only *Oxalis* is native to North America.

Plants with oxalic acid are commonly used in external cancer remedies to literally etch away the offending tumor. One recipe suggests fermenting the bruised, oxalate-rich leaves in a crock-pot in the ground or 6-8 weeks. The resulting black salve is placed on the tumor and is left in place until it draws out the cancer and falls off. It is reported to be extremely painful (Cummings). This fermentation process would involve fungi, probably with antibiotic effects and other unknown properties.

Key Words
Small plants with shamrock leaves and flower parts in 5's.

Oxalis—Woodsorrel, Shamrock (850/31/2) • Like other plants that contain oxalic acid, over-consumption of woodsorrel can block the body's ability to absorb calcium. The oxalic acid gives a tart, lemon-like flavor. The leaves can be used sparingly in salads or steeped and chilled for ice tea. Some species have edible, tuberous roots (Zomlefer). Medicinally, oxalic acid is an irritating stimulant to the digestive system, helpful for digestive problems. It is used externally as an astringent wash for skin problems.

Balsaminaceae—Touch-Me-Not Family

Jewelweed really stands out when you come across it. It has translucent, watery stems and a distinctive irregular blossom. There are 3 (rarely 5) sepals of unequal size, the lowest one forming a spur. There are 5 petals, two of which are united, plus 5 stamens. The ovary is positioned superior. It consists of 5 united carpels (syncarpous) with the partition walls present, forming an equal number of chambers. Each carpel produces 2 to numerous seeds. The fruit is usually a capsule that explodes when touched, hence the common name of the family. The leaf has a silvery appearance when held underwater.

World-wide there are 4 genera and 500 to 600 species. Middle Eastern and African species have been used to produce red, yellow, and black dyes. The house/garden plant *Impatiens* is a well-known member of this family. Be sure to notice the spur on the back. Only 2 species of *Impatiens* are native to North America. Additional species have escaped cultivation.

Key Words:
Delicate, juicy plants
with irregular flowers and spurs.

Impatiens—Jewelweed, Touch-Me-Not (419/10/3) • Young jewelweed shoots up to 6 inches tall are reported to be a good potherb. The seeds are also edible. Medicinally, jewelweed is astringent; it is often used as a poultice or wash for skin irritations, especially for poison ivy, bee stings and athlete's foot. A European species also contains a bitter principle; it is used as a laxative.

Jewelweed is not common in my part of Montana. I have only seen a half-dozen plants, and they are all gone now. I think it perfers a more humid environment.

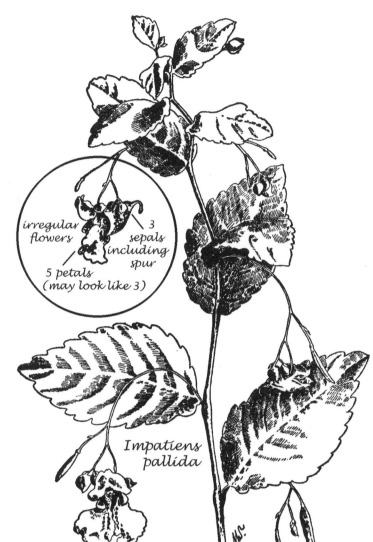

irregular flowers
3 sepals including spur
5 petals (may look like 3)

Impatiens pallida

Geraniaceae—Geranium Family

If you have a geranium at home, stop and look at it. The regular, bisexual flowers have 5 sepals and 5 petals with 5, 10, or 15 stamens. Note however, that some varieties have been bred to have multiple layers of petals. The ovary is positioned superior. It consists of 5 united carpels (syncarpous) with the partition walls present, forming an eqal number of chambers. It matures as a "schizocarp", a dry fruit which splits apart into individual carpels (mericarps) when dry. The styles are fused together, making a distinctive 5-parted, star-like stigma at the end.

The most striking pattern of this family is the schizocarp or seed pod. It forms as the flower wilts away, and looks like a needle emerging from the center of the blossom. It has 5 cells,

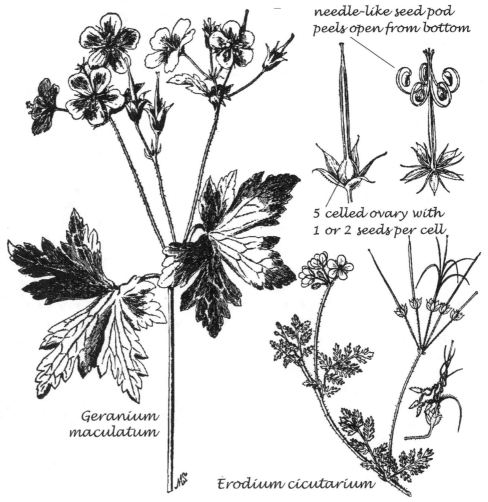

needle-like seed pod peels open from bottom

5 celled ovary with 1 or 2 seeds per cell

Geranium maculatum

Erodium cicutarium

with 1 or 2 ovules in each cell. At maturity the pod starts at the bottom and "peels" open to release its seeds. Indoor geraniums are seldom pollinated, so they do not form seed pods. It would be worth setting one outside so the bees can pollinate it, just so you can see the distinctive seed pod. This floral pattern is common to all the members of the family. World-wide there are 11 genera and 780 species. Only *Erodium* and *Geranium* are native to North America. Domestic geraniums come from the genera *Monsonia* and *Pelargonium*.

The members of this family contain significant quantities of **tannic**, **ellagic**, and **gallic acids**, making them quite astringent. The roots are especially acid.

<u>Key Words</u>
Flower parts in 5's with a "stork's bill" pistil and a 5-parted stigma.

Erodium—Stork's Bill (75/9/1) • Stork's bill is an introduced weed from Europe. The young leaves are edible as a salad or potherb (Duke) before becoming too astringent. The roots are also edible. Warm days with freezing nights may cause the plant to accumulate toxic concentrations of nitrates (Bigfoot). Medicinally, it is a mild astringent and diuretic. The root and leaves are used as tea for an afterbirth remedy (Moore).

Geranium—Wild geranium (375/33/6) • Geranium is a potent astringent, containing tannic and gallic acid, and the power is in the root. The powdered root is a good poultice for drawing ut pus and inflammation or to stop bleeding. The roots or leaves are used in tea for sore throat; used as an enema for bleeding piles or hemorrhoids; or as a douche for vaginitis (Moore). The roots of some species are used as food (Sturtevant). The stems of the sticky geranium are covered with anti-bacerial resins useful for protecting injured tissues (Klein).

Pelargonium—Domestic Geranium (250/D/D) • The leaves are edible (Sturtevant, Fern). Martha Stewart has mentioned using the scented geraniums for culinary purposes.

Linaceae—Flax Family

Flax plants wake up with a cheer every morning. In spite of their wispy little stems and small leaves that may nearly disappear in dry weather, flax plants open up a whole bouquet of fresh flowers each day with the rising sun. The plants often droop under the weight of their own exuberance, and all the petals fall off by noon—but just wait until tomorrow, and they will do it all again.

Linum usitatissimum

Linum lewisii

Flax is often planted in wild flower mixes. The flowers are bisexual and regular, with 5 sepals, 5 delicate petals, and 5 stamens. The sepals are alternate with the petals. The ovary is positioned superior and consists of 5 (rarely 3 or 4) united carpels (syncarpous), with the partition walls present, forming an equal number of chambers. It often looks more like ten carpels due to intrusion of the midrib. It matures as a capsule (rarely a drupe) with each cell containing 1 or 2 seeds. The capsule splits apart longitudinally like the sections of an orange.

World-wide there are 12 genera and 290 species. Only *Hesperolinon* and *Linum* are native to North America. Flax plants supply fibers for linen, and seeds for linseed oil. ***Linseed oil*** is used as a drying agent in paints and varnishes and is also used in the manufacture of linoleum. *Reinwardtia* is a small shrub from India sometimes planted in conservatories.

Key Words
Flower parts in 5's. Seed capsules like the sections of an orange.

Hesperolinon— (12/-/0) *Hesperolinon* is sometimes included within *Linum*. It is native to the Pacific coast states.

Linum—Flax (230/35/4) • The seeds contain cyanide, but it is easily destroyed by cooking, and the seeds are quite edible and nutritious. Flax seed is rich in oils, including linoleic and linolenic essential fatty acids, also known as Omega 6 and Omega 3 . Essential means that we need the substances to function normally, but our bodies do not produce them. Essential fatty acids are obtained only through our diets (Healty Cell). These substances help lower cholesterol and block platelets from clumping together in the bloodstream (Willard), also helpful to relieve arthritis, PMS, auto-immune disorders, and chronic inflammation of the colon (Hobbs).

In order for our bodies to properly utilize these essential fatty acids, they should be consumed together with a sulfur-rich protein source, as for example, flaxseed oil combined with cottage cheese. This combination reportedly alleviated anemia, reduced cancerous tumers, and increased vitality in patients (Healty Cell).

Flax stalks are the source of fibers for linen, and make an excellent cordage material. Bundles of mature stalks are soaked in water for up to two weeks to loosen the fibrous outer bark. The fibers can then be stripped and twisted into cordage while wet or dry. Be sure to read my book *Participating in Nature* for additional instructions on making cordage.

Millegrana—All Seed (-/-/0) All seed is a native of Europe, but naturalized in North America along the coast of Nova Scotia.

Polygalaceae—Milkwort Family

Flowers of the Milkwort family look superficially like those of the Pea family, but there are some significant differences. Milkwort flowers are irregular and bisexual. There are 5 sepals—usually 3 green outer sepals, and 2 petal-like inner sepals. There are 3 petals, usually joined to the stamens, and the lower petal is often fringed. There are 8 stamens (sometimes less), fused together like a tube, but split open. The ovary is positioned superior. It consists of 2 (rarely 5) united carpels (syncarpous) with the partition walls present, forming an equal number of chambers. It matures as a capsule, nut, or "drupe", (a fleshy fruit with a stoney pit.)

World-wide there are about 13 genera and 800 species in the Milwort family. The two genera below are found in North America. Milkworts are somewhat rare in the north and west, much more numerous in the east, especially in the south and southwest.

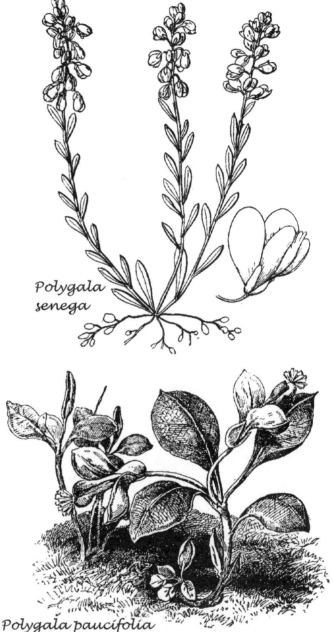

Polygala senega

Polygala paucifolia

Key Words
Irregular flowers with milky stems.

Monnina— (80/1/0) *M. wrightii* grows in Arizona and New Mexico.

Polygala—Milkwort, Snakeroot (500/60/2) Seneca snakeroot is *P senega*, native to eastern North America. The roots contain 8 to 16% triterpenoid saponins. The saponins irritate the stomach lining, causing nausea which subsequently stimulates bronchial secretions and the sweat glands (Tyler). A tea of the dried root stimulates salivation and circulation; it is considered beneficial for lung disorders, but it is irritating to inflamed tissues. (Hutchins). A tea of the leaves is taken for coughs, bronchitis, and other chronic lung ailments. The plants are useful as digestive stimulants (Lust). Some species of milkwort were once believed to increase milk production in cows (Schauenberg), and herbal books still list milkwort as an herb to stimulate milk flow from nursing mothers (Lust). Milkwort is also used as an expectorant (Weiner).

114

Apiaceae (Umbelliferae)—Parsley Family

<u>Key Words:</u> Compound umbels. Usually hollow flower stalks.

If you want to find plants from the Parsley family just open your spice cabinet! Most members of the family contain rich, aromatic volatile oils, and many of them are common culinary spices, including: anise (*Pimpinella*), celery (*Apium*), chervil (*Anthriscus*), coriander (*Coriandrum*), caraway (*Carum*), cumin (*Cuminum*), dill (*Anethum*), fennel (*Foeniculum*), and parsley (*Petroselinum*). There are also a number of edible roots in the family including the carrot and parsnip. The herb gotu cola (*Hydrocotyle*) is also a member of this family.

For identification, the most distinctive pattern of the Parsley family is the "**compound umbels**". Notice that all the stems of the flower cluster radiate from a single point at the end of the stalk, kind of like an umbrella. At the end of each of these flower stems there is another umbrella of even smaller stems, hence the "compound umbrella" or "compound umbel". Looking closer you will also find that the tiny flowers have 5 sepals (small and underneath), 5 petals, and 5 stamens. The ovary is positioned inferior. It consists of 2 united carpels (bicarpellate) with the partitions present, forming an equal number of chambers. It matures as a "schizocarp", a dry fruit which splits apart into individual one-seeded carpels (mericarps) when dry.   World-wide there are 300 genera and 3000 species. About 75 genera are native to North America.

Although so many plants of this family are quite *edible*, the family also includes some of the most *deadly* plants in North America, and people die every year thinking they have discovered wild carrots or something like it. When you see the compound umbel, let it be your warning—you *must* get positive identification of these plants!

Medicinally, the *volatile oils* of the Parsley family are stimulating and warming, causing the body to open up and sweat; thus most of the plants are diaphoretic or sudorific. This property can help you break a fever. A fever is the body's way of "cooking" the microorganisms that cause infections. Using a diaphoretic herb can help raise a mild fever just high enough to kill a virus, thus "breaking" the fever. Note, however, that diaphoretics can be dangerous where there is already a high fever, and other compounds, such as aspirin, should be used to reduce the fever. Diaphoretics tend to be most effective if used at the very onset of a cold. Volatile oils also have a decongestant effect, as you'll notice when your nose runs after a spicy meal. Intensely diaphoretic plants may even stop venereal diseases.

Plants with volatile oils are also used as carminatives to expel gas. They are often anti-viral as well. Some members of this family stimulate menstruation (emmenagogue) and relieve menstrual cramps. They are sometimes used in conjunction with child-birth, but may be dangerous during a pregnancy. Celery contains furanocoumarins. The juice on the skin can cause dermatitis when exposed to sunlight.

Poisonous Plants in the Parsley Family

Berula—Creeping Water Parsnip (1/1/1) *B. erecta* is reported to be poisonous (Pammel).

Cicuta—Water hemlock (-/7/2) • Water hemlock is the deadliest plant in North America! The whole plant is toxic, with the highest concentrations in the roots and the base of the stalks (Harrington). It affects the central nervous system, causing convulsions and quick death. Some victims chew their tongues to shreds. Remarkably, it has been used medicinally as an emetic (with mixed results!), and as a poultice for snake bites (Hart). Numerous people have died from eating hemlock.

Conium—Poison hemlock (2/1/1) • *Conium* is a little less poisonous than *Cicuta*, but not much. The most toxic parts are in the leaves and stems. *Conium* was used to execute Socrates (Lust). It causes paralysis rather than convulsions (Harrington).

Sium—Water parsnip (-/-/1) The leaves and stems are reported to be deadly to livestock. The roots may be edible, but the plant looks so much like *Cicuta*, that it should be avoided.

Cicuta maculata

115

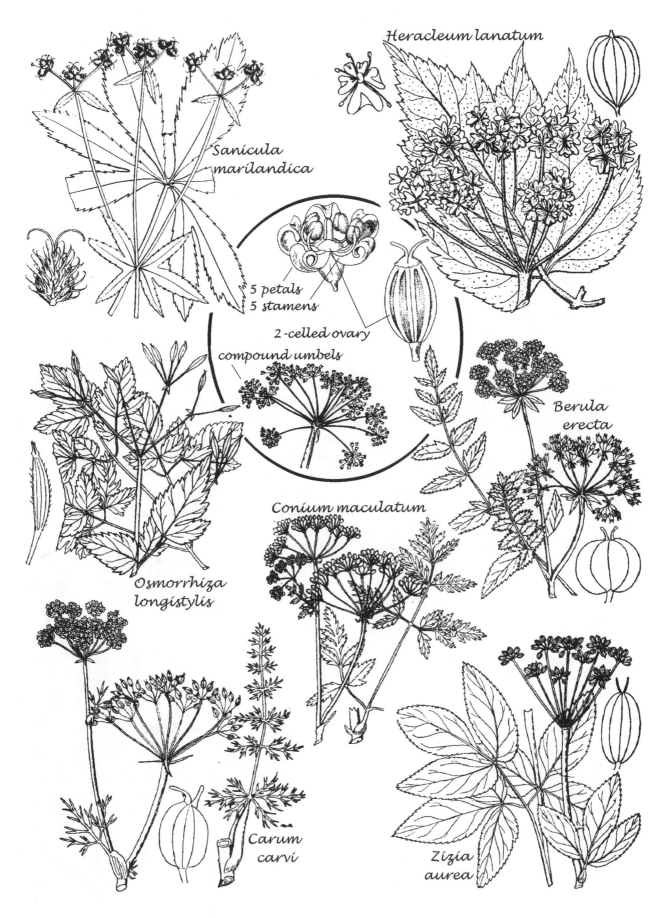

Sanicula
marilandica

Heracleum lanatum

5 petals
5 stamens

2-celled ovary

compound umbels

Berula
erecta

Osmorrhiza
longistylis

Conium maculatum

Carum
carvi

Zizia
aurea

116

Edible an Medicinal Plants in the Parsley Family

Angelica—Angelica, Don Quai (50/21/4) • The peeled, boiled roots of *A. archangelica* are edible (Brown), but most other species of *Angelica* are strongly medicinal. The roots and seeds are diaphoretic, diuretic, antispasmodic, and carminative. The boiled seeds are an aromatic bitter for indigestion. A tea of the root is a menstrual stimulant and antispasmodic for cramps (Moore). It may relieve severe headaches. Excess dosage may affect heartrate and blood pressure (Brown). Angelica increases the sugar level in the blood. The plants contain coumarins (Schauenberg). I sometimes chew on the raw root for its anti-viral qualities, a substitut for *Linguisticum* (below). Angelica is not recommended for people of "weak constitution" (Hobbs). Note: Don Quai is *A. polymorpha* from China.

Bupleurum— (-/3/1) Several species of *Bupleurum* are used in Chinese medicine. The root is bitter and slightly acrid. It is used torestore normal liver function, especially in patients with hepatitis (Hobbs).

Carum—Caraway (25/-/1) • Caraway is a domestic herb and spice that is often found growing wild. Medicinally, it is antispasmodic, carminative, and stimulating to digestion, menstruation, lactose production, and as an expectorant. The leaves and root are edible. Some species have bigger roots than others (Sturtevant).

Cymopterus—Biscuit Root (-/31/5) The roots, leaves, and flowers are edible (Sweet). The seeds are used as a digestive aid. The leaves are used to stimulate sluggish menstruation and to help urinary infections (Moore). I've never been able to determine the difference between *Cymopterus* and *Lomatium*.

Daucus—Carrot (60/2/1) • Wild carrots produce edible roots and seeds The domestic carrot was bred fromthis wild plant (Harrington). Wild carrots are not very common in Montana. Carrot seeds are carminative, anthelmintic, and stimulant. The potassium salts make carrot seeds and roots diuretic. Te root is also high in carotene, used by the body to make vitamin A (Lust).

Heracleum—Cow Parsnip (60/2/1) • Cow parsnip contains a potent volatile oil (Densmore) and a furanocoumarin (Schauenberg). The young stalks are minimally edible. The root and seeds are antispasmodic, carminative and expectorant (Willard). A tea f the root is good for nausea, gas and indigestion. The fresh root is acrid and should be dried prior to using. A bath, poultice, or tea of the fresh root is used to treat paralysis (Moore, Willard). The mature, green seeds have an analgesic effect on the teeth and gums (Tilford).

Ligusticum—Osha, Lovag (-/11/5) • The seeds and leaves are dried and used as spice. The root is chewed as a potent diaphoretic, anesthetic, bitter and expectorant. Osha is a popular and effective herb, particularly favored for viral infections (Moore). It is listed as emmenagogue and diuretic (Lust) and is also taken for headaches (Willard).

Lomatium—Biscuit root (-/78/11) • Some biscuit rots are strongly medicinal, while others are quite edible and easy to harvest. The individual species are all very different from each other and often similar in appearance to other parsleys, including some poisonous ones. These plants are not for amateurs. Be sure of what you have before you start working with these. A one-hour harvest of *L. cous-cous* in the Pryor Mountains of south-central Montana yielded a quart of delicious, starchy roots. I spent an additional two hours washing and peeling the roots, but this coud probably be done significantly faster.

Medicinally, *L. dissectum* is valued for its antiviral propertie, especially for repiratory infections like the flu or pneumonia, plus tonsilitis and pharyngitis (Klein). I use it as a good substitute for osha (*Ligusticum*).

Musineon— (-/-/2)

Orogenia—Indian potato (-/2/1) • The roots are edible raw or cooked (Craighead, Harrington). Olsen considers it one of thetastiest foods in the west.

Osmorhiza—Sweet Cicely (11/9/5) • Sweet cicely root has a powerful anise-like aroma, although the intensity varies by species. Most people like the smell, but some find it intensely repelling. I have used a tea of the root for flavoring cookies. Medicinally, the root has antiviral, expectorant, and mildly laxative properties (Willard). It contains a volatile oil composed mostly of anethol (Densmore). It is listed as carminative, expectorant, and a digestive stimulant (Lust). Sweet cicely may help to balance the blood sugar , while also inhibiting fungal infections of the digestive and reproductive systems (Tilford).

Pastinaca—Parsnip (14/1/1) • *P. sativa* was introduced from Europe. The roots are edible and delicious, either raw or cooked. The green plant contains furanocoumarins and may cause dermatitis on contact with sweaty skin (Pammel).

Perideridia—Yampa (-/13/1) • Yampa roots are one of my favorite wild edibles. They are okay raw, but abolutely delicious cooked. Using a simple digging stick I found I could dig 1 cup of roots per hour. This was in grainy soil that did not hold moistre very long. In better soils the roots can be three times as large; this suggests that you may be able to dig up to 3 cups per hour of work. Also, the seeds can be used as seasoning (Willard). Medicinally, eating the seeds is good for indigestion (Sweet).

Sanicula—Sanicle (40/17/1) The plant contains saponins, tannic acid, bitters, and volatile oils (Schauenberg); it is used as an astringent, expectorant, and nervine (Lust).

Zizia— (-/3/2)

Araliaceae—Ginseng Family

Aralia nudicaulis

The next time you see a building covered with ivy (*Hedera*), stop and notice the umbels of flowers or berries. Note that they form single umbels, not compound like the closely related Parsley family. A few members of the family produce flowers and berries in dense heads or elongated spikes rather than umbels. Botanically, these plants typically produce very small greenish-white flowers with 5 small sepals, 5 petas (sometimes 4 or 10), and usually 5 stamens (sometimes 3-numerous). The stamens are alternate with the petals. The flowers are regular and may be either unisexual or bisexual. The ovary is positioned inferior. It consists of 5 (sometimes 2-15) united carpels (syncarpous) with the partition walls present, forming an equal number of chambers. It matures as a red or purple berry with one seed per carpel. The fruit splits apart at the carpels in some species. The plants of this family prefer moist environments.

World-wide there are 70 genera and 700 species. The genera listed below are native to North America. *Volatile oils* are common in the Ginseng family, useful as diaphoretics to stimulate sweating. Read more about volatile oils in the Medicinal Properties section of this book.

English ivy (*Hedera helix*) also contains volatile oils, and it is very bitter. It has been used externally to treat dermatitis, inflammations and burns. Ivy has been used internally to expel parasites and to treat gout, rheumatism and bronchitis, but caution is advised since the plant is mildly toxic, probably due to the triterpene saponins. *Schefflera* is a common house plant. Note that ginger (*Zingiber*) is in a separate family, *Zingiberaceae*.

Key Words
Plants of the damp forest
with umbels (not compound) and berries.

Aralia—Wild Sarsaparilla, Spikenard (30/4/1) • Wild sarsaparilla is considered a substitute for the true sarsaparilla (*Smilax spp.* of the Lily family), and either may be used for flavoring rootbeer. Medicinally, it contains an acrid resin (Densmore). It is diaphoretic and stimulant. It also has demulcent properties (Willard). A tea of the root is commonly used for colds and coughing, even pneumonia. It can also stimulate menstruation, if it has been delayed by health stress (Moore). A poultice of the root is used on burns, sore, ringworm, and skin eruptions. It is also used for intestinal gas, and is reportedly a strong antidote for deadly poisons (Willard). Note: sasparilla is an unrelated tree, also used in the production of rootbeer.

Oplopanax—Devil's Club (1/1/1) • *Oplopanax* is used similarly to *Aralia*, as a respiratory stimulant and expectorant for chest coldss. It also has a history of use as a hypoglycemic, to lower blood sugar and reduce or eliminate the need for injected insuin in cases of adult onset iabetes. A poultice of the root has analgesic properties. A tea and bath of the root is used for rheumatism and arthritis (Willard). Herbalist Keith Hess reported that the cut stalks will often take root when inserted into the moist ground.

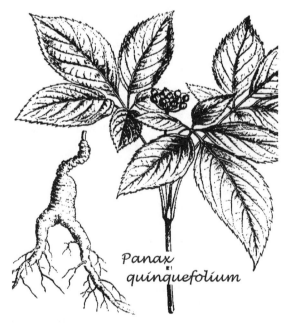

Panax quinquefolium

Panax—Ginseng (6/2/0) Ginseng is rich in volatile oils, used especially as a diaphoretic, but also to counteract nausea and the double vision that can accompany dizziness (Kadans).

Gentianaceae—Gentian Family

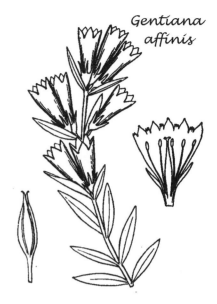

Gentiana affinis

The gentians have distinctive, cup-shaped blossoms. They are usually bisexual and regular with 4 or 5 separate sepals, 4 or 5 united petals, and 4 or 5 stamens. The stamens are inserted on the corolla tube and alternate with the lobes. The ovary is positioned superior. It conists of 2 united carpels (bicarpellate), forming a single chamber. It matures as a capsule with many seeds. The leaves are mostly opposite, but some species of *Frasera* have leaves in whorls of three or four.

World-wide there are 70 genera and 1100 species. Thirteen genera are native to North America, including *Bartonia, Eustoma, Obolaria, Nymphoides, Nephrophyllidium, Sabbatia* and the genera listed below. Some botanists include the Buckbean family (*Menyanthaceae*) with the Gentians.

Most members of the Gentian family contain potent *bitter* principles that stimulate the digestive system. You must taste the bitterness in your mouth for it to take effect. The bitter taste signals the nervous system to release digestive fluids all the way down, from saliva to gastric acid, to bile. Sampling bitter herbs shortly before a meal will help get your digestive system ready for the main course; this can help prevent indigestion. The release of fluids throughout the digestive system also helps loosen the bowels to relieve constipation.

Volatile oils are also present in the Gentian family, and some species have been used to expel worms. This anthelmentic effect may be due to the combination of bitters and volatile oils. For additional informaton about bitters and volatile oils be sure to read the Medicinal Properties section of this book.

<u>Key Words</u>
Plants with opposite leaves and tubular flowers with parts in 4's or 5's.

Centaurium—Centaury (40/15/1) The plant is stimulating to the digestive system, benefiting the liver and kidneys. It is also used as a diaphoretic, suggesting the presence of volatile oils (Hutchins).

Frasera—Deer's Tongue (15/-/2) • The plant has mild bitter qualities, while the raw root is emetic and cathartic, at least in some species. The dried root is used as a bitter, but caution is advised as large doses of the powdered root have been fatal (Fern). A tea of the plant was taken as a contraceptive (Vogel). The seeds are very bitter.

Gentiana acaulis

Gentiana—Gentian (200/56/7) • Gentian root contains some of the most bitter compounds known in the plant world. Gentian bitters were once used in beer making and in many medicines (Fern). The root or chopped herb is steeped for use as a bitter tonic for indigestion and as an appetite stimulant (Moore). Gentian is used as a blood-builder to increase the number of white blood cells (Lust) It is also used to expel worms (Bigfoot). Excess consumption of gentian can lead to nausea, vomiting, or diarrhea. Gentian has mild anti-inflammatory properties. A tea of the root was used externally by some ative Americans to relieve back pains (Weiner).

Gentianella— (-/-/5) Gentianella is similar to the true gentian and may be substituted for it (Fern).

Halenia— Spurred Gentian (-/2/1)

Lomatogonium—Felwort (1/1/1) *L. rotatum* is found from Alaska to Maine and south through the Rocky Mountains.

Swertia—Cebadilla (100/15/1) The powdered, dried root is steeped for a bitter tonic; it is stronger and more irritating than *entiana*, potentially laxative or cathartic. The root can be used as a fungicide for ringworm, athlete's foot, also for lice and scabies (Moore). The leaves may be toxic (Bigfoot).

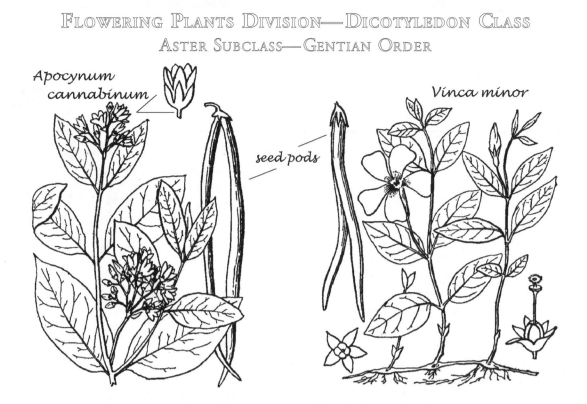

Apocynum cannabinum

Vinca minor

seed pods

Apocynaceae—Dogbane Family

The herbs, shrubs and trees of the Dogbane family typically have a milky, latex sap, and most are poisonous to some degree. The flowers are bisexual and regular, with 5 united sepals, 5 united petals (forming a funnel), and 5 stamens. The stamens are attached at the base of the corolla and alternate with the lobes. The ovary is positioned wholly or mostly superior. It consists of 2 carpels, usually separate in Norh American genera, united only at the styles. Each carpel matures as a separate "follicle", a pod-like dry fruit with a seam down one side. There are many seeds, often with a tuft of hair attached at one end. Some genera produce berries or capsules.

World-wide there are 200 genera and 2000 species, including 11 genera in North America. This family is closey related to th Milkweed family. Periwinkle (*Vinca*) is often used in landscaping. The oleander (*Nerium oleander)* is grown as an ornamental (and toxic) shrub in warmer parts of our country. Oleander contains cardiac glycosides (Geller). Children have died after roasting hot dogs on the sticks.

<u>Key Words</u>
Plants with opposite leaves and milky juice. Tubular flowers with parts in 5's

Apocynum—Dogbane (7/6/3) • All dogbanes produce durable fiber in the stalks that can be used for cordage, but *A. cannabinum* is the best of them. This dogbane is more potent than other species and should not be used medicinally (Moore). The root of *A. androsaemifolium* is used internally as a vasoconstrictor. It raises blood pressure and slows, but strengthens the heart rate. It is a potent diuretic, an irritating stimulant to the kidneys. Externally the root can be used as an irritating poultice to stimulate blood flow (vasodilator) and speed healing, or as a rinse to irritate the scalp and stimulate hair gowth (Moore). Dogbane is also listed as diaphoretic, cathartic, and expectorant (Lust). It contains resins, a volatile oil, a bitter substance (Densmore) and cardiac glycosides (Phillips). It should not be used internally by amateurs.

Vinca—Periwinkle (6/4/D) • *Vinca* and *Catharanthus* are closely related and both called periwinkle. They are ommonly domesticated and often escape into the wild. *Vinca* is used medicinally as an internal astringent for excess menstrua-tion, hemorrhoids, bleeding ulcers and diarrhea (Willard). As a capillary constrictor it may be useful for migraine headaches (Tilford). The dried leaves have been smoked as a hallucinogen, but with serious side effects. It causes an immediate reduction in the white blood cell count, and makes the hair fall out (Emboden)! Vinblastine and vincristine are two indole alkaloids derived from a species of periwinkle, used in the treatment of blood and lymph cancers.

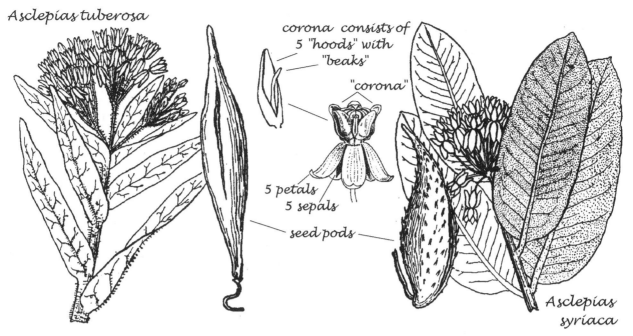

Asclepias tuberosa

corona consists of 5 "hoods" with "beaks"

"corona"

5 petals
5 sepals

seed pods

Asclepias syriaca

Asclepiadaceae—Milkweed Family

The Milkweeds are perennial herbs, shrubs, or rarely trees usually with acrid, milky juice and opposite or sometimes whorled leaves. The flowers are bisexual, and regular, typically grouped in clusters. There are 5 sepals and petals, plus a "corona" (different from the "corolla") that looks like an extra set of petals. The corona consists of 5 hood-like forms facing towards the center of the flower. Inside the corona there are 5 stamens fused to the ovary. The ovary is positioned superior. It consists of 2 mostly separate carpels. Each carpel matures as a separate "follicle", a pod-like dry fruit with a seam down one side. The pods are filled with numerous seeds with silky tufts. World-wide there are 250 genera and 2000 species, mostly native to the tropics. The waxplant (*Hoya*) is a common house plant from this family. There are 5 genera across the United States including *Cynanchum*, *Gonolobus*, *Matelea*, and *Sarcostemma*.

Key Words:
Plants with opposite leaves, milky juice, and big pods. Irregular, crown-like flowers.

Asclepias—Milkweed (80+/77/5) • In the northeast states and possibly elsewhere, milkweeds contain a bitter, milky sap that is poisonous when raw, but the young shoots, tender tops, flower buds, or young seed pods can be eaten as a potherb when properly cooked. Note: the toxic alkaloid becomes fixed if placed in cold water and gradually boiled. The proper method is to plunge the herbs into rapidly boiling water for two minutes, drain the water, then repeat the process two more times. If all bitterness is gone then the herbs are safe (Gail). Narrow-leafed species typically have more toxins than wide-leafed species (Tilford). The blossoms are high in sugar and can be boiled down to make a syrup (Willard). Milkweeds in other parts of the country are completely free of bitterness and are safe to eat either raw or cooked without any special preparation, although moderation is certainly advised. The silk from tender young pods is also edible raw or cooked (Thayer).

    The constituents of the genus include a volatile oil, resins (Densmore) and a cardiac glycoside (Phillips). Medicinally, at least some milkweeds have a bitter latex sap that can be used to irritate and stimulate the body. The boiled root dilates the bronchioles, stimuating lymph drainage from the lungs for lung infections. It is used as a menstrual stimulant, lactose stimulant, laxative, bitter diuretic, diaphoretic, expectorant, and the root powder can be snuffed to promote sneezing to clear the sinus. Some species may poduce nausea (Moore). Long-term consumption may lead to depression or death (Willard). The latex sap can be applied repeatedly to remove a wart (Hutchins). A boiled tea of the herb applied to the eyes may have some effect on blindness (Hart).

    A. tuberosa is the Pleurisy Root or Butterfly Weed. It is diaphoretic, carminative, expectorant, and diuretic. A tea of the dried or cooked root is used for colds, flu, and bronchitis. The raw root may be poisonous (Lust).

    Milkweed, particularly *A. speciosa*, is an excellent fiber plant like it's cousin the dogbane. It produces a beautiful, silky white cordage. This species can frequently be found growing in semi-moist ditches along the highways.

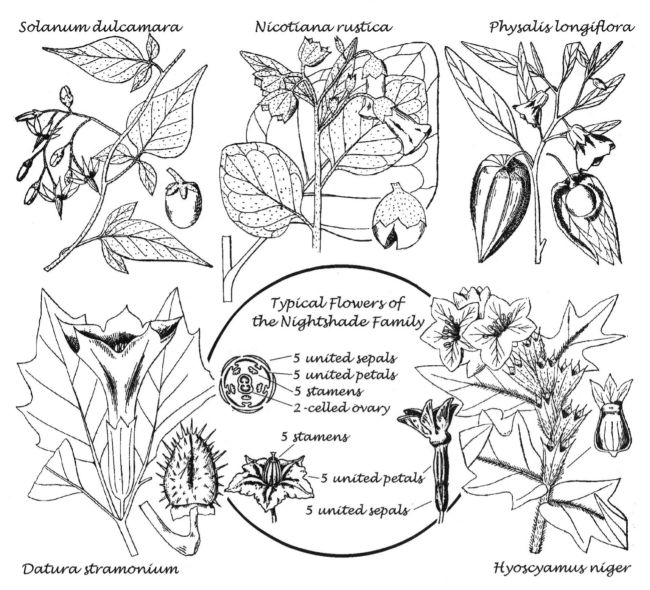

Solanum dulcamara

Nicotiana rustica

Physalis longiflora

Typical Flowers of
the Nightshade Family

5 united sepals
5 united petals
5 stamens
2-celled ovary

5 stamens

5 united petals

5 united sepals

Datura stramonium

Hyoscyamus niger

Solanaceae—Nightshade Family

Stop and study the next tomato, potato, or pepper flower you come across and you will quickly learn the Nightshade family. These are herbs with alternate leaves and colorless juice. They have solitary, bisexual, regular flowers with 5 separate or united sepals (rarely 3, 4, or 6) and 5 united petals. There are 5 stamens inserted on the tube. The ovary is positioned superior. It consists of 2 united carpels (bicarpellate) with the partition walls often present, but more obvious in wild species than domestics. Cut across a maturing berry (like the tomato) or a capsule (like a *Petunia*) and you will usually see the two chambers inside. World-wide there are 85 genera and 2300 species, including many of our favorite foods. Thirteen genera are native to North America. The tomato is the genus *Lycopersicon*. Bell peppers, chili peppers, jalapeno peppers, paprika, and tabasco all come from the *Capsicum* genus. *Physalis* is the tomatillo. *Solanum* includes the potato and egg-plant. Belladonna is *Atropa*, and the petunia flower is from the genus *Petunia*. The genus *Nicotiana* gives us tobacco.

Chemically, the pattern of this family is alkaloids and lots of them. Many species of this family are narcotic. A **narcotic** is any alkaloid that depresses the central nervous system; they are toxic in excess. They are used especially for their analgesic properties. An analgesic numbs the body's sense of pain, like opium or morphine. For similar reasons, a few of these species are useful as sedatives. Some depressants can cause hallucinations, including *Atropa*, *Datura*, *Hyoscyamus*, and *Mandragora*. Our European heritage of witches flying on broom sticks comes from these hallucinogenic plants. An ointment containing *Atropa* and *Hyosyamus* was rubbed on the broom stick, then absorbed through the vaginal tissues, by "riding" the broom (Emboden). The "witches" then experienced "flying". It should be noted that these plants are all extremely poisonous, with a toxicity that varies from plant to plant. Many individuals have died while attempting to hallucinate. Symptoms of poisoning include an unquenchable thirst, dilation of the eyes, delirium, hallucinations, convulsions and coma. The alkaloid scopolamine is used medicinally today to treat seasickness or vertigo. Soldiers in the Persian Gulf War carried the alkaloid atropine with them as a treatment for nerve gas attacks (Duke). The juice of *Atropa* was used by Italian ladies as eyedrops to dilate the pupils, hence the common name belladonna, meaning "fair-lady" (Klein). Plants with parts that are free of alkaloids are often our food plants.

Key Words
Alternate leaves. Flower parts in 5's with united petals and a two-celled ovary.

Capsicum—Red Pepper, Bell Pepper, Chilis, Jalapeno, Cayenne, Tabasco (35/-/D) Peppers are mostly native to Central and South America, and a few wild species are found as far north as our southern states. Any wild or domestic members of the genus with a pungent fruit should contain capsaicin and other active constituents. Capsaicin is applied topically as an analgesic. It works by depleting "substance P", the compound which mediates the transmission of pain impulses from the peripheral nerves to the spinal cord. Capsaicin doesn't stop the pain, but it prevents the signal from reaching the brain. It is especially helpful for people who still feel pain weeks or months after surgery. A commercial product is marketed as "Capsaicin P". It takes about three days to become effective. People who eat hot peppers develop higher and higher tolerances, apparently due to the numbing effect of the capsaisin ("Hot Stuff"). Cayenne pepper is good to have in the first aid kit. Internally it increases circulation, stimulates digestion and helps to treat shock. Externally the powder can be applied to stop bleeding, reduce pain, and increase circulation (Sheff).

       Peppers may be used as irritants to warm the skin without causing blisters, but caution is advised to avoid getting it in your eyes. Pepper oils are not easily soluble in water, so traces can remain on your hands even after you washed them. I learned this after making jalapeno salsa. On the way to the airport later that evening, my eyes suddenly felt like they were on fire. The more I rubbed my eyes the more it hurt! It took me a few minutes to make the connection. If you do get it in your eyes, or your mouth is on fire, just use a little olive oil or some other vegetable oil to wash it out. Don't use water, as that will repel the oil and drive it in even more.

Datura—Jimson Weed (18/7/1) • Narcotic. Contains scopolamine, hyoscyamine, and atropine. *Datura* is a very dangerous plant, and many individuals have died from misusing it. Do not ingest any part of the plant, period. A small amount of smoke from the leaves can be used to numb and relax the bronchials for asthma and bronchitis; it also brings temporary sinus relief, probably by numbing the area. A poultice or bath of the fresh plant can be used for its analgesic properties (aching joints, etc.) An extended bath can result in absorption of alkaloids through the skin and lead to drowsiness (Moore). The poultice may have some effect on rattlesnake or tarantula bites (Hutchins).

Chamaesaracha— (-/4/0)

Hyoscyamus—Henbane (15/1/1) • *H. niger* was introduced from Europe. It is now widespread in areas of disturbed soils. My grandmother picked henbane during World War II; it was used as an analgesic for wounded soldiers. Henbane contains atropine, hyoscyamine, and scopolamine (Schauenberg). It should never be eaten. The plant is used similarly to *Datura* (Hutchins).

Lycium—Matrimony Vine (110/-/1) The red berries are edible fresh or cooked. They are said to have a "bitter-astringent" taste, and can be mixed in equal portions with food clay (bentonite) to remove the bitterness (Harrington). A tea of the leaves is taken to dry the lungs in pleurisy. A tea of the berries is taken as an eye tonic to improve vision (Bigfoot).

Margaranthus—

Nicotiana—Wild Tobacco (100/12/1) Wild tobacco is rare in the north, but more common in the south. The fresh herb is used as a poultice or bath for an analgesic. The leaves can be smoked (Moore). Nicotine is a toxic alkaloid, chemically similar to the poisonous water hemlock. It was one used as a pesticide, but caused numerous human fatalities (Schauenberg). It should never be taken internally.

Petunia— (14/-/D) •

Physalis— Husk Tomato (110/34/3) • As I understand it the tomatillo (i.e.: green salsa) was bred from this genus. Our species produce yellow fruits. They are initially sweet, but with a slightly bitter, lingering after-taste. I think they are a real treat when I can find them. The green fruits should not be eaten raw (Bigfoot).

Saracha— (-/-/0)

Solanum—Nightshade, Bittersweet, Potato, Buffalo Bur (1500/40/5) • Most species of *Solanum* contain the toxic alkaloid solanine, especially in green parts of the plants (i.e.: green potato peels). *S. jamesii* produces an edible wild potato found in the southwestern states. *S. nigrum* has edible black berries, while the other species with green or red berries are toxic. Medicinally, members of this genus are used externally as an analgesic poultice or bath (Hutchins). The fresh plant is too dangerous to be used internally without expert assistance.

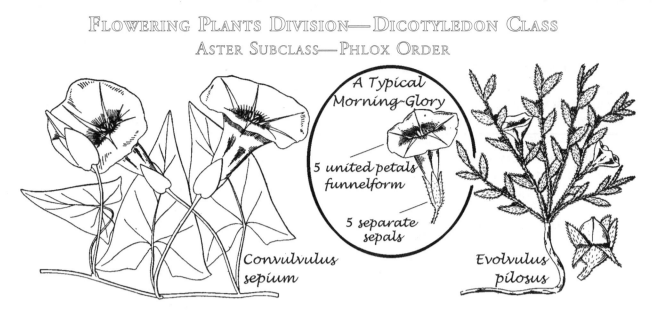

A Typical Morning-Glory

5 united petals funnelform

5 separate sepals

Convulvulus sepium

Evolvulus pilosus

Convolvulaceae—Morning-Glory Family

If you have ever seen a morning-glory blosom then you will know this family. The flowers are regular and bisexual with 5 separate sepals and 5 united petals. The corolla (petals) is often slightly twisted, and it may have a star pattern inside. There are 5 stamens attached at the base of the flower tube. The ovary is positioned superior. It consists of 2 (someimes 3-5) united carpels (syncarpous) with the partition walls present, forming an equal number of chambers. It matures as a capsule with 1-2 seeds per carpel. World-wide there are 50 genera and 1400-1650 species, including 10 genera in North America. The sweet potato belongs to the genus *Ipomoea*. Several members of this family contain ***ergoline-type alkaloids***, similar to those found in the ergot fungus (see *Poaceae*). Kids have purchased morning-glory seed packets and ingested them to get high.

Key Words:
Often vining plants with tubular, funnel-form flowers, parts in 5's. Sepals separate, petals united.

Convolvulus—Bindweed (250/28/2) • The bindweeds contain glycosides with potent purgative properties (Pammel).

Cuscuta—Dodder (170/-/7) Dodder is a parasitic plant, sometimes separated into its own family. At maturity the plant is generally yellow-orange in color, with no apparent roots or leaves. It feeds off of many different plants, but especially legumes. Medicinally, it contains the strongly laxative anthraquinone glycosides (Schauenberg) (see Glycosides), also used to reduce inflammation in the spleen and lymph nodes (Moore).

Evolvulus— (-/6/1)

Ipomoea—Bush Morning Glory, Sweet Potato (400/51/1) • The sweet potato is a member of this genus. Other species have similarly enlarged taproots that are edible, although sometimes bitter. Our species in Montana is *I. leptophylla*. It can have roots 1 foot thick and 4 feet deep. The boiled or roasted root is reported to be qite exceptional, although older plants with bigger roots may have some bitterness (Harrington). *I. pandurata* is the wild potato vine of the southeastern states. It also has remarkably large roots. It is edible, but may require a couple changes of the water to remove the bitterness (Hall). The bitterness comes from the milky sap present in the fresh roots of each of these species, an indication of mild latex and/or alkaloid properties. Bush morning glory is more prevalent south of Montana. The root of *I. jalapa* is listed as cathartic (Lust). The seeds of many *Ipomoea* species have psychoactive properties (Emboden).

Menyanthaceae—Buckbean Family

This is a small family of aquatic plants. The flowers are regular, bisexual, and tubular. There are 5 sepals, mostly separate, and 5 petals, united into a funnel form. There are 5 stamens, attached to the corolla tube. The ovary is positioned superior and consists of 2 united carpels (bicarpellate), forming a single-celled capsule with many seeds. Our species are semi-aquatic, preferring marshy soils. Wold-wide there are 5 genera and 33 species.

Menyanthes—Bogbean, Buckbean (-/2/1) Bog bean contains a bitter substance. The fresh plant is emetic. The dried plant functions as a bitter to stimulate digestion, relieve gas, and act as a cathartic. It is high in vitamin C, iron and iodine, and is thus used as a tonic for general health (Willard). The roots are sometimes crushed and washed to remove the bitterness, then used as flour (Sturtevant).

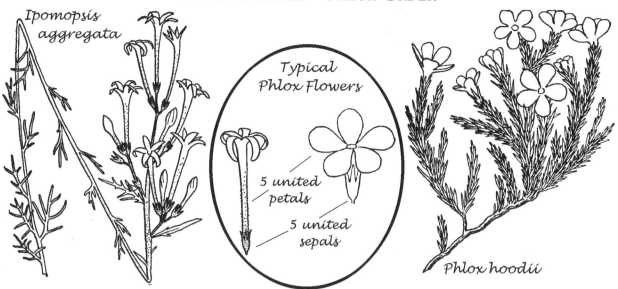

Ipomopsis aggregata

Typical Phlox Flowers

5 united petals

5 united sepals

Phlox hoodii

Polemoniaceae—Phlox Family

Members of the Phlox family are usually small plants with narrow leaves adapted to arid environments, especially the western states. A few species take the form of shrubs or trees in other parts of the world. The delicate flowers are regular and bisexual, usually forming a tube at the base and flattening out to form a dish-like face. There are 5 united sepals, but they may appear mostly separate. There are 5 united petals, usually twisted in the bud stage. There are 5 stamens attached to the corolla and alternate with the petals. (In a few species there are 4 sepals, petals and stamens.) The ovary is positioned superior. It consists of 3 (sometimes 2 or 5) united carpels (syncarpous) with the partition walls usually present, forming an equal number of chambers. It matures as a capsule with 1 to numerous seeds.

World-wide there are 18 genera and 320 species, mostly in the Western hemisphere. Eleven genera are present in North America, as listed below. Medicinally, many of these plants have seeds containing mucilage. The plants also contain inulin polysaccharides, saponins, and flavanoids (Zomlefer).

<u>Key Words</u>
5 united petals forming tubular flowers with a flat face. Usually narrow leaves.

Collomia— (14/11/4) • The seeds contain significant amounts of mucilage (Craighead).

Eriastrum (Hugelia)— (-/12/0)

Gillia— (56/70/3) • Some species may contain saponin (Craighead).

Ipomopsis— (-/-/5)

Langloisia— (-/4/0)

Leptodactylon— (-/-/2)

Linanthus— (-/35/2)

Microsteris— (1/1/1) • *M. gracilis* grows from Alaska to Baja California and east to the Rocky Mountians.

Navarretia— (30/30/3) The seeds of *N. squarrosa* are reported to be edible, typically parched and pulverized. A tea of *N. leucocephala* was used on swellings (Sweet).

Phlox— (61/60/11) • We have large patches of *P. longifolia* on our property. This phlox especially loves the drought years, blooming as a spectacular carpet of white and pinkish flowers with dozens of blossoms on every little plant. It is a refreshing reminder that drought is not the tradgedy we often make it out to be, but part of the natural flow of things. Medicinally, the boiled leaves are used as a drawing poultice (Murphey).

Polemonium— (23/20/4) A tea of the herb has diaphoretic properties (Kadans).

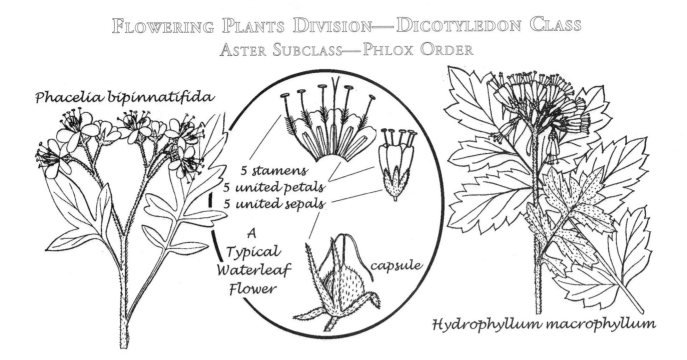

Phacelia bipinnatifida

5 stamens
5 united petals
5 united sepals

A Typical Waterleaf Flower

capsule

Hydrophyllum macrophyllum

Hydrophyllaceae—Waterleaf Family

The flowers of this family often have a "dainty" appearance because the stamens stick so far out of the little blossoms. The flowers are typically small and often clustered together. The flower stalks often curl over, much like a scorpion tail. The flowers are regular and bisexual with 5 united sepals, 5 united petals and 5 stamens attached to the base of the petals. The ovary is positioned superior. It consists of 2 (rarely 4) united carpels (syncarpous), forming a single-celled ovary. It matures as a capsule with a variable number of seeds. The plants are usually hairy and may be confused with members of the Borage family. World-wide there are 20 genera and 270 species. Sixteen genera are native to North America, as listed below. The species I am familiar with seem mildly *astringent*.

<u>Key Words</u>
Small, hairy plants with parts in 5's, united.

Draperia— (1/1/0) *D. systyla* is found in the mountains of northern California.

Ellisia—Aunt Lucy (1/1/0 *E. nyctelea* is found from the plains eastward.

Emmenanthe—Whispering Bells (1/1/0) *E. penduliflora* is found in the Arizona, southern Utah, and southern California.

Eriodictyon—Mountain Balm (10/-/0) Mountain Balm is native to the desert southwest The plant contains resins and phenols; it is smoked or madeinto tea for ue as an expectoant and bronchial dlator. Also use for mild infection of the urinary tract (Moore).

Eucrypta— (2/2/0) Both species of *Eucrypta* grow in the southwest.

Hesperochiron— (2/2/2) *Hesperochiron* grows from the Rocky Mountains west to the Pacific.

Hydrolea— (-/5/0)

Hydrophyllum—Waterleaf (8/-/1) • The leaves and shoots are edible in a salad. The roots are edible cooked (Kirk.

Lemmonia— (1/1/0) L. californica is found across the southern two-thirds of California.

Nama— (-/21/0) Most species of *Nama* are found in the southwestern states.

Nemophila—Baby Blue Eyes (11/11/1) •

Phacelia—Phacelia, Scorpionweed (130/8) • *P. racemosissima* was reportedly used b the Indians as a potherb (Kinucan). The flowers of some species have a unique smell that is sweet to some people and very offensive to others.

Pholistoma— (-/2/0) Both species grow in the southwest.

Romanzoffia—Mist Maiden (-/4/1)

Tricardia— (1/1/0) *T. watsonii* is found in Utah, Arizona, and southeastern California.

Turricula— (1/1/1) *T. parryi* is found in the mountains of southern California.

Verbenaceae—Verbena Family

Verbena hastata

The Verbena Family includes herbs, shrubs and a few trees. The leaves are usually opposite or whorled and sometimes aromatic. *Verbena* has squarish stems and may be confused with the Mints until you examine the flowers.

The flowers are mostly bisexual and slightly irregular. They bloom in elongated spikes. There are typically 5 united sepals and 5 united petals, forming a tube with unequal lobes. There are 4 stamens (sometimes 2 or 5 outside the continent). The ovary is positioned superior. It consists of 2 (rarely 4 or 5) united carpels (syncarpous) with the partition walls present, forming an equal number of chambers. (Additional false partitions may be present in some species.) The fruit matures as 1-2 nutlets per carpel within North America and often as a drupe or capsule in other parts of the world.

World-wide there are about 75 genera and 3000 species, including teak wood (*Tectona*) and the fast growing "white teak" (*Gmelina*). Fifteen genera are found in North America, mostly across the southern states. Only *Verbena* is widespread.

**<u>Key Words</u>: Opposite or whorled leaves.
Flower parts in 5's, united. Slightly irregular.**

Avicennia—Black Mangrove (11/-/0) Native to Florida.

Bouchea— (1/1/0) *B. prismatica* grows from Arizona east to Texas.

Callicarpa—French Mulberry (100/-/0) A native of the southern states.

Citharexylum—Fiddlewood (-/-/0) A native of the southern states.

Clerodendron—Glory-Bowers (390/-/0) Introduced from China.

Duranta—Golden-Dewdrop (25/-/0) A native of the southern states.

Lantana— (160/-/0) *L. horrida* is a toxic shrub native to and cultivated across the southern states from Arizona to Florida.

Lippia–– (-/-/0)

Phyla—Frog Fruit (15/-/0)

Priva—Velvet Bur (-/1/0) *P. lappulacea* grows from Arizona to west Texas.

Siphonanthus—Turk's Turban (-/-/0) Introduced from the East Indies.

Stachytarpheta (1/1/0) *S. jamaicensis* is found in Florida and southern Alabama.

Tetraclea— (-/2/0) Tetraclea grows in the southwest.

Verbena—Verbena, Vervain (230/47/3) • *Verbena* contains glycosides, tannins, bitters, and volatile oils (Schauenberg). Medicinally it is sedative, diaphoretic, diuretic, antispasmodic, and bitter tonic. The tea is considered an ideal treatment at the beginning of a virus cold, to relieve cold symptoms. It is also used to settle the stomach. The tea is bitter, and too much can cause nausea and vomiting (Moore). Verbena is also listed as astringent and as a lactose stimulant (Lust).

Vitex—Monk's Pepper, Chaste Tree (270/-/0) Introduced from the far East.

Boraginaceae—Borage Family

If you have ever pulled "beggar's ticks" (flat, tear-drop shaped stickers) from your clothes, then you have met one member of the Borage family, also called "hound's tongue" (*Cynoglossum spp.*) The plants of this family are often rough and hairy, usually with simple, alternate leaves. The flowers are bisexual and mostly regular. They have 5 separate sepals and 5 united petals. There are 5 stamens; these are attached to the corolla tube, alternate with the petals. The ovary is positioned superior. It consists of 2 united carpels (bicarpellate) and produces 4 separate nutlets or sometimes achenes (dry seeds). (False partitions may make the ovary appear 4-chambered.) Notice the variations in the nutlets among the examples. Some genera produce fewer than 4 nutlets due to abortion. You will usually be able to see the aborted nutlets around the developed ones. World-wide there are approximately 100 genera, representing about 2,000 species. About 22 genera are native to North America.

The flower spikes often curl like a scorpion tail with the flowers blooming on the upper surface, similar to members of the Waterleaf family (*Hydrophyllaceae*). Most members of the Borage family are also very hairy.

Medicinally these plants are primarily *astringent*, good internally as tea or externally as poultices for pretty much any wounds or excretions that need an astringent to tighten up the tissues. A few members of the family are also *mucilaginous*, useful for their *emollient* properties. Some contain volatile oils, and may serve as an antidote to poisons by functioning as diaphoretics. Many members of this family have irritating hairs that may cause dermatitis on some individuals. Also, several plants contain minute amounts of *poisonous alkaloids*, making them toxic with sustained use.

<u>Key Words</u>: Hairy plants with flower parts in 5's. 4 nutlets.

Amsinckia—Tarweed, Fiddlenick (20/14/2) The seeds are reported to be edible, ground on a metate and used as flour (Olsen). The protective hairs may irritate the skin. The seeds may be poisonous to cattle (Kinucan).

Anchusa—Alkanet (-/3/3) The leaves of at least some species are edible as a salad (Sturtevant). *A. officinale* contains alkaloids, tannin, and mucilage, used internally as an expectorant, "blood purifier", and to stop diarrhea. (Schauenberg).

Borago—Borage (3/1/1) • *B. officinale* is a European herb, often planted domestically in the U.S. The very young leaves can be used in salads or as potherbs. The plants have mucilaginous, astringent, diuretic, and diaphoretic properties. It is used to reduce fevers, stimulate milk production and calm nerves. As with other members of this family, long-term consumption is not recommended.

Cynoglossum—Hound's Tongue, Beggar's Ticks (68/6/1) • No doubt you have pulled the flat, tear-drop shaped seeds of this plant from your socks or woolens. *C. officinale* is a European weed that is now wide-spread across this country. Medicinally, hound's tongue contains allantoin (Tilford). The plant or root is principally astringent and demulcent, useful externally a poultice for burns, internally for sore throat or diarrhea (Hutchins). Hound's tongue is similar to comfrey (Moore) and includes similar, potentially carcinogenic alkaloids (Tilford). One alkaloid, cynoglossine, is toxic to cold-blood animals, but has little effect on mammals (Schauenberg); it may be useful as a fish poison.

Heliotropium—Heliotrope (220/23/1) A tea of the plant was reportedly taken as an emetic (Murphey). A European species contains a poisonous alkaloid (Pammel).

Lithospermum—Stoneseed; Gromwell (50/18/3) • Indians reportedly ate the root of *L. incisum* (Craighead), and *L. linearifolium* (A. Brown), however some species of gromwell contain toxic alkaloids and estrogen-like compounds that interfere with hormonal balances in the female reproductive system (Tilford). Some species were used by Native American women as a female contraceptive. Extended use may cause sterility (Vogel).

Mertensia—Bluebell (40/23/8) • Some species of *Mertensia* have wide leaves that serve well as a lid for steaming foods over a campfire. I eat bluebell leaves in limited quantities. They seem mildly astringent and mucilaginous.

Symphytum—Comfrey (17/4/1) • Comfrey is often planted domestically for its herbal properties. The root and leaves are astringent, mucilaginous and contain allantoin, useful externally on cuts and burns, internally as an expectorant and demulcent. The astringency makes comfrey useful for stopping bleeding and healing ulcers, while the mucilage soothes the irritated tissues.

Comfrey contains pyrrolizidine alkaloids which are toxic to the liver tissues. Toxicity is variable from species to species. People have died from chronic use of this herb (Tyler), but many herbalists consider it safe in moderation.

Other selected members of the Borage family:

Asperugo—Catchweed, Creeping Jenny (-/-/1) • … *Cryptantha*—Miner's Candle (150/113/13) • … *Echium*—Viper's Bugloss (50/2/1) … *Eritrichum*—Alpine Forget-Me-Not (-/6/2) • … *Hackelia*—Stickseed Forget-Me-Not (-/25/5) • … *Lappula*—Stickseed (-/-/2) … *Myosotis*—Forget-Me-Not (80/10/3) • … *Onosmodium*—Marble seed (-/3/1) … *Plagiobothrys*—Popcorn flower (60/46/2)

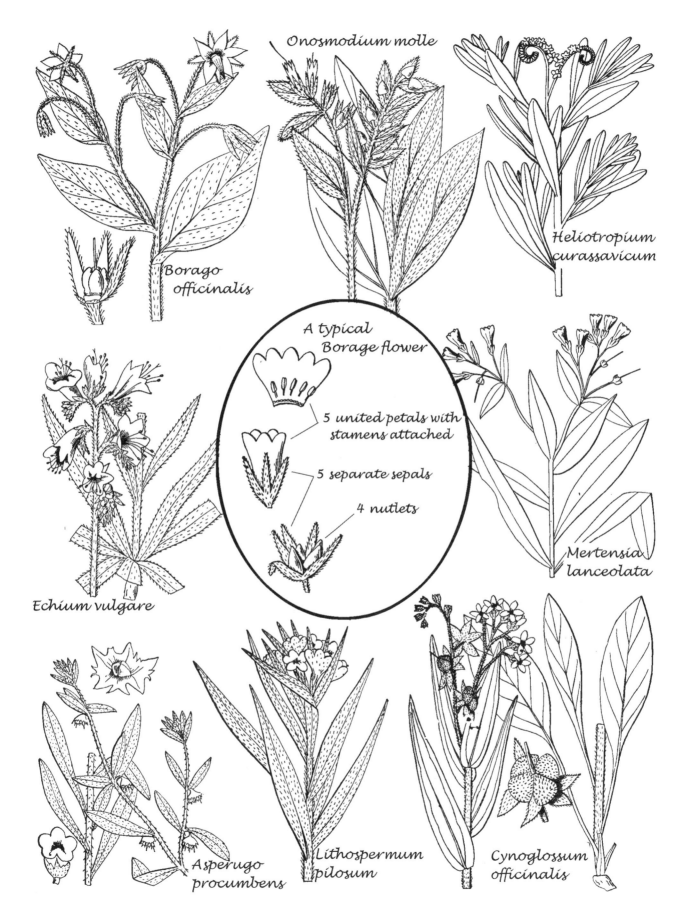

Onosmodium molle

Borago
officinalis

Heliotropium
curassavicum

A typical
Borage flower

5 united petals with
stamens attached

5 separate sepals

4 nutlets

Echium vulgare

Mertensia
lanceolata

Asperugo
procumbens

Lithospermum
pilosum

Cynoglossum
officinalis

129

Lamiaceae (also Labiatae)—Mint Family

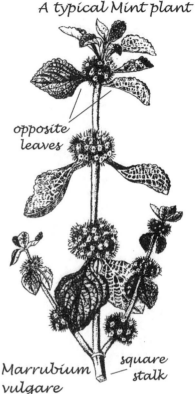

A typical Mint plant

opposite
leaves

square
stalk

*Marrubium
vulgare*

Key Words
Square stalks and opposite leaves. Usually aromatic.

If you pick a plant with a distinctly squarish stalk and simple, opposite leaves it almost certainly a member of the Mint family. The flowers of this family are bisexual and irregular. The calyx (sepals) is 5-toothed, and often 2-lipped. The corolla (petals) is tubular and 2-lipped, usually with 2 lobes to the upper lip, and 3 lobes to the lower lip. (*Mentha* is barely irregular at all.) There are 4 stamens, with one pair longer than the other. The ovary is positioned superior. It consists of 2 united carpels (bicarpellate) and matures as a capsule containing 4 nutlets. (False partitions may make it appear 4-chambered.) World-wide there are about 180 genera representing some 500 species. Approximately 50 genera are found in North America. Other plants with square stems and opposite leaves which may be confused with the Mints are found in the Loos-estrife, Verbena and Stinging Nettle families.

Many species from the Mint family are popuar kitchen *spices*, including: rosemary (*Rosmarinus*), lavender (*Lavandula*), marjoram (*Origanum*), mint, peppermint, spearmint (*Mentha*), germander (*Teucrium),* thyme (*Thymus*), savory (*Satureja*), horehound (*Marrubium*), sage (*Salvia*) (not sagebrush!), and basil, (*Ocimum*). An ornamental houseplant from this family is the *Coleus*.

Medicinally this family is rich in **volatile oils**, especially menthol. These spicy oils are stimulating and warming, causing the body to open up and sweat; thus most of the plants are diaphoretic. This property can help you break a fever. A fever is the body's way of "cooking" the microorganisms that cause infections. Using a diaphoretic herb can help raise a mild fever just high enough to "cook" a virus, thus "breaking" or ending the fever.

Warming the body also opens up the vessels, allowing blood to flow more freely. This means they have a vasodilator effect, useful for relaxing the blood vessels in cases of hypertension, or for stimulating delayed menstruation, called an emmenagogue. Volatile oils are also carminative (expels gas) and anthlementic (expels worms). The oils also apparently calm the nerves, so many of these plants are described as nervine, antispasmodic, and sedative.

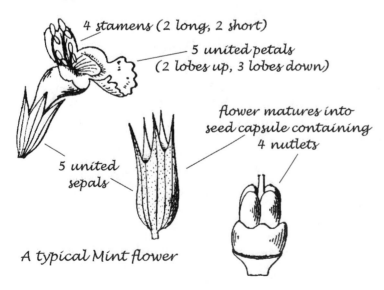

4 stamens (2 long, 2 short)

5 united petals
(2 lobes up, 3 lobes down)

flower matures into
seed capsule containing
4 nutlets

5 united
sepals

A typical Mint flower

Most members of this family are **astringent**, but a few are **bitter**, resulting in significantly different uses between them. The astringent mints are sometimes recommended as menstrual regulators, apparently because he volatile oils stimulte menstruation, whle the astringents suppress it. This, in theory, has a balacing effect. Th bitter mints like pennyroyal (*Hedeoma*), horehound (*Marubium*), mints (*Mentha*), and false horemint (*Monardella*) tend to have a more pronounced vasodiating effect.

Some of these herbs may be dangerous during pregnancies, due to their anthlementic (worm killing) and emmenagogue (menstrual stimulating) properties. The most dangerous ones are those that are also bitter (irritating).

130

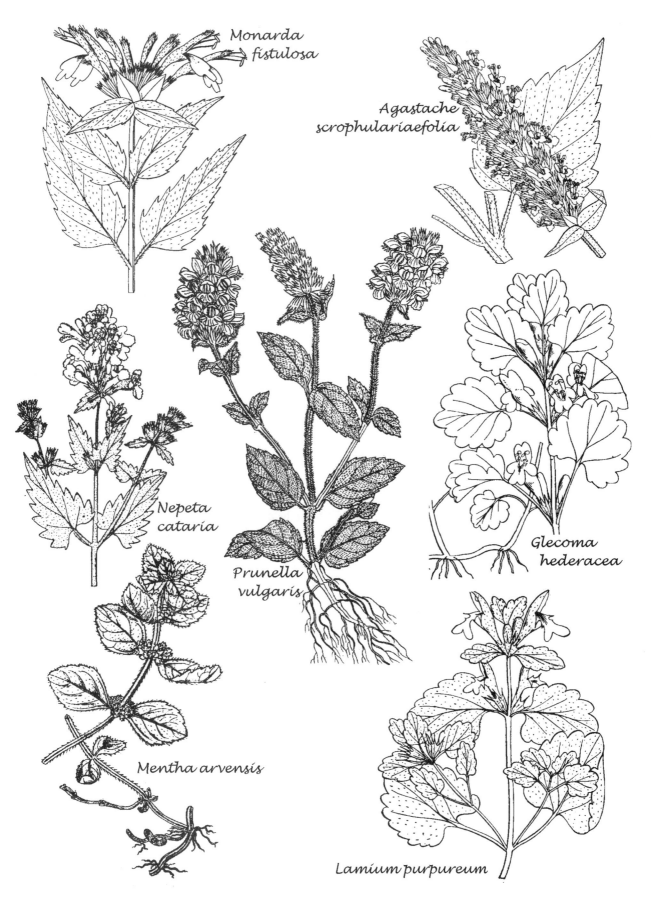

Monarda fistulosa

Agastache scrophulariaefolia

Nepeta cataria

Prunella vulgaris

Glecoma hederacea

Mentha arvensis

Lamium purpureum

131

Edible and Medicinal Properties of the Mint Family plants

Agastache—Giant Hyssop (-/14/2) • *Agastache* is astringent, diaphoretic, and carminative.

Dracocephalum—False Dragonhead (-/4/1) • The seeds can be ground into flour, or cooked into mush, and eaten (Olsen). The plant is probably astringent.

Glecoma—Ground Ivy (5/1/1) *G. hederacea* was introduced from Europe. It contains tannins, bitters and volatile oils (Schauenberg). The herb has been used for respiratory ailment, including bronchitis, pneumonia, and coughs (Tilford).

Galeopsis—Hemp Nettle (-/3/1) A tea of the plant is astringent, diuretic, and expectorant. It is used especially for clearing bronchial congestion. Also used as a blood purifier (Lust).

Hedeoma—Pennyroyal (-/14/2) Pennyroyal is diaphoretic, antispasmodic, and bitter. It is used as a tea to stimulate a sweat, or to stimulate digestion. The tea is also a menstrual stimulant and vasodilator, and it can be used to stimulate contractions in an overdue pregnancy (Moore). At least one person has died from ingesting pure, distilled pennyroyal oil to cause an abortion. Nervine (Hutchins). Also carminative (Lust).

Hyssopus—Hyssop (-/1/1) *H. officinalis* was introduced from Europe. It is carminative, tonic, expectorant, vasodilator, and anthlementic (Hutchins). Also reported as astringent and emmenagogue (Lust), used for nose and throat infections.

Lamium—Dead Nettle, Henbit (40/5/2) • Henbit contains tannin, mucilage and many flavanoids; it is used as a mild astringent and expectorant (Schauenberg). The whole plant is edible (Tilford).

Leonurus—Motherwort (-/3/1) Antispasmodic, nervine, emmenagogue, anthlementic, laxative (Hutchins). Also astringent (Lust). The plant contains bitters, tannins, volatile oils, and an alkaloid (Schauenberg). Motherwort is used to slow and strengthen the heartbeat while lowering high blood pressure. It is also used as an uterine tonic and antispasmodic, hence the common name (Tilford).

Lycopus—Bugleweed, Water Horehound (-/-/3) Bugleweed is edible, but tough and bitter (Tilford). Medicinally, bugleweed is mildly astringen, useful internally or externally to stop bleeding (Moore). It also contains some bitters (Schauenberg), useful as an expectorant (Tilford). Bugleweed is often used for its mild antispasmodic, nervine, and sedative properties, much like the hops vines of the Hemp family (Moore).

Marrubium—Horehound (30/1/1) • *M. vulgare* is a native of Europe, now widespread on this continent. The plant is aromatic and extremely bitter and therefore useful as a digestive aid or as a cough suppressant and expectorant. The herb is often added to cough syrups. Horehound candy is much easier to consume than the bitter herb or tea. Excessive use may lead to hypertension (Moore) Horehound also contains tannic acid (Schauenberg).

Mentha—Mint, Spearmint, Peppermint (15/11/2) • As a child I loved finding and picking peppermint on outings with my grandmother. Today I still nibble on the leaves to freshen my breath as I walk. I often eat peppermint when drinking from streams to help kill microbes in the water. Mints are the main source of the menthol, a volatile oil used for its penetrating vapors to relieve congestion or as a carminative to aid digestion. These are the original "after dinner mints".

Moldavica—Dragonhead (-/1) •

Monarda—Horsemint, Bee Balm, Bergamot (-/15/1) • *Monarda* is diaphoretic, refrigerant, carminative, anthlementic, mildly sedative and diuretic. A poultice can be use for headaches (Willard). The cool tea is used as an emmenagogue (Moore). At least some species contian tymol, an antiseptic compound used in commercial mouthwashes. Native Americans used it as a tea for mouth and throat infections (Tilford). Oil of bergamot is reported to have a calming effect on birds if it is rubbed on the bil, near the nostrils (Verrill).

Monardella—False Horsemint (20/22/0) The plant is used identically to *Hedeoma* above (Moore).

Nepeta—Catnip (150/2/1) • The young leaves and buds may be added to a salad (Tilford). Medicinally, catnip containsvolatile oils (Densmore) with mild antispasmodic, nervine, and sedative properties (Moore). It makes a wonderful and mildly relaxing tea. Catnip is also carminative, useful to expel gas or aid indigestion (Tilford). It is an effective emmenagogue (Hutchins). The reason cats like the smell of catnip is because it is chemically similar o the anal glands of cats (Klein)! Lions, tigers, leopards and jaguars are affected by lavender instead (Verrill).

Prunella—Self Heal (5/-/1) • Heal-all is edible as a salad or potherb (Tilford). Medicinally it is carminative, anthlementic, diuretic, antispasmodic, astringent, and mildly bitter. (Willard, Klein).

Salvia—Culinary Sage, Chia (500/56/2) • *S. columbarae* is chia; the seeds are edible, high in protein, and mucilaginous (Bigfoot). Many species of Salvia are richly aromatic and can be used as spices or anit-microbials. Ornamental varieties often lack aromatics. Sagebrush (*Artemisia*) belongs to the Aster family, and tastes nothing like culinary sage.

Scutellaria—Skullcap (200/42/3) Skullcap cntains a flavonoid called scutellarin, with antispasmodic, nervine, and sedative properties, used especially in cases of acute or chronic nervous tension or anxiety (Tilford). It also acts as a vasodilator to reduce high blood pressure (Hutchins) and to increase menstruation (Lust).

Stachys—Hedge Nettle, Betony (200/30/1) The roots of some species are starchy and edible (Sturtevant. The seeds are edible parched or roasted and ground into meal (Olsen). *Stachys* contains up to 15% tannic acid (Schauenberg), useful for diarrhea and irritations of the mucous membranes (Tyler).

Plantaginaceae—Plantain family

Our members of this family are low, green plants with inconspicuous flowers. The leaves initilly appear to have parallel venation like monocotyledons, but there are smaller, netted veins in between the main veins. The flowers are greenish, forming on a slender stalk. If you look close you will see that the flowers are regular and bisexual with 4 united sepals and petals and 4 stamens . The ovary is positioned superior and consists of 2 united carpels (bicarpellate) forming a single chamber. It matures as a circumscissile (lidded) capsule with 1 or more seeds per cell, or sometimes as a nut.

World-wide there are only3 genera and 270 species, mostly of *Plantago*. North American genera are listed below. *Plantago psyllium* is raised commercially for its seeds. These are marketed as a bulk laxative in products like *Metamucil*. The seed husks swell up in water, resulting in softer, larger stools that are easier to pass. It is importnt to drink plenty of water with psyllium seeds, or they will suck the water out of the body and contribute to further obstructing your bowels. Plantain seeds have also been used to absorb toxins present in the intestinal tract (Klein).

Plantago lanceolata

Key Words:
Dicots with parallel veins.
Slender flower stalks with small, greenish flowers,
parts in 4's and lidded capsules.

Littorella— (3/-/0) *Littorella* is an aquatic plant found from Minnesota to through the northeastern states.

Plantago—Plantain (260/-/8) • The broad-leaf plantain (*P. major*) was introduced from Eurasia. It is the most widespread and easily recognized member of the genus. The leaves are delicious batter-fried, or they can be boiled as a potherb and the leaf fibers removed. Plantain is rich in the vitamins A, C, and K (Tilford).

The seeds are edible as a "cereal grain". In a timed study of *P. major* I stripped the standing seed stalks with two fingers, caught the seed capsules in my hand and dropped them in a bag. One hour of picking yielded 1.5 quarts of rough material. I spent 20 minutes winnowing out the chaff for a final yield of 1.75 cups. A better way to harvest them might be to cut and collect the whole stalks, then to rub them between the palms to loosen the seeds.

Plantain is a gentle astringent for stomach ulcers, bee stings, etc. The fresh leaf can be secured over a wound as a bandage (Willard). The leaves contain allantoin, useful for soothing skin sores (Duke). Eating the mucilaginous seeds before a meal can decrease the absorption of "bad" cholesterol.

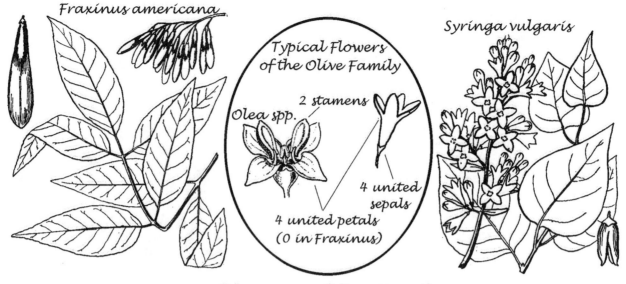

Fraxinus americana

Syringa vulgaris

Typical Flowers of the Olive Family

Olea spp.

2 stamens

4 united sepals

4 united petals (0 in Fraxinus)

Oleaceae—Olive Family

If you live in the northern states then you may know the lilac already. Stop and take a closer look the next time you see one. The leaves are opposite in most members of the family, sometimes on squarish stems. The flowers are regular and bisexual. There are 4 united sepals and 4 united petals (may be lacking in *Fraxinus*), plus 2 stamens—a rare combination in the plant world. The ovary is positioned superior and consists of 2 united carpels (bicarpellate) with the partition walls present, forming 2 chambers. It matures as a capsule, a pair of winged seeds, or sometimes as a berry or drupe (a fleshy fruit with a stoney pit).

World-wide there are 29 genera and about 600 species, including 5 genera in North America. All are shrubs or trees. The olive tree is the genus *Olea*, and jasmine comes from *Jasminum*. Other cultivated genera include *Abeliophyllum*, *Chionanthus*, *Fontanesia*, *Forsythia*, *Ligustrum*, *Noranhia*, *Notelaea*, *Nyctanthes*, *Osmanthus*, *Osmarea*, *Parasyringa*, and *Phillyrea*.

Key Words
Trees or shrubs with opposite leaves and 4 sepals, 4 or 0 petals, 2 stamens.

Fraxinus—Ash (50+/-/2) • Ash is stimulating, diaphoretic, diuretic, and laxative. Drink a tea of the inner bark for depression or tiredness; a strong tea for a laxative (Willard). A tea of the bark is used to reduce fever, and to expel worms. A tea of the leaves is used as a laxative (Lust).

Olea—Olive (20/-/0) • A tea of the leaves or inner bark is diaphoretic, astringent, and sedative. Olive oil is useful internally as a laxative, or externally as an emollient to soothe the skin (Lust).

Syringa—Lilac (30/-/D) • Several species of lilac are planted domestically. The Latin *Syringa* is confusing, because it is also one of the common names of *Philadelphus* of the Hydrangea family.

Fraxinus americana

Scrophulariaceae—Figwort or Snapdragon Family

If you have ever seen a common domestic snapdragon then you know the Figwort family. I used to play with them as a kid, squeezing the sides of the blossoms to make the "mouth" open and close.

The flowers are bisexual and mostly irregular. There are 4 or 5 sepals, at least partially united. There are 4 or 5 petals united as a tube, usually 2-lipped with 2 lobes above and 3 lobes below. There are usually 4 stamens in 2 pais, but a fifth stamen is present in som. The ovary is positioned superior and consists of 2 united carpels (bicarpellate) withthe partition walls present, forming 2 chambers. It matures as a capsule containing many seeds, or sometimes as a berry.

When you have identified a plant as a member of the Figwort family you can continue by reading the descriptions of the three subfamilies to find out which group your specimen belongs to. World-wide there are about 220 genera, representing some 3000 species. About 40 genera are found in North America. The common garden snapdragon belongs to the genus *Antirrhinum*.

Key Words: Irregular flowers with 3 lobes down and 2 lobes up. Capsules with numerous seeds.

Figwort Subfamily

Members of the Figwort Subfamily are distinguished from other Figworts by the presence of a *small* 5th stamen (except in *Mimulus*). Also, most of these plants have opposite leaves near their base.

Collinsia—Blue-eyed Mary (20/19/1) •
Gratiola—Hedge Hyssop (-/-/2) *Gratiola* contains cardiac glycosides (Schauenberg). It is listed as cardiac, diuretic, purgative, and vermifuge, considered too dangerous for amateurs to use (Lust).
Linaria—Butter and Eggs Toadflax (150/12/1) • *Linaria* is astringent, diuretic, and cathartic. It is primarily used for its diuretic / antilithic properties (Lust).
Mimulus—Monkey Flower (120/89/9) • The plant is edible, but bitter, as a salad or potherb (Craighead). The root is astringent (Sweet). Juice of the plant is soothing on minor burns (Tilford).
Penstemon—Penstemon (300/210/25) • The plant is astringent (Moore), and diuretic (Sweet).
Scrophularia—Figwort (150/8/1) Figwort contains saponins (Schauenberg). It has sedative, astringent, and antifungal properties (Moore). It is also diuretic. It is used especially as a skin wash (Lust).

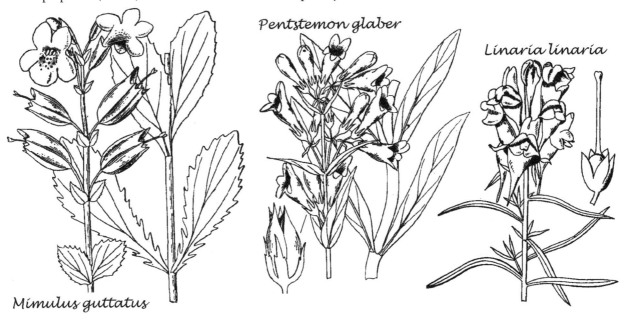

Mimulus guttatus

Pentstemon glaber

Linaria linaria

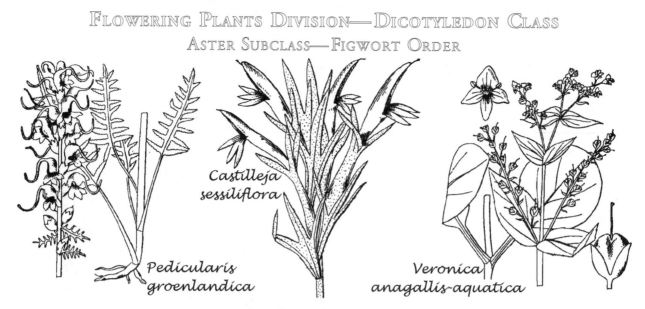

Castilleja
sessiliflora

Pedicularis
groenlandica

Veronica
anagallis-aquatica

Rattleweed Subfamily

If you find a figwort with 2 or 4 stamens, and the 5th stamen completely lacking, then it is a member of the Rattleweed Subfamily.

Castilleja—Indian Paintbrush (200/109/22) • The blossoms are edible, but they may absorb selenium from the soil, so you should not eattoo many of them. The plants have been used for "women's diseases" and for rheumatism; the uses possibly related to the selenium content (Willard). It functions as an astringent to stop menstrual flow (Vogel).

Digitalis—Foxglove (21/4/1) • Digitalis is often planted domestically. It contains dangrous cardiac glycosides used fr heart arrhythmia. Just touching the plant may cause rashes, nausea, and headache (Lust).

Euphrasia—Eyebright (-/11/1) Eyebright is astringent, used in typical ways, but especially as an eyeash (Lust).

Melampyru—Cow Wheat (-/1/1) *M. lineare* is found across Canada and the northern states.

Orthocarpus—Owl Clover (30/24/2) •

Pedicularis—Lousewort, Elephant Head (600/40/10) • The root and plant of some species is edible raw or cooked (Willard), but the plants are partly parasitic and may absorb toxins from neary poisonous plants such as groundsels (*Senecio spp.*). Please refer to Michael Moore's *Medicinal Plants of the Pacific West* for detailed information on this plant.

Rhinanthus—Rattleweed (-/2/1)

Synthyris—Kittentail (-/2/2)

Veronica—Speedwell, Brooklime (300/30/9) • The plat is edible raw or cooked, but bitter (Harrington). Medicinally the various species are mildly diuretic, diaphoretic and expectorant (Lust). The plants may be mistaken for members of the Mint family, but the stems are not quite square.

Mullein Subfamily

Mullein is in its own subfamily, due to the presence of a fifth stamen.

Verbascum—Mullein (320/7/2) • Mullein is a popular medicinal herb imported from Europe. It grows in disturbd soils all across North America. Mullein has sedative, astringent, and mildly mucilaginous properties. The leaves can be smoked or made into tea to relax the bronchials in the initial stages of an infection. A tea of the root is diuretic and astringent for the urinary tract (Moore). A strong tea or dry powder of the leaves can be applied o a wound as an effective astringent (Brown). The small amount of mucilage makes the tea useful as a demulcent to soothe a sore throat. The blossoms and seeds also contain a small amount of saponin, useful for emporarily paralyzing fish.

Verbascum
thapsus

Other selected genera of the Figwort family:

Bacopa—Water Hyssop (-/9/1) • ... *Beseya*—Kittentail (-/6/2) • ...
Chonophila—Snowflower (-/-/1) ... *Cordlanthus*—Bird's Beak (-/29/1) ...
Limosella—Mudwart (-/-/1)

Orobanchaceae—Broom-Rape Family

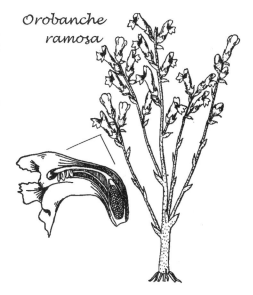

Orobanche ramosa

If you find a plant with Figwort-like flowers and no chlorophyll, then it is likely a member of the Broom-Rape family. Plants of this family are parasitic on the roots of other plants. They have no leaves, but the stalk is wrapped with alternate bracts. The flowers are bisexual and irregular. The corolla is tubular with an upper and lower lip, similar to the Figwort family. The are 2-5 united sepals, 5 united petals, and 4 stamens, appearing in pairs. The ovary is positioned superior and consists of 2 united carpels (bicarpellate) forming a single chamber. It matures as a capsule with many seeds.

World-wide there are 13 genera and 180 species. Four genera are native to North America. Note that the Heath family also includes a few parasitic species without chlorophyll.

Key Words
Parasitic plants with Figwort-like flowers.

Boschniakia—Ground Cone (2/3/0)
Conopholis—Squaw Root (2/2/0)
Epifagus—Beech Drops (1/1/0) *E. virginiana* grows in the eastern states.
Orobanche—Broomrape (100/16/4) • Some species have swollen starchy edible roots (Olsen). *O. fasciculata* is edible in salad or roasted. Medicinally, broomrapes are highly astringent, useful externally as a powerful drawing poultice; internally the tea is a uterine homeostatic (Moore). A tea of the blanched or powdered seeds reduces swelling for toothaches or joint inflammation (Willard).

Campanulaceae (including Lobeliaceae)—Harebell family

The delicate flowers of the Harebell family are bisexual and mostly regular (except *Lobelia*). There are 5 separate sepals (sometimes 3, 4, or 10), 5 united petals (rarely 4), and 5 stamens. Flowers are most often blue or white. The ovary is positioned inferior or partly so, and consists of 2, 3, or 5 united carpels (syncarpous) with the partition walls present, forming an equal number of chambers. (False partitions may make it seem like more cham-

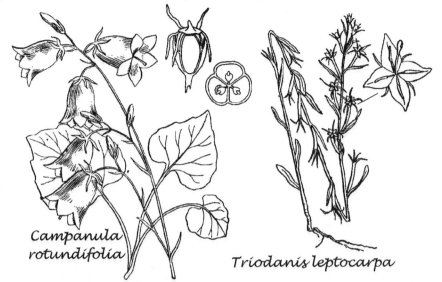

bers.) It matures as a capsule (rarely a berry) with numerous seeds. Most members of the family are herbs with simple, alternate leaves and usually milky juice. There are also a few shrubs and/or trees in Hawaii, Florida and other tropical/subtropical climates around the world.

This family is known by some as the "Bluebell" family, but that is confusing since *Mertensia* of the Borage family is also popularly called bluebell. World-wide there are about 70 genera and 2000 species. Twelve genera are found in North America. Many plants in this fam-

Campanula rotundifolia

Triodanis leptocarpa

ily contain inulin polysaccharides and cyanogenic glycosides (Zomlefer). *Laurentia* provides isotomin, a heart poison. Little information is available about wild species of the family, other than *Lobelia*.

Key Words: Bell-shaped flowers, usually with milky juice in the stems.

Campanula—Harebell (300/29/6) • The leaves and roots are edible (Willard, Harrington, Sturtevant). Flowers are edible.
Heterocodon— (-/1/0) *H. rariflorum* grows in the Pacific Coast states and British Columbia.
Howellia— (-/-/1)
Jasione—Sheep's Bit (-/1/0) *J. montana* was imported from Europe. It is naturalized in the east coast states.
Porterella— (-/-/1)
Specularia—Venus' Looking Glass (-/8/0)
Sphenoclea—Chicken Spike (-/1/0) *S. zeylanica* was imported from Europe. It grows from South Carolina to Texas.
Triodanis—Venus' Looking Glass (-/-/2)

Lobelia Subfamily

Although part of the Harebell family, the Lobelias look distinctly different with their irregular flowers. Also, the stamens of the Lobelias are united at their anthers, where other members of the Harebell family have completely separate stamens.

Key Words:
Irregular flowers with 2 petal lobes up and 3 down.

Lobelia inflata

Downingia— (-/13/1)
Lobelia—Lobelia, Cardinal Flower (380/29/2) *L. inflata* is a popular and potent herb for the lungs. Other species are used similarly but vary in potency. Lobelia has a milky sap containing pyridine alkaloids. It first stimulates the nervous system, then depresses it. In moderate doses it dilates the bronchials and increases respiration. Over-doses lead to respiratory depression, low blood pressure and coma (Tyler). Large doses has been used as an emetic, but this is dangerous and has resulted in at least one death (Moore). Externally it can be used as a stimulating poultice (Lust). The plant can also be smoked for asthma (Bigfoot).

Rubiaceae—Madder Family

Our members of this family are small plants or vines with squarish stalks and whorled leaves. The tiny flowers are regular and usually bisexual with 4 or 5 separate sepals, 4 or 5 united petals and 4 or 5 stamens The ovary is positioned inferior or rarely superior and consists of 2 (sometimes 4) united carpels (syncarpous) with the partition walls present, forming an equal number of chambers. Most members of the family produce a capsule or a berry with numerous seeds, but *Galium* produces a fuzzy fruit with just two seeds. It looks—well, like little green fuzzy testicles.

The Madder family is large, consisting of some 500 genera and 6000-7000 species, most of them in tropical climates. There are about 20 genera native to the United States, mostly in Florida with some species occurring in the southwestern states. Members of this family provide us with coffee (*Coffea*), ipecac (*Cephaelis*), and the anti-malarial alkaloid quinine (*Cinchona*). The *Gardenia* is a common ornamental plant from this family.

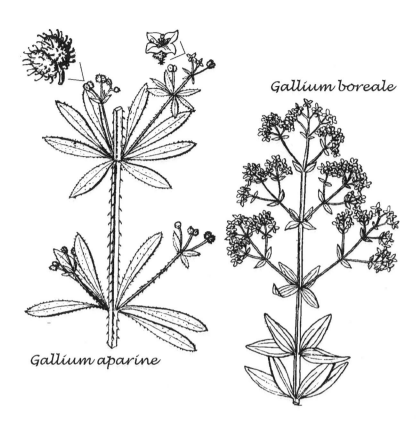

Gallium boreale

Gallium aparine

Key Words (*Galium spp.*)
Squarish stalks with whorled leaves. Fruits like small, green testicles.

Coffea—Coffee (50+/0/0) Coffee beans contain the purine-type alkaloid caffeine which prolongs the useful lie of many hormones, but epecially adrenaline. Thi gives coffee its stimulant efect. Coffee can be used as a stimulant to counter the effects of depressant alkaloids and as an anti-emetic to keep you from vomiting. It also has a diuretic effect (Kadans).

Galium—Bedstraw, Cleavers (300/78/6) • The young shoots are edible as a salad or potherb (Hall), but the hairy varieties may irritate the throat. A tea of the plant is recommended for dissolving calcium stones and as a general diuretic, astringent (Willard), anti-inflammatory, and lymphatic tonic. Pure bedstraw juice is considered very beneficial for stomach ulcers (Tilford). Bedstraw is also useful for modest healing without irritation in cases of hepatitis (Moore).

The roots of some species yield a bright red dye (Willard). *G. odoratum* contains high levels of coumarins (Duke). *G. aparine* is a fun plant to play with. The vines are covered with Velcro-like stickers that cling to the clothing of whomever you throw them at! The common name "bedstraw" comes from the practice of filling mattresses with the plants. Apparenly the plants do no pack down flat, but retain a certain amount of "loft"

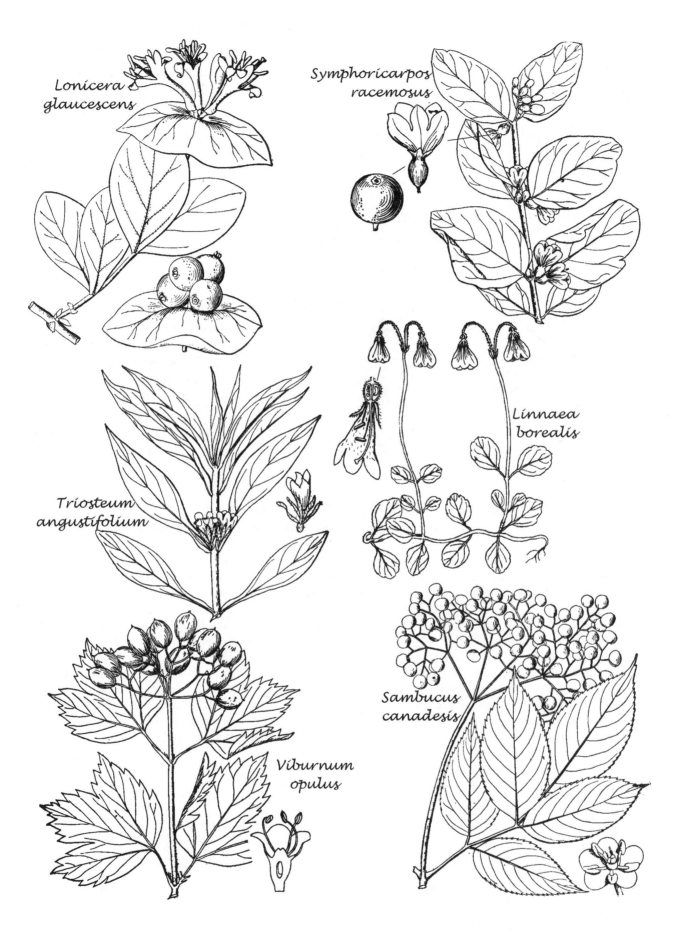

Lonicera glaucescens

Symphoricarpos racemosus

Linnaea borealis

Triosteum angustifolium

Sambucus canadesis

Viburnum opulus

140

Carifoliaceae—Honeysuckle Family

If you see a bush (sometimes an herb) with flowers or berries in pairs, then it may be a member of the Honeysuckle family.   Berries also form in clusters or umbels. Members of the family are mostly bushes with opposite leaves and often "pithy" stems, as if there were styrofoam in the core. The flowers are regular, except in some species of *Lonicera*. The bisexual flowers include 5 small, united sepals, 5 united petals, and usually 5 stamens, but sometimes 4. The ovary is positioned inferior and consists of 2, 3, 5, or 8 united carpels (syncarpous) with the partition walls either present or absent. It matures as a fleshy berry or sometimes a drupe, meaning a fleshy fruit with a stoney pit. The remains of the calyx can be seen attached to the fruit. World-wide there are 15 genera and 400 species. Many of them are planted domestically as ornamentals. Seven genera are native to North America.

This is a chemically complex family. Most of the species are border-line between being minimally edible and slightly toxic. Many, but not all of the species produce *edible berries*, with significantly bitter and/or astringent qualities. Some plants have *toxic alkaloids* present in either the fruits or vegetation. The vegetation is typically diaphoretic, and laxative but astringent.

<u>Key Words</u>
Bushes with opposite leaves and flowers/berries usually paired or in clusters. Pithy stems.

Linnaea—Twin-Flower (1/1/1) • *L. borealis*, the plant or berries might be edible. The plant has been used as a tonic for pregnancy and for painful or difficult menstruation (Fern). It is probably mildly astringent.

Lonicera—Honeysuckle (180/-/4) • Honeysuckle berries are edible, but usually bitter. A frost may improve their flavor (Willard). A European species may be poisonous. The bark and leaves contain bitter principles with emetic properties (Schauenberg). The plant is also used as an expectorant and laxative (Kadans).

Sambucus—Elderberry (25/-/4) • The blue or black elderberries are edible. The light-blue berries seem to be the sweetest. The seeds of all elderberries contain a form of cyanide and the bitter sambucine alkaloid, which may cause nausea and diarrhea in large enough amounts. Cooking destroys the cyanide, but intesnifies the bitter flavor of some species. Note that the red-berried species contain much higher concentrations of cyanide. Most authorities regard red elderberries as toxic, although Indian tribes reportedly used and even prefered them (Harrington). Drying sweetens the taste of the elderberries and probably destroys the cyanide, even in the red berries, but caution is advised. Elderberries are easy to gather in abundance. They are especially high in iron (Hutchins). The flowers can be batter-fried.

Cyanide and sambucine are present in the leaves and bark as well (Moore).   These are present in toxic concentrations in the red-berried species and in "medicinal" amounts in other species. The cyanide is likely destroyed by cooking, leaving the alkaloid. A tea of the leaves and flowers is diaphoretic; the leaves are also laxative. The flowers and dried berries are diuretic, used to treat arthritis and rheumatism (Moore). Th berries are astringent (Hutchins). Elderberry is an effective remedy for the flu. A property of the elderberries reportedly bnds to the "spikes" on the flu virus, disarming it from penetrating and entering body cells. A clinical trial with a trade-marked elderberry extract called "Sambucol" revealed that 90% of a flu-infected group fully recovered after three days, while most individuals in the control group needed six days to recover (Eliman).

The pithy stems of elderberries are useful for bowdrill and handdrill fire sets, as well as for making flutes, but keep in mind that the stems may be toxic until dried.

Symphoricarpos—Snowberry (15/-/4) • The leaves, bark, and berries have astringent properties; the poultice is used for wounds, and the tea as an eye wash (Hart). The berries contain saponins, and may be used as a soap substitute or fish poison (Fern). The berries are considered emetic (Willard), probably due to the taste of the saponins.

Triosteum—Feverwort (8/-0) A tea of the leaves is used as a diaphoretic to bring down a fever, hence the common name. A tea of the roots contains an alkaloid; it is considered diuretic and cathartic. In addition to urinary disorders, it is used for menstrual disorders and constipation. A poultice of the root is used on snakebites and sores (Fern).

Viburnum—High-Bush Cranberry, Snowball Tree (120/-3) • The true cranberry is a member of the Heath family. *Viburnum* berries are edible but bitter. A frost may improve them. It is recommended that you cook the berries with sugar and strain out the big seeds (Hall). Medicinally, the bark contains isovalerianic acid (like *Valerian*) and simple phenol glycosides (Densmore, Geller, Schauenberg). It is used for its antispasmodic, nervine, astringent, and diuretic properties. The boiled tea is recommended for the last two to three months of a pregnancy to eliminate nervousness and cramps (Willard).

Dipsacaceae—Teasel Family

The Teasel family is not native to our country, but a few plants, particularly teasel, have become widely naturalized here. The flowerheads could easily be mistaken for those of the Aster family. The individual flowers are bisexual and slightly irregular, clustered in a dense head. There are 5 sepals and 4 or 5 united petals, plus 4 stamens. The ovary is positioned inferior and consists of 2 united carpels (bicarpellate), but aborts one, forming just 1 chamber. It produces a dry seed (an achene) enclosed in a sac. World-wide there are 10 genera and 270 species. Three genera were introduced from Europe.

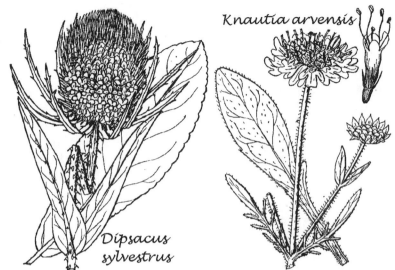

Knautia arvensis

Dipsacus sylvestrus

**Key Words:
Aster-like blossoms with slightly irregular flowers.**

Dipsacus—Teasel (15/2/1) • Teasel is not very common in Montana, but is quite prolific in warmer climates, usually near water. To a beginning botanst it might look a lot like a thistle. The spikey flowerheads were once used to raise the nap on new woolen textiles, a process called "teasing" or "fulling" the cloth (Baumgardt). The upper leaves of the teasel have evolved to catch water and drown insects. The nutrients are absorbed as the bodies naturally decompose (Verrill). *Dipsacus* contains a simple phenol glycoside (Schauenberg).

Knautia— (*Scabiosa*) Blue Buttons, Pin Cushion Flower (40/1/1) • *K. arvensis*, the plant contains tannic acid and bitter principles (Schauenberg). A tea of the plant or roots is used externally as a wash for cuts, burns, and bruises, internally as a "blood purifier".

Valeriana sylvatica

Valerianaceae—Valerian Family

North American members of this family have small flowers in clusters. The flowers can be bisexual or unisexual, regular or slightly irregular. The sepals are inconspicuous. There are 5 united petals, often with a spur at the base of the flower. There are 1-4 stamens. The ovary is positioned inferior and consists of 3 united carpels (tricarpellate) but aborts two, forming just 1 chamber. It produces a dry seed, called an "achene". World-wide there are 13 genera and 400 species. Three genera are found in North America.

Key Words: Plants with basal and opposite leaves. Small flowers with tiny spurs. Roots with pungent aroma.

Plectritis— (15/3/1)

Valeriana—Valerian, Tobacco Root (250/19/5) • My home is at the base of the Tobacco Root Mountains, which are named after this plant. *V. edulis* (Harrington) and *V. obovata* (Craighead) produce large, edible roots. These are traditionally cooked in a steam pit for two days prior to being eaten. The two species in the Tobacco Root Mountains have small, inedible roots. The roots of all valerians have a characteristic "dirty sock smell", due to the presence of isovaleric acid. Many people consider the odor repelling.

 Valerian is a well-known sedative, and no, it is not related to Vallium. Valerian sedates the central nervous system, although it also stimulates digestion and the cardiovascular system. About one if five people will react to valerian as a stimulant rather than a sedative. Long-term use can result in depression (Moore). Robin Klein told a story of driving down the road with freshly-dug valerian roots in the front seat. The sun shone in on the roots, warming up the constituents, until she grew so tired she suddenly pulled off the road and slept for two hours!

Valerianella—Corn Salad (60/-/0)

Asteraceae (Compositae)—Aster or Sunflower Family

Despite the simple outward appearance of the plants, the Asters are possibly the most complex family of plants yet evolved. Most other families of plants have floral parts in a similar order: a ring of sepals on the outside, then a ring of petals, a ring of stamens and the pistil or pistils in the middle. A few of the parts may be missing, but the basic order is always the same. The Aster family, however, is very different. The "sepals" are actually bracts (modified leaves), and these often appear in multiple layers. The "petals" make it appear that there is just one big flower, but look closely inside and you will discover many much smaller flowers—dozens or even hundreds of them! In the sunflower for example, *every seed* is produced by *one small flower within the larger head*. These itsy-bitsy flowers, called **disk flowers**, each have their own microscopic sepals and petals, stamens and pistil. Even the big "petals" are flowers, although they are often infertile, without stamens or a pistil. They are properly called **ray flowers**. Members of the Aster family have disk flowers, ray flowers, or both.

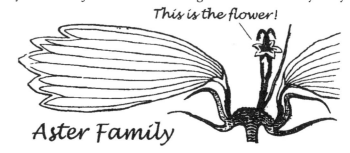

Among the Asters the true sepals have been reduced to small scales, or often transformed into a hairy "pappus", or sometimes eliminated altogether. One of the best clues for identifying members of this family is to look for the presence of multiple layers of "false sepals" (actually bracts) beneath the flowers. In an artichoke, for instance, those are the scale-like pieces we pull off and eat. Most members of this family do not have quite that many bracts, but there are frequently two or more rows. This is not a fool-proof test, only a common pattern of the Aster family. Next, look inside the flowerhead for the presence of the many smaller flowers. These are often quite small. Even the common yarrow, with its tiny flower-heads, usually has a dozen or more nearly microscopic flowers inside each head, and the inside of a sagebrush flower-head is even smaller. Also, please note that many members of this family have no obvious outer ring of petals, including sagebrush.

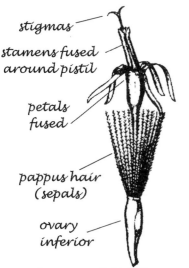

The Asters are the largest family of flowering plants, at least after the Orchids which inhabit mostly tropical areas. World-wide there are about 920 genera and 19,000 species, including 346 genera and 2,687 species in the U.S. and Canada. Many are cultivated as ornamentals, including Marigold (*Tagetes*), *Chrysanthemum*, *Calendula*, and *Zinnia*. Surprisingly few are food plants. Some that are include: lettuce (*Lactuca*), artichoke (*Cynara*), and endive (*Cichorium*).

Once you have identified a plant as a member of the Aster family just read about the Dandelion Subfamily and the eleven tribes of the Aster Subfamily (Artichoke, Ragweed, Mutisia, Boneset, Ironweed, Camomile, Everlasting, Groundsel, Aster, Sunflower, and Sneezeweed) to get a sense about which group your specimen belongs to.

Besides being botanically complex, the Aster family is also chemically complex. Except for the Dandelion Subfamily, most members of the family are *resinous*, or otherwise contain *volatile oils* to varying degrees. Thus they are often medicinally diaphoretic (to make you sweat), stimulating (to increase lactose production, also as a menstrual stimulant or emmenagogue), vasodilating, and carminative. Most members of this family are somewhat astringent and diuretic as well. The diuretic properties are especially used for cleansing the urinary tract. The astringents close off secretions, and they are typically used to heal open wounds, reduce inflammations, control diarrhea, and decrease menstruation. Thus, a number of plants in this family have properties to both increase and decrease menstruation—which generally used as menstrual regulators. Be sure to read more about volatile oils, resins, and astringents in the Medicinal Propeties section of this book.

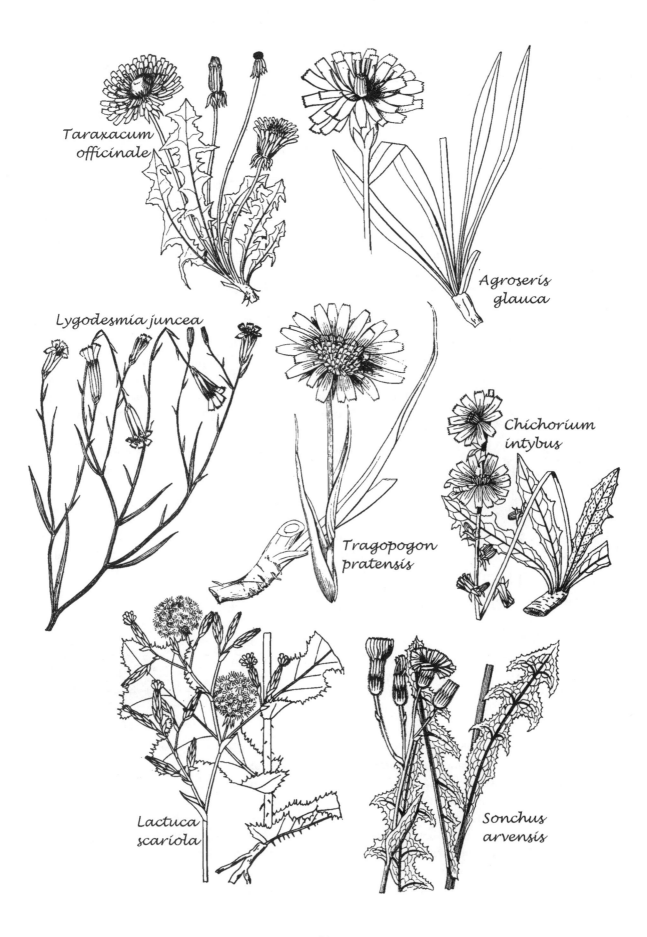

Taraxacum
officinale

Agroseris
glauca

Lygodesmia juncea

Tragopogon
pratensis

Chichorium
intybus

Lactuca
scariola

Sonchus
arvensis

144

Dandelion Subfamily

The Dandelion Subfamily is the most distinct sub-grouping of the Aster family. Botanically speaking the distinguishing feature is the "strap-shaped" petals—the petals have mostly parallel edges like a strap, instead of tapered edges like the petals of other flowers. Also, these strap-shaped petals (actually ray flowers) over-lap all the way to the center of the flower like a dandelion. There are no disk flowers like you would find in a sunflower. Another pattern of the subfamily is the milky juice in the stems. Most, if not all, members of the Dandelion Subfamily are *edible*, but bitter due to the milky juice. The bitterness makes these plants valuable as digestive aids. Dandelion leaves especially are known as a "spring tonic", to cleanse the liver after a long winter of eating hard-to-digest foods. Please note that many unrelated plants have milky juice and some are poisonous, so check the flower to make sure it is a member of the Dandelion subfamily before you eat it!

Agoseris—False Dandelion (-/8/4) • The leaves are edible. The hardened milky juice can be chewed as gum (Olsen).

Cichorium—Chicory (8/1/1) • *C. intybus* was imported from Europe. The leaves are edible as a salad or potherb, especially after blanching to reduce the bitterness. The bitterness is useful as a digestive aid and liver stimulant. The young roots are edible raw or cooked (Willard). They contain up to 58% inulin polysaccharides, favorable for diabetics (Hobbs). Chicory is similar, but more mild than dandelion (see *Taraxacum*, below) (Moore). The roots can be gently roasted and ground for a coffee substitute (Harrington). Caffix is one commercially available coffee substitute made with chicory roots. Roasting converts the inulin into oxymethylfurfurol, the compound with the coffee-like aroma (Tyler).

Crepis—Hawksbeard (200/22/9) The young leaves are edible as a potherb. (Olsen).

Hieracium—Hawkweed, Mouse Ear (800/56/6) A tea of the plant is astringent/diuretic, used in conventional ways (Lust).

Lactuca—Lettuce, Prickly Lettuce (100/-/5) • Domestic leaf lettuce belongs to this genus. Note that prickly lettuce has a row of prickles down the midrib underneath the leaf. Sow thistle (*Sonchus*) does not. Prickly lettuce is edible as a salad green or potherb. The leaves are extremely bitter at times.

> Prickly lettuce is sometimes called "lettuce opium", because the sap is reminiscent of the milky white latex from the opium poppy. The sap does have a very mild analgesic effect, safe enough even for children (Moore). It includes two bitter principles, lactucin and lactucopicrin, which were shown to have a depressant effect on the nervous systems of small animals. However, the bitter principles are very unstable, so any commercial preparations are functionally useless (Tyler).

Lapsan— (-/-/1) The plant is reported to be minimally edible as a salad or potherb (Sturtevant).

Lygodesmia—Skeletonweed (-/7/2) • A tea of the plant is used to increase lactose production (Willard), suggesting the presence of stimulating resins.

Malacothrix— (-/14/1)

Microseris— (-/17/4) The roots are edible (Sturtevant).

Prenanthes—Rattlesnake Root (-/12/1) A tea of the root is both astringent and bitter, used for diarrhea (Lust).

Sonchus—Sow Thistle (70/-/4) • *Sonchus* is edible as a salad or potherb. The stem has a milky, latex type sap (Harrington).

Stephanomeria—Wire Lettuce (-/13/2)

Taraxacum—Dandelion (70/-/5) • Dandelions are one of the most nutritious plants on earth, yet every year people senselessly spend millions of dollars on chemicals trying to kill them, then buy lifeless, nutritionless lettuce for the table.

> Dandelion leaves and roots are rich in vitamins A, B, C, & E and the minerals iron, phosphorus, potassium and calcium (Hutchins). Dandelions are bitter, useful as a digestive aid. Most people think the greens are too bitter to eat at first, but just try a small amount mixed in with other greens. You can develop a taste for them until they hardly seem bitter at all. I keep a simple digging tool in a handy spot and harvest the dandelions root and all. Most of the time I put the greens on an egg sandwich for breakfast. The roots I clean and dry. When I save up enough roots I roast them and grind them for a delicious coffee substitute. I also pay my kids five cents for each dandelion root they dig up, cut and wash for me. Roasting dandelion roots sweetens them by breaking the inulin polysaccharides down into fructose (Hobbs). The roasted, powdered roots make a delicious coffee substitute, much like chicory roots (see above).

> Medicinally, dandelion roots and leaves are most bitter in the spring, useful as a diuretic and stimulating to the liver, spleen, and kidneys. The plant is safe for long-term use, making it ideal for dissolving calcium stones (Moore). Dandelions, especially the roots, are high in sodium, recommended for breaking down acid in the blood. Dandelions may lower blood sugar, good for diabetics. The latex sap from the stems is used on warts (Willard).

Tragopogon—Salsify, Goat's Beard, Oyster Plant (45/5/3) • Salsify produces edible, slightly bitter foliage and large edible roots. It is sometimes planted as a garden vegetable. It is a biennial, producing an edible root the first year which turns woody the second year. The purple flowered species are best. The yellow flowered species are more fibrous and bitter (Tilford). I once dug up a field mouse "cellar" with nearly two gallons of salsify and grass roots! Medicinally, salsify is used as a diuretic and digestive stimulant (Lust).

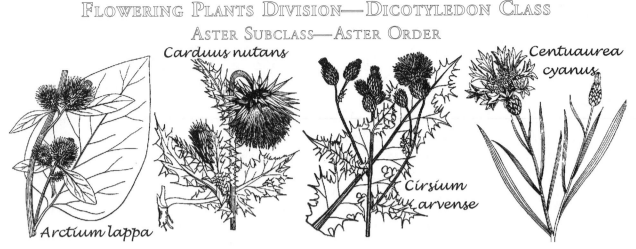

Carduus nutans

Centuaurea cyanus

Cirsium arvense

Arctium lappa

Artichoke Tribe

If you find an Aster with its head protected inside a tight wrapping of bracts like an artichoke, then it belongs to the Artichoke Tribe. Most of these plants have at least some prickly parts, especially those bracts around the flowerheads. Except for their spines, coarse texture, and fibrous nature, these plants are *edible* and *bitter*. The plants are often used in bitters formulas to stimulate digestion. The artichoke belongs to the *Cynara* genus. Teasel of the related family *Dipsacaceae* could be mistaken for a thistle.

Arctium—Burdock (6/-/2) • Burdock is a biennial with an edible taproot. The first year it produces basal leaves and stores starch in the root. The second year it uses the starch to send up a flower stalk, set seed, and die. The roots are edible during the first year, especially in June and July, and later become woody. It has been cultivated in Europe and Japan (Harrington). In a one hour study I dug up about a quart of roots with a primitive digging stick. I cannot eat too many roots by themselves, but they are good cooked as a side dish to a meal. The big leaves are ideal for covering a steam pit to keep dirt out of the food. The burrs can be used as "Velcro". The roots contain 45% inulin polysaccharides (Schauenberg). Burdock root is a very popular medicinal, especially for facilitating liver function. It is bitter and diuretic in effect (Hobbs, Tilford). Overall, burdock is considered a very gentle and cleansing herb.

Carduus—Thistle (100/5/2) The musk thistle (*C. nutans*) is a favorite wild snack. There is a technique to peeling the stalk while avoiding the stickers. Thistles are only good when the stalks are still fleshy; as summer progresses they become woody and inedible. Carefully grasp the tip of a budding flower and bend the stalk over to see how much of the plant is still succulent and where it has become too woody. With a quick slice of a knife, cut through the stalk taking only the top succulent part.

Do not cut all the way through the stalk, but rather, leave the "rind" intact on one side and let the thistle top hang down from that rind. Carefully grab the thistle top and pull it gently away from the parent stalk. This action peels the rind off the side of the stem that is still attached to the main stalk. The peeled side of the stem provides a safe, stickerless place for your fingers. The rest of the process is like peeling a banana. Enjoy!

Medicinally, musk thistle leaves and seeds are useful as a bitter tonic to stimulate liver function. (Lust).

Centaurea—Knapweed, Cornflower, Bachelor's Buttons (500/27/8) • *C. cyanus* is the cornflower or bachelor's button. It is native to Europe, but commonly cultivated in the U.S. as an ornamental flower. The knapweeds include several species of noxious weeds introduced from Eurasia. Spotted knapweed (*C. maculosa*) covers more than 5 million acres just in Montana, often to the exclusion of all other plnats. The leaves and roots of many species of *Centaurea* are edible (Sturtevant). Medicinally, knapweed is both bitter and astringent (Klein).

Cirsium—Thistle (250/92/9) • Thistles are biennial, tender and edible the first year, turning woody and fiberous the second year when the flower stalk forms. The bull thistle (*C. vulgare*) is especially delicious. The roots are crunchy but good when raw, and even better cooked. The young leaves can be cooked as greens, effectively wilting the spines (Kallas). Thistle roots and foliage contain mineral electrolytes and have an energizing effect when you are exercising (Bigfoot). The stalk of the elk thistle (*C. scariosum*) is edible and delicious (see *Carduus* above). Medicinally, the plants are mildly bitter, an some species are used in bitter formulas (Hobbs).

Onopordum—Cotton Thistle, Scotch Thistle (-/5/1) • The roots are reasonably edible, just fibrous.

Silybyum—Milk Thistle (2/1/0) *Silybyum* was introduced from Europe. It is now found in the Atlantic and Pacific coast states. The young leaves are edible as a salad or potherb. The young stalks are edible after peeling, soaking to remove the bitterness, and cooking. The root is also edible (Sturtevant).

Medicinally, milk thistle is used as a bitter to stimulate liver function. It also contains the flavonoid silymarin which has been shown to protect the liver from toxins. It has been given to patients who ingested toxic amanita mushrooms. The silymarin molecules attach to the liver where the amanita toxins would normally attach, so the toxins pass through the body harmlessly (Klein).

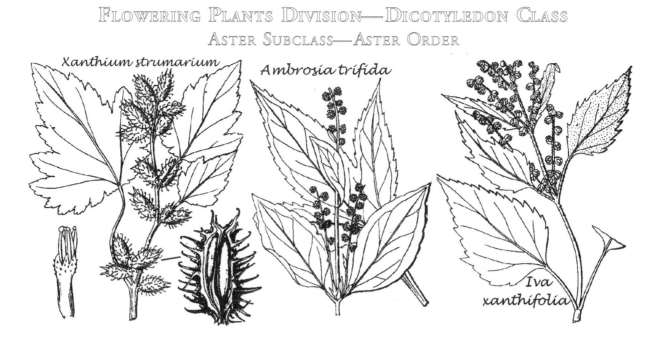

Xanthium strumarium

Ambrosia trifida

Iva xanthifolia

Ragweed Tribe

The flowers of the Ragweed Tribe do not look at all like a typical "sunflower", but they are indeed part of the same family, just a different tribe. Ragweed flowers are usually unisexual, with male and female flowers appearing separately on one plant, an oddity within the Aster family. Another distinguishing feature of the ragweeds is that the anthers (the tips of the stamens) are mostly separated from one another, whereas the anthers are fused together in other members of the family. It would be easy to confuse *Ambrosia* and *Iva* with the "green globby flowers" of the Goosefoot family. The cocklebur is the most noticeable member of the Ragweed tribe. Its sharp cockleburs, a "composite" of two female flowers, are often underfoot along lakes and streams across the West. Note the cross-section of the bur above, showing the two mature seeds inside.

Ambrosia—Ragweed (50/-/3) A tea of the plant was used by the Cheyenne as an antispasmodic and astringent for bowel cramps and bloody stools (Vogel). It is also used for menstrual cramps, but excess consumption can lead to nausea (Bigfoot). The root can be crushed and used as a poultice to remove warts. A tea of the leaves is bitter, useful especially for relief from allergies (Bigfoot).

Iva—False Ragweed, Giant Pigweed (15/-/2) •

Xanthium—Cocklebur (5/-/2) • The leaves are diuretic. The seeds are a more potent diuretic and astringent, with analgesic and antispasmodic effects. A boiled tea of the seed pods is used for persistent diarrhea, also for arthritis. Excessive consumption can be toxic to the intestines and liver (Moore).

Mutisia Tribe

The most distinctive feature of the Mutisia tribe is that the disk flowers are **irregular**. Look close and you will see a two-lipped flower with two petal lobes up and three petal lobes down. Also, the blossoms have no outer ring of petals (the ray flowers). The flowers of this tribe are found in the southern states from coast-to-coast, but **not** in the north.

Chaptalia—Sunbonnets(-/5/0)
Gerbera—Transvaal Daisy (50/-/0)
Perezia—Brownfoot, Desert Holly (-/5/0)
Trixis— (-/2/0)

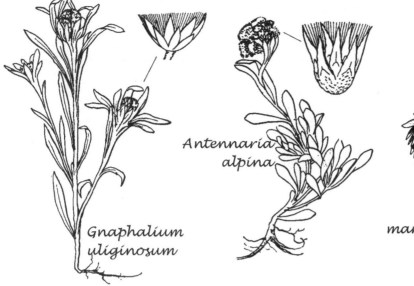

Antennaria alpina

Gnaphalium uliginosum

Anaphalis margaritacea

Everlasting Tribe

If you find a member of the Aster family with grayish vegetation and papery, often colored bracts surrounding a flower with disk flowers but no ray flowers then it is probably a member of the Everlasting trbe. (Only *Inula* has ray flowers.) The bracts around the flowers are properly described as "scarious"—which means thin, dry, and translucent. Please note that the plants of the Camomile tribe also have somewhat scarious bracts, but the Chamomiles have a strong odor, whereas the Inulas do not.

Adenocaulon—Trail Plant (-/1/1) A. bicolor grows from the Great Lakes west to British Columbia and south to California.

Anaphalis—Pearly Everlasting (50/1/1) • *A. margaritacea*, a tea ofthe plant is principally astringent an diaphoretic, also with expectorant properties. It is used in the expected ways, for colds, fevers, sore throats, and to expel worms. The smoke is inhaled to relieve headaches (Willard). Pearly everlasting has a mildly antihistamine effect. It has been used in the treatment of asthma (Tilford).

Antennaria—Pussytoes (85/85/12) • *Antennaria* contains tannin, volatile oils, resin, and bitters (Schauenberg). It is astringent and diuretic; the tea is used for liver inflammations and for irritations of the upper intestines. As an astringent it is useful as a vaginal douche (Moore). It may act as a vasoconstrictor, and raise blood pressure (Lust).

Gnaphalium—Cudweed, Everlasting (150/29/6) *Gnaphalium* is astringent, diuretic, and diaphoretic, used especially as a gargle for sore throat; also moked for headache, o used to expel worms (Lut).

Filago—Fluffweed (-/11/2)

Inula—Elecampane (-/1/0) *I. helenium* was introduced from Eurasia.

Inula helenium

Camomile Tribe

The Camomile tribe includes some of the most richly *aromatic* plants of the Aster family. The other distinguishing characteristic is that the bracts surrounding the flower base are somewhat "scarious"—that is they are thin, dry, and translucent. Please note that the members of the Everlasting tribe also have scarious bracts (much more translucent), but the plants lack the odor characteristic of the Chamomiles. If your specimen has *both* the odor and the translucent bracts then it belongs with te Chamomiles.

Achillea—Yarrow (100/5/2) • Yarrow contains a volatile oil and a bitter principle (Densmore). It is astringent, diuretic and diaphoretic. The Latin name comes from the warrior Achilles who reputedly used yarrow to stop the bleeding from wounded soldiers (Hart). Internally, the tea can be used to decrease menstruation or shrink hemorrhoids, also to stimulate sweating in a dry fever (Moore). Drinking the tea will speed up childbirth and will aid in expelling the afterbirth. It is apparently a lactose stimulant. Also used to ease the transition of menopause (Willard). I have found that a little yarrow tincture on a tissue, stufed up the nostril, will stop a bloody nose in seconds. My grandma always gave me yarrow tea with honey when I had a cold, or sometimes just to enjoy.

Anthemis—Dog Fennel, Camomile (110/8/1) Camomle tea is useful as a antispasmodic and carminative for the digestive system; also as a mild sedative, especially for restless children. The flowers can be used in a rubbing oil on painful joints (Lust). Also used for migraine headaches (Schauenberg).

Artemisia—Sagebrush, Wormwood, Tarragon (250/100/19) • *Artemisia* is prolific all over the west. We have 6 different species growing just on our 5 acre "homestead" in southwest Montana. Some species are commonly used as a smudge for purification before entering sweatlodges and other ceremonial events. Please note that the *Artemisia* specie are not related to culinary sage, which belongs to the Mint family.

The *Artemisias* contain potent volatile oils, some tannins, and a bitter substance. Medicinally, the bitter tea acts as a digestive aid, but the volatile oils in some species can lead to permanent nervous disorders with prolonged use (Schauenberg). The *Artemisias* are useful as a menstrual stimulant and as a vermifuge. Some species of *Artemisia* will decrease the effects of rancid fats (called lipid peroxides, such as in old donuts, etc.) on the liver (Moore). *A. drancunculoides* and *A. dracunculus* are the culinary spice called tarragon, used in tartar sauce, hollandaise, and bé arnaise.

Chrysanthemum—Oxeye Daisy (200/18/2) • Imported from Europe. The leaves are edible. A tea of the herb is diuretic and astringent useful in predictable ways for stomach ulcers, and bloody piles or urine. Also used as a vaginal douche for cervical ulceration (Willard). The daisy is aromatic, used as an antispasmodic for colic and general digestive upset.

Matricaria—Pineapple Weed, Caomile (50/5/2) • Pineapple weed is a sweet-smelling herb often found in lawns and driveways. The fresh plant is edible. It is an excellent tea, similar but milder than chamomile. It is listed as diaphoretic, antispasmodic, stimulant, and sedative. It is a mild remedy, safe for children, used for stomach pains, colds, fevers, and as a menstrual stimulant (Hutchins). It is also a lactose stimulant (Willard). The tea is said to aid in delivering the placenta (Hart). The aromatic constituents act as a mild anesthetic and antispasmodic to the mouth and stomach (Moore). Also carminative and anti-inflammatory (Lust). Some species are not aromatic.

Tanecetum—Tansy (-/-/3) • Tansy was introduced as a medicinal herb. It is now a noxious weed in many parts of country. It contains a bitter principle (Densmore), plus resins, volatile oils, tannic and gallic acids, gums, lime, and lead oxide, amongst other things. In small doses the tea is used as a diaphoretic and emmeagogue. In large doses it can cause convulsions, vomiting, reduced heart function and coma (Hutchins). It should not be used at all without much additional research, and should never be used during pregnancies. Some individuals have died using oil of tansy to cause abortions.

Achillea millefolium

Artemisia tridentata

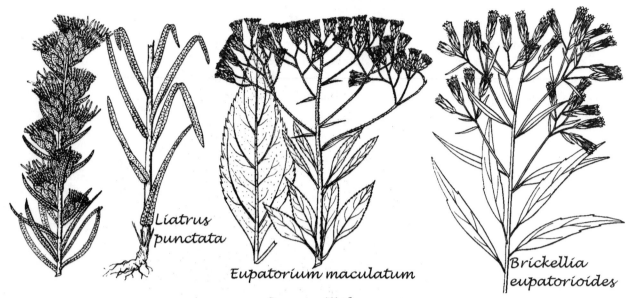

Liatrus punctata

Eupatorium maculatum

Brickellia eupatorioides

Boneset Tribe

Members of the Boneset Tribe are distinguished from oher composites by the shape of their stigmas, which are thickened in the ends much like a baseball bat is. It is a pretty nit-picky distinction, but then it is botany! Otherwise the flowers lack an outer ring of petals (the ray flowers) and none of the blossoms are pure yellow. These plants are most easily confused with the Ironweed Tribe.

Brickellia—Thoroughwort (-/12/3) • A tea of the leaves is reported to be useful for insulin-resistant diabetes (Bigfoot).

Eupatorium—Joe Pye Weed, Boneset (600/50/2) Boneset contains tannins and bitters (Schauenberg).. The hot tea has been used for centuries as a diaphoretic to treat fevers, including dengue, also known as "breakbone fever", from which it gets its common name. This common name as led to some confusion so that some recent herbalists have recommend boneset to aid in knitting broken bones. There is neither the history nor scientific basis to support that use. Boneset may act as a cathartic or emetic (Lust).

Gutierrizia—Snakeweed (-/-/1) A tea of the plant is used in a bath to reduce inflammation from arthritis and rheumatism. It is safe for repeated, long-term use. The tea is also used to decrease menstruation (Moore).

Liatris—Gay Feather (34/34/2) • In August our place is covered with the blossoms of *Liatris*, one of my favorite flowers. Medicinally it is astringent and diuretic. The roots are burned and the smoke inhaled for headache, nosebleed, sore throat, and tonsil inflammation. A tea of the root is similarly used for sore throat and laryngitis (Moore).

Ironweed Tribe

Members of the Ironweed Tribe can be distinguished from the Bonesets and other composites by the shape of their stigmas, which are long, thread-like, and hairy. Similar to the Bonesets, there are no ray flowers and virtually none of the blossoms are pure yellow. The Ironweeds are found in the southern and eastern states, **not** in the northwest or the Rocky Mountains.

Veronia—Ironweed (600/22/0)
Elephantopus—Elephant's Foot (-/4/0)

Vernonia noveboracensis

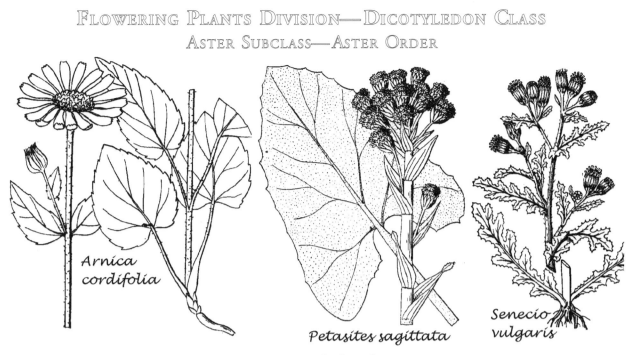

Arnica cordifolia

Petasites sagittata

Senecio vulgaris

Groundsel Tribe

Many memers of the Aster family grow a "pappus" of white hair around each of the little flowers inside the larger head. The Goundsels are distinguished from other Asters by the *soft, silky quality* of the pappus hair. The hair is usually pure white and very abundant.

Arnica—Arnica (-/32/13) • Arnica has been used externally for centuries to treat bruises, arthritis and other inflammations. It may be used fresh as a poultice or otherwise as a tea, tincture, oil or salve (Moore). The active constituents are believed to be sesquiterpenoid lactones (Tyler). Arnica stimulates and dilates the blood vessels near the surface, improving circulation to the injured area. In rare cases it causes severe dermatitis (Moore). Arnica may be used as a mouth rinse to aid sore throat, or taken in small doses to treat bruises and inflammations from the inside—but only if you are physically strong and do not have any diseases of the kidney, liver, or blood vessels (Moore). Please note: arnica is toxic to the heart, and it can significantly raise blood pressure (Tyler). It has put children in comas (Kinucan).

Petasites—Butterbur, Coltsfoot (including *Tussilago*) (20/-/1) *Petasites* are our native genera of coltsfoot. *Tussilago* was introduced to the northeastern states from Europe and may or may not be a separate genera (Moore). Coltsfoot leaves and stems are edible as potherbs. The plant has a salty flavor and may be used as a salt substitute (Tilford).

Young coltsfoot leaves contain traces of pyrrolizidine alkaloids, but virtually none at maturity. Other constituents of the leaves include a sesquiterpene ester, saponins, and mucilage. A tea of the leaves is especially useful as a cough suppressant and expectorant. The leaves may be smoked for chronic coughing.

The roots contain volatile oils and resins. A poultice of the crushed root is useful to lessen the pain and inflammation of an injury. It sedates the nerves and depresses the rate of nerve-firing, at least when applied to a part of the body with many sensory nerves (Moore).

Senecio—Groundsel (1500/120/24) • Groundsels are diuretic, astringent, and diaphoretic (Hutchins). In larger quantities the plants may be emetic or purgative (strongly laxative) (Willard). The plants contain pyrrolizidine alkaloids, which can damage the live..

The Sunflower, Aster, and Sneezeweed Tribes

If you have a composite flower that does not belong to the Dandelion subfamily or to any of the previous tribes of the Aster subfamily, then chances are it belongs to either the Sunflower, Aster, or Sneezeweed tribes. These tribes include many showy "sunflowerlike" flowers, and they can be tricky to distinguish from one another.

First, to distinguish the Sunflower Tribe, pull apart the flowerhead and look for the presence of a small bract attached at the base of each disk flower. The Sunflowers have them; the other tribes do not. Members of the Sunflower Tribe usually also have opposite leaves *at the base* of the plant; upper leaves can be alternate or opposite.

Once you have ruled out the Sunflower Tribe then you can distinguish the Asters from the Sneezeweeds by comparing the layers of bracts surrounding the flower head. Members of the Aster Tribe usually have multiple layers of bracts of unequal length, while most of the Sneezeweeds have only one row of bracts, and none have more than three rows. Also, the Sneezeweeds often have glands or dots of resin on the leaves.

151

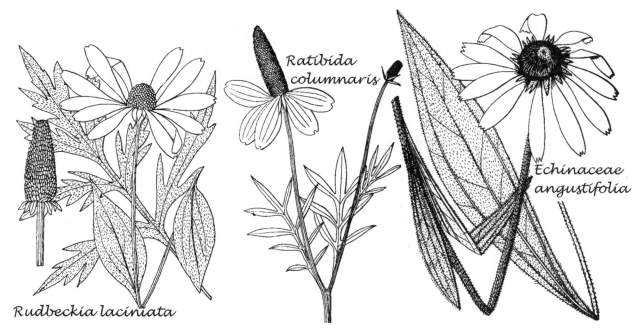

Ratibida columnaris

Echinaceae angustifolia

Rudbeckia laciniata

Suflower Tribe

Most members of the Sunflower Tribe are noticeably *resinous*. Just taste or smell any part of a sunflower head and you will notice the pitchy quality. Resins are especially useful as *expectorants* to help clear out mucous after a cold. Be sure to read more about resins in the Medicinal Properties section of this book. *Echinacea* has become a prominent member of the tribe in recent years, due to its *immunostimulating* qualities. The plant is now endangered and should not be picked in the wild. Other members of the tribe may have similar properties.

Balsamorhiza—Arrowleaf Balsamroot (12/11/3) • The young leaves and shoots are said to be good as a salad or potherb. The root, according to Willard, is good raw, boiled, or prepared in any other way. According to Hart it was cooked for three or more days in a steam pit. I cooked the root for four hours in the microwave without phasing it. (It was too fibrous.) I will have to try again. The seeds are edible (Willard).

    The medicinal part of arrowleaf balsamroot is the thick, resinous bark of the root. A tea of the root bark coats the throat with the sticky resins, soothing a sore throat and acting as an expectorant. Balsamroot also contains volatile oils, useful as a diaphoretic. Balsamroot has immunostimulating properties similar to *Echinacea*, but not quite as potent (Tilford).

Bidens—Beggerstick (-/30/3) A tea or tincture of certain species is used for irritation, inflammation, pain and bleeding of the urinary tract mucosa (Moore).

Coreopsis—Tickseed (-/40/2)

Echinacea—Purple Coneflower (7/7/1) • *Echinacea* was the fad herb of the 1990's. The plant and root have been shown to stimulate the immune system, useful for both preventing and curing viral infections The effectiveness of *Echinacea* is well-documented, but the reasons why it works are the subject of continued debate. It is most useful for "surface" conditions like the common cold, while other herbs are more appropriate for deep immune deficiencies (Hobbs). Even I have been hooked on the wonders of *Echinacea*—after trading copies of this book for the tincture. In addition to other measures (reduced dairy and sugar intake), the *Echinacea* helped me get through an entire winter without succumbing to the flu. I start taking the tincture at the earliest symptoms of a cold.

    Echinacea is considered highly effective for candidis and vaginal yeast infections (Hobbs). Also, the smoke is inhaled for headaches and the juice is used on burns. *Echinacea* is used for inflammations, mumps, measles (Willard) and just about anything else that ails you. Unfortunately the herb has been seriously over-harvested in the wild. Please only purchase formulas made with cultivated *Echinacea*.

Franseria—Bursage (-/-/2) The plant may be poisonous (Bigfoot).

Galinsoga—Quickweed (-/-/2)

Haplopappus—Goldenweed (-/-/15) The plant is resinous and aromatic. A tea is used externally for skin fungus (Bigfoot).

Helianthus—Sunflower, Jerusalem Artichoke, Sun Tubers (100/50/5) • *H. annus* is an annual, weedy sunflower, often producing 50 or more sunflower heads per plant. Early botanists brought this sunflower back to Europe, and then to Russia, where it was convinced to develop one big head with big seeds, rather than dozens of little heads with little seeds

(Hutchins). All sunflowers produce edible seeds that are high in oil. I eat them shells and all; it is simpler than trying to extract the tiny seeds. It is recommended that you harvest them with a seed beater and grind them on a metate for use as mush (Olsen). Sunflower seeds are rich in phosphorus, calcium, iron, fluorine, iodine, potassium, magnesium, sodium, thiamin (vitamin B), niacin, vitamin D, and protein (Hutchins), beneficial as a nutritional supplement.

The Jerusalem artichoke (H. tuberosus) is a perennial sunflower often cultivated for its enlarged, starchy roots. The popular name is quizical, since the plant was native to eastern North America and the edible part is more like a potato than an artichoke. I started calling them "sun tubers", which is much more descriptive.

Their roots are high in inulin polysaccharides, good for diabetics (Gibbons). Sun tubers are delicious simply boiled, and even better the following day, after more of the inulin has converted to fructose. Read more about inulin in the Medicinal Properties section of this book.

Sunflower plants and flowerheads are quite resinous, listed as diuretic and expectorant, used for coughs, kidneys, and rheumatism (Willard).

Madia—Tarweed (-/17/3) • I always smell tarweed before I see it. The odor is powerfully resinous, but also almost sweet. I like to put a stem on the dashboard of the car for fragrence, but usually have to keep the windows open to breathe! The seeds are extremely rich in oil, used in cooking (Sturtevant).

Ratibida—Prairie Coneflower (6/4/1) • The roots are mildly diuretic. The plant may have qualities similar to *Echinacea.*

Rudbeckia—Coneflower (30/24/2) • A tea of the root or leaves is a stimulating diuretic, also acting as a mild cardiac stimulant (Moore).

Thelasperma—Cota, Greenthread, Navajo Tea (-/13/1) *Thelasperma* is mildly diuretic. It is a popular tea where it is abundant in the southwest (Moore).

Viguiera—Golden-Eye (-/11/1)

Wyethia—Mule's Ears (-/14/2) • The seeds are edible. The root of *W. helianthoides* is edible after extensive cooking (Olsen). The poultice is used for rheumatism (Murphey).

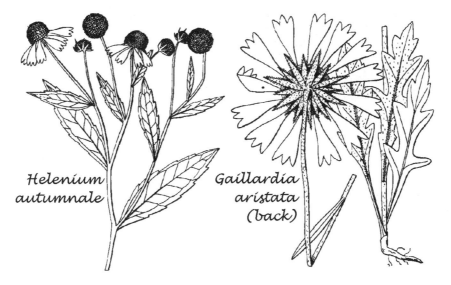

Helenium autumnale

Gaillardia aristata (back)

Sneezeweed Tribe

Little information is available on the properties or uses of the wild members of the Sneezeweed tribe. Marigold (*Tagetes*) can be included in this tribe or separated into its own.

Bahia— (-/11/1)

Chaenactis—Dusty Maiden (-/22/2) • The flower has three rows of unequal bracts. A tea of the plant is reportedly used as a fever medicine for children, but it may act as a sedative on the heart (Murphey).

Dyssodia—Dogweed (-/15/1)

Eriophyllum— (-/11/1)

Gaillardia—Brown-Eyed Susan, Blanket Flower (-/14/1) • *Gaillardia* is apparently astringent (Willard).

Helenium—Sneezeweed (40/20/1) The crushed blossoms are used as an inhalant for hay fever (Murphey).

Hulsea— (-/8/1)

Hymenopappus— (-/12/1)

Hymenoxis—Bitterweed (-/22/4) The root contains a latex that may be used as chewing gum. It is a potential source for commercial rubber (Fern).

Aster foliaceus

Grindelia squarrosa

Erigeron subtrinervis

Solidago neglecta

Chrysothamnus nauseosus

Aster Tribe

Although a number of the Asters are mildly astingent, there are many other qualities within the tribe that do not offer a clear pattern. Based on its properties, gmweed seems like it should be part of the Sunflower tribe.

Aster—Aster (500/150/28) • Asters are astringent; some may be mild enough for alads.

Baccharis—Seep Willow (400/-/0)

Bellis—Wild Daisy (10/1/1) *B. perennis* was introduced from Europe. The tea is used as a digestive aid, antispasmodic, laxative, expectorant, and demulcent (Lust). Te leaves can b used as a potherb (Sturtevant). The flowerheads contain saponins (Schauenberg).

Chrysopsis—Golden Aster (-/39/1) •

Chrysothamnus—Rabbitbrush (12/-/2) • The young shoots are edible, and the latex can be chewed as gum (Olsen).

Erigeron—Fleabane Daisy (250/140/30) • The fleabanes are astringent and diuretic, usful in every conventional way (Willard). *E. canadensis* is known to cntain a volaile oil (Densmore).

Grindelia—Gumweed (50/33/2) • *Grindelia* is rich in amorphous resins, tannic acid, volatile oils, and contains the alkaloid grindeline (Hart). A tea of the plant orflowers has expectant properties, probably due to the resins. It is principally used for the lungs, for coughing, athma, bronchitis, and such. A poultice of the plant can be used as a stimulant to bring healin to rheumatim, sores, and rashs (Willard). Also used as a diuretic (Hutchins). Gumweed may absorb selenium from the soil (Lust).

Solidago—Goldenrod (100/90/11) • Goldenrod seeds are edible as mush or as a stew thickener (Olsen), and the young greens are edible as a potherb. The dried flowers make a pleasant tea. Goldenrod contains saponins, tannins, bitters, flavonoids and a volatile oil (Schauenberg). Goldenrod is a source of pollen allergies, but it may also be useful in building resistance to such allergies. The dried, powdered plant was once used to stop bleeding on battlefields (Tilford).

Townsendia—(-/22/6)

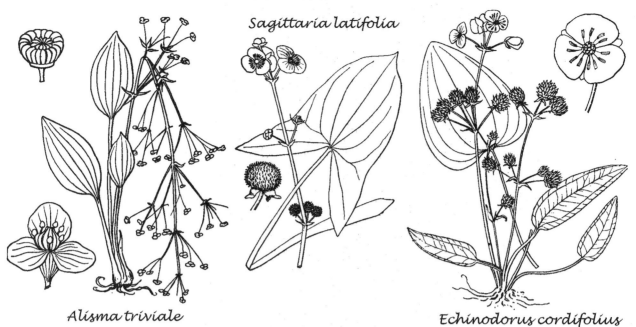

Sagittaria latifolia

Alisma triviale

Echinodorus cordifolius

Alismataceae—Arrowhead Family

If you were to compare the blossoms from *Sagittaria* of the Arrowhead family to the blossom of a typical buttercup (*Ranunculus*) you would see some striking similarities, especially the numerous pistils clustered together in a ball or cone shape in the center of the blossom and the numerous stamens around them. Of all the monocot plants, the plants of the Arrowhead family have retained the most ancestral characteristics, while the same is true for the Buttercup family among the dicot plants. So even though these families are categorized in completely different classes, they are still somewhat related.

Members of the Arrowhead family are aquatic herbs with 3 green sepals and 3 white petals. There may be 3, 6, or numerous stamens. These primitive flowers have 6 or more simple pistils (apocarpous). The pistils are positioned superior to the other parts. Each pistil matures as a single dry seed, called an achene. The leaves are basal, and either erect or floating. World-wide there are 13 genera and 90 species. Five genera are native to North America, including Burhead (*Echinodorus*), *Lophotocarpus*, and *Machaerocarpus*, plus the genera below. Another Latin name for this family is *Alismaceae*. Many species produce starchy, *edible* roots.

<u>Key Words</u>: Monocot flowers with parts in 3's and numerous simple pistils.

Alisma—Water Plantain (10/4/2) • The roots are acrid raw, but edible after thorough cooking or drying (Olsen). The young, cooked plants are also edible and salty tasting. Medicinally, the acrid leaves can be applied as a stimulating poultice for bruises and swellings. The root is reported to lower cholesterol and blood sugar levels, and reduce blood pressure. The powdered seed is astringent, used to stop bleeding. It may cause sterility (Fern).

Sagittaria—Arrowhead, Wapato (20/16/2) • The slender, long roots of the arrowhead plant form starchy swellings in the fall that reportedly can be as large as an egg. These can be boiled or roasted and eaten. These plants are somewhat rare in my region, and the swollen roots I found were the size of small marbles.

    In Oregon, where Wapato grows larger and more abundant, John Kallas reports harvesting 88 tubers in fifteen minutes, ranging from 3/4 to 2 inches long and 3/4 to 1 1/4 inches wide, weighing a total of 1 pound 10 ounces. He conducted his test in late May, just as the tubers were beginning to sprout new shoots. His technique was to gather the roots in shallow water, by stomping around on a small area until the tubers were dislodged and floated to the surface. Kallas wrote that it was important to work a small area really well to knock the tubers loose, and suggested that a person's body weight might be a factor in how well the technique works, since a heavier person will have more impact (Kallas).

Juncaginaceae—Arrowgrass Family

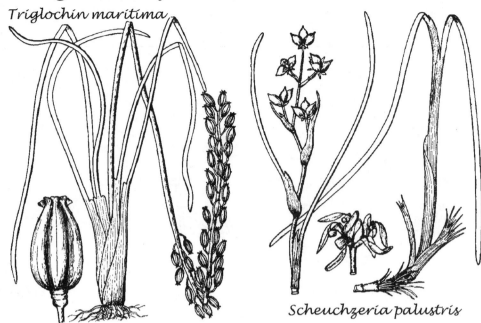

Triglochin maritima

Scheuchzeria palustris

Members of the Arrowgrass family are perennial herbs, typically growing in shallow fresh or salt water or in damp meadows. The flowers can be either bisexual or unisexual. The flowers are small, with 3 sepals and 3 petals or 6 "tepals" a term used when the sepals and petals cannot be distinguished from each other. There are usually 6 stamens (sometimes 4, and only 1 in *Lilaea*). There are 3-6 simple pistils (apocarpous), wholly separated or united only at the base, forming 1 or a few seeds per cell. The pistils are positioned superior to the other parts. Each pistil matures into a dry fruit called a "follicle" (a capsule that opens along a single seam).

World-wide there are 4 genera and 26 species. North American genera are featured below. *Scheuchzeria* is sometimes separated into its own family, *Scheuchzeriaceae*.

Key Words: Grassy plants with non-showy flowers and 3-6 simple pistils.

Lilaea—Flowering Quillwort (1/1/1) *L. scilloides*.
Scheuchzeria— (-/1/1)
Triglochin—Arrowgrass (15/3/3) • The plant and seeds contain a type of cyanide. They are quite poisonous raw, but cooking destroys the cyanide (Olsen). The leaves may also be edible with cooking (Harrington). The ashes of the plant are rich in potassium, useful for making soap (Fern).

Najadaceae—Water Nymph Family

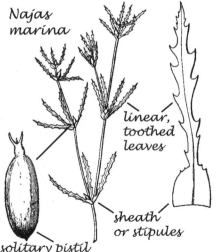

Najas marina

linear, toothed leaves

sheath or stipules

solitary pistil

Members of the Water Nymph family are truly aquatic plants that live and even pollinate fully submerged in the water. The leaves are linear and toothed with either stipules or sheathing bases. The flowers are unisexual, usually with male and female flowers appearing on the same plants (monoecious). Staminate (male) flowers consist of a single stamen enclosed by a bract. Pistillate (female) flowers consist of a single simple pistil (unicarpellate), naked, or sometimes enclosed by a membranous bract. The pistil matures as a dry seed called an achene.

World wide there is only 1 genus and about 50 species. Half a dozen species are found in North America, mostly in the eastern states. Two species are found in lakes and ponds of western states. The genus and family names are often spelled with an "i" rather than a "j", as in *Naiadaceae*.

Key Words:
Submerged aquatic plants with toothed, linear leaves.

Najas—Water Nymph (50/6/2)

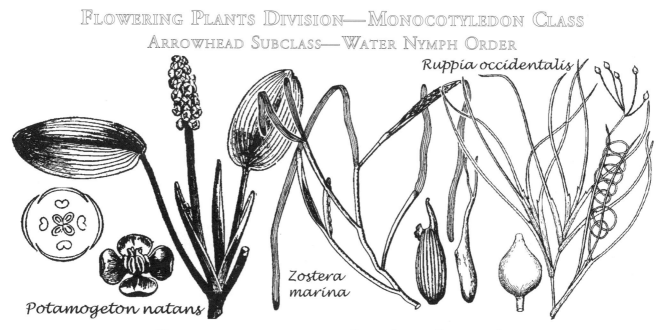

Ruppia occidentalis

Zostera marina

Potamogeton natans

Potamogetonaceae—Pondweed Family

Members of Pondweed family are perennial, aquatic herbs, usually found in fresh or salty water rather than swamps. The plants have both narrow, submerged leaves and broad, floating leaves. The flowers are usually bisexual, except for a few species that produce male and female parts in separate flowers on the same plant (monoecious). There are 4 scale-like "tepals", a term used to describe either petals or sepals, and 4 stamens. There are 1-4 simple pistils (apocarpous), each maturing as a single dry seed (an achene), or sometimes as a drupe (a berry with a stony seed) or nutlet.

World-wide there are 9 genera and 100 species. Our native genera are listed below. Some botanists split *Ruppia*, *Zannichellia*, and *Zostera* into their own families, *Ruppiaceae*, *Zannichelliaceae*, and *Zosteraceae*

Key Words: Monocots with submerged and floating leaves. Flower parts often in 4's.

Cymodocea—Manatee Grass (-/1/0) Manatee grass is found along coastal bays and creeks from Florida to Louisiana.

Halodule— (-/1/0) *Halodule is found in bays, creeks and reefs off southern Florida.*

Phyllospadix—Surf Grass(-/2/0) *Northwest coast Indians surf grass and eel grass to generate steam for bending wood (Turner), probably by placing the fresh plants on hot rocks.*

Potamogeton—Pondweed (100/30/21) The root stalks can be cooked in stew (Olsen). They are reported to have a nutty flavor. The rind should be removed (Fern).

Ruppia—Ditch Grass (2/2/1) Ditch Grass is found across North America.

Zannichellia—Grass Wrack, Horned Pondweed (-/-/1) Grass wrack is found across most of North America.

Zostera—Eel Grass (-/1/0) Eel grass is found in coastal waters.

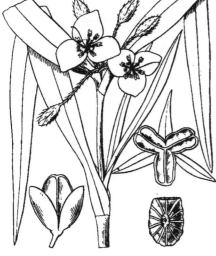

Tradescantia virginiana

Commelinaceae—Spiderwort Family

If you have a succulent, vining house plant with purple leaves and parallel veins, then you certainly have a member of the Spiderwort family. The Spiderworts have *nearly* regular, bisexual flowers with 3 sepals and 3 petals, usually with two broad petals and the third reduced in size. The petals range from blue to violet, pink, white or rose-colored, never yellow. There are 6 stamens, and the filaments (stamen stems) are often covered with bright hairs. The ovary is positioned superior and consists of 3 (rarely 2) united carpels (syncarpous) with the partition walls present, forming an equal number of chambers. It matures as a capsule with a few seeds per cell.

The leaves are alternate, succulent, and sharply folded with the leaf base sheathing the stem. The plants and roots are mucilaginous. The spiderworts could easily be mistaken for lilies, but most lilies have sepals and petals of approximately equal size and color, while the Spiderworts have smaller, usually green sepals.

World-wide there are about 40 genera and 600 species, mostly in the tropics. Six genera are native to North America. Several others are cultivated. A number of plants in this family are called "wandering Jew", and are grown as house plants.

Key Words
Lily-like flowers with small sepals and mucilaginous stems.

Aneilema— (-/1/0) *Aneilema* is found in the south from Texas to Georgia and Florida. The sepals are the same size and color as the petals.

Commelina—Wandering Jew, Day Flower (150/8/D) • *Commelina* grows wild across the eastern and southern states. The tender shoots are edible as a salad or potherb (Duke). The roots of many species are known to be starchy and edible (Sturtevant). Medicinally, a tea of the mucilaginous leaves is used as a gargle for sore throat. The plant has antibacterial properties (Fern).

Commelinantia—False Day-Flower (-/1/0) Grows in central Texas.

Tradescantia—Spiderwort (30+/21/2) • The plant is edible in salads. The stem has a white, mucilaginous sap (Bigfoot). Medicinally, a poultice of the leaves is used on insect bites and cancers. The roots are considered laxative, also used in tea for stomach aches (Fern).

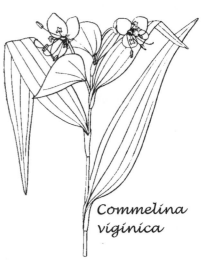

Commelina viginica

Juncaceae—Rush Family

The plants of the Rush family might best be described as "lilies-turned-to-grass". The flowers are similar to lilies, with 3 sepals, 3 petals and 6 stamens (sometimes 3) surrounding a pistil with a 3-celled ovary and a 3-parted stigma. The ovary is positioned superior and matures as a capsule. The only significant difference from the lilies is that rush flowers are small and green, and the plants look more like grasses or sedges.

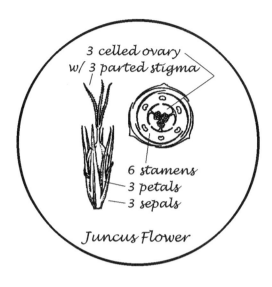

3 celled ovary
w/ 3 parted stigma

6 stamens
3 petals
3 sepals

Juncus Flower

World-wide there are 9 genera and 400 species, mostly of *Juncus*. Two genera are found in North America, as listed below. Members of the family are well-represented in the fossil record as far back as the Cretaceous period, mostly because the plants grow in wet habitats where fossils are made. The vegetation is tough enough to fossilize well, and it leaves recognizeable imprints in the mud.

Key Words: "Lilies-turned-to-grass."

Juncus—Rush (220/-/28) • The seeds of at least some species were used as food. An edible sugar may be found on top of some plants as well. Medicinally, a tea of the plant may have emetic qualities (Moerman).

Luxula—Woodrush (70/-/6) The seeds of at least some species may be cooked and eaten (Fern).

Juncus tenuis

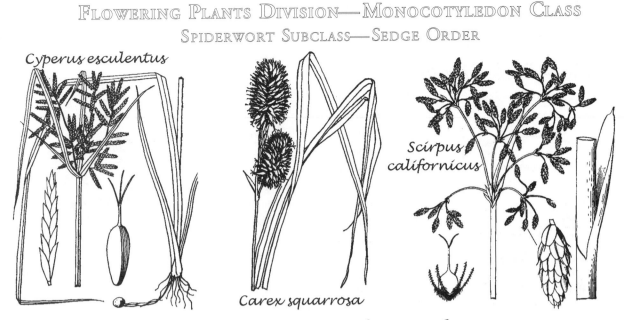

Cyperus esculentus

Carex squarrosa

Scirpus californicus

Cyperaceae—Sedge Family

"Sedges have edges, but grasses have knees" is the familiar rhyme used to remember the distinction between sedges and grasses. Only the grasses have lumpy nodes on the flower stems, while most sedges have a triangular leaf structure. Note however, that *Scripus*, one of the most abundant and visible sedges, has very round stems. It is often found growing with cattails and may be confused with them. You should also read about the characteristics of the Rush family.

Botanically, the sedges have flowers with bristles, hairs, or scales in place of sepals and petals, or none at all. There are typically 3 stamens (sometimes 6 or 1). The ovary is positioned superior and consists of 2 or 3 united carpels (syncarpous), forming a single chamber. It matures as an achene (a dry seed) or a nutlet. The fruit is either lens-shaped or 3-sided, the shape dependant on the number of carpels. World-wide there are about 90 genera and 4,000 species. Twenty-four genera are found in North America. Members of the Sedge family are mostly *edible*, although very few are worth harvesting. The small, but starchy roots are used similar to cattail roots.

Key Words: "Sedges have edges, but grasses have knees."

Carex—Sedge (1100/-/40+) • Medicinally, a tea of sedge roots is diuretic and diaphoretic. It contains silica, and could irritate the kidneys, especially if they are already inflamed (Lust). I've experimented with harvesting the seeds of various species of sedge. I gathered useable quantities from a couple species, but the seeds seemed so small and flat that they did not seem digestible, even after extensive cooking. Sprouting may help.

Cyperus—Chufa (600/-/4) Some species of chufa were cultivated by the Egyptians for their starchy tubers. They can be eaten fresh or cooked, or dried and made into flour (Hall). Optionally the tubers can be roasted and used as a coffee substitute (Angier).

Eleocharis—Spike Rush (-/-/9) The seeds (Olsen) and tubers (Sturtevant) are edible.

Scripus—Bulrush (250/-/14) • Bulrush roots are very similar to cattail roots, and used similarly. Flour can be obtained from the roots by drying them, pounding, and sifting out the fibers. Another method is to cook the roots into mush and then separate out the fibers. The younger roots are rich in sugar; these can be bruised and boiled down to produce a syrup. The pollen can be collected in season and used as flour. The seeds are reported to be edible (Hall), but I have found that they are not very digestible, even after grinding through a flour mill and boiling as mush. Probably they just needed to mature a couple more weeks on the plants. Sprouting the seeds before cooking may help too.

Medicinally, the starchy roots may be used as a drawing poultice, especially if first soaked in a tannic acid solution (Brown). Bulrushes can also be made into a sort of candle. First, carefully strip away the outer layer, revealing the pith. Leave a narrow strip of the outside intact for structural support. Saturate the pith in some type of fat or oil, such as lard, and the "rush light" is ready for use (Mabey).

Other selected genera from the Sedge family include: *Bulbostylis*— (-/-/1) … *Dulichium*—(1/1/1) … *Eriophorum*—Cotton grass (15/-/6) … *Hemicarpha*—Dwarf bulrush (-/-/1) … *Kobresia*— (50/2)

Poaceae (Gramineae)—Grass Family

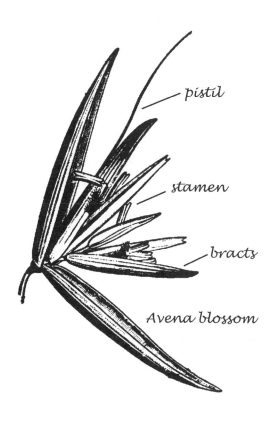

pistil

stamen

bracts

Avena blossom

We do not normally think of the grasses as flowers, yet they are. They only lack the showy petals and sepals because they are *wind pollinated*, and do not need to attract insects. The flowers typically have 3 stamens (rarely 2 or 6). The ovary consists of 3 united carpels (syncarpous/tricarpellate), forming a single chamber. It matures a single seed called a caryopsis (grain) or rarely an achene (a dry seed) or a berry. The flower is contained by modified leaves, called bracts. These are the chaff that is later winnowed out of harvested grain. World-wide there are about 600 genera and 10,000 species of grass. About 180 genera and 1,000 species appear in North America

All of our **cereal grains** belong to this family, including wheat (*Triticum*), rice (*Oryza*), wild rice (*Zizania*), corn (*Zea*), oats (*Avena*), barley (*Hordeum*), millet (*Echinochloa*), and rye (*Secale*). The seeds of virtually all other grasses are also considered edible, if they are not infected by the ergot fungus (see sidebar). A notable exception is rye grass (*Lolium*), which is used as a sedative and vasodilator. It is considered poisonous in excess (Lust). Although most grass seeds are edible, they are not all necessarily *economical*. Some seeds are too small, or otherwise difficult to process into a useable product. For instance, the very small seeds can be difficult to digest. They can be too small to grind on a metate, and too small to swell and turn to mush when cooked as a hot cereal. The best grasses to work with are those with big seeds, much heavier than the surrounding chaff. This makes it easier to blow the chaff away, while keeping the seeds.

There are three main techniques of **harvesting** cereal grains with crude implements. One method is to simply strip the whole seed heads by hand, collecting the material in a container. Another method of harvesting is to beat the seed heads with a stick, while catching the seeds in a pan or tarp. The third method is to cut the whole stalks, place them on a tarp, and then beat the seeds out. The plants can be dried on the tarp to make the seeds drop easier.

The next step in the process is to break the seeds free from the chaff. **Rubbing** the rough material between the palms is sufficient for most grains. Some seeds, however, are encased in a husk that is impossible to rub free of the grain. These seeds are ground up husk and all, for a high-fiber cereal. Also, a few grass seeds can be parched and then rubbed to remove the husk. Grasses that are hairy or sharp should be avoided, as they could cause irritation or injury to the throat.

Winnowing is the next step, to remove the chaff once it is broken free of the seeds. Winnowing is a little like gold-panning, where you catch the weighty metal and wash the lighter debris away; in fact, I recommend using a gold-pan for this process. Swirling the pan, and occasionally tossing the grain lightly in the air, brings the light chaff to the surface, so it can be blown away.

Another commonly used method is to toss the rubbed material in the air, such that the seeds will fall straight down on a tarp, and a light breeze will carry the chaff away, beyond the tarp. I have not had good results with this method, so I prefer the gold-pan/blowing technique, where I can precisely control the flow of wind. In either case you will not be able to completely clean out the chaff. There is always some left. That is okay. It is good roughage for the digestive system.

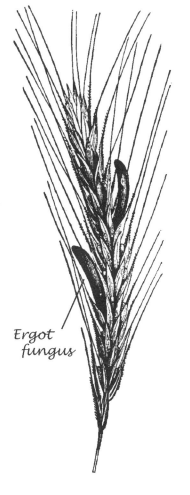

Ergot fungus

161

Harvested grains can be cooked whole as a hot cereal, or ground into flour and used for bread or mush. Cooking them whole may reduce the labor involved, but the grains must be cooked almost to mush or they will pass through your system undigested. The very small seeds may not ever soften enough to become digestible. Another alternative is to **sprout** the seeds. This makes the material digestible, although it also converts much of the starch and oil content into proteins. Some wild grasses that have a known history of use as cereal grains include:

Agropyron—Wheatgrass, Quackgrass (60/-/2) • The seeds are harvested with a seed beater and ground on a metate for use as mush or flour (Olsen).

Agrostis—Bentgrass, Redtop (125/-/12) The seeds are harvested with a seed beater and ground on a metate for use as mush or flour (Olsen).

Beckmannia—Sloughgrass (-/-/1) The seeds were eaten by the Indians in Utah (Sturtevant).

Bromus—Bromegrass, Cheat Grass (100/-/14) • The seeds of many species of bromegrass are known to have been eaten by the Indians (Duke). Cheat grass is a weedy species of *Bromus* introduced from Europe.

Ergot Fungus

Be sure to inspect the seeds of all grasses for the presence of ergot fungus (*Claviceps purpurea* or *C. paspali*). Ergot consumes the grass seeds, forming a black or purplish powder. Ergot can stimulate uterine contractions and abortions. A derivative of ergot is used as a medicine for migraine and cluster headaches. Ergot is also a source of LSD.

Ergot contamination in cereal grains can be extremely dangerous. *C. paspali* effects the nervous system. causing trembling, staggering, and paranoia. The witch hunts of Salem, Massachusetts in the 1600's are believed to have been a result of ergot contamination in stored grains. Many people were burned at the stake by the Puritans running around on LSD. *C. pupurea*, on the other hand, restricts the blood flow to the extremities, slowly killing the flesh on the fingers, toes, and ears, with long-term consumption. Gangrene bacteria, similar to botulism, rots away the dead tissues, often forming a foul gas. A religious order was formed to deal with this disease; the medics torched the rotting flesh off the victims and prayed they lived. They group adopted St. Anthony as their patron saint, and the disease came to be known as St. Anthony's Fire. In 1916 Federal Government regulations restricted the use or ergot-infested grain to .3% of weight for making flour. This virtually ended the disease of ergotism in this country. Needless to say, ergot is potentially very dangerous, and should not be used without expert supervision.

Deschampsia— (-/-/5) The seeds are harvested with a seed beater and ground on a metate for use as mush or flour (Olsen).

Digitaria—Crabgrass (300/-/2) • The seeds are a substitute for rice in Poland. One plant can produce 150,000 seeds (Duke).

Echinochloa—Barnyard Grass, Millet (20/-/2) • The cultivated millet is a species of this genus (Duke). The seeds are harvested with a seed beater and ground on a metate for use as mush or flour (Olsen).

Elymus—Wild rye, Wheatgrass (50/-/19) The seeds are harvested with a seed beater, or stripped by hand. They are winnowed and ground on a metate for use as mush or flour (Olsen). The stems were used as temporary arrows (Turner).

Festuca—Fescue (100/-/14) • The seeds are parched to remove the husk, ground into flour, or cooked as mush (Olsen).

Glyceria—Mannagrass (35/-/4) The is reported to be one of the better tasting grains found in the West. The seeds are gathered with a seed beater and winnowed to remove the chaff. They are used as a thickening for stews, or ground into flour (Olsen).

Hordeum—Barley, Foxtail Barley (25/-/6) Cooking hulled (pearled) barley produces a mucilaginous substance, useful as a demulcent for a sore throat. It is mixed with milk to soothe the stomach and intestines (Lust). Some wild species are known to have been used by Native Americans (Duke).

Oryzopsis—Rice Grass (-/-/4) • Rice grass is common across the desert southwest. The grains are large and easy to process. I think it has potential as a commercial cereal grain. Note that wild rice belongs to *Zizania*.

Panicum—Switch Grass (600/-/5) Several species of *Panicum* have been cultivated for grain (Sturtevant).

Phalaris—Canary Grass (15/-/2) • Preliminary tests indicate the reed canary grass has excellent potential as a cereal crop. The season is very short, near the end of July, and I have not yet been able to do a timed study.

Phleum—Timothy Grass (10/-/2) • Strip the seeds off by hand, or collect the whole stalks and rub or beat the seeds out. They are easy to winnow, and are really quite a beautiful seed. I hand-stripped the seed heads for my studies and came up with about 1 quart of rough yield per hour. Twenty minutes of winnowing left me with over a cup of pure seed.

Poa—Bluegrass (250/-/30) • The mature seeds can be harvested with a seed beater for a short time before they drop (Olsen).

Setaria—Bristlegrass, Foxtail (125/-/4) The seeds are edible (Duke).

Zizania—Wild rice (3/-/1) Wild rice is most common across the eastern states with cold climates; it is virtually absent from Montana and other western states. The grain is collected by beating the seed heads over a boat. The collected seeds are

Phragmites australis

Polypogon monspeliensis

Bromus brizaeformis

dried, then parched, rubbed and winnowed, to remove the husks. There is only a few days to collect the seeds upon maturity, before the seeds drop (Hall).

Grasses can also be eaten as **greens**, except that you only swallow the juice and spit the fiber out. Chewing on the tender grasses, and particularly the immature seed heads, is an excellent way to get a healthful and sustaining dose of vitamins and minerals. In fact, many health enthusiasts grow wheat and barley sprouts, and process them through a juicer. You do not have to do all that work, though, if you just graze on the tender grasses as you walk through the woods. Grazing on grass is just the kind of health tonic that every person in this country desperately needs. Please note, however, that some grasses produce cyanide compounds as they wilt. This may be an evolutionary strategy to ward off foraging animals when the plants are already stressed from heat or drought.

Some grasses are also a source of **sugar**. Sugar cane (*Saccharum*), corn (*Zea*), and *Sorghum* for instance, are all processed commercially for sugar. The concentrations of sugar are usually found in the roots or the base of the stalks. Two wild grasses that are known to produce useable amounts of sugar are *Phragmites* and *Sorghum*.

Phragmites—Common Reed (2/-/1) • The young stalks or roots can sometimes be processed for sugar, by drying and beating into a flour. This sugary flour can be moistened and heated over the fire as a substitute marshmallow. The seeds can be processed out by searing away the fluff. Then the seeds are ground with the hull, for a high-fiber meal. (Duke).

Sorghum—Johnson grass (35/-/1) The seeds are edible. Some species of sorghum were once widely grown for sugar. Plants that are stressed from heat, drought, or frost, are prone to producing cyanide (Duke).

A few grasses have notable aromatic properties. Lemon grass, for instance, is often added to commercial herbal teas. Sweet grass or *Hierochloe* (-/-/2) is often burned as a ceremonial incense by Native Americans.

Other selected genera from the Grass family

Aegilops—Goat Grass (-/-/1) … *Alopecurus*—Foxtail (-/-/5) • … *Andropogon*—Bluestem (113/-/3) … *Aristida*—Three-Awn (200/-/1) … *Arrhenatherum*—Tall Oatgrass (-/-/1) … *Bouteloua*—Grama (50/-/4) … *Buchloe*—Buffalo Grass (1/1/1) … *Calamagrostis*—Reed Grass, Pine Grass (-/-/9) … *Calamovilfa*—Prairie Sandreed (-/-/1) … *Catabrosa*—Brookgrass (-/-/1) … *Cenchrus*—Sandbur (-/-/1) … *Cinna*—Woodreed (-/-/1) … *Crypsis*— (-/-/1) … *Cynosurus*—Dogtail (-/-/1) … *Dactylis*—Orchard Grass (3/-/1) • … *Danthonia*—Oatgrass (-/-/5) … *Distichlis*—Saltgrass (-/-/1) … *Eragrostis*—Lovegrass (250/-/4) … *Helictotrichon*—Spike Oat (-/-/4) … *Holcus*—Velvet Grass (8/-/1) … *Koeleria*—Junegrass (-/-/1) … *Leersia*—Rice Cutgrass (-/-/1) … *Leptochloa*—Sprangletop (-/-/1) … *Leucopoa*—Western Grass (-/-/1) … *Melica*—Melicgrass, Oniongrass (60/-/1) … *Monroa*—False Buffalo Grass (-/-/1) … *Muhlenbergia*—Muhly (100/-/11) … *Phippsia*—Icegrass (-/-/1) … *Polypogon*—Rabbitfoot Grass (-/-/1) … *Puccinellia*—Alkali Grass (-/-/4) … *Schedonnardus*—Tumblegrass (-/-/1) … *Schizachne*—False Melic (-/-/1) … *Schlerochloa*—Hard Grass (-/-/1) … *Scolochloa*—Prickle Grass (-/-/1) … *Spartina*—Cord Grass, Slough Grass (16/-/2) … *Sphenopholis*—Wedgegrass (-/-/2) … *Sporobolus*—Dropseed (100/-/5) … *Stipa*—Needlegrass (150/-/10) … *Trisetum*—Wheat (14/-/5)

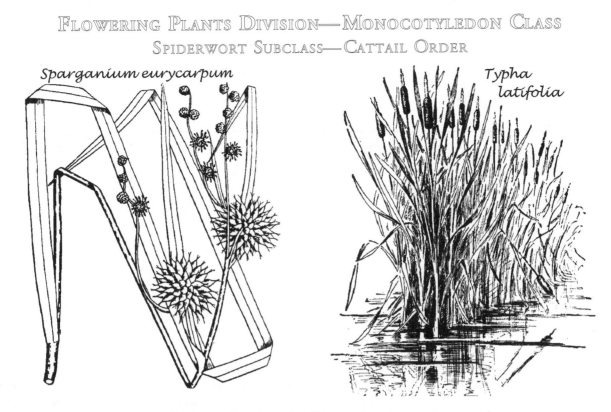

Sparganium eurycarpum

Typha latifolia

Typhaceae—Cattail Family (including Sparganiaceae)

The cattail is probably one of the most recognized wild plants in North America. It can be found in most swamps with its long, slender, flat leaves and a seed head that looks like a hot dog on a stick. The seed head starts developing early in the season; at first it looks like two hot dogs on a stick. The top portion is comprised of thousands of minute male flowers. It produces pollen for about two weeks early in the summer. Cattails are cross-pollinated by the wind, so the sepals and petals have been reduced to minute threads, bristles, and scales around each of the tiny flowers. There are 2-5 stamens with each flower. This upper hot-dog-on-a-stick withers away through the summer and eventually drops off. The female part of the stalk is also comprised of thousands of minute flowers. Examine the flowers under a microscope and you will find that the ovary is positioned superior and consists of a single carpel (unicarpellate), producing a single seed. The seeds are almost microscopic in size; they are carried away in the wind by the fluffy cattail down when the seed heads are broken apart. World-wide there is 1 genera of cattail, with 15 species.

I have included the closely related Bur-reed family here as a matter of convenience. Although the flower heads are round, they still develop with male and female flowers in separate heads like the cattails, with the males above the females. The flowers of either sex have 3-6 membranous "tepals" (meaning either sepals or petals). Male flowers have 3 or more stamens. Each female flower produces a single seed. World-wide there is 1 genera and 20 species. About 10 species are found in North America, especially in the eastern states. The plants of these two families produce starchy, *edible* roots, and some *mucilage* in between the leaf stalks.

Sparganium—Bur-reed (20/10/5) The roots and bulbous stem bases are edible like cattails (Olsen).

Typha—Cattail (15/4/2) • Almost any boy scout knows the cattail, and how to harvest food from it at any time of the year—at least, that is what I always read and heard. For years I was rather embarrassed that I knew so little about the cattail, especially considering that it is my profession to know about such things. Now that I have finally taken the time to do methodical studies of the cattail I know there is a lot more to it than is generally acknowledged.

Cattails send out horizontal undergound stems, called rhizomes, that extend out up to two feet from the plant where they bud out and send up new cattail plants. I will call them roots, since that is what they look like. These roots store starch in the winter time, which is used to rebuild the plants in the summer. Consequently, the rhizomes are very rich from fall until early spring, but pretty worthless in the summer. To harvest the roots, look for a swamp free of contamination from railroad tracks, busy roads, factory sites, etc. Ideally you should be able to reach your hands down through the muck beside the stalks to feel the horizontal shoots. Then pull up from underneath, gradually working your way along the roots until you get to the end, usually after pulling up several plants. Try not to break the roots up too much, as that contaminates the inside with mud and unclean water. If the roots are anchored in hard mud or under rocks, then you might want to shop around for an easier site to work.

Plunge the muddy roots in the water to wash away the globs of mud, then you can eat the **starchy cores** raw right there in the swamp. Simply cut away the contaminated ends, then peel pack the foam-like outer layer to reveal the starchy core. Chew up the core, then spit out the fibers that remain. I like to pop a few berries in my mouth while eating the starch to give it some flavor. You can also roast the roots on the hot coals of a fire prior to peeling and eating them.

A more refined product can be obtained by separating the starch out for use as **flour**. There are two common ways of doing this. The wet method involves shredding and mashing the roots in water, then allowing the starch to settle to the bottom, and pouring off the water. The advantage to this method is that the roots can be processed immediately, assuming you have a pot to work in. However, this method misses a significant amount of starch that is difficult to separate from the fibers. Also, even after settling over-night, there is still a lot of fine starch suspended in the water, that is lost when the water is poured off. This method requires about an hour of labor per cup of flour. Other types of dry flour can be added to soak up the moisture if you want to bake with it right away. Under semi-primitive conditions I have processed cattail roots in a shallow gold pan. I saved the water, after settling out the starch, and used that water to cook my hot amaranth cereal (*Amaranthus spp.*). The cereal took over an hour to cook, so I kept adding more starch water. This thickened into a whitish "milk-like" substance, a nice compliment to the otherwise seedy cereal.

The other method for obtaining flour involves drying the roots, then pounding out the starch. Drying the roots whole can take a week or more, but you can speed up the process considerably by separating out just the starchy core. The starchy mass will dry within a few hours. Then pound the starch out between two rocks. The flour can be used on its own, except that it contains no gluten to hold it all together. It works best mixed with an equal amount of wheat flour. I was able to obtain a cup of flour per hour of processing effort this way. You might do considerably better however, since the cattails in my area seem smaller on average than in other regions of the country.

Attached to the end of the roots will be another plant, or sometimes the bud or shoot that will become another plant. Those buds or shoots are probably the best delicacy of the cattail, because they are rich with starch, but lack the fibers found in the rest of the root. Fortunately the buds and shoots seem to linger a little longer into the summer too. I like to stir fry the sliced buds and shoots with a mix of other goodies.

Cattail **pollen** can also be used as a source of flour. Shake the flower stalks over a can or basket, or in a bag to catch the pollen. The season is very short and easy to miss if you are not around the cattails every day. Also you need a couple calm days for the pollen to accumulate on the flower heads before you harvest; even a slight breeze will shake all the pollen loose into the water. In my area the pollen season runs from the end of June to mid July. The pollen is often mixed with other sources of flour. Optionally, the entire male flower head can also be stripped off by hand and used as meal.

The green **flower heads** are edible, at about the same time as the pollen. They can be steamed or boiled and eaten just like "corn on the cob". These are quite delicious. The tender **young shoots** are also edible early in the spring. Later in the summer you can pull apart the main stalks to find tender new leaves forming inside the base. Basically, if it is tender enough to cut easily with a knife than it is edible. If the knife doesn't cut through easily, then the shoots are building cellulose for structural support, too fiberous to eat.

Lemnaceae—Duckweed Family

Spirodela polyrhiza

The Duckweed family includes the world's *smallest flowering plants*. The plants form a thallus (not differentiated into leaves and stem), typically no more than a 1/4 inch in diameter. The little plants float in the water with thread-like roots dangling below. While the plants are tiny, the flowers are microscopic—and no, I am not going to suggest that you need to identify the flower parts!

If you did look at a duckweed under the microscope, however, you would see separate male and female flowers on the same plant, lacking sepals or petals. Male flowers have one or two stamens, while female flowers consist of a simple pistil (unicarpellate), producing 1-7 seeds. Worldwide there are four genera and 25 species. All four genera occur in North America. The Duckweeds could be confused with the Water Fern family, so you should read about those as well.

Lemna—Duckweed (7/-/3) • The plant is edible (Fern), probably when cooked. It is used as a poultice (Moerman).
Spirodela—Greater Duckweed (3/-/1) The plant is edible (Fern), probably when cooked.
Wolfiella—Bogmat (2/-/0)
Wolffia—Water Meal (12/-/2) The cooked plants are edible and rich in protein and carbohydrates (Fern).

Araceae (Aroideae)—Arum Family

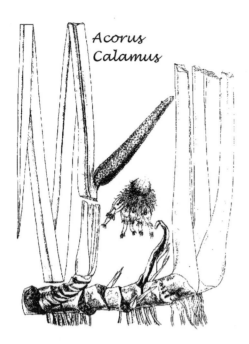

Acorus Calamus

Members of the Arum family are unique plants with minute flowers crowded on a fleshy stalk that is often surrounded by a large, colored bract called a "spathe". There are 4-6 small, scale-like "tepals", a term used when the sepals and petals cannot be distinguished from one another. There are typically 6 stamens (sometimes 1, 2, 4, or 8). The ovary is positioned superior and consists of 2 or 3 (sometimes 1-9) united carpels (syncarpous) with the partition walls present, forming an equal number of chambers. It matures as a berry with 1-numerous seeds. The plants have mostly basal leaves.

World-wide there are 115 genera and 2,000 species, most of them tropical and subtropical. Eight genera are native to North America, as listed below. Some of our common house plants come from this family, including *Philodendron*, *Dieffenbachia*, *Alocasia*, and *Anthurium*. Many members of this family emit foul smells to attract carrion insects; the insects transport pollen from one plant to another. The foliage of a number species contain needle-like *calcium oxalate crystals*. These crystals can mechanically injure the mouth and throat, when eaten, or can precipitate out in the kidneys, plugging the tubules. Some members of the family have *acrid* roots and potent *volatile oils*.

Key Words
Flower stalks with minute flowers in a spathe.

Acorus—Sweet Flag (2/1/1) *A. calamus*, the young leaves are edible. The root is spicy. The tender, young roots can be made into candy. Wash, peel and chop the roots; then boil them at least eight hours. The water should be changed frequently to reduce the potency of the root. Finally, add sugar and boil into a heavy syrup, drain, and allow to dry (Hall). Medicinally sweet flag is carminative, diaphoretic, emmenagogue, sedative, and a digestive stimulant (Lust). It contains a volatile oil much like terpene (Densmore). Our North American species is considered safe, but varieties of the same species found on other continents produce varying amounts of cis-aioasarone, a known carcinogen. *A. calamus* is banned as a food or food additive in the U.S. (Tyler).

Arisaema—Jack-in-the-Pulpit (130/4/0) The acrid root is pounded and applied as an irritating poultice to stimulate healing for rheumatic joints (Gilmore). It contains calcium oxalate crystals. Much of the acridness can be removed by drying. The dried, powdered root was taken as an expectorant and diaphoretic (Angier).

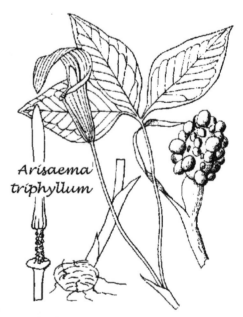

Arisaema triphyllum

Arum—Arum (12/-/0) Arum does not grow in Montana; it may be more common in the eastern forests. The fresh root is extremely acrid, but many species can be utilized as a source of starchy food after cooking or drying (Sturtevant). A tea or syrup of the dried root is used internally as a diaphoretic and expectorant, for asthma, bronchitis, gas, and rheumatism (Lust).

Calla—Water Arum (1/1/0) *C. palustris* is native to the northeastern states and provinces.

Lysichiton—Western Skunk cabbage (1/1/1) *L. americanum*. The plant contains oxalates (Phillips). The is starchy and edible, but it must be thoroughly cooked (Fern). Native Americans roasted, dried and ground the roots to make flour (Couplan). Otherwise the leaves were used by Native Americans for improvised drinking cups, plus to line berry baskets and steam pits (Turner).

Peltandra—Tuckahoe (-/1/0)

Orontium—Golden Club (-/1/0) Golden club is found in the southeastern and eastern states.

Symplocarpus—Eastern Skunk Cabbage (1/1/0) *S. foetidus*.

Liliaceae—Lily Family

Key Words: Monocot flowers with parts in 3's. Sepals and petals usually identical.

If you find a plant with parallel veins in the leaves, and regular flowers with parts in multiples of three, chances are you have a member of the Lily family. The flowers have 3 sepals and 3 petals, but these are sometimes described as 6 "tepals", because the sepals and petals are usually identical in size and color. Members of this family have 6 stamens, but three of them may be lacking anthers. The ovary is positioned either superior or inferior or in between and consists of 3 united carpels (syncarpous/tricarpellate) with the partition walls present, forming an equal number of chambers. It matures as a capsule or a berry with 3 to numerous seeds.

World-wide there are about 250 genera and 3,700 species, including about 75 genera in North America. Botanists disagree about the makeup of the Lily family, and there have been many attempts to break it into smaller families—up to 70 of them! The conglomerate family includes many ornamental plants such as the hyacinth (*Hyacinthus*), lily (*Lilium*), tulip (*Tulipa*), spiderplant (*Chlorophytum*), *Aloe, and Amaryllis*. Onions, garlic, chives, and leeks all belong to the *Allium* genus. *Asparagus* is another well-known edible plant of this family. I have retained the traditional family grouping, and simply listed the plants within five of the most clearly defined subfamilies. Please note that the Amaryllis Subfamily, including daffodils (*Narcissus*), is not covered in this text. Once you have identified a plant as a "lily" you can read the summaries for each subfamily for clues as to which group your specimen belongs to. Also be sure to read about the Iris family.

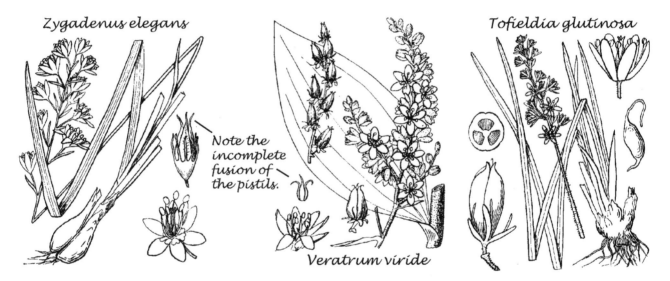

Zygadenus elegans

Note the incomplete fusion of the pistils.

Veratrum viride

Tofieldia glutinosa

Bunch Flower Subfamily

The Bunch Flower subfamily is named after *Melanthium spp.*, a plant native to the eastern states. Like other members of this subfamily, *Melanthium* grows lots of small flowers close together in bunches—hence the name. Also note the incomplete fusion of the pistils. (This characteristic may also be present in other lilies.)   It is very important to learn these plants right away because most of them are quite **poisonous**.

Veratrum—False Hellebore (48/7/2) • *Veratrum* contains dangerous alkaloids that depress the nervous system, resulting in a slower heart rate and lower blood pressure (Hall). It is powerfully medicinal; considered too dangerous for amateurs to work with (Lust). Indians inhaled the dried, powdered root to induce sneezing to clear the sinuses (Klein).

Xerophyllum—Beargrass (-/2/1) The baked root is edible (Fern). The leaves may be used for cordage.

Zigadenus (including *Amianthium*)—Death camas (15/15/3) • *Zigadenus* contains a toxic alkaloid that may be twice as potent as strychnine (Harrington). Ingestion can cause vomiting, diarrhea, and death (Hall). I once read that a single bulb mistakenly harvested with blue camas would sometimes kill an entire family of Indians. Yet I have also heard that you would have to eat 50 or more of them to die from it. Clearly there needs to be a controlled study of how many bulbs it takes to kill a person, but as yet I do not know of anyone willing to participate in the study! Medicinally, the raw roots were reportedly used externally as a poultice for inflamed joints (Murphey).

Other selected genera include: *Stenanthium*— (-/2/1) … *Tofieldia*—False asphodel (-/6/1)

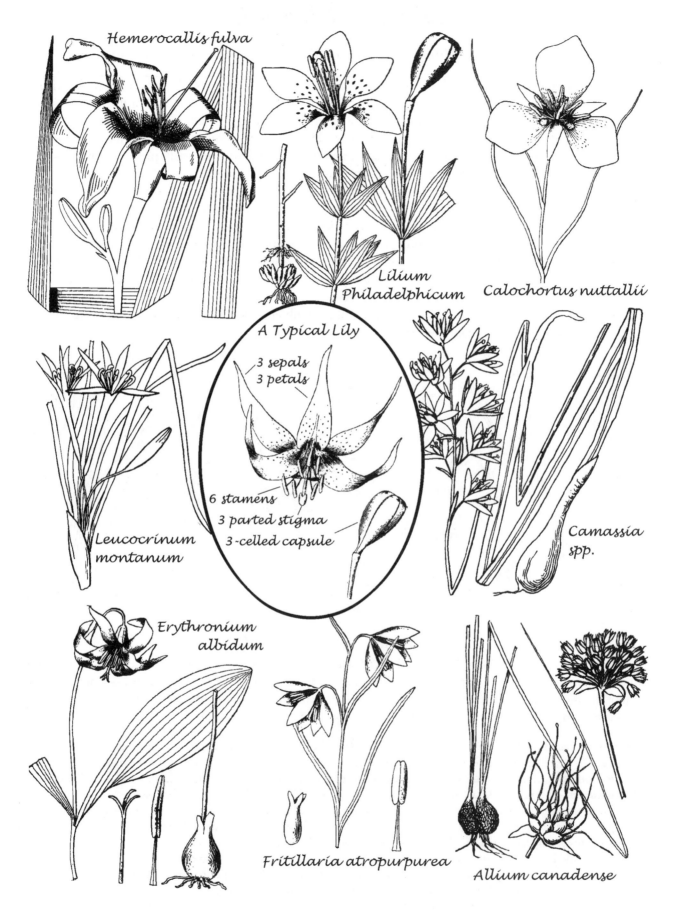

Hemerocallis fulva

Lilium Philadelphicum

Calochortus nuttallii

A Typical Lily

3 sepals
3 petals

6 stamens
3 parted stigma
3-celled capsule

Leucocrinum montanum

Camassia spp.

Erythronium albidum

Fritillaria atropurpurea

Allium canadense

168

Lily Subfamily

The plants of the Lily Subfamily usually have larger, more showy blossoms than other lilies. Most of these plants have bulbs and most are *edible*, but be extremely cautious—the plants of the Bunchflower Subfamily also have bulbs, and some of them are highly poisonous. Be especially careful gathering blue camas and onions. They do not look much like their poisonous relatives to someone who has studied plants for a long time, but amateurs can and do confuse them easily before the blossoms come on. This error has cost many people their lives. If you have any doubt about an onion, just crush the plant and smell it. If it smells like an onion then it is. Blue camas should only be gathered when in blossom; its flowers are blue, whereas death camas is white. *Allium* and *Triteleia* properly belong to their own subfamily, but are included here for convenience. Most bulbs in the Lily subfamily are rich in inulin polysaccarides. Read more about that in the Medicinal Properties section of this book.

Allium—Onion, Garlic, Chives, Leeks (300/80/11) • Wild onions make a great addition to almost any wilderness meal. The various species grow in many different environments from semi-swampy mountain meadows to very dry, south-facing foothill slopes. Medicinally, the *Allium* species contain volatile oils and sulfur glycosides. They act as a digestive stimulant, expectorant, anthelmintic, and carminative (Lust). Garlic, especially is recommended for colds; it has also been shown to lower cholesterol and blood pressure.

Calochortus—Sego Lily (46/46/7) • The bulb is delicious roasted or boiled, similar in texture and flavor to camas.

Camassia—Blue Camas (5/5/1) • Blue camas looks similar to death camas (*Zigadenus spp.*) before it blooms. Always be extra careful to be sure you have the right camas. One wrong bulb in the bunch can spell disaster. Blue camas bulbs are starchy and nearly tasteless, varying from marble size to golf-ball size and larger. I have found them growing in clumps along the creeks of south-central Idaho where you could reach down and yank up a whole meal. More often the plants grow individually in the sod along intermittent creeks or in damp meadows. Camas was a major food source for the Native Americans. It is always a thrill to me to find some.

Camas bulbs are mostly made up a carbohydrate called inulin plus a dietary fiber called hemi-cellulose. Neither are digestible raw so they ferment and produce gas in the gut. However, the inulin can be converted to fructose through extended cooking. Native Americans cooked camas bulbs in a steam pit for 10 to 72 hours. The more the roots are cooked the more of the inulin that is converted to fructose. In kitchen experiments John Kallas found that pressure-cooking the roots at 257ºF for 9 hours produced the sweetest tasting roots (Kallas).

Erythronium—Glacier Lily, Adder's Tongue, Dog-tooth Violet (20/18/1) • Glacier lily roots are crisp and sweet. There are acres and acres of them in my area, carpeting the ground in yellow below the aspens and fir trees, blooming in May and early June. They are somewhat difficult to dig with a primitive digging stick, because the roots are so deep in the soil, about 4 to 6 inches down. Fortunately, they often grow close enough together that you can dig out one, then pry each next one into the hole left behind. The roots can vary tremendously in size, so I would suggest doing a number of tests to find the best patch before doing an extensive harvest. A good patch can yield one to two cups of roots per hour of digging. Washing will take an additional 10 minutes or so. The leaves are edible as a salad or potherb, but there is a lingering bite to them, which can be emetic in excess. A poultice of the leaves is used for a skin condition called scrofula (Lust). Be careful to avoid over-harvesting glacier lilies. The plants take years to grow to maturity.

Fritillaria—Yellowbell, Leopard Lily (100/19/2) • The whole plant is edible, both raw or cooked. The corm (bulb) is delicious and almost melts in your mouth like butter. I have been able to dig up almost a cup of yellowbell corms per hour of work. Yellowbells seldom grow in enough abundance to justify collecting a significant quantity of them. The leopard lily is even more rare. Please note that a European species contains highly toxic alkaloids (Schauenberg); a species in China is also poisonous (Klein).

Hemerocallis—Day lily (16/2/D) • The day lily grows wild in the eastern states. It is cultivated or escaped in the West. The flowers and buds are edible as a cooked vegetable. The tubers can be harvested any time and eaten raw or cooked (Hall). There have been isolated cases of adverse reactions (nausea, vomiting, diarrhea), possibly do to environmental factors or genetic variants. People who successfully consumed the plant for many years still became ill (Kallas).

Leucocrinum—Sand lily (-/1/1) •

Lilium—Wood lily (75/25/2) • The pulverized flower was applied by the Dakota Indians to a certain brown spider bite (Gilmore). The bulbs of many *Liliums* are known to be edible (Sturtevant).

Lloydia—Alpine lily (-/1/1)

Triteleia—(including *Brodiaea*) (37/37/1) • The cooked bulb is edible and delicious; it has a buttery texture and flavor like the closely related *Fritillaria*. The plants in my area are small and rare, but I had the opportunity to dig up several cups full in eastern Oregon... a real treat.

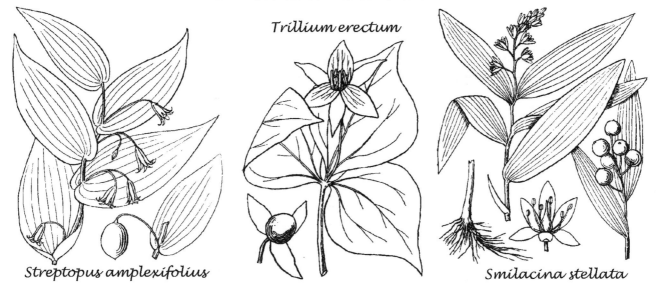

Trillium erectum

Streptopus amplexifolius

Smilacina stellata

Asparagus Subfamily

If you find a plant with berries *and* parallel veined leaves it is almost certainly a member of the Asparagus Subfamily of the Lily family. Look closely at the berry and you should also be able to see that it is divided into thirds in some way. Some berries are round, except for faint lines marking the division. Other berries are slightly lumpy, with three distinct sides. I do not know of any exceptions to this rule in the northern latitudes, although there are probably exceptions in warmer regions of the world. The asparagus and most of its allies are at least minimally *edible*, with the exception of *Convallaria*, which contains dangerous cardiac glycosides. None of the berries are particularly exciting, and some of them may act as powerful *purgatives* (laxatives) if eaten in excess. *Smilax* should be separated into its own subfamily, but it is included here for convenience.

Asparagus— (300/1/1) • *A. officinalis* is the cultivated asparagus. It has escaped from gardens and now grows wild in some areas, particularly along roads and fence lines. It is always a delight to find a patch in the spring. Medicinally, asparagus is diuretic, acting to increase cellular activity in the kidneys; it is not recommended for inflamed kidneys. Asparagus is also a bulk fiber laxative. The powdered seeds are used as a diaphoretic and to calm the stomach (Lust).

Clintonia—Queen's Cup (-/4/1) The plants are edible; the very young leaves in salad, older leaves cooked (Fern).

Convallaria—Lily-of-the-Valley (2/2/0) Convallaria's cardiac glycosides can cause an irregular heartbeat (Lust).

Disporum—Fairy Bell (-/5/2) • The berries are edible (Williams).

Maianthemum—False Lily-of-the-Valley (3/2/1)

Polygonatum—Solomon Seal (30/4/0) The young shoots and starchy, mucilaginous roots are edible as potherbs (Sturtevant). The tea is used as a demulcent, expectorant, and cough suppressant.. A poultice of the root is used as an emollient, possibly with mildly astringent properties.

Smilacina—False Solomon Seal (25/5/2) • The berries are edible and laxative (Williams). Medicinally, it is used identically to the true Solomon seal (*Polygonatum*) above.

Smilax—Greenbrier, Sarsaparilla (300/5/1) • The young leaves and shoots are edible as a salad or potherb. The roots contain a gelatin-like substance that can be extracted by crushing and washing them (Hall). Medicinally, a tea of the root is listed as diaphoretic, carminative, diuretic, and as a blood purifier (Lust). It has been used in the production of rootbeer. See also *Aralia* of the Ginseng family.

Streptopus—Twisted stalk (-/4/1) • The tender leaves and stalks are edible. The berries are juicy, but flat-tasting, and cathartic in excess (Angier).

Trillium—Birthroot, wake robin (30/26/1) • Trillium is listed as astringent, diaphoretic, and expectorant. The tea is used internally for asthma, bronchitis, hemorrhaging from the lungs, and as menstrual stimulant. The poultice is used externally for insect bites and stings (Lust). It contains some saponin.

*Smilax
herbacea*

Yucca sp.

Yucca flowers are pollinated only by the yucca moth, Pronuba yuccasella. The moth larvae eat the developing seeds, but enough seeds survive to produce more yuccas.

Agave Subfamily

The members of the Agave Subfamily are distinctive desert-type plants, largely native to the southwestern states. These plants grow a rosette of basal leaves surrounding a central flower stalk. The leaves are often useful for fiber. The stalks are useful for bowdrill and handdrill fire sets.

Agave

americana

Agave— (300/26/0) • Agave is a well-known plant growing in the southwestern states. The juice from the leaf is reported to be acrid. The young flower stalk is edible raw or cooked. It is commonly cooked in a steam pit for two to three days to convert the starches to sugar (Bigfoot). Sisal fiber comes from a species of *Agave*. A. americana is listed as antiseptic, diuretic, and laxative (Lust)

Dasylirion—Sotol (25/-/0) The young flower stalk of the plant is rich in sugar, sometimes used to make alcohol. It be cooked and eaten (Bigfoot, Fern).

Yucca—Yucca, Joshua Tree (35/38/1) • The flower stem and flowers, but especially the root, contains saponin, used as a soap substitute. A tea of the of the plant or root has been used both for heartburn and arthritis. The seed pods have a laxative effect (Bigfoot). The flowers and pods of some species of yucca are edible (Sturtevant), but many are too bitter to be palatable. The leaves contain some salicin (Pamell).

Aloe Subfamily

Aloe spp.

By their general appearance the Aloe plants seem like they should be included with the Agave Subfamily, but there are significant differences, both in the flowers and the leaves. Especially, the Agaves tend to have dense fibrous leaves while the Aloes are highly *mucilaginous*. Please read more about mucilaginous plants in the Medicinal Properties section of this book.

Aloe vera is neither native nor naturalized in the United States, but I chose to include it in this text because it is such a well-known medicinal plant and a popular house plant, but also because I grew up using it more than any other plant.

Aloe— (250/D/D) • *Aloe vera* is originally from Africa. Other *Aloe* species grow wild in Florida. My Grandma always treated my sunburns with *Aloe vera*. She split the leaf down the middle and rubbed the slimy, mucilaginous gel over any burns. Often my burns tanned over without peeling after this treatment. It is a family tradition to keep an *Aloe vera* around for such occasions. The treatment should be repeated several times a day for maximum effect. The beneficial properties of *Aloe vera* may break down in storage, so that many commercial products have little therapeutic value. Some may even retard healing (Tyler).

Aloe vera also has cathartic properties (strongly laxative) due to anthraquinone glycosides (Geller) in the bitter yellow latex found immediately beneath the surface of the leaf (Tyler).

Iridaceae—Iris Family

Stop and look closely at an iris or gladiolus the next time you come across one in a yard, in a bouquet, or at the florist. Members of this family produce regular, bisexual flowers with parts in multiples of 3. There are 3 sepals, colored to look like petals, and 3 true petals, plus 3 stamens. The ovary is positioned inferior and consists 3 united carpels (syncarpous/tricarpellate) with the partition walls usually present, forming an equal number of chambers. It matures as a capsule containing many seeds. The styles of the pistil are often distinctive; in the *Iris* they look like a third set of petals and the stamens are hidden underneath—this is well worth looking at! Overall, the flowers of the Iris family look much like the Lilies. One key difference is that the leaves of the Irises all lay together at the base of the plant in a flat plane. Also note that the Lilies have six stamens, while the Irises only have three.

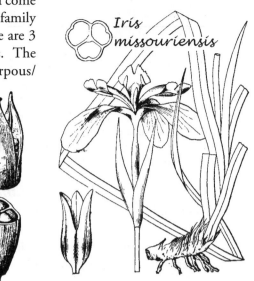

Iris missouriensis

World-wide there are 70 genera and about 1500 species. Five genera are native to North America. The expensive saffron spice is made from the stigmas of *Crocus sativus*. The *Iris* and *Gladiolus* are commonly cultivated members of this family.

<u>Key Words</u>
"Lilies with leaves in a flat plane."

Alophia— (-/3/0) *Alophia* is found in Texas.

Belamcanda—Blackberry Lily (-/1/0) The blackberry lily was introduced from Asia. It can be found from Conneticut to Texas.

Eustylis—Pinewoods-Lily (-/1/0) The Pinewoods-Lily is found in Texas, Arkansas, Oklahoma, and Louisiana.

Gladiolus— (250/D/D) • *Gladiolus edulis* of South Africa produces an edible bulb (Sturtevant).

Iris— (200/36/2) • The irises have starchy, but typically acrid roots. Several of them around the world are edible, but a few may be potentially dangerous, including the common *I. versicolor* (Pammel). Irises with acrid qualities are listed as cathartic, emetic diuretic, and as a saliva stimulant. A tea of the root is used for chronic digestive disorders, including heartburn and vomiting, and for migraine headaches caused by indigestion (Lust). The iris is used as a liver and lymph stimulant (Bigfoot). For additional information, be sure to read about acrid substances in the Medicinal Properties section of this book. Iris roots were boiled by some Native Americans and applied as a poultice on wounds (Weiner). Iris leaves were can be used for cordage. Some Irises were preferred by the Indians for making deer snares (Moerman).

Nemastylis—Celestial Lily (-/4/0) The Celestial Lily is found in Texas and other nearby states.

Sisyrinchium—Blue-eyed grass (80/44/2) •

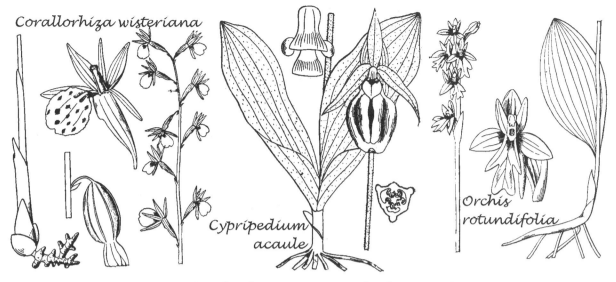

Corallorhiza wisteriana

Cypripedium acaule

Orchis rotundifolia

Orchidaceae—Orchid Family

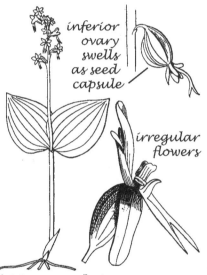

inferior ovary swells as seed capsule

irregular flowers

Listera cordata

The orchids are the only monocot plants in the northern latitudes with distinctive, *irregular* blossoms. It is worth a trip to the floral store to see the unique flowers. The flowers are bisexual, with 3 sepals and 3 petals. The sepals can be green or colored like the petals. The lower petal is often modified into a sort of "lip". There are 1 or 2 stamens combined with the pistil into a column. The ovary is positioned inferior and consists 3 united carpels (syncarpous/tricarpellate) with the partition walls present, forming an equal number of chambers. It matures as a 3-valved capsule with numerous seeds. The inferior ovary is one of the more distinctive patterns for identifying members of this family. It elongates into a seed capsule while the flowers are still present.

The Orchid family is the biggest family of flowering plants, most of which inhabit the tropics. World-wide there are about 735 genera representing some 20,000 species. Vanilla flavoring is extracted from the immature pods of *Vanilla planifolia*. There are 88 genera and 285 species of orchid in the U.S. and Canada, mostly in the south. Many are rare species and should not be harvested.

Key Words: Irregular monocot flowers. Distinctive inferior ovary.

Calypso—Fairy Slipper (-/1/1) • *C. bulbosa*, the plant and root is edible raw or cooked (Willard).

Corallorhiza—Coral Root (15/6/5) • A tea of the root is used as a sedative and nervine (Moore).

Cypripedium—Lady Slipper (50/10/4 • Lady slipper is considered a non-narcotic sedative (Weiner). A tea of the root is used as a tranquilizer for nervousness or spasms. Over-dosing may cause hallucinations. The fresh root may irritate the skin (Lust). It contains a volatile oil and a glucosidal resinoid (Densmore). Hairs on the stems of some species can cause a dermatitis reaction (Pammel).

Epipactis—Helleborine, Stream Orchid (20/2/2) *Epipactis* contains resins, volatile oils, and bitter glycosides. It is antispasmodic and sedative, and uplifting rather than depressant (Moore).

Goodyera—Rattlesnake Plantain (100/4/2) The plant is mucilaginous and astringent; the fresh plant or dry powder is used as a drawing poultice (Moore). The leaves or roots have emollient properties for use on skin conditions (Lust).

Habenaria—Bog Orchid (450/35/7) • This species is common in my area. The cooked roots are edible, but please do not over-harvest the plants.

Listera—Twayblade (30/7/4)

Orchis—Spotted Orchid (50/2/1) The roots of many species are starchy and mucilaginous, edible after drying and cooking (Sturtevant).

Spiranthes—Ladies' Tresses (35/25/1)

The Properties of Plants

I. Knowledge and Knowing

A number of natural, unflavored foods were placed before a group of infants in a study. These infants demonstrated over a period of time that they could select a nutritionally balanced diet for themselves from the selections at hand. If an individual initially binged on starchy foods, he would later seek out foods high in protein. If at first he ate foods lacking a particular vitamin, he would later eat what was needed to make up the deficit. Without any logical knowledge of diet or nutrition these infants demonstrated an innate ability to make healthy choices.

We lose this innate ability very quickly as we grow up. Our parents teach us which foods are known to be good for us, and that if we can choke them down we will be rewarded with foods that are known to be bad for us. Even without this perverse sense of dietary rewards, we grow up, learn language and logic and lose our innate abilities. We eat from the fruit of Knowledge, and forever leave the Garden. We acquire Knowledge, but we lose Knowing.

Chimpanzees have exhibited a similar Knowing when ill, by seeking out specific plants for their medicinal properties. Today there are researchers following these animals through the jungles for the purpose of seeing what medicinal plants they use. When an animal significantly alters its behavior, stops eating, and starts consuming different herbs, the researchers then send those plants to the lab for analysis. They hope to find new and beneficial drugs for people.

> *"Today there are researchers following the chimpanzees through the jungles for the purpose of seeing what medicinal plants they use. When an animal significantly alters its behavior, stops eating, and starts consuming different herbs, the researchers then send those plants to the lab for analysis."*

The study of edible and medicinal herbs and stone-age skills (which I also teach) is often an attempt, in part, to get back into the Garden. It is an effort to tune into nature, to harvest from the abundance, to live healthy, and to be "one" with nature. Those of us who pursue this goal are on the path of knowledge, picking up the pieces of information that will allow us to again become part of the Whole. Unfortunately, it is impossible to reassemble the whole by picking up its pieces. Through Knowledge we can achieve a life in balance and harmony with nature, but it is very different from the experience of our ancestors. It is still the path of fragmented Knowledge.

We might guess at the nutritional needs of an infant and provide a carefully balanced meal based on what we think, but it can never be as good as what the infant innately knows. We could come close on the obvious, major nutrients, vitamins, and minerals, but there are an infinity of micronutrients and microminerals that we can never fully comprehend. Most importantly, however, the needs of every individual at every moment are completely unique to him- or herself. There are an infinite number of parts to the whole, and it is simply not possible to pick them all up. Even if we could pick up all the pieces, the Whole would still be greater than the sum of its parts.

> *"Nearly 40% of our pharmaceuticals contain constituents originally found in herbs."*

It is important to note that fragmented knowledge is not all bad. There are obviously life-threatening ailments that neither infants nor apes are able to treat. The fragmented knowledge of science has given us the ability to isolate certain compounds and develop procedures that mean the difference between life and death for people all over the world. The best herbalists among our ancestors still lost patients to ailments as simple as dysentery (severe, bloody diarrhea). Through the science of fragmented knowledge researchers have been able to isolate and often synthesize specific compounds from medicinal plants. Nearly 40% of our pharmaceuticals today contain constituents originally found in herbs.

Those of us with an interest in herbalism are often drawn to it because it is "closer to the whole", or less fragmented, than conventional medical science. Most herbalists, myself included, maintain that there is a difference between using a whole herb, versus using a single "active" constituent isolated from it. Some plants have a remarkable record of successful use, yet modern science cannot isolate a single constituent to account for the effects. Herbalists claim that it is the action of multiple constituents working together, sometimes from multiple herbs.

THE PROPERTIES OF PLANTS

Similarly, herbalists can treat certain conditions that medical doctors are unable to even diagnose—because the doctors cannot isolate any specific ailment. People may go to the doctor feeling lousy but the M.D. might not find anything wrong with them. These "subclinical" conditions are within the realm where herbalists excel. Herbalists can use whole plants and life-style changes to promote more efficient functioning of the body's systems, so that the body is better able to help itself.

Herbalism has its place, just as Western medicine or acupuncture have theirs. All are ultimately fragments belonging to the whole. Each can achieve independent results that are beyond reach of the others, and none is complete in itself. The individual must shop around and find what seems to work best for a particular situation. More importantly, however, the individual must learn to tune into the feelings inside for direction. It is not enough to merely seek treatment after becoming ill; the path of health is to intuitively select what the body needs at each moment *to maintain good health*.

> *"Herbalism has its place, just as Western medicine or acupuncture have theirs. All are fragments belonging to the whole. Each can achieve independent results that are beyond reach of the others, and none is complete in itself."*

In this pursuit of good health, many people have turned to eastern philosophies or other sources to find a "natural diet". But now there is a "natural diet" promoted by every health guru. Each has developed their own strict diet of what you can and cannot eat to be healthy and live naturally. But these diets are not natural at all, as they are products of fragmented thinking. These diets teach you to eat from the outside, with knowledge, instead of from the inside, with knowing.

The scope of this particular book is to help you build on your *inner knowing*. The process is quite logical, but you may find the results to be surprisingly intuitive. For instance, you will first learn to *consciously* recognize the patterns of plants in appearance, smell, taste, and chemistry. With practice, however, the process of recognition becomes more and more *automatic*. Soon you will discover that you often *know* a plant, even if you have never seen it before in your life. You will often know the edible and medicinal uses of a plant even before you know its name.

Please keep in mind that this guide is intended to identify plants and their properties only. There is a big difference between knowing the properties of a plant and knowing how and when to apply them to the body. The process of diagnosis and medication requires, in essence, a "field guide to the body", and no guide to *plants* can provide an adequate substitute.

For starters, I recommend Christopher Hobbs' book, *Foundations of Health: Healing with Herbs & Foods*. (ISBN: 0-9618470-8-5) The book rings true to the old herbalists' axiom that "the only true disease is constipation". Poor digestive function leads to many other ailments, and the *Foundations of Health* is an excellent resource for understanding and facilitating the digestive processes.

II. About Edible, Medicinal, and Poisonous Plants

This book covers edible, medicinal, and poisonous plants. Most of the material is on medicinal uses. This is simply because there are more medicinal than edible plants available. Indeed, *all plants are medicinal in some context*, regardless of whether or not they are otherwise considered edible or poisonous. For example, oatmeal, potato soup, or chicken soup are all foods, but are sometimes used as mild medicines. On the other end of the spectrum, water hemlock—the most poisonous plant in North America—was also once used medicinally. A piece of the root the size of a small marble is enough to kill a person, but smaller portions have been used medicinally (*with variable results!!!*).

From the perspective of a person looking for *edible* plants, there are surprisingly few truly poisonous plants. There are only a small handful of plants across the nation that are potent enough to kill a normal, healthy adult. People do die from eating wild plants every year, but it always turns out to be the same half-dozen species or so—out of *tens of thousands* of different plants across the United States. Once you know these few poisonous plants well, then it is relatively difficult to seriously hurt yourself on all the others. Simply put, most poisonous plants taste bad, and you are not going to eat enough of them to cause any harm.

From the perspective of a person looking for *medicinal* plants however, there are many more potentially poisonous plants. If you are looking for a cure then you are simply going to ingest many kinds of plants that you would not otherwise touch as "food". In addition, many herbal preparations extract and concentrate the medicinal qualities from the plants, making potent concoctions out of otherwise relatively benign herbs. Besides that, we

The Properties of Plants

Americans are just prone to overdosing anyway. As Robyn Klein puts it, we tend to think, "If a little is good, more is better!", and we pour all kinds of toxins down the hatch in the name of good health! For these reasons, people die every year from using medicinal plants, sometimes from herbal extracts bought at health food stores.

It is commonly assumed that ancient peoples learned the edible and medicinal qualities of plants strictly by trial-and-error. There are hundreds of thousands of species of plants around the world, and we blindly think that past cultures approached each specimen without prior insight, eventually discovering by pure chance what was edible or not, and what medicinal effects every plant has. But the reality is that there are only a handful of basic constituents throughout the Plant Kingdom, and most of these are recognizable with the five senses. In fact, even *you* can learn to determine the uses of many plants without ever knowing their names!

> *"There are only a handful of basic constituents throughout the Plant Kingdom, and most of these are recognizable with the five senses. In fact, even you can learn to determine the uses of many plants without ever knowing their names!"*

For instance, you chew up a leaf and have the sensation of "cotton mouth", or you just seem to run out of saliva; this typically indicates the presence of *tannic acid*, one of the most prevalent plant constituents. Once you learn to recognize this constituent and know what it is used for, then you know the approximate use of thousands of plants around the world.

In herbal classes the students typically follow the instructor around copying down precise recipes and uses for each plant along the way, but the instructors often gained *their* knowledge through direct experimentation. They would just start trying all different plants when they were ill—sometimes at random—to see what worked. The result is that each herbalist seems to have a unique recipe and different uses for the same plant. This is one of the reasons that herbalism has not been accepted by the medical establishment; to the outsider the prescriptions and dosage seem completely arbitrary and inconsistent.

Most herbalism is simple and straightforward. Tannic acid for example, has a definable *astringent* effect. The acid binds with proteins, drawing water out of the cells, causing tissues to constrict. This is a quantifiable effect, and it can be used medicinally for *hundreds* of different situations. As you learn this broad picture you will develop a much more flexible knowledge of herbalism. You will not be limited to any set of recipes or uses, but you will be able to experiment for yourself and see what really works for *you*. This is the essence of true herbalism.

For these reasons I have intentionally avoided including any formulas, recipes, or dosage for using the medicinal herbs—I would rather help you gain the ability to *think for yourself.*

Also, most herbalists prepare herbs as alcohol tinctures and other herbal extracts. These tinctures are considered useful because the alcohol can dissolve out medicinal constituents that are not very water-soluble. This increases the potency of the herbal preparations. Still, most herbs can be used without tincturing and work just fine. In fact, I have often had better results when I just chewed on raw hunks of root, or drank medicinal teas, than when I have used tinctures.

I should emphasize that you do not want to go randomly sampling the greenery. It is important for safety to know what every plant is before you put it in your mouth. At the very least, you should be positive of what a plant *isn't.* If you can rule out every lethal plant in your area then you may be able to experiment more liberally with other plants.

III. Plant Properties

The allure of western science is great, and modern herbalism has become increasingly focussed on the fragments—the specific constituents of the plants. Everyone, myself included, wants to know what the active constituents are in the plants they are using. Some plants may have pages worth of constituents, and we all want to know what they are and what they do in the body. Sometimes it is helpful to know what is happening at the molecular level to better understand and communicate why a certain herb is used in a certain way. But there are so many variables to deal with when you break a plant apart into its constituents, that the information gained is often inaccurate.

For example, in earlier editions of this book I wrote that the immuno-stimulating properties of *Echinacea* and several other herbs were do to their polysaccharide content. It was hypothesized that these complex sugars looked similar to the cell walls of bacteria, thereby stimulating the immune system into action. That hypothesis has been rejected, but the concept will still be referenced in the herbal literature for decades to come.

The greatest danger in pursuing plant constituents is that some herbal products on the market are no longer representative of the whole plants they were derived from. Partly there is a problem with adulteration, where companies either knowingly or unknowingly substitute other herbs for those on the package label. But also, certain constituents may be highly concentrated through the extraction process. The whole plant may be harmless, but a strong dose of one of its chemicals can be dangerous. Pennyroyal for instance, is a benign plant as a whole, but individuals have died from overdosing on pure pennyroyal oil, used to cause abortions. These kind of extracts are hardly herbal medicine. They are pharmaceutical concoctions derived from plants. The plants themselves have been fragmented into their constituents. They can be used with remarkable results by expert hands, but are sometimes dangerous for the amateur to utilize. The few words on the label can nowhere begin to accurately prescribe the proper conditions for use. Even the seemingly benign herbal supplements may initially energize you, only to cause withdrawals when you stop taking them. Some are more like pharmaceuticals than herbs.

For the purposes of traditional herbalism there is rarely a need to know all the individual constituents of the plants. Herbalism is rooted in the basic properties, such as "astringent", "mucilaginous" or "aromatic". In many plants you can gather the all the information you need about the active ingredients with your five senses.

> *"Any plant may be chemically dissected into hundreds, even thousands of isolated constituents. Yet learning each of these constituents may ultimately teach you less about the plant, not more. Do not focus too much on any one of these chemical properties, or you will begin to open a Pandora's box of new questions and fragments to get into. Each of the individual substances may have different uses on its own than when combined with the whole of the plant. It is the overall pattern of constituents within the plant that is important.*

For instance, plants with a white, milky sap contain some type of *latex*. Those that form suds when beaten in the water usually contain *saponin*. Aromatic plants contain *volatile oils*. Plants with a clear, slimy juice are considered *mucilaginous*. It is really pretty basic stuff!

These observable constituents could be called the basic properties. I have further defined these into their more specific properties. There are for instance, some 30,000 known volatile oils, which can be consolidated into a dozen or so main groups based on their chemical structure. Fortunately you do not need to learn every individual volatile oil, or even their chemical groups, because they tend to have roughly similar effects on the body. I have provided these details to help you understand that not all volatile oils or alkaloids, etc. are the same, but that there are differences—both subtle and extreme—within the basic properties.

You only need to study and learn the few basic properties found in plants, and you will have a framework for understanding plants all over the world. Use the more fragmented details as a reference guide only. The majority of alkaloids for instance, have a narcotic effect on the body—that is they depress the central nervous system, but some alkaloids such as caffeine are stimulants or have other effects. You can read through the alkaloid chemical types to get a better sense of the variations. Wherever possible, I have mentioned these details for the individual plants. As an example, if you see a plant that contains "pyrrolizidine alkaloids", then you can turn to the section on alkaloids for additional information on that specific chemical type.

Please remember to always keep the big picture in mind. Any plant may be chemically dissected into hundreds, even thousands of isolated constituents. Yet learning each of these constituents may ultimately teach you *less* about the plant, not more. Do not focus too much on any one of these chemical properties, or you will begin to open a Pandora's box of new questions and fragments to get into. Each of the individual substances may have different uses on its own than when combined with the whole of the plant. It is the overall *pattern of constituents* within the plant that is important. The specific definitions presented here are a sort of crutch that you can use to help you get around. Just accept the broader definitions without trying to understand their intricacies. *You must eventually throw away the crutch of knowledge and use the knowing.*

THE PROPERTIES OF PLANTS
Carbohydrates

The basis of all sugars are the elements carbon, hydrogen, and oxygen. The word **carbohydrate** is derived from these three words, and is used for any type of sugar. Plants make sugars from the air, water, and sun light. They use the sun's energy to break apart H_2O (water), and CO_2 (carbon dioxide), and to recombine these elements into CH_2O (sugar) and O_2 (the oxygen we breathe). These sugars are a means of storing energy. We eat the sugars and release the energy, allowing the molecules to revert to H_2O and CO_2.

We rarely taste the sweetness in most carbohydrate foods because we chew and swallow our food so quickly. But there are enzymes in saliva that break carbohydrates apart into simple sugars, so you can taste the sweetness simply by chewing your food a little longer. Sugars that are improperly digested can ferment in the gut and cause gas.

Starch: Many plants like potatoes or cattails store energy in their roots in the form of starchy carbohydrates. This energy reserve is built up over the course of the summer, then used to give the plants a fast start in the spring. Most seeds also include a starch reserve called the endosperm. Most starchy roots and seeds are *edible*, but some to contain dangerous alkaloids or acrid substances. Starchy roots can be used medicinally as *drawing poultices* to absorb toxins or to draw down an inflammation. The effectiveness of these poultices can be increased by soaking the starchy root first in tannic acid.

Monosaccharides: Monosaccharides are simple sugars, including glucose, fructose, and galactose (a milk sugar). These are metabolized through digestion for energy. They have no known medicinal functions.

Disaccharides: When two simple sugars are combined they are called a disaccharide. Sucrose, for example, is made of a unit of glucose and a unit of fructose. Maltose is a combination of two units of glucose. Lactose is made of glucose and galactose. Most disaccharides are easily broken down through digestion into monosaccharides, and then used for energy. A few of them are indigestible and become "roughage" in our systems. An **oligosaccharide** is a combination of 2 to 10 sugar molecules.

Polysaccharides: Polysaccharides are complex carbohydrates made of many sugar units. Wood is made of one form of polysaccharide called **cellulose**.

Inulin: The word "inulin" is often confused with the unrelated word "insulin". Inulin is a non-digestible carbohydrate which can be converted to fructose through extended exposure to heat and moisture. Undercooked inulin tends to produce copious gas in the gut. Plants that contain inulin (usually in the roots) are good for diabetics, since they are able to eat fructose. Inulin is especially abundant in the Aster family. Dandelion roots are roasted to break the inulin down into sweet-tasting fructose. Jerusalem artichoke tubers (*Helianthus tuberosus*) are sweetest the day after they are cooked. The onion, blue camas, and other bulbs of the Lily family are also rich in inulin.

Mucilage: Mucilage is a slimy, moist polysaccharide, found in *Aloe vera* and other herbs, that moistens tissues. It is especially useful for mild burns and sun burns. The fluid between your body cells is a "mucopolysaccharide hydrogel". The polysaccharides help strengthen this hydrogel after damage. It is typically described as an *emollient* when it is used externally on irritated skin, and as a *demulcent* when used internally, as for soothing a sore throat. It has a mildly *expectorant* quality, probably by increasing the sliminess of the phlegm enough to release it. Mucilage is sometimes used as a *bulk laxative*. Mucilage also coats the intestinal tract, reducing irritation and sensitivity to chemicals, acids, and bitters. The Cactus, Mallow, Flax, Purslane, Borage and Plantain families are all high in mucilage. Mucilage is also found in the Violet family and several members of the Rose family.

Pectin: Pectins are complex polysaccharides used medicinally for ulcers, wounds, and intestinal problems, such as diarrhea. Kaopectate is a commercial remedy for diarrhea that includes pectin. Pectin also contains calcium and phosphorus, bound with a strong electrical charge that attracts toxic chemicals, heavy metals and radioactive compounds. The toxins are then eliminated through the bowels. Apples and some other fruits contain enough pectin to jell without adding commercial pectin. Pectin is especially found in fruits of the Rose family, but also in citrus fruits (*Rutaceae*), and in the Barberry, Mallow and Aster families.

Gum: Gums are similar to mucilage, but thicker and more sticky. Gums are commonly used as *stabilizers* in the cosmetic, pharmaceutical and food-processing industries. The gums prevent the other ingredients from separating out of a mixture. Agar gum appears on the labels of many products; it is extracted from a seaweed of the same name. Gums are present in the Pea family and are especially common in the Aster family,

THE PROPERTIES OF PLANTS
Glycosides

A glycoside is a sugar combined with an non-sugar (a-glycone) compound. Herbalists are most interested in the aglycone part; the sugar itself has little therapeutic value. In fact, other than saponins, most glycosides are inactive until separated from the sugar component. Crushing a plant and soaking it in warm water is usually sufficient for the plant's own enzymes to break apart the glycoside and release the active constituents into the water, called hydrolyzation. Please note that cold water may not always activate the enzyme activity, and hot water can alter the chemistry, occasionally producing toxic substances (Schauenberg).

Sulfur Glycosides: Sulfur glycosides, like glucosinolate and thiocyanate, contain nitrogen in combination with sulfur. They are especially found in the Mustard, Caper, Nasturtium and Mignonette families, plus in *Allium* of the Lily family. Sulfur glycosides are mostly *acrid and irritating*. In small amounts they stimulate digestion; in larger amounts they can cause heartburn. These plants are often used as a *rubifacient poultice*; the glycosides irritate the area of application, *stimulating* circulation and healing. Sulphur from these food sources is also useful to metabolize and excrete acetaminophen (Tylenol), which could otherwise build up to toxic levels in the body. Along with iodized salt, the popularization of mustard may have contributed to the virtual disappearance of goiter in the modern world, but please note that *excessive consumption* of these plants can block the body's ability to absorb iodine, and *cause* goiter.

Cyanide Glycosides: Cyanide appears in many forms with many names, including cyanophore, cyanogen, hydrocyanic acid, and prussic acid. Cyanide glycosides contain nitrogen in combination with hydrogen and carbon. Cyanide occurs widely in nature, especially in the Rose, Honeysuckle, and Flax families. Amygdalin, also called **Laetrile** or **Vitamin B17**, is a glycoside containing cyanide. Laetrile has been promoted as an *anti-cancer* agent, but with inconclusive results. An overdose of Laetrile can cause death. Cyanide reacts with a body enzyme called cytochrome oxidase, which normally links oxygen to the individual cells. The cyanide interrupts this process and causes the individual cells to asphyxiate. Plants containing cyanide are sometimes listed as *sedative*, because they literally choke off the metabolic processes.

The body handles trace amounts of cyanide by adding a molecule of sulfur to create thiocyanate (see Sulfur Glycosides). But excess dosage over-whelms and poisons the body. Chronic consumption of trace amounts will rob the body of sulfur and iodide, leading to thyroid disorders (Klein).

Phenol Glycosides: Phenols come in many different forms, but they are all carbon based. Phenols are a component in the other glycosides to follow, including flavanoids, coumarins, anthroquinone and cardiac glycosides and saponins.

-Simple phenols, like salicylin (i.e.: salicylic acid, willow, **aspirin**) are an important class of their own. Salicylic acid affects the "thermo-regulatory centers" and the peripheral blood vessels to relieve fevers, pain, and inflammation. The simple phenols are used especially for **urinary tract infections, arthritis, rheumatism, and other inflammations**. Some forms pass through the digestive tract before they are hydrolized (separating the active component from the sugar) in the presence of alkaline urine in the bladder. Hydrolization forms potent disinfectants especially useful for urinary tract infections. Sodium bicarbonate must be taken with the herbs when the urine is acid. Simple phenols are found in the Willow and Heath families, plus *Spiraea* and pear from the Rose family.

-Flavonoids: Flavonoid glycosides include flavones, flavonals, flavonones, isoflavones, chalcones, and aurones. Plants that are rich in flavonoids have long been used as dyes—in fact, the word "flavonoid" comes from the Latin "flavus", meaning yellow. The fall colors, both the reds and the yellows, are flavonoids— always present in the leaves, but hidden by the chlorophyll until fall. Flavonoids are safe to people and animals, but toxic to microorganisms. Plants produce them to protect against disease. Many flavonoids are known to have antiviral and anti-inflammatory properties for people, but they are especially valued as *antioxidants* to help protect the body from *free radicals*.

Free radicals occur when otherwise healthy body cells lose electrons at the molecular level. This creates an imbalance in the electrical charge, and makes the cells highly reactive. The deficient cells have a sort of magnetic attraction that will bind them to anything that will balance out their charge. The imbalanced cells are called "free radicals" because of this highly reactive nature. These free radicals are especially prone to combining with oxygen molecules, hence the term "antioxidants". The imbalanced cells react with the oxygen molecules in the cells, causing damage. Antioxidants are foods or supplements that provide a source of electrons to stabilize the cells before they are injured. Our body cells are constantly being injured by normal biological processes. Youthful bodies are able to repair the damage quickly, but this ability tends to slow with age. Antioxidants are a means of neutralizing the free radicals before they injure any tissues.

THE PROPERTIES OF PLANTS

Flavonoids are generally diuretic and relieve cramping. They also affect the heart and circulatory system and strengthen the capillaries. There are about 500 known flavonoids, including Vitamins C, E, and P. The best way to get your flavonoids is to eat lots of fruits and vegetables. The fruits, including wild berries, tend to be especially rich in flavonoids. Flavonoids are found throughout the Plant Kingdom.

-**Coumarins**: There are more than 100 kinds of coumarins within the general types: hydroxycoumarins, methoxycoumarins, furanocoumarins, pyranocoumarins, and dicoumarols. Coumarins have a sweet smell. Medicinally they have *anti-inflammatory* and *antibacterial* properties. The Indian breadroot (*Psoralea*) and sweet clover (*Melilotus*) of the Pea family contain coumarins, as do many plants of the Parsley family.

Dicoumarols act as anticoagulants. Vitamin K is produced by bacteria in the small intestine and used by the liver in the manufacture of prothrombin, a blood-clotting enzyme. Dicoumarol destroys vitamin K, so it is used to reduce blood clots in heart patients. Excess consumption can prevent the scabbing of clots, or lead to spontaneous internal bleeding. Concentrated doses of dicoumarols are used in rat poison. Dicoumarols are formed when sweet clover (*Melilotus*) is fermented.

Furanocoumarins can have *phytotoxic* effects, causing a rash when the skin is exposed to ultraviolet light. Juice from celery leaves (Parsley family) can make the skin sensitive to sunlight. Furanocoumarins are often toxic to fish.

-**Anthraquinone glycosides** (also known as Anthracenosides): Anthraquinone glycosides have *purgative* (strongly laxative) properties. The glycosides are digested by the bile, absorbed by the small intestine, and passed on to the large intestine hours later as purgatives. The glycoside is found in diverse, mostly unrelated plants.

Anthraquinone glycosides are violent purgatives, especially those found in senna *(Cassia)* and *Aloe vera*; they can cause blood to be released with the stools. *Rhamnus*, however also contains a form of cyanide that gives the laxative a calming effect so it can be used for several days without irritation. Rhubarb root (*Rheum*) is considered relatively gentle. *Cuscuta* and *Hypericum* also contain this purgative glycoside, but the latter is fat-soluble, not digestible by the bile, so it has no effect. Anthraquinones can have a "griping" effect on the bowels, so spicy herbs like ginger (see Volatile Oils) are often taken with the laxatives for their antispasmodic property. Also note that excess use of laxatives can weaken the bowels and result in laxative dependency.

-**Cardiac Glycosides**: There are a number of diverse plants with steroid glycosides that stimulate heart contractions. Among the most well-known are *Digitalis* of the Figwort family and *Convallaria* of the Lily family. Other plants with cardiac glycosides include *Helleborus* and *Adonis* from the Buttercup family, *Nymphaea* from the Water Lily family, and *Gratiola* from the Figwort family (Schauenberg). These are very dangerous plants and should not be used internally by amateurs. The Dogbane and Milkweed families also contain cardiac glycosides. Water retention can be symptomatic of a weak heart and kidneys. Through increased heart function, cardiac glycosides can remove fluids from the body, a *diuretic* effect.

Some plants with cardiac glycosides were used to stun fish. The plants were broken up, tossed into pools, and the fish scooped out by hand. The fish are reportedly safe to eat (Nyerges).

-**Saponin**: Saponin is a glucoside poison; it destroys the membranes of red blood cells and releases the hemoglobin. Fortunately saponin is not easily absorbed by the digestive system, and most of what we eat passes straight through the body. Saponin is widely found in plants, including many vegetables like beans, spinach and tomatoes. There are many forms of saponin, all with varying potency. Saponin breaks down with prolonged cooking.

Plants that contain saponin can usually be worked into a "lather", and are used as *soap substitutes*. Saponins are effective at removing dirt but not oils. They are sometimes used as cleansers in cosmetics. Some specific plants that are rich in saponins include: yucca root (*Yucca*), buckbrush flowers and berries (*Ceanothus*), snowberries (*Symphoricarpus*), bouncing bet (*Saponaria*), white cockle (*Lychnis*), horse-chestnut (*Aesculus*), and *Cyclamen*.

Medicinally, saponins are sometimes used as irritants in the form of sneezing powders or emetics, but more often to stimulate digestion. Saponin may be valuable in certain cases of arthritis where the pain is combined with indigestion or headaches. Saponins clean the intestinal walls and facilitate the body's use of certain substances like calcium and silicon. Saponins also have a diuretic effect.

Saponin-rich plants are often used as *fish poison*. Fish directly assimilate saponin into the blood stream through their gills, destroying their red blood cells. Adding a significant quantity of an herb with saponin to a small, still pond may effectively stun or kill the fish, without harming the fisherman who eats them.

THE PROPERTIES OF PLANTS
Acids

Tannic Acid: An *astringent* is an acid substance that causes tissues to constrict. The most common natural astringent is tannic acid. Gallic and malic acids are also astringent. The act of constricting tissues is medicinally useful in a number of ways.

First, it closes off secretions, especially of the digestive system and is therefore useful for "drying up" **diarrhea**. (Dysentery is a severe, often bloody type of diarrhea.) Similarly, astringents tighten up ulcerated tissues, thus speeding the healing of stomach ulcers and bloody urine, as well as cuts, excema and eruptions on the skin, often used as a poultice or wash. Since they cause wounds to tighten-up and stop bleeding, they are sometimes listed as *hemeostatics* or *coagulants*.

> *If you get the sensation of cotton-mouth or seem to run out of saliva when you bite into an herb, then the plant is said to be astrigent.*

Astringents even tighten up inflamed tissues, thus being beneficial to swellings, sunburns, pimples, blisters, sore throats, inflamed or tired eyes, or as a sitz bath after childbirth to speed the healing of inflamed tissues. A few astringent plants have been used on headaches and to a limited extent on arthritic-type conditions, again to reduce inflamed tissues. Thus astringent herbs are sometimes listed as being *anti-inflammatory*. Astringent herbs are sometimes used as a poultice to diminish varicose veins.

Since acids are generally harmful to bacteria, astringent plants are often also listed as being *antiseptic* or *antibiotic*.

Through the act of tightening tissues, astringents act as a sort of *toner* or *strengthener*. For example, you can buy astringent facial toners at the store. Similarly, the leaves of astringent plants can be put in shoes to tighten tissues and protect against blistering. Internally, astringents can tone and strengthen mucous membranes, such as in the urinary tract. Many plants that have astringent properties are also *diuretic* in nature, meaning they make you urinate more. The diuretic effect may be due in part to the tannins drawing water out of the cells, but also to the simple phenol glycosides (see glycosides) that are often found with tannic acid.

Tannic acid is also used for tanning hides. That drying, puckering sensation that you get when you taste an astringent is the same action that works on the hides, drawing out the binders, so the hide becomes more flexible. Over-consumption of these tannins is potentially dangerous, and countries where black tea is popular tend to have high rates of stomach cancer. Incidentally, milk in tea reduces the tannin effect. The tannin binds with the milk protein, instead of binding with the proteins of your stomach lining.

Oxalic Acid: The lemony-sour taste in rhubarb and many other plants comes from oxalic acid, also called oxalate. (Please note that the true lemon taste comes from citronellal, a potent volatile oil found in lemons.)

Like other acids, oxalate acts as an *astringent* when used as a wash for skin problems. But oxalic acid is much more harsh than other acids. Internally it acts as an *irritating stimulant* to the digestive system. It irritates the system to increase secretions, rather than decreasing them as many other acids do. Thus it is helpful as a digestive aid, for heartburn, or for constipation. Intermittent consumption of this acid is okay, but too much can excessively irritate the system, leading to diarrhea and even hemorrhaging. Oxalic acid can also precipitate into oxalate crystals in the kidneys and plug the tubules.

> *A plant with a lemony-sour taste like rhubarb usually contains "oxalic acid".*

Plants with oxalic acid are commonly used in external *cancer remedies*, to literally etch away the offending tumor. One recipe suggests fermenting the bruised, oxalate-rich leaves in a crock-pot in the ground for 6-8 weeks. The resulting black salve is placed on the tumor and is left in place until it draws out the cancer and falls off. It is reported to be extremely painful (Cummings). This fermentation process would involve fungi, probably with antibiotic effects and other unknown properties.

Most plants with oxalic acid are *edible* to some degree, but long-term consumption of oxalic acid can block the body's ability to absorb calcium. (Ironically, many plants that contain oxalic acid are also high in calcium.) Drinking milk, or taking some other calcium supplement may sufficiently neutralize the effect. Pregnant or nursing women should avoid consumption of plants with oxalic acid. The **Buckwheat** and **Wood-Sorrel** families are especially rich in oxalic acid. Several plants in the **Purslane** and **Goosefoot** families also contain oxalates.

The Properties of Plants

Citric and Tartaric Acid: Citric and tartaric acids cleanse the mouth, stimulate saliva flow, and reduce the number of cavity-causing bacteria. The acids are considered laxative because they are absorbed very slowly through the intestines, so stools remain soft. Citric and tartaric acids are useful after surgery or in cases of hemorrhoids, to reduce the muscle action of the lower abdomen. Citric and other plant acids can also bind with and remove heavy metals and other toxins in the body. Citric acid is especially found in the Citrus family (*Rutaceae*), but also in raspberries and other fruits of the Rose family, plus members of the Grape family.

> *If you have ever brushed against stinging nettles or been bitten by the wrong kind of ant, then you know what "formic acid" is!*

Formic Acid: Formic acid is a defensive mechanism used by biting ants and several members of the Stinging Nettle family. Both the ants and the nettles inject the acid under the skin, causing a temporary inflammation. The formic acid easily breaks down with cooking, making both nettles and ants *edible*.

Medicinally, formic acid has been used as an *irritant* to *stimulate* healing in cases of arthritis. The arthritic joints are whipped with stinging nettles; the irritation causes improved circulation and healing. This is a cure for the desperate!

Acrids

An acrid substance causes a hot, biting sensation, much like horse radish, when it hits your tongue. Herbs with acrid properties are often used as *irritating poultices* to stimulate healing under the skin. These poultices can be used on bruises, aches, or arthritis to stimulate healing activity inside, but be careful, because the poultices can cause blistering if left in place too long. The poultices can stimulate activity even in cases of mild paralysis.

Acrid substances can have a similarly stimulating effect when taken internally. In moderate amounts they warm the body, *dilating* the blood vessels, decreasing blood pressure, and equalizing the blood flow to the extremities. For this reason acrid plants are often listed as *emmenagogue* (stimulates menstruation), *diaphoretic* (causes sweating), *diuretic* (causes increased urination), and *galactagogue* (increases milk flow). The hot, acrid quality opens you up from the inside out.

Larger doses of acrid substances can cause a vomiting reaction (*emetic*). Similarly, acrid substances are sometimes used as *expectorants*, by irritating the mucous membranes to loosen phlegm. Caution is advised is using either of these remedies.

Acrid plants are also used for **warts**. The plant juice is smeared on the wart a few times each day until the wart disappears. Likewise, acrid plants can be used as a hair rinse to get rid of lice.

Acrid poultices can even be used on external **cancerous tumors**. A strongly acrid poultice is placed over the cancer and the caustic effect literally burns out the growth. The body often encases these cancerous cells to separate them from healthy ones, and the acrid substances reportedly burn out everything within that casing, leaving a hole which later heals over. This treatment is said to be extremely painful.

The acrid substance in mustard, radish, and horseradish (Mustard family) and garlic (Lily family) and cow parsnip (Parsley family) comes from a thiocyanate glycoside (see Glycosides for more information). The Buttercup, Arum, and Iris families also include many acrid plants.

Latex

Many plants, from dandelions to milkweeds, contain a milky white sap. This sap is an indicator of latex. Latex is used in house paints and caulking. It was originally the source of rubber for making tires, until the industry switched to synthetic oil products.

Medicinally, latex is typically acrid, but sometimes bitter; it is most often used to *irritate*, and thus *stimulate* the body. It stimulates the secretions of digestive acids, promoting digestion, and functioning as a *laxative*. Latex-rich plants are sometimes used to irritate and stimulate (dilate) the bronchials to aid lung infections. This leads to *expectorant* properties as well. They often used by women to stimulate lactose production (*galactagogue*) and menstruation (*emmenagogue*). Caution: latex sap often contains dangerous alkaloids.

The acrid property of latex makes it useful for removing warts. Put the milky sap of a plant on a wart, and the acridness will eat away the growth. Do this several times a day until the wart disappears.

THE PROPERTIES OF PLANTS
Alkaloids

There are approximately 5,000 known alkaloids. Alkaloids contain nitrogen and have a very basic (alkaline) pH. Alkaloidal plants do not fully utilize all the available nitrogen for protein production, so the nitrogen circulates in the sap, or accumulates in parts of the plants in the form of alkaloids. Alkaloids are especially produced during periods of rapid growth; somehow the accelerated metabolism apparently uses the nitrogen less efficiently. Overall, alkaloidal plants are more common—and more potent—in hot climates than cold ones.

Alkaloids mixed with acids form salts. Alkaloids usually end in a suffix such as -in, ine, or -ane. Most are named after the plant they are discovered in, hence the name "cicutine" for the toxic alkaloid found in *Cicuta* (water hemlock).

> *A narcotic is any alkaloid that depresses the central nervous system.*

Alkaloids are *bitter* to taste, and some are used to stimulate digestion, but many alkaloids also produce a strong reaction in the nervous system. Alkaloids rarely effect the heart directly, but they may depress or excite the central nervous system, affecting circulation, respiration, and blood pressure. Most alkaloids are water soluble.

A *narcotic* is any alkaloid that *depresses* the central nervous system; they are toxic in excess. They are used especially for their *analgesic* properties. An analgesic numbs the body's sense of pain, like opium or morphine of the Poppy family. For a similar reason, a few of these species are useful as *sedatives*. Some depressants can cause *hallucinations*, including *Datura* and *Hyosyamus* from the Nightshade family, but the toxicity varies from one area to another, and a slight overdose causes death. Symptoms include an unquenchable thirst, dilation of the eyes, delirium, hallucinations, convulsions, and coma.

Indole Alkaloids: There are over 1,200 indole alkaloids, with diverse medicinal applications. Ergotomine, from the ergot fungus (see the Grass family) has been used as a vasoconstrictor for migraine headaches. LSD is a related compound with hallucinogenic effects. Serotonin, tryptamine (like tryptophan), and adrenaline are all indole alkaloids. Most indole alkaloids are found in the Dogbane, Madder, and Logania (not covered in this text) families.

Quinoline Alkaloids: Quinine is an anti-malarial alkaloid of this group.

Isoquinoline Alkaloids: Morphine and several other analgesic isoquinoline alkaloids are derived from members of the Poppy family. Mescaline is the hallucinogenic alkaloid in peyote of the Cactus family.

An isoquinoline alkaloid that is non-narcotic is berberine from the Barberry family, also found in goldenseal (*Hydrastis*) and gold thread (*Coptis*) of the Buttercup family. Berberine is extremely bitter, used especially to stimulate liver function. It is also strongly anti-viral. It may be effective against giardia. Ipecac is another non-narcotic alkaloid of this group, derived from a plant in the Madder family.

Purine Alkaloids: Purine alkaloids can prolong the useful life of many hormones, particularly adrenaline. Caffeine is a purine-type alkaloid. In large amounts caffeine can lead to nervousness, insomnia, a rapid and irregular heart beat, elevated blood sugar and cholesterol levels and heartburn (Tyler).

Pyrrolidine and Tropane Alkaloids: These alkaloids act on the central nervous system, blocking parasympathetic nerve activity. Atropine, hyoscine, hyoscyamine, and scopolamine come from the Nightshade family. Cocaine also belongs to this group; it is derived from coca leaves (*Erythroxylum coca*) of the Coca family. Please note that coca is unrelated to the source of our chocolate, cocoa (*Theobroma cacao*) of the Sterculia family.

Pyridine and Piperidine Alkaloids: These alkaloids tend to act first as an *irritating stimulant*, then as a *nerve paralyzer*. Cicutine and coniine, from water hemlock and hemlock of the Parsley family are extremely toxic, fast-acting alkaloids of this group. They cause progressive paralysis of the nervous system, and eventually death. Nicotine from the Nightshade family is a similar alkaloid, but not as potent; smokers reduce their life-spans by about 8 minutes per cigarette. Lobeline from the Harebell family also belongs to this group.

Pyrrolizidine & Quinolizidine Alkaloids: Many of these alkaloids are toxic to people and livestock. *Senecio spp.* from *the* Aster family contains the pyrrolizidine-type alkaloid. Comfrey, hound's tongue, and borage from the Borage family contain lesser amounts of this alkaloid type. Apparently the unsaturated forms are more toxic than the saturated forms. Quinolizidine alkaloids are prevalent in the Pea family.

Terpenoid Alkaloids: Some members of the Buttercup family, including *Aconitum* and *Delphinium* contain highly poisonous terpenoid alkaloids. The popular sedative Valerian from the Valerian family, also contains a terpenoid alkaloid.

THE PROPERTIES OF PLANTS
Volatile or Essential Oils

Volatile oils are unstable, as the name implies. They easily separate from the plant material and vaporize into the air. Any plants with a strongly aromatic odor contain significant quantities of these oils. Our culinary spices are inherently rich in volatile oils. Medicinally, these oils are usually easy to assimilate into the body, again due to their tendency to vaporize out of the plant material. Conversely, medicinal plants rich in volatile oils often have a short shelf-life, because the desired properties are vaporized away. Oils and resins are best extracted in alchohol.

Medicinally, these spicy oils are *stimulating* and warming, causing the body to open up and sweat; thus most of the plants are *diaphoretic* or *sudorific*. This property can help you break a fever. A fever is the body's way of "cooking" the microorganisms that cause infections. Using a diaphoretic herb can help raise a mild fever just high enough to "cook" a virus, thus "breaking" or ending the fever. Note, however, that diaphoretics can be dangerous where there is already a high fever, and other compounds such as aspirin should be used to reduce the fever. Diaphoretics tend to be most effective if used at the very onset of a cold. Volatile oils also have a *decongestant* effect, as you'll notice when your nose runs after a spicy meal. Intensely diaphoretic plants may even stop venereal diseases.

Warming the body also opens up the vessels, allowing blood to flow more freely. This means they have a *vasodilator* effect, useful for relaxing the blood vessels in cases of hypertension or for stimulating delayed menstruation, called an *emmenagogue*.

Diaphoretics can warm you up and make you sweat, but sweating is also the body's way of cooling itself. Thus a diaphoretic herb can act as a *refrigerant* (also called a *febrifuge*). Old evaporation coolers worked on a similar principle, where a damp cloth was laid over the food and placed in a breeze. The food was cooled as the moisture in the cloth is evaporated away. Our bodies are thus cooled when we sweat, and the sweat evaporates away from our skin. It is no coincidence that hot, spicy food (like Mexican cuisine) originates in hot climates. Chili peppers and jalepeno peppers contain volatile oils that really make you sweat, and that helps to cool you off even when it is extremely hot out. (Besides, anything feels cool after sweating through a hot jalepeno pepper!) In cold, northern climates we eat fatty foods like ice cream to give us calories to burn for warmth!

A hot tea of a spicy herb has a diaphoretic effect because the volatile oils are expelled through the pores of the skin. The same tea served cold may has a diuretic effect, as the volatile oils are expelled through the urine.

Herbs with volatile oils are often listed as being *anthelmintic*—that is, they kill or expel worms (also called a *vermifuge*). If you imagine yourself being totally inundated with volatile oils, you can sense that they would probably have a similar effect on you. For similar reasons, aromatic herbs are often *antibiotic or antimicrobial* in character. They are also used externally to kill lice and ringworm fungus.

Volatile oils are frequently listed as being *carminative* (dispels gas). Apparently, the volatile oils act similarly to bitters, stimulating secretions from the salivary, stomach, and intestinal glands to improve digestion. Either the gas is more completely digested, or the food producing the gas is more completely digested. Also, the volatile oils easily vaporize into a gas and may directly interact with and break down the digestive gases.

Plants with volatile oils are sometimes listed as *antidotal* for eliminating poisons, such as from snake bite. Apparently the increased sweating would eliminate the toxins through the skin. The effectiveness of this treatment is questionable for serious poisons, and I have not listed specific antidotal plants in this text. Seek professional medical assistance for such cases if in any way possible. Sweating is, however, a reliable means of cleansing to remove ordinary body pollutants.

Finally, some plants with volatile oils have mildly *sedative* properties. Like alkaloids, volatile oils are generally alkaline, and they may have remotely related chemistry. From what I can determine in the literature, it seems that the volatile oils act on the central nervous system similar to the alkaloids, but more mildly. As a result of these nerve-calming properties, many plants with volatile oils are described as *nervine* and *antispasmodic*.

The Aster, Birthwort, Birch, Cypress, Heath, Ginseng, Parsley, and Mint families all contain significant quantities of volatile oils. Note: many of these herbs may be dangerous during pregnancies, due to their anthlementic (worm killing) and emmenagogue (menstrual stimulating) properties. The most dangerous ones are those that are also bitter (irritating).

More specifically now, volatile oils are combinations of **aromatic molecules**. There are approximately 30,000 different aromatic molecules found in plants, mostly comprised of carbon, hydrogen, and oxygen. They can be separated into a number of subgroups according to their chemical make-up and their effects on the body. Any

THE PROPERTIES OF PLANTS

plant may contain just a few aromatic molecules belonging to one subgroup, or may contain hundreds of these molecules belonging to multiple subgroups. Plants are usually placed in whichever chemical-type they contain the most of. Individual aromatic molecules are typically named after the plant they predominately occur in. These often end in a suffix indicating the chemical subgroup it belongs to. Peppermint plants (*Mentha piperita*), for example, contain an alcohol volatile oil named **menthol**. This is the root word of the mint genus combined with the -ol suffix from alcohol. Menthol is a common ingredient in many cough drops. Listed below are a few of the common chemical groups that aromatic volatile oils belong to.

Alcohols: Alcohol volatile oils are generally considered energizing and non-toxic. These are non-irritating and safe to use. The suffix -ol generally indicates a member of this or the phenol group.

Aldehydes: Aldehyde volatile oils are anti-inflammatory, antiseptic, sedative, and may be irritating to the skin. Citronellal is an aldehyde found in lemons, lemon-grass, and other lemon-scented herbs. Cinnamon contains significant concentrations of cinnamic aldehyde.

Coumarins: Coumarin volatile oils can damage the liver, and may lead to photosensitivity. They also thin the blood and act as anticoagulants. (Read more about coumarins with the Glycosides).

Esters: Ester volatile oils are typically very fragrant. They are considered antispasmodic, antifungal, and relaxing. Esters are the product of a reaction between an alcohol and acid, forming an acetate.

Ethers: Ether volatile oils have antispasmodic, carminative, stimulant, expectorant, and antiseptic properties.

Ketones: Ketone volatile oils dissolve fats and mucus. Some are quite safe, but others can be toxic in excess. The toxins seem to effect the nervous system leading to convulsions, stupefaction, seizures, or abortion. Junipers (*Thuja*) of the Cypress family contain a toxic ketone volatile oil called thujone. Thujone is also found in wormwood (*Artemisia absinthium*) and tansy (*Tanacetum vulgare*) of the Aster family. Pulegone is a similarly toxic ketone found in pennyroyal *(Hedeoma pulegioides)*. *Hyssop* also contains ketone volatile oils. Some plants with non-toxic ketones include jasmine and fennel. The suffix -one often indicates a member of this chemical group.

Oxides: Eucalyptol is an oxide volatile oil found in the *Eucalyptus* tree.

Phenols: Phenol volatile oils can be irritating to the skin and toxic to the liver. They should be used only in small amounts for short periods of time. Some plants that contain phenol volatile oils include: cloves, thyme, oregano, and savory. The suffix -ol generally indicates a member of this or the alcohol group.

Sulfurs: Volatile oils containing sulfur are typically acrid, like onions and radish. (See Acrids and Sulfur Glycosides for more details.)

Terpenes: Terpene volatile oils can be irritating to the skin. They are sub-grouped according to the number of carbon atoms they contain. Monoterpenes, including menthol, camphor, and thujone, contain 10 carbon atoms. Sesquiterpenes such as azulenes and bisabolol contain 15 carbon atoms. Terpenes with 20, 30, and 40 molecules are rare in plants. The 30 and 40 molecule terpenes are plant steroids and hormones. The suffix -ene generally indicates a member of this group.

Resins

Plant resins are sticky-gummy substances, like pine pitch. Resins are formed from **oxidized volatile oils**; they are complex compounds that form solids at room temperatures. Resins do not contain nitrogen. They are insoluble in water, so organic solvents like alcohol are often needed to extract them from the plants. The digestive system produces some such solvents.

Resins are especially useful for their *expectorant* qualities, to help expel phlegm during a cold. When you drink a warm tea of a resinous plant your throat becomes coated with the sticky substance. This protects tissues from irritation when coughing. Moreover, the stickiness seems to slick up the passageways in the body, so phlegm can be more readily coughed up.

Resins typically contain potent **volatile oils**, such as the turpentine in fir trees. Resins thus have *warming* or *stimulating* properties, useful when applied to arthritic joints. Internally, resins often have *expectorant, diaphoretic* and *diuretic* properties. However, plants with resins may lead to kidney troubles with excessive use. The resins do not break down easily in the body, and they can irritate and plug the tubules of the kidneys. The Pine, Cypress, and Aster families are especially rich in resins.

THE PROPERTIES OF PLANTS

Bitters

Herbs with a *bitter* taste *stimulate* the body's systems and are most commonly used as digestive aids. You must taste the bitterness in your mouth for these to take effect. The bitter taste signals the nervous system to release digestive fluids all the way down, from saliva to gastric acid to bile. Sampling bitter herbs shortly before a meal will help get your digestive system ready for the main course; this can help prevent indigestion. Consuming bitter herbs after the fact, when you already have indigestion, can help your system to catch up. It may seem odd that you would use bitter herbs to increase acidity when you are already experiencing hyperacidity, but the bitters also stimulate the release of bicarbonate from the liver, pancreas and the "Brunner's" glands. Bitter herbs influence and balance the whole digestive system, whereas most commercial remedies just neutralize the acid and impair the natural processes. Because bitter herbs help stomach problems, they are often listed as *stomachic*.

Please note that many astringent herbs have a bitter taste, but they are not true bitters. We are used to such bland and sweet foods that many people cannot distinguish between bitter and astringent tastes. At first it all tastes the same. If an herb gives you a sensation of "cotton mouth", or if you seem to be lacking in saliva, then you are sampling an astringent, not a bitter.

Another primary use of bitters is as laxatives. The fluids from your digestive system help to loosen up your bowels and relieve constipation. This also stimulates muscle contractions to help move matter through the bowels. A mild laxative is sometimes called an *aperient*. An ordinary *laxative* is in the middle of the scale. A *purgative* is stronger and literally "purges" your system. A *cathartic* intensely stimulates bowel movement. Purgative and cathartic herbs can be dangerous.

A third use of bitter herbs is to increase the flow of bile from the liver to the gall bladder and thence into the small intestine. This stimulated flow enhances the liver's ability to evacuate toxins from the body. Herbs that help the liver are often listed as *hepatic*. Increasing the flow of bile also dilutes it. This is important to prevent the formation of gall stones. These stones are formed when bile becomes concentrated in the gall bladder. The bilious acids essentially dry out and precipitate into salts, forming a salt crystal in the gall bladder. In addition to diluting the bile, bitter herbs trigger its release back into the digestive tract where it is used to break down fats. Consuming bitter herbs as a regular part of the diet can help maintain a healthy system. Bitters are especially helpful to revitalize the body after exhaustion, chronic disease, or lack of appetite and weakness of the digestive system. Please note that bitter herbs can cool and contract the digestive system in some people, so spicy herbs (rich in volatile oils) are often taken to counteract the effect.

Bitter principles are very common in herbs. The Gentian and Buckbean families are especially rich in bitter principles. The Dandelion subfamily and the Artichoke tribe of the Aster family are bitter throughout, with other bitters appearing scattered throughout the family. The Barberry family and a few members of the Buttercup family contain a potent bitter alkaloid known as berberine.

Gelatin

Gelatin is a type of protein. It is the substance that makes Jell-O® set. Gelatin is most commonly derived from animal hooves and hides, but it is found in a few plants as well. Powdered gelatin can be dusted over an open wound to stop the hemorrhaging. One plant that contains gelatin is *Smilax* of the Lily family. Some lichens also contain gelatin.

Bibliography

_____. "Hot Stuff: Chili pepper can ease lingering pain after surgery". <u>Bozeman Daily Chronicle</u>. May 21, 1996. Pg. 13

_____. <u>Text-Book of Western Botany</u>. Ivison, Blakeman & Co.: New York & Chicago. 1885.

Amrion, Inc. "Grape Seed Extract". Promotional Pamphlet. 1995.

Andrews, E. F. <u>A Practical Course in Botany</u>. American Book Company. New York, Cincinatti, Chicago. 1911.

Angier, Bradford. <u>Survival with Style</u>. Stackpole Books: Harrisburg, PA. 1972.

Angier, Bradford. <u>Living off the Country</u>. Stackpole Books: Harrisburg, PA. 1956, 1971.

Angier, Bradford. <u>Field Guide to Medicinal Wild Plants</u>. Stackpole Books: Harrisburg, PA. 1978.

Asch, John. <u>The Story of Plants</u>. G. P. Putnam's Sons: USA 1948.

Bailey, L. H. <u>Standard Cyclopedia of Horticulture</u>. Macmillan Co: New York. Vol. I, 1900, 1914. Vol. 2, 1900, 1914.

Bastin, Harold. <u>Plants Without Flowers</u>. Philosophical Library, Inc.: New York. 1955.

Baumgardt, John Philip. <u>How to Identify Flowering Plant Families</u>. Timber Press: Portland, OR. 1982, 1994.

Bell, Peter R. <u>Green Plants: Their Origin and Diversity</u>. Dioscorides Press: Portland, OR. 1992.

Benson, Lyman. <u>Plant Classification, 2nd Edition</u>. D.C. Heath & Co.: Lexington, MA & Toronto. 1957, 1979.

Bigfoot, Peter. <u>Useful Wild Western Plants</u>. Reevis Mountain School: Roosevelt, AZ.

Booth, W. E. & J. C. Wright. <u>Flora of Montana—Part II</u>. Montana State University: Bozeman, MT. 1959, 1962, 1966.

Britton, Nathaniel Lord, Ph.D. & Hon. Addison Brown. <u>An Illustrated Flora of the Northern United States, Canada, and the British Possessions</u>. Charles Scribner's Sons: New York. Volume I: 1896. Volume II: 1897. Volume III: 1898.

Brown, Annora. <u>Old Man's Garden</u>. J. M. Dent & Sons (Canada) Limited: Toronto, Vancouver. 1954.

Brown, Tom Jr. <u>Tom Brown's Guide to Wild Edible and Medicinal Plants</u>. Berkeley Books. New York. 1985.

Campbell, Douglas H. <u>The Evolution of the Land Plants</u>. Stanford University Press: Stanford University, CA. 1940.

Corner, E. J. H. <u>The Life of Plants</u>. University of Chicago Press: Chicago & London. 1964.

Craighead, John J., Frank C. Craighead, & Ray J. Davis. <u>A Field Guide to Rocky Mountain Wildflowers</u>. Houghton Mifflin Co: Boston. 1963.

Crellin, John K. and Jane Philpott. <u>Herbal Medicine Past and Present: A Reference Guide to Medicinal Plants</u>. Duke University Press: Durham and London. 1989.

Coon, Nelson. <u>Using Plants for Healing</u>. Hearthside Press: New York. 1963.

Coulter, John M., A.M. Ph.D. <u>Plant Relations</u>. D. Appleton & Co. New York. 1899.

Coulter, John M., A.M. Ph.D. <u>A Text-Book of Botany</u>. D. Appleton & Co: New York. 1910.

Coulter, John M., A.M. Ph.D., Charles R. Barnes Ph.D., Henry C. Cowles Ph.D. <u>A Textbook of Botany, Volume II: Ecology</u>. American Book Company. New York, Cincinnati, Chicago. 1911.

Couplan, Francois Ph.D. <u>The Encyclopedia of Edible Plant of North America</u>. Keats Publishing: New Canaan, CT. 1998.

Culpeper, Nicholas. <u>Culpeper's Complete Herbal</u>. W. Foulsham & Co., Ltd.: London.

Cummings, Elsie, J. & Wavie J. Charlton. <u>Survival: Pioneer, Indian and Wilderness Lore</u>. Self-published. Missoula, Montana. 1971, 1972.

Dana, Mrs. William Starr. <u>How to Know the Wild Flowers</u>. Charles Scribner's Sons. New York. 1909.

Dayton, William A. <u>Important Western Browse Plants</u>. USDA Handbook No. 101. July 1931.

Densmore, Frances. <u>How Indians Use Wild Plants for Food, Medicine, & Crafts</u>. Dover Publications, Inc.: New York. 1974.

Dorn, Robert L. <u>Vascular Plants of Montana</u>. Mountain West Publishing: Cheyenne, WY. 1984.

Duke, James A. <u>Handbook of Edible Weeds</u>. CRC Press: Boca Raton, Ann Arbor, London, Tokyo. 1992.

Duncan, Ursula K., M.A. <u>A Guide to the Study of Lichens</u>. Scholar's Library: Gracie Station, NY. 1959

Emboden, William A. Jr. <u>Narcotic Plants</u>. The Macmillan Company: New York. 1972.

Fern, Ken. <u>Plants for a Future Database</u>. http://www.axis-net.com/pfaf/plants.html. Jan.-Feb. 1997.

Fukuoka, Masanobu. <u>The Natural Way of Farming</u>. Japan Publications, Inc.: Tokyo & New York. 1985 and 1986.

Geller, Cascade Anderson. *"Pharmacognosy Basics: Predominate Constituent Groups in Common Plant Families"*, <u>1995 Gaia Symposium Proceedings—Naturopathic Herbal Wisdom</u>. Gaia Herbal Research Institute: Harvard, MA. 1995.

Gibbons, Euell. <u>Stalking the Wild Asparagus</u>. David McKay Company, Inc.: New York. 1962-1973.

Gillaspy, James, Ph.D. *"Purslane: A Personal Perspective"*. <u>Bulletin of Primitive Technology</u>. Society of Primitive Technology. Volume 1. No. 7. Spring 1994. Pgs. 54-55.

Gilmore, Melvin R. <u>Uses of Plants by the Indians of the Missouri River Region</u>. University of Nebraska Press: Lincoln & London. 1991.

Glimn-Lacy, Janice and Peter B. Kaufman. <u>Botany Illustrated. Introduction to Plants, Major Groups, Flowering Plant Families</u>. Van Nostrand Reinhold Company: New York. 1984.

Green, James. <u>The Herbal Medicine-Maker's Handbook</u>. Simplers Botanical Co.: Forestville, CA. 1990.

Hale, Mason E. <u>How to Know the Lichens</u>. Wm. C. Brown Co. Publishers: Dubuque, Iowa. 1969, 1979.

Hall, Alan. The Wild Food Trailguide. Holt, Rinehart, & Winston: New York. 1973 and 1976.

Hart, Jeff. Montana: Native Plants and Early Peoples. Montana Historical Society Press: Helena, MT. 1976 & 1992.

Harrington, H. D. Edible Native Plants of the Rocky Mountains. University of New Mexico Press: Albuquerque. 1967.

Hayes, Doris W. & George A. Garrison. Key to Important Woody Plants of Eastern Oregon and Washington. Agriculture Handbook No. 148. USDA. December 1960.

Healthy Cell News. "Flaxseed As Food and Medicine". Healthy Cell News. Spring/Summer 1997. Page 1.

Healthy Cell News. "Oil-Protein Combination". Healthy Cell News. Spring/Summer 1997. Page 2.

Hobbs, Christopher. Foundations of Health. Botanica Press: Capitola, CA. 1992.

Holmes, Sandra. Outline of Plant Classification. Longman Group Ltd.: London & New York. 1983.

Hutchins, Alma R. Indian Herbology of North America. Shambala Press: Boston & London. 1973.

Jaeger, Ellsworth. Wildwood Wisdom.

Kadans, Joseph M., N.D. Ph.D. Modern Encyclopedia of Herbs. Parker Publishing Company, Inc.: West Nyack, NY. 1970.

Kallas, John. "Amaranth—Staple Food Source for Modern Foragers." The Wild Food Adventurer. Vol. 3, No. 2. July 1, 1998.

Kallas, John. "Bull Thistle." The Wild Food Adventurer. Vol. 2, No. 4. November 15, 1997.

Kallas, John. "Edible Blue Camas—Preparation Old & New." The Wild Food Adventurer. Vol. 3, No. 2. July 1, 1998.

Kallas, John. "Grounnut—Pearls on a String." The Wild Food Adventurer. Vol. 5, No. 2. June 15, 2000.

Kallas, John. "Oregon Grape: Not for the Faint of Taste." The Wild Food Adventurer. Vol. 2, No. 2. June 15, 1997.

Kallas, John. "Tawny Day Lily—Unpredictably Tainted Fare." The Wild Food Adventurer. Vol. 5, No. 2. June15, 2000.

Kallas, John. "Wapato, Indian Potato." The Wild Food Adventurer. Volume 1, No 4. Dec. 10, 1996.

Kallas, John. "Wild Spinach: Delicious, Nutritious and Abundant" The Wild Food Adventurer. Vol. 1, No 2. June 30, 1996.

Kirk, Donald R. Wild Edible Plants of the Western United States. Naturegraph Publishers: Healdsburg, CA. 1970.

Kirtikar, K. R. & B. D. Basu. Indian Medicinal Plants. India. 1918.

Kinucan, Edith S. & Penny R. Brons. Wild Wildflowers of the West. Kinucan & Brons: Ketchum, ID. 1979.

Klein, Robyn. "The Mountain Herbalist" Montana Pioneer: Livingston, Montana. Articles 1992-1994.

Klein, Robyn. "The Simple Wort... and the Rest of the Story." Community Food News: Bozeman, MT. Summer 2000. Page 18.

Kloss, Jethro. Back to Eden. Woodbridge Press Publishing Co.: Santa Barbara, CA. 1981-1983. Kloss 1939.

Krakauer, Jon. Into the Wild. Anchor Books (Doubleday): New York. 1996.

Kramer, Miriam Darnall & John Goude. Dining on the Wilds. Videos. JEG Development. Yucaipa,CA.

Lust, John, N.D., D.B.M. The Herb Book. Bantam Books: New York. 1974. 16th printing: 1983.

Mabey, Richard. Plantcraft: A guide to the everyday use of wild plants. Universe Books: New York. 1977.

Mathews, F. Schuyler. Familiar Trees and Their Leaves. D. Appleton & Co. New York. 1898.

Mcmenamin, Mark A. and Dianna L. S. Hypersea: Life on Land. Columbia University Press: New York. 1994.

Merwood, Anne. "Plants of the Apes". Wildlife Conservation. March-April 1991. Pgs.54-59.

Mills, Simon Y. Out of the Earth: the Essential Book of Herbal Medicine. Viking Arkana: London. 1991.

Moerman, Dan. American Indian Ethnobotany Database. http://www.umd.umich.edu/cgi-bin/herb. Jan-Feb. 1997.

Moore, Michael. Medicinal Plants of the Mountain West. Museum of New Mexico Press: Sante Fe, NM. 1979.

Moore, Michael. Medicinal Plants of the Desert and Canyon West. Museum of New Mexico Press: Santa Fe, NM. 1989.

Moore, Michael. Medicinal Plants of the Pacific West. Red Crane Books: Sante Fe, NM. 1993.

Murphey, Edith Van Allen. Indian Uses of Native Plants. Mendocino County Historical Society: Ukiah, CA. 1959, 1987.

Nyerges, Christopher. " Plants Which Stun Fish". Wilderness Way. Volume 3, Issue 4. 1997. Pgs. 49-54.

Olsen, Larry Dean. Outdoor Survival Skills. Brigham Young University: Provo, UT. 1967 & 1972.

Orr, Robert T. & Margaret C. Wildflowers of Western America. Galahad Books: New York. 1974, 1981.

Pammel, L. H., Ph.D. A Manual of Poisonous Plants. The Torch Press: Cedar Rapids, Iowa. 1911.

Pendell, Dale. Pharmako/poeia: Plant Powers, Poisons, and Herbcraft. Mecury House: San Francisco. 1995.

Phillips, Wayne. "Poisonous and Medicinal Plants" (class hand-out.) HOPS Primitive Fair. 1995.

Platt, Rutherford. Our Flowering World. Dodd, Mead & Co.: New York. 1947.

Platt, Rutherford. This Green World. Dodd, Mead & Co.: New York. 1942 & 1988.

Rothschild, Michael. Bionomics. John Macrae / Henry Holt and Company: New York, NY. 1990.

Rogers, Robert D., AHG. Sundew Moonwort: Medicinal Plants of the Prairies. Volumes I, II, III. Jan 1997.

Schauenberg, Paul. Guide to Medicinal Plants. Keats Publishing, Inc.: New Canaan, CT. 1990.

Sheff, Elaine. "Nature's First Aid Kit". Community Food News. Bozeman, MT. Sept/October 1997. Pg. 4.

Smith, James Payne Jr. Vascular Plant Families. Mad River Press, Inc.: Eureka, CA. 1977.

Spellenberg, Richard. The Audubon Society Field Guide to North American Wildflowers. Alfred A. Knopf: New York. 1979.

Sturtevant, Dr. E. Lewis. Sturtevant's Edible Plants of the World. Dover Publications: New York. 1972.

Sunset. Western Garden Book. Lane Publishing Co.: Menlo Park, CA. 1988.

Sweet, Muriel. Common Edible and Useful Plants of the West. Naturegraph Publishers: Happy Camp, CA. 1976.

Thoreau, Henry David. Faith in a Seed: The Dispersion of Seeds and Other Late Natural History Writings. Island Press /

Shearwater Books: Washington, D. C. & Covelo, CA. 1993.

Thayer, Sam. "The Milkweed Phenomenon." The Forager. Volume 1, No. 2. June-July 2001. Pages 2-4.

Tilford, Gregory L. The EcoHerbalist's Fieldbook. Mountain Weed Publishing: Conner, Montana. 1993.

Tilford, Gregory L. Edible and Medicinal Plants of the West. Mountain Press Publishing Co.: Missoula, MT. 1997.

Tompkins, Peter & Christopher Bird. The Secret Life of Plants. Harper & Row, Publishers: New York. 1973.

Turner, Nancy J. Plant Technology of First Peoples in British Columbia. UBC Press: Vancouver. 1998, 2000.

Tyler, Varro E., Ph.D. The Honest Herbal, 3rd Ed. Pharmaceutical Products Press (Haworth Press): New York. 1982, 1993.

Uphof, J. C. TH. Dictionary of Economic Plants. H. R. Engelmann: New York. 1959.

Venning, Frank. A Guide to Field Identification—Wildflowers of North America. Golden Press, Western Publishing Co.: New York. 1984.

Verrill, A. Hyatt. Wonder Plants and Plant Wonders. D. Appleton-Century Company: New York, London. 1939.

Vitt, Dale H., Janet E. Marsh, & Robin B. Bovey. Mosses, Lichens, & Ferns of Northwest North America. Lone Pine Publishing: Edmonton, Alberta. 1988.

Vogel, Virgil J. American Indian Medicine. University of Oklahoma Press: Norman, OK. 1970.

Weiner, Michael. Earth Medicine-Earth Food. Fawcett Columbine: New York. 1972, 1980.

Willard, Terry, Ph.D. Edible and Medicinal Plants of the Rocky Mountains and Neighboring Territories. Wild Rose College of Natural Healing, Ltd.: Calgary, Alberta. 1992.

Williams, Kim. Eating Wild Plants. Mountain Press Publishing Co.: Missoula, MT. 1977.

Wohlberg, Beth. "Barberry bush beats bacteria." High Country News. July 31, 2000. Pg. 8.

Zimmer, Carl. "Hypersea Invasion", Discover. October 1995. Pgs. 76-87.

Zomlefer, Wendy B. Guide to Flowering Plant Families. University of North Carolina Press: Chapel Hill, NC & London. 1994.

Index of Plants by Genus

Index of Plants by Genus

INDEX OF PLANTS BY GENUS

INDEX OF PLANTS BY GENUS

INDEX OF PLANT FAMILIES BY LATIN NAMES

INDEX OF PLANTS BY COMMON NAMES

Index of Plants by Common Names

Index of Plant Families by Common Names

Names high-lighted in **bold** indicate families you should learn first.

—Direct Pointing to Real Wealth—

Thomas J. Elpel's Field Guide to Money

All living organisms consume energy, modify resources from the environment and produce waste. That is an inescapable fact of life. But in nature all material wastes are recycled as inputs to other living organisms. The only true waste is diffuse, low-grade heat.

In order to create a truly sustainable economy we must mimic the ecosystem so that the waste of every household and business becomes resource inputs to other enterprises, and the only waste produced is diffuse, low-grade heat from renewable resources like solar.

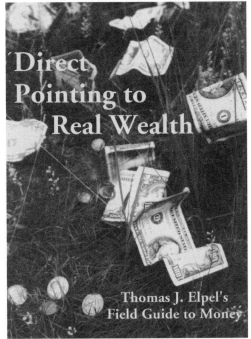

In *Direct Pointing to Real Wealth* author Thomas J. Elpel demonstrates that it is inevitable that we will create an ecologically sustainable economy. Tom turns conventional thinking on its head and outlines steps you can take to increase your prosperity right now while closing the loop on waste and speeding the transition to a greener world.

Direct Pointing to Real Wealth is an enlightened look at the nature of money. Discover how the economy is like an ecosystem and how money is a token we use to represent calories of energy in the ecosystem. Tom's unique approach to money takes you beyond the numbers game to a direct examination of the laws of physics, biology, and economics. These laws are the same today as in the Stone Age, when people worked only a few hours per day and had much more leisure time than we do now.

Whether you are raising a family or running a business, Tom's book gives you a fresh new look at economics, ecology and how to achieve your Dreams. Break through perceived limitations to discover a world of prosperity and abundance!

"You have been a tremendous inspiration to us. Your books positively took ideas that had been running around in my head for years and tied them together for the foundation of my thinking. Without your books and ideas, I would still be trying to fit all my ideas and philosophies into one big picture. You've helped me get all those thoughts into goals, realistic goals, and I thank you."

—John Y. / Wausau, Wisconsin

"This is the third book of Tom's that I have read. There is no way to say enough to describe how this book has affected me. It comfined, for me ways that I veiwed money and my personal views of finances. It also gave me the inspiration and insight to approach finances from a different level. I bought the book on a gut feeling (I wasn't interested in it, that I knew of) and I am really glad I did. Bravo Tom, great information, Thank you!"

John C. /Spring Mount, PA

—Living Homes—

Thomas J. Elpel's Field Guide to Integrated Design & Construction

The house of your Dreams does not have to be expensive. The key is all in the planning. How much a house costs, how it looks, how comfortable it is, how energy-efficient it is—all these things occur on paper before you pick up even one tool. A little extra time in the planning process can save you tens of thousands of dollars in construction and maintenance. That is time well spent!

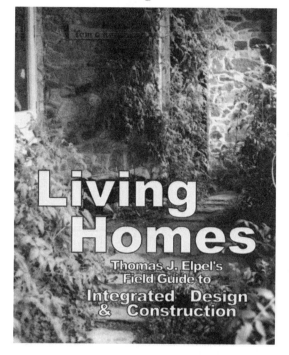

Living Homes takes you through the planning process to design an energy and resource efficient home that won't break the bank. Then, from the footings on up to the roof, author Thomas J. Elpel guides you through the nuts and bolts of construction for slipform stone masonry, tilt-up stone walls, log home construction, building with strawbales, making your own "terra tile" floors, windows & doors, solar water systems, masonry heaters, framing, plumbing, greywater, septic systems, swamp filters, painting and more! Living Homes includes an incredible 300+ photos and drawings.

Environmental Note—Everything but the cover is printed with soy ink on 100% post-consumer recycled paper, bleached without chlorine. $1 from every book sold is donated to the Institute for Solar Living to support their work promoting sustainable living through inspirational environmental education.

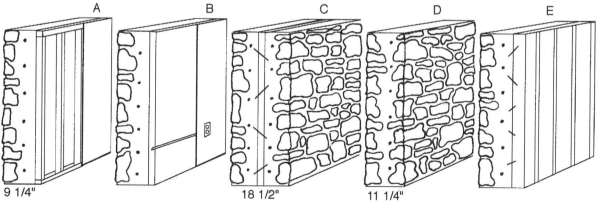

9 1/4"   18 1/2"   11 1/4"

Slipform Wall Options

The method of stone masonry we use is called "slipforming". Short forms, up to two feet tall, are placed on both sides of the wall to serve as a guide for the stone work. You fill the forms with stone and concrete, then "slip" the forms up for the next level. Slipforming makes stone work easy even for the novice.

—Participating in Nature—
Thomas J. Elpel's Field Guide to Primitive Living Skills

"Primitive living is a metaphor we participate in. We journey into the Stone-Age and quest to meet our basic needs. We learn to observe, to think, to reach inside ourselves for new resources to deal with challenging and unfamiliar situations. We return with knowledge, wisdom, and strength to enrich our lives in contemporary society."

—Thomas J. Elpel, Participating in Nature

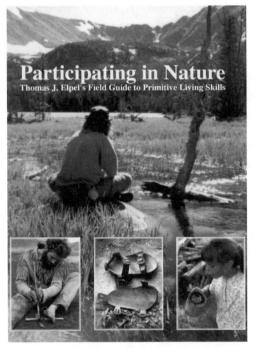

Discover nature by using it! Primitive skills allow you to get closer to nature by experiencing nature directly. Instead of merely hiking through, or camping in nature, primitive living allows you to move in and become part of the process. Learn about nature as you use it to meet your daily needs for shelter, clothing, fire, water, and food. Connect with the land iin an intimate way as you learn about all the plants and trees and rocks and animals, and all their uses.

Tom's guide gives you a direct, hands-on experience of the world around you. With this book you will discover the thrill of staying warm and comfortable without even a blanket! Experience the magic of starting a fire by friction. Learn about the edible plants of the Rocky Mountain region and the techniques to process them, plus "primitive gourmet" cooking skills.

Braintan the hides from your fall hunting trip and manufacture them into durable clothing. Also covered are: sinews, hide glue, backpacking, felting with wool, fishing by hand, stone knives, wooden containers, willow baskets, twig deer, cordage, stalking skills, trapping and tire sandals.

Participating in Nature includes dozens of innovative skills and nearly 200 illustrations, plus an encompassing philosophy. Tom does extensive experiential research. He places an emphasis on publishing new information that is not found in any other source.

"I've read MANY books on survival. Enough that I rarely find fresh ideas in a new one I read. But yours is full of things that I haven't read in many other books. Thanks not only for the fresh ideas, but also for the fresh format. The narrative is wonderfully inspirational. I almost feel like I'm out in the field with you. I don't know if we'll ever meet (I hope we do), but if not I feel like I know you through your writings."

—David W. Attala, AL